Praise for *Press On: Living Victorious After*

"John Putch is a man with deep conviction, determination, and resilience who has established, through faith, a personal mission of ministry to those battling through the struggles of divorce. John proposes a Christ-centered approach to help readers rely on a God who is the ultimate healer."

—*Greg Blanchard, Plant Manager, Ascend Performance Materials*

• • •

"What a great resource for someone who is going or has gone through divorce! This devotional is well done and encourages the reader to put their eyes on the Lord daily. I highly recommend this book!

—*Pastor Ron Hindt, Calvary Houston*

• • •

"Having been pastor to the young John Putch and his family, I knew him to be a dedicated Christian and a serious student of the Word of God. He has always been a man of character in business, home and religion.

"The keys of this character are conveyed in this book, *Pressing On*. Here is the answer to those who are going through the terrible storm and aftermath of divorce: character for the storm, as defined in the Word of God and available to all who will live by faith; and trusting God to supply strength to meet every need one day at a time.

"John calls it a devotional. I call it a prescription for restoring meaning, hope and joy to those who look for purpose in life when it seems all is lost. It is really a heart-to-heart message to those who are saying *"What now?"* I'm thankful for this book and expect it to be a resource of great help to many wounded and hurting people in days to come."

—*Dr. Wayne Hudson, DTh; President, Texas Theological University; Staff Evangelist, Metropolitan Baptist Church, Fort Worth, Texas*

Lee,

I hope something in this book helps you. I have learned so much from your life and the experiences you have been through. I appreciate you, and your service to the USMC!

May God bless you!

Love,

[signature]

Philippians
3: 13-14

PRESSING ON

PRESSING ON

Living Victoriously After Divorce

A 365-Day Devotional
For Encouragement

By

JOHN D. PUTCH

XULON PRESS

Xulon Press
2301 Lucien Way #415
Maitland, FL 32751
407.339.4217
www.xulonpress.com

Cover: Kristen King, Owner and Designer, Graphique Motif LLC
Editor: Cheryl Suarez

Unless otherwise indicated, Scripture quotations taken from the English
Standard Version (ESV). Copyright © 2001 by Crossway, a publishing
ministry of Good News Publishers. Used by permission. All rights reserved.

Printed in the United States of America.

Paperback ISBN-13: 978-1-6628-1727-4
Dust Jacket ISBN-13: 978-1-6628-1728-1
eBook ISBN-13: 978-1-6628-1729-8

Preface

I write this devotional to all people who are experiencing the horrors of divorce. I am a graduate of Baptist Bible College (1991) and a graduate of Trinity Valley Baptist Seminary (2003). Like many people, I dreamed of being a pastor and serving our Lord in full-time service. I met my wife at college; we were married 19 years. We served God to the best of our abilities. God gave us two wonderful sons. We were the model couple—or so it seemed. In September 2010 she told me she had a boyfriend and that we must get a divorce. To make matters worse, my oldest sister died of breast cancer that very same week. My life was in complete turmoil! I preached my sister's funeral and then resigned my pastorate.

God knew this tragic event would take place in my life and He sent help immediately. Help started coming in from everywhere. My father slept on my couch each night while I worked, so my two sons would not be home alone. As I was left with no transportation, a great friend let me borrow his car. Church members spent time with me and my sons. Friends and coworkers came out of the woodwork to offer help. One friend even dreamed about me, and the message he received from the dream was to tell me that "you win!"

God did allow me to win! The purpose of this book is to share God's Word as a way of encouragement. It is a simple format: a text is given for each day of the month, an explanation of the text follows, then there is a short Suggested Prayer. My hopes and prayers are that this book will help you win! If the reader can catch a few handfuls on purpose to help him get through life's journey, it is well worth my feeble efforts.

A special thank you to Linhong, whom God used to help me continue this project after I decided to quit. A special thank you to my two sons, Ben and Grant, because "You are those who have stayed with me in my trials" (Luke 22:28).

My primary audience is men, women, and families whose lives have been ripped apart by divorce, but this book can be used as a daily devotional for any Christian who desires a closer walk with Christ.

Let us believe the words of my dear friend, "you win!" The great news is that we do win through our Lord Jesus Christ!

John Putch

A New Year Filled with Great Opportunities

Jeremiah 29:11
For I know the plans I have for you, declares the LORD, plans for welfare and not for evil, to give you a future and a hope.

What are our plans for the coming year? Many of us are so discouraged that we really cannot plan anything. We are just hoping to get through the day and cannot plan weeks and months ahead. Add to that the fear of failing at yet one more thing, so we choose not to plan at all. When we aim at nothing, we hit it every time.

God says He has great plans for us. The verse almost seems like a contradiction. God would allow His people to be captured by the Babylonians, and Israel would be out of their homeland for seventy years. But God brought them back into the land as He promised.

At the right time He sent His Son to redeem us. One day Jesus will come back to rule and reign with Jerusalem as the social, political, and religious center of the world. It may seem like our plans, hopes, and dreams are shattered, but God is working out an awesome plan for us. His plan is for our welfare. He has our best interests in mind with everything He allows to enter our lives. His plan will give you hope and make your future bright. The will of God is a process. Israel has yet to realize the plans God has for her, and we really do not understand what God has in store for us either. May we trust that He is working an awesome plan in and through us.

Suggested Prayer
Dear Lord,
I want Your plans for my life! Please show me Your perfect plan for me. Let me realize that the plan is for my welfare. Let it bring hope back into my life. May Your plans for me enlighten my spirit and give me a purpose for this year. In the Name of Jesus I pray, Amen.

God's Word Will Pull You Through

Hebrews 4:12

For the word of God is living and active, sharper than any two-edged sword, piercing to the division of soul and of spirit, of joints and of marrow, and discerning the thoughts and intentions of the heart.

The Bible is truly the most unique book ever written. It is composed of sixty-six books by some forty authors. However, both the Old Testament and the New Testament form one unified whole without any errors. What sets the Bible apart is that it is a living book. There are many helpful books in the world but they are not alive. God's Word is alive and applicable to any time period and every culture. If we would read just three chapters a day, we could read the Bible through in one year. The most important thing is that this living Word begins to change my life and helps me through life's problems. The Word is "active," and it works on my heart, comforts my spirit, teaches me what I need to do, and even rebukes me when I go against its precepts. The Bible is "sharper than any two-edged sword," penetrating deep into our hearts. The power of the Word exposes my thoughts and intentions and aligns them with God's will.

The scriptures were written with the finger of God and preserved for us. Someone has said that prayer is talking to God and reading the Word is God talking to us. Determine in your heart that you want God to speak to you this year. Do this by spending some time in His Word. Ten to fifteen minutes a day in the living Book may make a difference in your life, not only today but throughout your life. God wants to fellowship with us. Make it a point to meet with Him in His Word. Try waking up twenty minutes earlier to read a little and pray before heading out the door. If we want life, we must read a living book. God has many truths in His Word that will pull you through your divorce, depression, health problems, family problems, or financial problems. Reading God's Book also will increase our faith. So, what are we waiting for?

Suggested Prayer

Dear Lord,
I know that You want to speak to me through Your Word. Lord, the Bible is alive, and I know it will speak to me. Help me to begin reading it and may it change my life. Let the Bible help me, and may You use me to help other people as You begin to change my life. God, help me be a person who knows and applies Your Word. In Jesus' name, Amen.

I Can't Seem to Forgive Them

Luke 23:34

And Jesus said, "Father, forgive them, for they know not what they do." And they cast lots to divide his garments.

When Jesus was crucified, He said these monumental words: "Father, forgive them, for they know not what they do." Jesus uttered these words in the present tense, meaning He continually said these words to His Father. The Jews and the Romans thought they knew what they were doing by killing Jesus. The religious leaders viewed Him as a religious threat, and Rome saw Him as a political threat. Both groups sinned out of ignorance and unbelief. The devil himself thought he knew what he was doing by orchestrating the death of God. God's purpose was to redeem mankind through the death of His own beloved Son. There was a bigger purpose involved at Calvary; one that only God knew about. No one really understood what was taking place until three days later when Jesus arose from the grave.

As we reflect on those who have harmed us, we too need to say, "Father, forgive them, for they know not what they do." We should also recognize that God has a purpose in these hurts that we have experienced. We might not know the purpose of the hurt immediately, but one day we will understand. So, the next time someone hurts you or trespasses against you, take the higher ground and forgive them. Forgive them because it will help you in your relationship with God, and it will help you see the great freedom of not being bound by roots of bitterness. If we do not forgive, our relationship with God will be hindered. The people who have hurt us are living their lives, yet we are allowing them to have unwarranted power over our lives.

Suggested Prayer ────────────────────────────────

Heavenly Father,
I ask that You forgive those who have hurt me. These people sinned against me out of ignorance and unbelief. May Your will be done through these hurts. Please bless those who have hurt me and my family. In our Savior's name, Amen.

Encourage Yourself in The Lord

1 Samuel 30:6

And David was greatly distressed, for the people spoke of stoning him, because all the people were bitter in soul, each for his sons and daughters. But David strengthened himself in the LORD his God.

David was greatly distressed as he ran from King Saul each day. Saul knew David would be king so he hunted David each day, and he would not be satisfied until the young shepherd was dead. Now what? David and his band of men and their families were raided by the Amalekites, and all the wives and children were taken as spoils of war. David's men were ready to kill him. They had put their trust in David, and as a result they had lost their families and possessions. Through all of David's turmoil he learned how to encourage himself in God. The Lord did restore David's and his followers' losses, and he became the shepherd King of Israel.

God, in His time, will restore your losses too. We need to encourage ourselves by prayer and the reading of the scriptures. David was also a musician and wrote most of the Hebrew Hymnbook known as the book of Psalms in our Bible. When David played his harp for God he encouraged himself and those around him. These songs are preserved for us so we might receive encouragement too. We must become our own motivational speaker! No one knows exactly what you are going through except God. So read, pray, and sing praises to God like never before. Cling to the promises found in His Word. Dig deeper and deeper in your walk with Him. Deliverance will come, so encourage yourself in the LORD.

Suggested Prayer

Dear Lord,
I am discouraged! Help me to be encouraged as I read Your Word. Help me sense Your presence as I pray and try to get through this rough time. By faith, I claim and receive the victory over my problems. Amen.

It Feels Like I Am on Death Row

2 Corinthians 1:9
Indeed, we felt that we had received the sentence of death. But that was to make us rely not on ourselves but on God who raises the dead.

P aul felt like he had received the death sentence for his life. How could this be? He is the great apostle who gave us so much of the New Testament! It has been said that not everyone in prison is behind bars. This is true! Family problems and financial difficulty often imprison our souls. Our bodies might be free, but our spirits are not free.

Sometimes we feel like we are serving a prison term. We count the days till we will be released from paying child support, hoping for better financial days in the future. We remember when we were free to go the movies and eat at our favorite restaurants. Now every penny must be accounted for.

This feeling of being in prison is to get us to rely on God and not ourselves. The real power in our lives comes from God who raises the dead. It is this resurrection power in our lives that we must tap into. If God can raise the dead, He can see us through any situation as we place our trust in Him. We can either trust ourselves and our power to go through life or we can begin to trust God and His resurrection power.

Suggested Prayer
Help me Lord!
I feel like I am trapped in prison. Lord, my body is free, but my soul is chained with heavy burdens. I am trapped because of this divorce, and because of my own bad decisions. Lord, You have all the power! Let me live in such a way that I depend not on myself but on You. In Jesus' name, Amen.

Life Is Not Over

Philippians 1:6
And I am sure of this, that he who began a good work in you will bring it to completion at the day of Jesus Christ.

We often feel discouraged, thinking maybe God is through with us. We feel that way because of our circumstances or perhaps because of our shortcomings. We think that God will not use us because of our continual sins. Can He continue to forgive me? We think to ourselves, "Surely I am doomed, and He has passed me by." A divorced person feels like God will not use them because of the event that they went through. The most important institution on earth is the family, and our biggest failure in life came the day we were divorced. Shame puts us in a place where we feel abandoned by God. We avoid people and places, feeling shunned.

Paul was confident that God had not given up on any of us. In fact, he explains that the Great Captain of our faith will always be faithful to guide us. Paul wants us to have that confidence too. "God did not abandon me! He is still working in my life! He will use me and give me a new purpose!"

He started a good work in us and will complete this good work. Let us also have confidence that it is a good work. You and I are a good work in His eyes. God will be with us till death or when He returns for us. God never quits. How many projects have we started and never completed? We have good intentions, but somewhere along the way we give up. Not so with our loving Lord. He will complete the work He started in you.

Divorce, separation, and loneliness are often tools used by God to bring about this good work in us. Let's be confident that He is working in us, and that He will complete this work. Look in the mirror and see yourself as God sees you. You investigate the glass and see a failure. God looks and sees a good work. Go to the mirror right now and say, "I am a good work in God's eyes! Life is not over. He is working in my life and will be faithful to me forever."

Suggested Prayer
Dear God,
I feel like life is over for me. However, I read that You are still working in my life. Let me see Your hand in my life. Let me be confident that You are working to complete Your perfect work in me. In Jesus name,. Amen.

Jesus Knows What We Are Going Through

Isaiah 53:3
*He was despised and rejected by men; a man of sorrows, and acquainted with grief;
and as one from whom men hide their faces he was despised, and we esteemed him not.*

Only God really knows what we are going through. Family and friends may be supportive, but only God really knows the facts. He is a man of sorrows. His life on earth was full of sorrow. He knows what it is like to be despised and rejected. Our Lord was well acquainted with grief. People hid from Jesus and they considered Him as nothing. However, we know He is God and He accomplished the greatest mission by dying for our sins. The One who did the most was esteemed the least. God's goal for our lives is to make us more and more like Jesus. We too must be rejected, laughed at, and esteemed as nothing. We also will be well acquainted with sorrow and grief before this life ends. If the world rejected and despised Jesus it will do the same to us.

The real hurt came when our former spouses rejected us. It is one thing for a stranger to reject us, but when it is family it is unbearable. Often people tell us the biggest lie by saying, "I know how you feel" when they are clueless. Many well-meaning people have done much damage when trying to comfort a hurting individual by saying such foolish things. Their words and advice hurt down to the very core of our being. However, Jesus does know how we feel. So rely on the Man of sorrows because He will never leave you or forsake you. He knows what you are going through.

Suggested Prayer
*Dear God,
I forgot that You know how I feel. Thank You that You and You alone know exactly what I am dealing with. Lord, give me Your perspective on my pain. Thank You that not only do You know but You are helping me as we go through this together. Lord, teach me what You want me to know through these sufferings. Help me to be sensitive to others who are going though pain. In the Name of Jesus I pray, Amen.*

Exercise Will Help

1 Timothy 4:7-8

Have nothing to do with irreverent, silly myths. Rather train yourself for godliness; for while bodily training is of some value, godliness is of value in every way, as it holds promise for the present life and also for the life to come.

Paul says that when we train ourselves in the ways of God it is always helpful. Godly training helps us in this life and in the life to come. Training yourself in the ways of God is the only thing that pays eternal dividends. He also says that physical exercise is good too. Beginning to exercise will be a major stress reliever.

A good daily walk will help you unwind from the daily pressures of life, along with the heavy burden that you are under. Exercise will clear the mind and help you focus. When going through a divorce the body, mind, spirit, and emotions are under severe stress. Listen to some motivating music as you exercise. Shedding a few extra pounds will also help us feel good about ourselves at a time when our self-esteem is at an all-time low.

You might make new friendships, whereby you can encourage each other. If a gym membership is too expensive, try walking or running in your local park. There might be someone who needs your help as you get into an exercise routine.

We never know what God has in store for us as we honor Him by taking care of the bodies that He has given us. Our bodies are the temple of the Holy Spirit and we must treat them as such. Exercise will motivate you, give you a purpose, and bring discipline into your life. If you are already exercising regularly, God bless you because you are well on your way to a spiritual recovery.

Suggested Prayer

Father,

I give my body to You. I commit myself to exercise my heart and mind in Your Word. I also commit to exercise. This body of mine houses the Holy Spirit. Help me honor You, both physically and spiritually. Help me develop new lasting friendships through this commitment. In Jesus' Name I pray, Amen.

Give Yourself to God

Romans 12:1-2

I appeal to you therefore, brothers, by the mercies of God, to present your bodies as a living sacrifice, holy and acceptable to God, which is your spiritual worship. Do not be conformed to this world, but be transformed by the renewal of your mind, that by testing you may discern what is the will of God, what is good and acceptable and perfect.

After a tragic life-changing event like divorce, we need to realize and recognize that God still has great plans for us. We will never see those plans come to fulfillment unless we first give ourselves to Him. We must offer our all to Him as a living sacrifice. All the Old Testament sacrifices were dead, but Paul begs and pleads that we give ourselves as a living sacrifice. We need to lay all on the altar; including ourselves. We should do this daily. We can now begin to live life by yielding to Him and His will.

When He puts us in His will a great transformation begins to take place. We desperately need this renewal of our minds that only comes as we yield to Him. We need this transformation from this present evil world. The world lies to us, especially when we are most vulnerable. The world says, "live it up, go have an affair yourself; God will understand!" God is in the transforming and renewal business. The world cannot make us better. The world does not have the answers we are looking for. However, when we are transformed we begin to live holy and we come to know God's will for our lives. It is a gradual transformation, so be patient. The rewards are great when you begin to do His work. Life is full of purpose, joy, and peace. God needs people who will be willing to give up everything to follow Him.

Suggested Prayer

Dear Lord,
I lived my own life, and everything fell apart! Today, right now, I give myself to You as a living sacrifice. I want to be holy and pleasing in Your sight. Most importantly, I want You to further Your kingdom through me. Amen.

Are We Free to Serve God?

Proverbs 22:7
The rich rules over the poor, and the borrower is the slave of the lender.

Solomon warns us that if we are in debt we are not free to serve God as we should. He says we are actually slaves to the lender. Slavery involves restrictions on our wills and spirits. The shackles of debt weigh our spirits down and we are ineffective for God. Jesus said that no man can serve two masters. We will either serve God or the financial lenders who we are indebted to. Debt brings about so much stress in our lives that we cannot focus on the things of God. We wake up thinking about debt and we go to bed thinking about it. We would be devastated if one of our children were sold into slavery. Yet we think nothing about a hasty purchase that will enslave not only ourselves but our children too. Debt will keep us from having new relationships because we simply cannot afford them. If we cannot take care of our existing family, God will not put a new family in our lives.

When divorce comes, we are tempted to buy a new car or something that will bring temporary comfort to our hurting hearts. But we must find our contentment in Christ, because we are only complete in Him. We must be able to distinguish between wants and needs. We must also be great planners with what God has given us. If we are not faithful with our current income, it is doubtful that God will entrust us with more. All our money belongs to Him, and we must be faithful stewards of His possessions. We should consider ourselves in a financial emergency when going through a divorce. This is not the time to splurge! A hasty financial decision may keep us from serving God for years to come. Do things really satisfy? Are you financially free? If you are not, devise a plan that will honor God and leave you free you to serve Him.

Suggested Prayer
*Dear Lord,
I give my finances to You. Help me make wise financial decisions, trusting You to supply my needs. Lord, let me realize that one hundred percent of my money belongs to You. Help me be a good steward. Protect me from hasty, unwise financial decisions. In the Name of Jesus I pray, Amen.*

It's Difficult to Go to Church

Hebrews 10:25
Not neglecting to meet together, as is the habit of some, but encouraging one another, and all the more as you see the Day drawing near.

When separation or divorce occurs, it is often very difficult to go to church. It is not that we do not love God, but our circumstances seem to overwhelm us. Church screams family! Sunday is God's day, and a day for the family. Now we suddenly find ourselves without a family. Now we are walking into God's house totally alone. Our friends at church are interested in our well-being, but we are tired of talking about our problems.

Through it all God wants us to go to church to be a blessing, and to receive a blessing. The church is where we receive spiritual encouragement through music, preaching, and the fellowship of His Word. In the Old Testament God primarily worked through the nation of Israel. In the New Testament God mainly works through His church. The coming of the Lord is getting closer so we cannot afford to neglect His house. We do not just go to church; we are the church. The word *church* means assembly or congregation. Many churches offer classes that help people cope with divorce. There are people in the building that are going through the same trials you are. You can encourage each other as you go through the divorce because you will go through it with God's help.

He wants to use His church, a group of believers, to help you through the tough trial. If your ex-spouse goes to your church and he or she is keeping you from going, go to another church. God understands! Go where the Bible is taught and the Name of Jesus is high and lifted up. Go through those doors alone! Yet, you are not alone! The Holy Spirit will help you because He will be with you. The devil wants to keep you from God's house. Determine in your heart that God is going to win this battle because the battle is not ours. The battle is the Lord's.

Suggested Prayer
*Dear God,
I do not feel like going to church. It seems like everyone is looking at me and judging me. Lord, it is hard to walk through those doors alone. I commit myself to You and to the attendance of Your house. Please give me grace. Help me find new friends and a renewed strength in You. Thank You. In Jesus' name, Amen.*

God's Love Is Unconditional

Romans 5:8

God shows his love for us in that while we were still sinners, Christ died for us.

God's love for us is unconditional, meaning He loves us no matter what we have done. The verse implies that we have done some very bad things. In fact, the chapter indicates that we are born sinners. It is in our fallen nature to sin. No matter what we do He still loves us. He loves us for who we are. We should not take advantage of this love by sinning against Him. The great demonstration of God's love for us was seen when He sent His only Son into the world. While we were still sinners, Christ died for us.

My salvation is not based on my works; it is solely rooted in the sacrifice of Jesus Christ on the cross. I simply do not have any works good enough to merit a place in heaven. He came to save sinners! If we will turn from our sins and trust in God's Son, we will be saved. When we stand before God on eternity's shore, and He asks us why He should let us in, what will we tell Him? The only correct answer is that we placed our faith in the sacrifice of Jesus Christ. He died, was buried, and rose the third day for our sins. The greatest motivation of our salvation is the love of God. The Lord did not want us to perish in our sins, nor did He want us to think we are good enough to reach heaven without Him. We cannot save ourselves. Only God can save us, so He sent us Jesus. God gave us His Son, His very best, to save us—the least deserving. Jesus is good enough!

Suggested Prayer

Dear Lord,

I am a sinner. I confess my sins and ask forgiveness. I see You loved me enough to send Jesus to die for me. I ask You to save me and give me eternal life. Thank You for saving me. In the Name of Jesus, I pray, Amen. Hallelujah!

I Have Lost So Much It Hurts

Job 1:21
And he said, "Naked I came from my mother's womb, and naked shall I return. The LORD gave, and the LORD has taken away; blessed be the Name of the Lord."

Divorce is a "Job-like" experience. In the great affliction of Job, he lost family, finances, and friends. He did not lose his faith, though! In the end God gave him twice as much as he had before the great test of faith started. Job realized that God had taken away his children, possessions, and even his health. He found out that God is sovereign and can do as He pleases. He can give as well as take away.

We need to praise Him through the trials. Many of us have lost family, finances, and friends. We are literally starting life all over again! Many people must sell their most prized possessions just to put food on the table. It is tough to lose friends. The worst pain is not being able to see our children daily. We cry out to God in our affliction, hoping that He will restore our losses. Let us resolve, like Job, to praise His name, knowing He allowed the trial to come.

Ultimately, God took away our family, friends, and finances. May we try to see the great hand of God in our losses. God never showed Job why he had to suffer. We may not receive an answer to our questions in this life, but we can still trust Him. One day God will still the storm, bring peace, and leave behind a blessing. May we trust Him! We can be like Job—we do not have to lose our faith.

Suggested Prayer
Dear Father,
I have lost so much! It hurts not to be able to see my children. It hurts to sell my possessions and lose everything that I have worked for. Lord, I dedicate my losses to You. If You restore my losses, I am thankful. If You chose not to restore my losses, I will be thankful and praise Your name, knowing this is Your hand in my life. Work out Your purpose in me. Amen.

Lord Teach Me to Pray

Matthew 6:9

Pray then like this: "Our Father in heaven, hallowed be your name."

When Jesus taught the people this model prayer, He was giving the people a *pattern* for prayer, more than something to be repeated. However, it is perfectly fine to repeat the prayer, because God knows the thoughts and intentions of our hearts. It is a good practice to make scriptures a prayer.

An old preacher once said, "the best way to pray is to pray." There is an element of truth in his statement. The more time we spend in prayer to God the more we will learn how to approach God. From this verse we can learn much about prayer. It is reverential as we address God as Father. It is positional as we see He is in heaven and we are on earth. It has an element of praise: "Hallowed be your name." Praise is lifting up the Name of God. It is not thanking Him for things. It is honoring Him for all that He is and all that He represents. He is omnipotent and omnipresent, He is Jehovah. He is Savior. He is love. He is grace.

We must lift up the Name of Jesus. The Name of Jesus means all that He stands for. Praise is worship, which means we show His worth in prayer. Begin praising God for who He is a couple of minutes a day. Begin to learn the different names of God and what those names mean. As we praise Him, we begin to see our problems in a different light. We begin to see the Great Jehovah who made a covenant with Abraham. We begin to see Him as our Great Shepherd. We see the miracle-performing God who will do a miracle for us in our hour of need. We see Him ascending to heaven and seated at the right hand of God to make intercession for us. Let us begin our prayer with praise. Let everyone and everything praise the Name of the Lord!

Suggested Prayer ————————————————————————

Lord, I praise You today! You are the Great Sovereign. You are Jehovah, the covenant-keeping God. You are Elohim the Creator God. You are the God of all comfort. You are love, mercy, and the God of all grace. You are my Savior and my King. I praise You. In the wonderful, precious Name of Jesus I pray, Amen.

Lord, I Really Want to Pray

Matthew 6:10
Your kingdom come, your will be done, on earth as it is in heaven.

As we continue to look at the model for prayer, we must remind ourselves that the two most important things we can do are pray and read the Word of God. Not only should we praise God (Matthew 6:9), we should be seeking His plan as we pray.

Jesus did not tell us what posture to pray in. Some people kneel, some stand, some walk, some are very still. The point is that we pray, not what posture we assume. He did not give specific times to pray. It is always a good time to pray.

In the text we see that we really need to know His plan for our lives. We know that God is accomplishing His plan in heaven. We should be praying that He ushers in His plan on earth too. We want God's plan for our lives. We should want His will above our own wills. We can pray for His will to be done through our divorce and the new difficulties we are facing. We should pray about every aspect of our lives. We should pray for His plan in our church, city, nation, and around the world.

As we pray for God's will, He will align our will with His plan. True satisfaction comes when we are walking in the will of God. We also need to pray that He will accomplish His will in the lives of our children and even that of our ex-spouse. God will accomplish His will with or without our help. Our lives will take on a totally new meaning when we see the will of God come to pass in us and through us. Not my will, but Thine be done.

Suggested Prayer
Father,
I want Your will. I want You to accomplish Your will through me. May Your kingdom come, and may You use me. I want Your will through all my troubles and trials. I want You to use my children. May You even use those who have hurt me the most. May You accomplish something great in our church, schools, nation, and around this world. Thy will be done. Amen.

JANUARY 15 | 15

Lord, Help Me Pray

Matthew 6:11
Give us this day our daily bread.

We have seen that prayer involves praise (Matthew 6:9) and planning (6:10). Prayer also has an element of provision. It is not wrong to ask God to supply our needs and the needs of the people around us. We should be encouraged that Jesus said it was part of prayer to ask God to supply our needs. It is true that God knows what we need. It is equally true that God is the one who supplies our needs. Yet God wants us to *ask* Him to supply our needs. As we pray for our needs, we begin to learn the difference between needs and wants. We also learn patience as we wait on Him to help. We learn to depend on God. Prayer shows that we are depending on God.

The reason why people have a hard time finding time to pray is because they are depending on themselves and not God. We do not pray to Him if we do not need Him. We should work like everything depends on us, but we should pray like everything depends on Him. As our needs are met, we can testify and give glory to God as we tell those around us about the wonderful God who supplies our needs.

Pray in a big way. Instead of just asking that your needs be met; ask God to bless you in such a way that you can have your needs met and that you can help those who are struggling around you. Pray for the needs of others that you know. Pray for the needs of the world. Rest in the fact that you can pray to God for your needs. Be comforted, knowing that He hears your prayers. Be cautious that you do not spend your whole time in prayer just asking for things. Remember to praise Him. Remember to pray for God's will to be done. Remember to pray for yourself.

Suggested Prayer
Our Father,
I have so many needs just now that I really do not know where to start. Please supply each need that I have. Lord, bless me so You can use me to bless others. I know You are listening to me and in due time You will give me the help that I need. In Jesus' Name I pray, Amen.

Forgiveness Is Essential to Prayer

Matthew 6:12
And forgive us our debts, as we have forgiven our debtors.

We have seen that prayer involves praise (Matthew 6:9), planning (6:10), provision (6:11), and it also involves pardon. We must ask forgiveness for our sins and we must forgive those who have trespassed against us. Forgiveness is a two-sided coin. On one side of the coin we must ask God to forgive us for our personal sins. The other side of the coin is forgiving those who have sinned against us. The problem with mankind is that we are all sinners. No matter how hard we try to live a holy life we are going to fall short. Unconfessed sin hinders our fellowship with God. Once we repent, we have our fellowship restored with God and we can begin to pray, knowing He is listening to our petitions. If we do not forgive those who have wronged us, our fellowship with God will be severed until we confess our anger or bitterness towards the offender.

The awesome thought here is that God loves us enough to forgive us and to restore our relationship with Him. We should confess sins daily and ask God to show us where we have trespassed against Him. One of the greatest feelings in the Christian experience is having a clean heart that has been forgiven. When we forgive others it often feels like a heavy burden has been lifted from our souls. If we want God to forgive us, we must forgive others. Our Christian walk will dwindle until we forgive others. Once God has forgiven you, learn to forgive yourself. God casts our sins as far as east is from west and keeps no record of them. We are the ones who have trouble forgiving ourselves and forgetting about it.

Suggested Prayer
Dear God,
I fell short again. Please forgive me for sinning against You. God, help me forgive those who have sinned against me. Thank You for forgiving and cleansing me. Holy Spirit, fill me with Your love. In the Name of Jesus I pray, Amen.

Pray for Power and Protection

Matthew 6:13
And lead us not into temptation, but deliver us from evil.

We have seen that prayer involves praise (Matthew 6:9), planning (6:10), provision (6:11), and pardon (6:12); it also involves power and protection. Jesus taught us to ask for protection in this evil world. We should daily ask God to protect us from temptation; we should ask God to protect our families as well. We need protection in our vehicles as well as our places of employment. We also want God to protect us from bad decisions. We should ask God to protect our children in all aspects of their lives. God's kingdom is a powerful realm. In fact, it is stronger than anything—including the devil and the forces of darkness.

We should ask for power to keep from sinning. We should ask for power to be good witnesses, parents, and servants for His kingdom. The devil has come to kill and to steal and to destroy the work of God. Without God's protection and power, we will live defeated lives and will not be able to further His kingdom. Through His power and protection we can have victory. Our families will thrive through His power. The kingdom of God will advance in this present evil world as we rely on His power and protection. The next time you fall into sin, ask yourself this question, "Did I pray for God's protection and power?"

Suggested Prayer ——————————————————————————
Dear Lord,
We are helpless. We need Your protection and power. Protect me and my children. Protect my going out and my coming in. Please hedge us about with Your protection. Please give me power to live victoriously. Give me power to be a witness and a good parent. Give me the power to further Your kingdom. In the resurrection power of Jesus, I pray, Amen.

Compromise

Nehemiah 6:2-3

Sanballat and Geshem sent to me, saying, "Come and let us meet together at Hakkephirim in the plain of Ono." But they intended to do me harm. And I sent messengers to them, saying, "I am doing a great work and I cannot come down. Why should the work stop while I leave it and come down to you?"

Nehemiah was used by God to rebuild the broken walls of Jerusalem. The Babylonian Empire destroyed the Holy City and her walls in 586 B.C. Israel had sinned against God, and He allowed the nation to be destroyed. After seventy years God, in His mercy, allowed the Jews to return to their homeland. The Lord raised up Nehemiah to rebuild the walls of Jerusalem. The enemies of the land made every attempt to stop the Jews from rebuilding. Sanballat, Tobiah, and Geshem, the main antagonists, sought a meeting with Nehemiah. Their intentions were to kill Nehemiah and stop the work. We have Nehemiah's response recorded for us in these verses.

We also have three main enemies: the world, our flesh, and the devil. We too are doing a great work, and the work should not stop. We are doing the King's business. We are not building physical walls, we are building our lives back. We are building our families back. We are strengthening fellow believers and witnessing to the lost without Christ. We are doing a great work and cannot compromise with the enemy.

Nehemiah finished the wall in just fifty-two days. We are building a life work that can be destroyed in fifty-two seconds. We must not come down to meet with the enemy. Let us continue to build spiritual walls for the King of Kings. Consider your life a great work that must go on for the glory of God.

Suggested Prayer

Abba, Father,
I purpose to finish what You have started in me. I refuse to come down to meet with the enemy. The work You gave me to do is a great work and must not be stopped. Let me never compromise with the flesh, the world, and the devil. In the Name and power of Jesus I pray, Amen and Amen!

Help God! I Want to Be A Good Parent

Ephesians 6:4
Fathers, do not provoke your children to anger, but bring them up in the discipline and instruction of the Lord.

Most people feel that the children are the ones who suffer the most when there is a divorce. A single parent must now be mom and dad. There is no spouse to discuss discipline with anymore. Some parents are too strict on the children. Often these parents take the frustrations of the divorce out on the kids. On the other hand, some parents become too lenient, offering no instruction or discipline at all. A single parent must find a balance and must make the children a priority.

Our relationship with God is first, then our children are our next priority. We must provide instruction, correction, rebuke, and encouragement. We might need to set aside dating for a period to make sure our children are being taken care of. If we cannot manage our existing household, we surely cannot manage a new home with another spouse and possibly more children.

Never speak evil of your former spouse. In time your children will develop their own opinions about the divorce. Try not to let your feelings get hurt if your child wants to spend some time with your former spouse. The children did not ask for a broken home. Let them know the divorce was mom and dad's fault and not theirs. Many children feel they were the reason that mom and dad divorced. Children even have thoughts like, "If I would have prayed more and read my Bible more, mom and dad would not have divorced."

We may have permanently lost our spouse but let us determine not to lose our children too. By the way, you will blow it and say or do something wrong and offend your children. When you do, acknowledge your guilt before God and ask your children to forgive you. Hang in there! Help is on the way in the form of God Himself!

Suggested Prayer ———————————————
Dear Father,
I want my children to prosper and to grow up serving You. Help me to be the best parent I can be. Forgive me for talking bad about my former spouse. Please give me the grace, wisdom, insight, knowledge, and patience I need to be an awesome parent. In the Name above all names I pray, Amen.

Be Content and See What God Has in Store

1 Corinthians 7:27
Are you bound to a wife? Do not seek to be free. Are you free from a wife? Do not seek a wife.

Paul, in 1 Corinthians chapter seven, answers the church's questions about marriage, divorce, and remarriage. If any person, single or married, wants answers to questions about marriage, this is the chapter to do an in-depth study on. Paul's primary concern was that Christians fulfill the will of God and the plans that God has for them. Paul was a single man, and he wished all Christians would remain single so they could serve the Lord without any distractions. Paul also believed it was God's will that people marry and enjoy their lives together, but he was appealing to some that they might remain single to serve God. He encouraged married people to stay married; he even encouraged those married to non-Christians to remain married, hoping that the unbelieving spouse might become a Christian. He encouraged the single not to seek to be married. This was not a command from God, but a recommendation from the apostle.

If we find ourselves single we should see what God has in store. He might lead you to a new spouse whereby you can serve Him together. He also may lead you to remain single. If He leads you to stay single you will be able to serve Him without distractions. A married man's attention is divided between God and his wife and family. Singleness is for a select few. If you have passions that are not under control or you must have the companionship of another person, singleness is definitely not for you. Some people must have a spouse because they simply cannot be alone. The loneliness overwhelms them. Open your heart before Him and see what He has in store.

Suggested Prayer
Dear Great Sovereign,
You know my heart and You see what is best for me. I give this decision to You. If You want me to remain single, then let me be content and let me accept Your will so I can serve You without distractions. Lord, if Your will is for me to be married, then please put an awesome Christian in my life so we can serve You together. Into Your hands I give this, Amen.

Lord, I Have Grown Impatient

Numbers 21:4

From Mount Hor they set out by the way of the Red Sea, to go around the land of Edom. And the people became impatient on the way.

The Israelites became impatient and discouraged because of the way they were being led to the promised land. We all become impatient from time to time, but these people were always impatient and spoke against God and against Moses. The problem was that they were walking by sight and not by faith. God put them in a place where they had to trust Him completely for everything. He fed them with manna and quail, they had fresh water, and their sandals even lasted forty years.

In this chapter we see that God sent serpents into the camp, and these snakes bit the impatient, complaining people. As they were beginning to die from the snake bites they confessed their sin, and Moses made a brass serpent and put it on a pole. Anyone who was bitten by the serpents could look at the brass serpent and be healed. They could look and live.

The answer for our impatience is the same today. The brass serpent represented Jesus Christ, who was suspended between heaven and earth for our sins (John 3:14-16). In the Bible brass is a symbol of judgment. Our sins were judged at Calvary. By faith we too look and live. We must confess our impatience and look to Jesus. He will forgive us! He will then show us the way of faith.

They were led by a cloud by day and a pillar of fire by night. We too must rely on God's leading. We may not come out of Egypt physically, but we did come out of a spiritual Egypt when we looked to Jesus. It took forty years to get Egypt out of the hearts of God's people. We too must get Egypt our of our hearts. Our wilderness-wandering might not take forty years, but it is a process and it requires patience. Let us rest in God's provision and His leading as He brings us into our promised land.

Suggested Prayer

Father,

You have me in a place where I can only trust You and look up. I have become impatient, and I ask that You forgive me. I look to You, Jesus. Let me live and walk as You would have me to. Holy Spirit, be that cloud and fire in my heart that leads me into Your promised possession. In Jesus' Name, Amen.

Peace for a Troubled Soul

John 16:33

I have said these things to you, that in me you may have peace. In the world you will have tribulation. But take heart; I have overcome the world.

On the eve of the crucifixion Jesus spoke these words to the disciples. He promised two things in this verse that at first glance seemed to be opposed to each other. First, He promised to leave His peace with us. We make peace with God when we trust Jesus for our salvation; this is known as peace with God. Then He also gives peace to believers as they fellowship with Him; this is known as the peace of God. The second promise in the verse is that we will have tribulation. It is not a matter of if I will experience a trial, it is a matter of when will it happen.

Jesus promised it would be a tough life for all who would follow Him. Various types of trials are our lot in this life. Jesus further admonishes us to be of good cheer, because He has overcome the world. Jesus overcame the world, sin, and the devil by rising from the dead on the third day. Jesus proclaimed victory before He was crucified. Victory was guaranteed before the world was even created. He truly was the Lamb slain before the foundation of the world.

We know that our trials only come as God allows them to. We also know that there will be victory, and that He is in control of everything. How do two seemingly opposing promises come together in our lives? The answer lies in the power of the resurrected Christ. As we go through tribulations, He gives us a peace in our hearts as we pray and surrender to Him. The power of Jesus working in us and through us brings peace.

Suggested Prayer

Dear Lord,
I am in much tribulation and distress. My heart is full of fear, anxiety, and confusion. I ask that You send me Your peace as I go through this storm. May Your power work through my situation. Help me be of good cheer, knowing You have already conquered the enemy. In Your Name I pray, Amen.

Music Is Therapeutic to The Soul

Colossians 3:16

Let the word of Christ dwell in you richly, teaching and admonishing one another in all wisdom, singing psalms and hymns and spiritual songs, with thankfulness in your hearts to God.

Did you ever think that music would help you? Paul tells us to let the Word of Christ dwell in our hearts richly. We are instructed also to teach each other and to warn each other in spiritual wisdom. Then, the apostle says, we should sing psalms, hymns, and spiritual songs, singing them with thankfulness to the Lord. One indication that you are walking with God is that you will sing songs to God out of a heartfelt gratitude to Him. This only happens as we let His words penetrate our hearts. He literally puts a song in our heart that will cause us to praise and adore Him.

So, what kind of music are we listening to? One of the biggest controversies facing churches and families is music. Often the friction lies in preferences and has nothing to do with scripture. Paul gives us some clues in this verse; he tells us the music should be Bible-based and something that is spiritual. Many songs are good but do not necessarily motivate us to worship God.

There might not be anything wrong with the music you listen to, but in the tough times we need music that motivates us in our walk with Him. Some people have been helped by listening to music with lyrics that refer to God; some are helped with purely instrumental music. Some have been helped by music that is even questionable with the established norm.

What music motivates you to get closer to Him or make decisions for Him? What songs encourage your spirit? What songs make you burst out in a spirit of praise? These songs should be the top priority to listen to. Music is such a vast arena and the types and styles vary, so in all your listening find something to encourage you as you walk with Him.

Suggested Prayer ————————————————————

Dear Father,

As I listen to music, help me worship You. Help me live under Your will and to do the right things. Please put a song in my heart in these dark days of mine, Amen.

Taking Responsibility for Our Actions

Psalms 51:4
Against you, you only, have I sinned and done what is evil in your sight, so that you may be justified in your words and blameless in your judgment.

King David was a man after God's own heart, but he was just a man. We might be good Christian people, but at the end of the day we are just sinful men and women—mere flesh. In a moment of weakness David committed adultery with a lady named Bathsheba. He also had her husband Uriah murdered, then he took Bathsheba as one of his wives. When David came to grips with himself he took complete responsibility for his actions. He saw his sin as a sin against God, and God alone. He also felt that God, since He is just, had to discipline him. The king yielded to any correction that God chose for his punishment. God forgave him and cleansed him of his sin, but there were consequences. Bathsheba had a miscarriage, David's daughter was raped, sons were murdered. God said the sword would not leave David's house, meaning there would be a lifetime of consequences for his actions. After all, David had broken two of the biggest commandments. King David was a murderer and an adulterer.

Today we need to take inventory of our sins and take full responsibility for our actions. We cannot always blame our ex-spouse for everything. Our spirits will be set free as we acknowledge our sins and confess them. As we take responsibility for our sins, God can begin the healing process in our lives. He will forgive and restore us, but there are always consequences. The Bible has a true law in its contents called the law of sowing and reaping. We truly reap what we sow. If we sin, there will be consequences!

Suggested Prayer
*Dear Lord,
I admit that I have messed things up. I take full responsibility for my wrong choices. Please cleanse me of my sins and help me make right choices. Discipline me in whatever way You choose. In Your wrath please remember mercy. Thank You for loving me enough to discipline me. In Jesus' Name, Amen.*

Surrender Your Worries To God

1 Peter 5:6-7

Humble yourselves, therefore, under the mighty hand of God so that at the proper time he may exalt you, casting all your anxieties on him, because he cares for you.

We humans try to do everything in our own strength without asking God for help. The result is a life filled with anxiety and stress. Then we feel so weighted down with stress that we cannot function properly. We cannot remember to do the simplest tasks because we are controlled by worries. Peter admonishes us to give all our worries to God.

Our Lord cares about us and wants to help us. We must humble ourselves and put ourselves under the power of His mighty hand, which possesses all power. Then we must lay all our troubles at His feet, trusting that He will take care of them. Once we cast these troubles on Him, we are not to go back to the altar and pick them up again. Leaving them in His hands, we can walk easier, knowing He is in charge and that He is helping us. Praise God!

At the proper time He will exalt us or lift us up. At the proper time we will be lifted from loneliness to joy. At the proper time we will be lifted financially. At the proper time our wounds of divorce will be healed. Our biggest problem in this matter is trusting God enough to cast our problems His way. There is something in our fallen nature that does not want to trust Him. If we go back to the altar and pick up those worries, we do not truly cast them. What a loving God we serve, who will bless us at the proper time.

Suggested Prayer —————————————————————————

Dear Lord,
Forgive me for trying to carry the burden alone. You care for me and want to help me. By faith I give you my worries and fears. I leave them with You this time! Thank You for taking these burdens off my heart. In Jesus' Name, Amen and Amen!

Rely on God's Wisdom

James 1:5
If any of you lacks wisdom, let him ask God, who gives generously to all without reproach, and it will be given him.

James invites us to ask for God's wisdom for the trials we are facing. God gives wisdom to all if we will just ask in faith. The word *all* includes you, whether you are rich or poor. God's desire is that we take on the character of His Son. There are no shortcuts to this sometimes painful process. We all need God's wisdom, not only for trials and troubles but for all aspects of our lives. D. Martyn Lloyd-Jones once said that wisdom is the ability to deal with a situation. God gives us this wisdom generously and He is not holding out on us.

We must be a people of prayer and we must ask for wisdom as we pray. Some feel like the book of James is the New Testament compliment to the Old Testament book of Proverbs. In Proverbs Solomon says, "The fear of the Lord is the beginning of knowledge" (Proverbs 1:7). The "fear of the Lord" means we have a holy respect for God and the things of God. It also includes the thought that God is watching me, my motives, and my actions, and that He will bring everything into judgment, not only in this life but in the life to come.

Solomon could have asked God for anything, and he chose to ask for wisdom to rule the Jewish people. As a result, God gave him riches and he was the wealthiest man on earth. However, Solomon said wisdom was more important than riches, or gold, precious stones. Wisdom is the most important thing that we could ask for and pursue. We have the promise of wisdom found in James as well as in Proverbs. We have this promise offered to "all." Wisdom's perspective will help us go through any trial in a way that will bring honor and glory to God.

Suggested Prayer
Dear Lord,
I do not understand the test that I am going through. Please give me Your wisdom so I will be able to go through this trial in a way that honors You. Lord, I want to do Your will, and I desperately want to do the right things. Thank You, Lord, for helping me and giving me wisdom. In Jesus' Name, Amen.

Getting to The Place of Blessing

Ruth 2:1

Now Naomi had a relative of her husband's, a worthy man of the clan of Elimelech, whose name was Boaz.

One question that many of us have is, "Will God send me another spouse?" The book of Ruth describes how a believing Gentile widow named Ruth married a Jewish man named Boaz. God arranged it all. Ruth came from Moab to Bethlehem during harvest time. She went to glean in a field belonging to Boaz. Ruth put herself in the place of blessing by committing her life to God. She also put herself in the place of blessing by being obedient to God, being faithful to her mother-in-law, and by leaving her country to come to live in Israel with God's people. The Bible in Ruth 3:11 says that Ruth was a "worthy woman." She was in the right place at the right time for the two to meet. Some call it coincidence; others call it providence.

A definition of providence would be that God sees to it beforehand. God sees what we need long before we ever know that we have a need. He knows our needs and supplies them. He works it all out. Boaz had to put himself in the place of blessing to receive a lovely lady like Ruth. Boaz was a kinsman-redeemer, which meant he could marry a widow of a deceased relative to carry on the family name. A kinsman-redeemer had to be near of kin, willing to redeem, and able to redeem.

For Christians to be near of kin means that our new spouse must be a believer in Christ. We must also be *willing* to marry the person. We must be *able* to marry the person. The last part is the toughest. Perhaps our finances make us unable. Maybe our present family obligations make us unable. If God has not put someone in your life, it may be that you are not quite prepared yet. Ruth and Boaz were prepared. We must ask God to show us what we need to do to be prepared so we can be in the place of blessing. So, we have two "worthy" people that God put together. God worked it all out, but both Ruth and Boaz put themselves in the place of blessing so God could do His work. If you desire a new spouse put yourself in the place of blessing. Be worthy!

Suggested Prayer

Lord, I want a Christian spouse. I am willing but I am not able at this time. Lord, I want to enter the place of blessing. Please prepare me so I can receive this blessing. Help me find meaningful things to do as I wait patiently for You to work in my life and my future spouse's life. In Your Name I pray, Amen.

Victory Ahead

1 John 5:4
For everyone who has been born of God overcomes the world. And this is the victory that has overcome the world—our faith.

The apostle John says that Christians are overcomers and that we have victory over this world. When the Bible speaks of the world it means this present evil system that is heavily influenced by Satan and his evil forces. We have all heard the saying, "it seems like the whole world is against me." The truth is that this evil system is against us and has plotted our downfall because it hates God and His people (Jews and Christians). With all this evil against us how can we overcome and have victory?

The answer lies in placing our faith in Jesus Christ. When we trust Him, we are born of God. At the moment of our salvation, we have victory over the world. The forces of darkness cannot take our victory away because we are sealed by the Holy Spirit. We are kept by God's power when we are born of Him. We also need a daily faith in our Lord because the world is trying to overtake us. We cannot become lost, but we can get out of God's plan for us. Faith is only as good as its object.

If we are trusting ourselves to get through this world, we will eventually fall short. However, if we place our faith in God, we will receive victory—not only in the life to come but right here and right now. The object of our faith is the sinless Son of God, who has all power. The world wants the tragedy that you experienced to be your death-blow spiritually. God wants you to trust Him daily, so you will get the victory and He can make something great out of all your troubles. As you depend on Him you will begin to receive this victory and begin overcoming the world. You will find that you can trust Him for your soul and your sorrow.

Suggested Prayer
Dear Lord,
I overcame the world when You saved me and made me your child. Lord, I am having trouble in this world with all its temptations. I place my faith in You and believe You will turn my tattered life into a victorious life that will help others. Father, into Your hand I give this, trusting only You. I die to my way and yield to Your way. In Jesus' Name, Amen.

Keep Up The Good Work

Titus 3:8

The saying is trustworthy, and I want you to insist on these things, so that those who have believed in God may be careful to devote themselves to good works. These things are excellent and profitable for people.

When Paul wrote to the younger pastor Titus, he instructed the pastor about many things concerning the church. Paul wanted Titus to tell his congregation to devote themselves to good works. Notice that good works are for believers, not because they had to work for their salvation, but rather they are working because of their salvation. Some are working, hoping to get to heaven. A believer is working because he or she is already going to heaven. There is a major difference, and the difference is a matter of life and death.

We believers need to be doing good things that will help others and further God's kingdom. We are God's hands and His feet for this task. He chooses to use us, and it is a privilege to be used by Him. We may have been victimized, but we are not victims. This is not a time to draw back and quit on God.

As we begin to work in His Kingdom our problems seem to get smaller and smaller. Our attention becomes outward instead of inward. We reap what we sow. As we help others, we receive the help that we need. Someone has well said that it is always too soon to quit. The devil and the hosts of hell would have us throw in the towel, but there is a race to run and a prize to obtain. Dust yourself off and get back in the race. What we do for God is the only thing that really matters anyway. Go to the Titus of your church and ask how you can be involved in serving.

Suggested Prayer —————————————————————————
Dear Lord,
Through all of my trials I stopped serving You. Forgive me, Lord, and help me to be zealous to serve You again. Lord, I don't know what to do or how to do it, but I am trusting You. Give me something to do and put some people in my life that I can encourage. In the Name of Jesus I pray, Amen.

Rejoice in God Despite the Circumstances

Habakkuk 3:17-19

Though the fig tree should not blossom, nor fruit be on the vines, the produce of the olive fail and the fields yield no food, the flock be cut off from the fold and there be no herd in the stalls, yet I will rejoice in the LORD; I will take joy in the God of my salvation. GOD, the Lord, is my strength; he makes my feet like the deer's; he makes me tread on my high places.

Habakkuk the prophet knew the Babylonians were coming to destroy Jerusalem. Nothing could change this fact. Israel had sinned and God was going to judge them. The Jewish people would be taken from their homeland for seventy years. Habakkuk saw that there would be desperate times and food would be scarce. He decided beforehand that he would rejoice in the Lord. He realized that God was his salvation, strength, and song. He also knew his steps would be sure and steady as he trusted God. There would be no shortcuts to this trial, so he decided to find his joy in God.

We might not have seen the disaster coming, but our admonition is the same: rejoice in the Lord. After seventy years God had accomplished His work and the Jews returned and rebuilt Jerusalem. God has a timetable for you too. It might be months or years before you are restored financially. You might have to struggle just to get by for years. It also may be years before God gives you another spouse. So, we should rejoice in Him and let Him do His perfect work. Rejoice in God now! Do not wait for everything to be perfect in your life before you begin to praise Him again.

Suggested Prayer ————————————————————————

Dear Father,
My life has been invaded by the enemy. Today I realize that there are no shortcuts to this trial. You have a perfect timetable in which You will work everything out. Today I choose to rejoice in You. You are my salvation, strength, and song. I choose to find my joy in You.

There Are No Shortcuts

Mark 14:34-36

And he said to them, "My soul is very sorrowful, even to death. Remain here and watch." And going a little farther, he fell on the ground and prayed that, if it were possible, the hour might pass from him. And he said, "Abba, Father, all things are possible for you. Remove this cup from me. Yet not what I will, but what you will."

The night before Jesus died on the cross He prayed in the garden of Gethsemane that the Father would let Him bypass Calvary. The word "Gethsemane" means oil press. People would take olives and roll a circular stone over them to release the oil. Jesus also went through the oil press, not to make olive oil but to redeem mankind. Theories abound as to why Jesus wanted to bypass Calvary. Some feel that He had never broken fellowship with the Father and His death would break this bond for a short time. Still others feel He wanted to escape the shame and the pain of crucifixion. The main point is there were no shortcuts. Jesus was the Lamb slain from the foundation of the world. God's plan was to send His Son to die for our sins long before there was such a thing as sin, or Adam and Eve for that matter (John 3:16). Jesus submitted to the Father's will and became sin for us so we could have eternal life. The road was paved with pain and suffering.

We too must submit to the Father's plan for us and there are no shortcuts. If God wants us to endure loneliness and discouragement, we should embrace these things. Keep in mind that it is only temporary, only until He works out His plan. Jesus was on the cross six hours before He died. Three days later He arose, never to die again. Your pain is only temporary, but unfortunately there are no shortcuts.

Suggested Prayer ——————————————————————————————

Lord,

I really do not like my situation and the things that I am going through. Not my will but Thine be done! I embrace the suffering. Remind me that the pain is only temporary. Accomplish Your will in me. I surrender to the Gethsemane and Calvary of my life trusting that a resurrection will occur. In the Name of Jesus I pray, Amen.

Christ Lives in Me

Galatians 2:20
I have been crucified with Christ. It is no longer I who live, but Christ who lives in me. And the life I now live in the flesh I live by faith in the Son of God, who loved me and gave himself for me.

Paul said his old life was actually crucified with Christ. When Jesus was crucified, so were our old sinful lives. Now we live, but it is not us living; it is Christ living through us. When we were born again all three persons of the godhead began to live in our hearts. This life that we are living in our flesh is through faith in Christ.

Paul emphasized the fact that God loves us and gave Himself for us. God could have let us all perish, but He chose to put love into action by dying for us. We now have new life in our spirits. Resurrection power flows through us. God can now control our minds, bodies, and emotions. God can live out His purpose in us. Each one of us was individually made by God. So, we need to ask God why He made us. What is His purpose for each of us? We have Christ in us, the hope of glory. We need not be like the world and trust the arm of flesh. We have the mighty hand of God in us to help us.

From this day forward, we need to see our old lives as dead and new life begun in Christ. We need to quit worrying and start worshipping. We need to quit pouting and start praising the all-powerful One who is working on our behalf. What power lies within us! Let us quit being discouraged and start realizing Christ lives in us. God is faithful and will not fail to keep us safe. Since He lives in us, He will never leave us or forsake us. We need to quit living defeated, discouraged lives and start depending on the power of Jesus to overcome this world.

Suggested Prayer
Dear God,
I have been defeated trying to do this all by myself. I realize that my old life is gone and I have new life in You. I count my old life as crucified and dead and buried to rise no more. Now I choose to live in your power by faith. When things become rough let me realize You live in me. In Jesus' Name, Amen.

Family and Friends Can Say Hateful Things

Job 8:4

If your children have sinned against him, he has delivered them into the hand of their transgression.

Job had seven sons and three daughters that all died in a tragic accident when a great wind destroyed the home that they were all in. All ten children died in this accident as they were having a family get-together. No doubt some died a painful death. Job had three friends that came to visit him with the purpose of comforting him. For seven days and nights they sat with Job and did not say anything. They were a tremendous help until they began to talk and analyze Job's situation. Bildad, one of the three friends, told Job the words we find in today's text. He was basically saying that Job's ten children got the punishment that they deserved. This is one of the most horrible verses in all of scripture.

We cannot imagine telling a friend who has lost a child that his son or daughter got what they deserved. These horrible, inaccurate words are recorded in the Word of God to let us know that family and friends can really be cruel. The problem lies in the fact that none of Job's friends understood the testing that he was experiencing. Job himself did not even know what was happening to him. In the end God gave Job twice as much as he had before the testing began. God gave him seven more sons and three more daughters. Now Job had fourteen sons and six daughters. Seven sons and three daughters were living with God in heaven, and the other seven sons and three daughters lived on earth with Job and his wife. He never really lost his first family because they are living with God.

Hold on! God has a purpose in your suffering! Keep in mind that well-meaning friends will be cruel and say horrible things. Take their horrible words to God in prayer. Ask God to forgive them and ask for forgiveness so their words do not hinder your walk. In the end, only God knows what is going on in our lives; not family, not friends, not even ourselves.

Suggested Prayer

Dear Lord,

I am hurt! My friends and family have hurt me, not with knives or guns but with hateful words. Lord, it hurts so much! Help me see Your purpose, if possible, in my suffering. Father, I forgive them for their hateful words. I ask that You heal me from all these words. In Jesus' Name, Amen.

FEBRUARY 4

Friends Can Bring Refreshment

Philemon 1:7
For I have derived much joy and comfort from your love, my brother, because the hearts of the saints have been refreshed through you.

Not all friends are like Job's miserable comforters. Philemon was a man who refreshed the soul of the apostle Paul like a glass of cold water on a hot day. It is a remarkable thing to be able to bring joy and comfort to the man who wrote so much of the New Testament. How was Philemon able to bring comfort to the apostle and other Christians? His great secret was found in his heart. In his heart he truly loved God and other people. He loved God and people unconditionally. He did not bargain with God and say he would serve Him under certain conditions.

He chose to love God with agape love, or unconditional love. He loved as Jesus loved. He also loved people with the same agape love too. He loved people unconditionally! Now this is a rare jewel that was found in Philemon's heart. He was not your average Christian. He poured out God's love to those he met. That is why people like Paul received joy, comfort, and refreshment from him.

Guess what? God has not changed. The Lord Himself will send you a good friend who loves Jesus and who will refresh your spirit. This friend will be there for you when you really need encouragement. In our weak hours and days of discouragement we need a friend who can strengthen us. A cry for help is not wrong; it is what the Great Physician prescribed. This friend will have an open heart, open hand, and an open home. Do not despair! Help is on the way!

Suggested Prayer
Dear Lord,
I feel dry in my spirit. I am reading Your Word and praying, but I also need a friend like Philemon. I am weak and need a strong friend who loves You. By faith I already receive this friend You are sending. Please give me this friend to help me, and may I also be a blessing to him or her too. Thank You, Jesus. Amen.

Comfort Me, Lord, and Put a Purpose in My Life

2 Thessalonians 2:16-17

Now may our Lord Jesus Christ himself, and God our Father, who loved us and gave us eternal comfort and good hope through grace, comfort your hearts and establish them in every good work and word.

When we go through a divorce our whole world is thrown upside down. We are on one big emotional roller coaster ride with seemingly no way off the ride. We lack comfort in our hearts, and we have lost our sense of purpose. Paul says that we have eternal comfort and a good hope through the grace of God who loves us. We understand that in the future there is comfort, but we need some comfort now.

The Father, Son, and Spirit work together to comfort our hearts. God loves us so much that when we cry out to Him, He fellowships with us and leaves His comfort in our hearts. He comes alongside us and brings this comfort. God could send angels down to comfort us, but this verse says that "Jesus himself" brings the comfort. God "himself" is personally working with me to bring about this comfort. Jesus is comfort, and the Holy Spirit is the Comforter. God is comfort, and this describes who He is and what He does. He is comfort and brings comfort.

Then Paul says he establishes our hearts in good words and works. As God works in us, we begin to speak comforting words to those around us. We begin to be used by God to be His mouthpiece. Then He gives us something to do. We begin doing the things that will make a difference in time and eternity. God comforts us and gives us a purpose, just because He loves us. As we work for Him and speak for Him, we begin to see that He really does have a purpose for us. It is an awesome thing to let God use you to do His work here on earth.

Suggested Prayer

Dear God,

I need Your comfort and Your purpose. Please flood my soul with Your comfort, and then establish my heart in good words and works. Help me be a comfort to others. Help me speak the gospel to the lost. Help me do things with these hands that will make a difference. In Jesus' Name I pray, Amen.

Our Children Need God's Word

Deuteronomy 6:6-7
And these words that I command you today shall be on your heart. You shall teach them diligently to your children, and shall talk of them when you sit in your house, and when you walk by the way, and when you lie down, and when you rise.

Before we can teach the Bible to our children we must treasure it in our own hearts. As we live by the Word and cherish its precepts, it will not be difficult to share it with our children. The Word will flow from our hearts to theirs as a natural result of our obedience to God and His Word.

We must be diligent and consistent in our teaching of the Scriptures. When you are at the dinner table, bring up a verse that you have recently learned. This method is informal and meaningful. It is also a topic of conversation and fits into the busiest of schedules. As you begin to share at the table the Holy Spirit begins to work on hearts and lives.

Beware—the enemy will make your phone ring, the dog will begin barking, and a whole host of distractions will come your way. Be diligent! The rewards are eternal. When you take your children places, be sure to show them how God's Word applies to the world around them. When the day is done and you lie down in bed, think of a verse in the Bible. Surprisingly, you will wake up thinking about the Word.

Your children will appreciate your spiritual leadership and thank you for guiding them in the right path. Your life and the lives of your children need to be anchored in the Word of God. The enemy has destroyed the family, but he does not need to destroy the wonderful lives of these precious children. Let's give them the foundation in the Word so they can live for God. May God bless your diligent efforts!

Suggested Prayer
Father,
Help me! I want to know and live by Your Word. Let me cherish it in my heart. May my heart overflow with Your Word. May I teach it diligently to my children, and may it change our lives. May I share it with everyone. Holy Spirit, make it real to us. We love You, Jesus, because You are the living Word. Amen.

Go Have Some Fun

John 21:3

Simon Peter said to them, "I am going fishing." They said to him, "We will go with you." They went out and got into the boat, but that night they caught nothing.

Peter decided that he was going fishing, and six other disciples decided to join him. They fished all night long and caught nothing. But then Jesus appeared, and they netted one hundred fifty-three keepers. The decision to go fishing opened a way for these seven men to have an encounter with Jesus.

Determine to have some fun and take your kids along. We all need a break from the stress of life and to just get away. Having fun is contagious. It encourages other stress-filled people to go have some fun too. More importantly, when Jesus makes Himself known to you and your children or friends, it makes for lasting memories and gives you strength for the journey.

Separated and divorced people often do not have the funds for enjoyable activities. Everything costs money, and this keeps many families from enjoying things. We should ask God for wisdom for what we can do for fun that will fit into our budgets. We can also ask Him to surprise us. It is an awesome thing to experience when someone calls you to give you free tickets to a concert or sporting event.

Our finances may be limited, but God is not limited. He owns everything. Pray to Him and explain your situation to Him. Then watch Him work. He will provide something for you to do that will draw your family closer to each other and closer to Him.

Suggested Prayer

Dear Lord,

I want to have fun with my kids, but my resources are very limited. Please give me wisdom to find some inexpensive things to do. Surprise me, Lord! You can do the impossible! You know my desires and what my children like to do. Please bring something about that we can enjoy and get closer to You and to each other. I thank You for what You are about to do. In Jesus' Name I pray, Amen.

Help Lord! I Am So Tempted!

1 Thessalonians 4:3-8

For this is the will of God, your sanctification: that you abstain from sexual immorality; that each one of you know how to control his own body in holiness and honor, not in the passion of lust like the Gentiles who do not know God; that no one transgress and wrong his brother in this matter, because the Lord is an avenger in all these things, as we told you beforehand and solemnly warned you. For God has not called us for impurity, but in holiness. Therefore whoever disregards this, disregards not man but God, who gives his Holy Spirit to you.

Paul plainly tells us that part of God's will for our lives is that we abstain from sexual immorality. God wants us to be set apart, holy for Himself. The word "sanctification" means to be set apart. Christians are set apart for God from this sinful world. At the right time He will send us a spouse. He expects us to control our thoughts, desires, and actions. If we reject this area of our lives, we are rejecting the Holy Spirit. No matter what our circumstances or how we feel, God expects us to be holy. Some feel that they are entitled to live lives of immorality and that God does not really care if we are holy or not. Some feel that they can get by with a little sin and that God will not judge them.

We must rely on the Holy Spirit when we are tempted. We will all be tempted, but our faithful God has made a way of escape for every temptation. When the dust settles, we fall short because we chose to sin. We thought our way was better than God's way. To save a lot of heartache we must rely on God. There is victory if we surrender our wills and passions to God. One destroyed family is one too many. We need to make sure that we are not the devil's instrument in destroying other families.

Suggested Prayer —————————————————————

Dear Lord,
I am tempted to sin against You. When sinful thoughts and desires come, please help me overcome the temptation. Holy Spirit, I do not want to reject You. Lord, keep me pure and holy, trusting that You will put another spouse in my life. Amen.

I Can't Go Through Another Year Like This

Isaiah 43:2

When you pass through the waters, I will be with you; and through the rivers, they shall not overwhelm you; when you walk through the fire you shall not be burned, and the flame shall not consume you.

Jesus said we would go through many trials in life. We are familiar with the saying, "out of the frying pan and into the fire." Our text says there will be waters to go through. Isaiah uses the word "when," letting the reader know that trials are coming, and it is just a matter of "when." God offers His presence as we go through these waters. The Holy Spirit in this verse plainly says, "I will be with you." We are not alone! God is with us each step of the way. We may not feel Him or see His work, but He is with us. Some trials are even harder and could be considered rivers to pass through. Again, God promises that these tough trials will not overwhelm us.

Isaiah speaks of going through the fire, which could be considered the most difficult trial we have ever encountered. He promises that we will not be burned through this difficult situation. We see God's great hand of protection in this text, knowing that these trying times are not going to harm us. In the end, it will all be for our good and His glory.

Trials vary in durations of time. It might not take long to go through the waters, but it might take years to go through the fires. In this verse Isaiah used the word "through" three times. With God's help we will get through the various trials that this year offers. Trials are difficult, but we are going through them. This verse is a promise of victory through various circumstances. There is still victory in Jesus. We are His possession. He created us, formed us, redeemed us, called us—and He owns us.

Suggested Prayer —————————————————

Dear Sovereign Lord,
I know this year will have many trials. I know that You will give me victory, because Your Word says I am going through each difficulty. Thank You for helping me get through my trials. In Jesus' Name, Amen.

God Is at Work

John 3:8
The wind blows where it wishes, and you hear its sound, but you do not know where it comes from or where it goes. So it is with everyone who is born of the Spirit.

Nicodemus, the leading religious teacher in Israel, was curious about Jesus and sought a private interview with Him. He recognized the fact that Jesus was from God because of the miracles that He was performing. Jesus told Nicodemus that he must experience a new birth if he were to ever enter heaven. He plainly told this Pharisee that he must be born again. Jesus' comment seems strange since Nicodemus was one of the best teachers in the land.

A person is born again when they believe the gospel and the Spirit of God makes them new in Christ. Jesus said the Spirit is like the wind. We cannot see the wind, but we can see the leaves and limbs of the trees swaying back and forth. We can hear the wind blow, but we cannot see it. We always have the wind, but do not notice it unless a strong gust comes our way. The Wind of the Holy Spirit is always blowing in our lives. Sometimes it is a recognizable gust and we feel God's presence. However, most of the time there is a gentle breeze on our hearts that often goes unrecognized.

The great truth is that God is always working on our hearts, just like the earth has the wind working on it. Rest assured, the Wind of the Spirit is blowing on your soul. May we earnestly strive to keep God first in our lives so we can sense His working in our midst! May God open our ears that we might hear the sound of the Holy Spirit working in our lives!

Suggested Prayer
Dear Lord,
I claim the fact that You are active and present in my life. Holy Spirit, let me see Your work in my life. I might not always see that You are working, but I trust that You are accomplishing Your will in my life. Let me be aware of Your presence. In Jesus' Name, Amen.

Dealing with Doubt

Matthew 11:2-6

Now when John heard in prison about the deeds of the Christ, he sent word by his disciples and said to him, "Are you the one who is to come, or shall we look for another?" And Jesus answered them, "Go and tell John what you hear and see: the blind receive their sight and the lame walk, lepers are cleansed and the deaf hear, and the dead are raised up, and the poor have good news preached to them. And blessed is the one who is not offended by me."

Jesus said that among men there was not a greater than John the Baptist, and yet John had doubts about his relationship to Christ. John was a hellfire-and-brimstone preacher. He called the religious establishment a generation of vipers and told them to repent. John lived in seclusion until he was thirty years old. At thirty he began a six-month ministry, telling the people to repent and trust the coming Messiah. He baptized Jesus, but was thrown in prison because he told Herod that his marriage to his brother Phillip's wife was wrong.

John was full of faith and assurance until he was thrown in prison. At that time John's mind began to wander. All he had was time to sit and think about his problems. 'Is this how it all ends? Is Jesus coming to rescue me? I preached about the coming King and now I am rotting away in prison.' John sent word to Jesus asking if He really was the true Messiah.

We also let our minds wander. When things are going well we do not worry about things. But when tragedy hits, our minds begin to wander and doubt replaces faith. Jesus' reply was that the lame walk, the blind now see, the dead are being raised, lepers are healed, the deaf can hear, and the poor are hearing the good news. Jesus' reply lets us know that He is real and He is working, even though it may not seem like it. If we have believed in Christ we are saved, no matter how we feel or what our circumstances. Our conditions and feelings change but God does not change. He is our Savior and His commitment to us is irrevocable.

Suggested Prayer

Dear Lord,

This idle time is bringing doubt upon my spirit. Help me use my time wisely, but more importantly, clear my mind from these doubts. Lord, please assure my heart in Your salvation. Let me see that my commitment to You is real and strong. Holy Spirit, please give me assurance. I believe in You, God. Amen.

God's Purpose in the Bad Things That Happen

Genesis 50:20

As for you, you meant evil against me, but God meant it for good, to bring it about that many people should be kept alive, as they are today.

Joseph suffered tremendously in his life. He had dreams from God that eventually saved his family, all of Egypt, and even preserved the Jewish nation. As a teen, his brothers hated him because he was daddy's favorite and because of his dreams. As a teen, his brothers threw him in a pit and then sold him as a slave. He went from the pit to Potipher's palace, where he was wrongly accused of having an affair with his master's wife. He was then thrown into prison.

In prison Joseph interpreted the dreams of Pharaoh's chief butler and chief baker. Eventually Pharaoh had a disturbing dream about a seven-year drought. Joseph interpreted the dream and Pharaoh made him prime minister of all of Egypt. During these years of drought Joseph's brothers came to Egypt to buy grain. Eventually Joseph and his brothers reunited. His brothers apologized, and that is when Joseph made the statement in this verse. Joseph realized that the suffering he endured was to preserve his family and Egypt in the seven-year drought. God also wanted the Jews in Egypt for four hundred years so they could become a great nation. After that time Moses brought them to the promised land.

What our ex-spouses and others meant for evil against us, God meant for good—to accomplish a bigger purpose. God is taking all this evil against us and accomplishing His will.

Suggested Prayer

God, I have been hurt to the core of my being. All this evil against me has destroyed my spirit. God, You meant all of this for good. Help me see Your hand in all of this. I trust that You are bringing about a bigger purpose for me. Forgive those who have wronged me. In the Name of Your Son Jesus, I pray, Amen.

Me, a Witness to the Gospel?

Acts 1:8

But you will receive power when the Holy Spirit has come upon you, and you will be my witnesses in Jerusalem and in all Judea and Samaria, and to the end of the earth."

Just before Jesus ascended to heaven He gave the apostles a job to do. It was more than a job—it would be a life changing mission that would impact the world. The impact of the task is ongoing, reaching to the farthest parts of the globe. He was commissioning the church to share the gospel with the whole world.

The gospel is the good news, or the God story. It includes Jesus' birth, life, death, resurrection, and ascension. Jesus said that the church would receive dynamic, miraculous power to share God's Word when the Holy Spirit would come upon the apostles. Jesus told them to share with people of their own city (Jerusalem), then their surrounding region (Judea), then the other regions of Israel (Samaria), and ultimately to the rest of the world. On the day of Pentecost, the church received the power of the Holy Spirit to witness. The church then began sharing the good news and people's lives were forever changed.

The mission for the church is still the same. We are to share the gospel in the power of the Spirit until Jesus comes back. When we yield to the Holy Spirit the words will begin to flow from our mouths. He will guide us to the people who need to hear. He will also guide us to share the good news with the rest of the world. He will give us creative ideas to share. You say, "Me? A witness? I can't do that!" If that is your idea you are exactly right. You cannot be a witness, but God can. Yield to Him and let His miraculous power flow out of your life. You will find that He does all the work. We just need to yield to Him and let Him speak through us.

Suggested Prayer ⎯⎯⎯⎯⎯⎯⎯⎯⎯⎯⎯⎯⎯⎯⎯⎯⎯⎯⎯

Dear Lord,
I tried to share the gospel and failed. I yield myself to You and ask that Your power will flow through me. Let me witness in my city, region, country, and around the world. Please use me. Holy Spirit, I yield to Your Sovereignty. In Jesus' Name I pray, Amen.

Giving Is Tough Right Now

Proverbs 3:9-10
Honor the LORD with your wealth and with the first fruits of all your produce; then your barns will be filled with plenty, and your vats will be bursting with wine.

Divorce often leads to desperate times financially. People cut and cut and cut some more to try to balance their dwindling resources. If we are not careful, we will cut out our giving. Some churches have not done a good job when it comes to teaching the subject of giving. Many teach on giving like it is a magic formula for riches and success. The church tells us to give ten percent but fails to tell us we need to be wise with the ninety percent.

Any Christian who gives to God must be wise with all his or her finances. All our money belongs to God and He expects us to be good stewards with it all. Our financial problems are not God's fault and His kingdom should not suffer by our not giving. Tithes and offerings honor the Lord. We should first give ourselves to God, then we can start to give to God in a financial way.

The text implies saving when it speaks of our barns being filled with plenty. There is a biblical balance with giving and saving. Instead of cutting God out of the picture, bring Him into the picture by praying and asking Him to lead and guide you and your finances. God will honor you as you honor Him in your giving.

God knows the trouble you are having and really wants to help you. Invite Him to work in this area of your life. Things might not happen as fast as you would like them to, but He will work things out. God often works through a process that teaches us and gets us closer to Him. God may work slowly, but He is sure. All of this takes time. In the end there will be great freedom as you are able to give and manage what is left over. You will have your needs supplied and the work of God will be well funded.

Suggested Prayer —————————————————————————
Dear God,
I am struggling to give. Right now, I give myself to You and I give You my finances. I invite You to lead me into a path that will help me give joyfully and still manage my household. Thank You for Your care and for helping me. Amen.

God Will Turn Your Finances Around

Proverbs 13:11

Wealth gained hastily will dwindle, but whoever gathers little by little will increase it.

God honors our honesty and integrity. He is more concerned about our behavior than our bank account. Praise God that He is actually interested in both. If we obtain wealth by fraud or cheating, God will make sure that our unrighteous efforts will dwindle down. We should never take advantage of people to make money. However, God says that He will honor our diligent work ethic. We will obtain wealth little by little as we work honestly and prayerfully. God will give us wisdom, knowledge, and insight to gain wealth if we ask Him.

It is not God's will for us to be in debt and to be worried all the time about money. We cannot live presumptuously with our finances. Many people spend what they want, never budgeting, trusting God will work it all out. People often do not think about finances and retirement until it is too late.

Spending money on things is deeply tied to our emotions. People that are going through a divorce feel horrible about themselves and often go out and buy things, hoping to find happiness. This spending habit does make them happy, but it is only a temporary happiness. So many have bought a new vehicle to feel better about themselves, only to find out that they feel worse now that they have accumulated a big debt.

As we find our well-being and worth in Christ, we will find that we do not need things to satisfy us. Resolve to curb unnecessary spending. Resolve to work honestly. Resolve to use God's wisdom in your finances. The result will be that little by little your wealth will increase. You will pay off your debts and begin saving. May God bless your efforts as you honor Him.

Suggested Prayer ———————————————————————

Dear Father,
I have tried so hard to get out of debt and to achieve financial freedom. Lord, I need Your wisdom. Please give me wisdom to handle Your finances. I purpose to do things honestly with integrity. Please bless me little by little. Help me gain confidence in You as I begin to see You work. In Jesus' Name, Amen.

Getting Our Finances Back in Order

Proverbs 24:27
Prepare your work outside; get everything ready for yourself in the field, and after that build your house.

S olomon gave some wonderful advice in this verse, basically saying a young man should establish his career first and then get married. If young people would follow this advice it would save them a lot of heartache. Bible professor James Sewell used to say, "Two can live as one half as long." Dr. Sewell would encourage his students to stay in school and finish their studies before marrying. His desire was to see God's purpose fulfilled in the lives of his young students.

So how does this verse apply to a divorced person? Before we decide to remarry, we should make sure we are firmly reestablished. Notice that Solomon says "your" twice and "yourself" once in this verse. We must do some things to prepare for the wonderful life God has planned for us. We might have good careers, but the effects of divorce have left us high and dry in many cases. We should establish ourselves financially. We should make sure our children are taken care of; then and only then can we build a new house under God's will and guidance. If we do not get our lives right and our finances right before a new marriage, the result will not be good.

Ask God to show you what exactly it is that you need to work on to establish your house. Once He shows you what you need to do; come up with a plan of action. Plan the work and work the plan! Trust God to work all things out for you. He knows your financial situation and He also know your need of a companion. In His time, it will all work out as you obediently wait on Him.

Suggested Prayer ———————————————————————————————
Dear Lord,
I am lonely and want a companion. However, I want to do things Your way and in Your time. I give myself to You. Help me establish my finances again and help me take care of my own family. Let me have finances that will honor You. Then, please send me a companion that I can serve You with. In the Name of Jesus I pray, Amen.

Do You Know Your Financial State?

Proverbs 27:23-24
Know well the condition of your flocks, and give attention to your herds, for riches do not last forever; and does a crown endure to all generations?

How many people live from paycheck to paycheck, never really thinking about retirement? If they want to purchase something, they just charge the item. Solomon warns us that riches do not last forever. He knows a king cannot always stay on his throne just like riches will not always be there for us. He says to know well the condition of your assets. Can you afford repairs on your housing and transportation? Do you have adequate funds for food and clothing? Will you help your children continue their education? Will you be able to retire?

Solomon also wanted the reader to pay attention to his possessions. If we do not pay attention to the resources that God has given us, we will pay a big price. Jesus said that if we are not faithful with such a small thing as money, He would not be able to trust us with bigger things. If we can be faithful in the small things God can entrust us with bigger things. We simply cannot do anything without the help of God. He is our Helper and He desires to help!

It is a good time to know well your financial condition and pay attention to what you have, especially after a divorce when half of your assets are gone. A divorce may set back your retirement several years. A divorce is a prime example of how riches can be here one day and gone the next. Take a financial assessment. Know well your financial condition. Pay attention to your wealth and determine that you will do your absolute best in this area of your life. We cannot wake up one morning five years from retirement and start a financial assessment. Now is the time to consider your ways and make the necessary adjustments.

Suggested Prayer
Dear Lord,
Help me honestly see where I am financially. Help me consider my wealth and pay attention to it. Help me make the right choices because wealth will not always be available to me. Lord, I want to be faithful with earthly riches so You can entrust me with heavenly riches. Amen.

You Are the Answer to Your Own Financial Problems

Proverbs 31:24-25
She makes linen garments and sells them; she delivers sashes to the merchant. Strength and dignity are her clothing, and she laughs at the time to come.

The virtuous woman described in Proverbs 31:10-31 did not worry about finances. Things that worry us did not bother her because she planned and prepared for the future. She was even able to reach out and help the poor. Two striking things were the keys to her success. The first key was she had a good relationship with God and followed His Word. She had the fear of the Lord that Solomon emphasizes in the book of Proverbs. She was an example of a person who had a holy respect for God and followed Him. The second key was that she found things that she was good at and made money doing these things. We are all good at something. She was good at making clothing, gardening, and real estate. She used those skills to provide for her home and she was well set financially. In other words, she was able to market her skills.

You probably already know what you are good at. If you are not sure what your expertise is, pray to God and ask Him. If you are still not sure, ask some trusted friends that know you well. Do not tell yourself that you are not good at anything. That is the voice of the enemy talking to your spirit. When you find out what you are good at, ask God to help you market those skills to help you get out of debt and become financially solvent. You are the answer to your problems. The virtuous woman has given you two keys to success. One key is to develop your relationship with God; the other key is to find out what you are good at and market your skill.

Suggested Prayer ————————————————————
Dear God,
I want to have an awesome relationship with You, so please teach me how. I understand it begins with a fear or holy respect for You. God, I also want financial freedom to serve You better. Show me what I am good at. Then please give me the wisdom to market my skill. Help me not only to become financially free, but to be blessed in such a way that I can help others. In the Name of Jesus I pray, Amen.

Be on Guard—the Devil Wants to Take Away Everything You Have Worked For

2 John 8

Watch yourselves, so that you may not lose what we have worked for, but may win a full reward.

John desires that we would not be led astray by false teachers who would destroy everything we have worked for. John wants us to receive a full reward on judgment day. We all want to hear the words "well done, my good and faithful servant." There are false teachers who deny the deity of Jesus Christ and spread a false doctrine that denies Christ and the truth of the gospel. Many deceivers are out there, and they are antichrists, powered by the devil himself. John emphasizes the truth of the gospel, which is centered around Jesus Christ. Beware! The devil will make sure that these false teachers find you.

We are all weak and vulnerable, especially when we have experienced personal tragedies. Any teaching that denies the doctrine of the deity of Christ is from Satan, the father of all lies. The truth is that **Jesus is God**. He was not an angel or a mere man. He was the God-man. He was one hundred percent God and yet he was in a human body, making Him also one hundred percent man.

The devil always offers shortcuts and only temporary help. Temporary satisfaction is a poor replacement for losing an eternal reward. A full reward comes by following our Savior, God manifested in the flesh—Jesus Christ. So be on guard and do not lose what you have worked for. Ask God to protect you from the enemy, because he is walking back and forth throughout the earth, seeking to devour the weak sheep of God's flock. Your divorce has made you weak emotionally. Beware!

Suggested Prayer

Dear Lord,
I am weak! Please put a hedge of protection around me. Help me discern when evil forces are at work in my life. Jesus, I believe in You. I commit myself to You. Holy Spirit, help me not to lose what I have worked for, but let me receive a full reward. In the Name and power of Jesus I pray, Amen.

Are Your Children Walking with God?

3 John 3-4
For I rejoiced greatly when the brothers came and testified to your truth, as indeed you are walking in the truth. I have no greater joy than to hear that my children are walking in the truth.

The apostle John loved the truth. He emphasized that he rejoiced greatly when he found out that his children were walking in the truth. In the strictest literal sense John is referring to fellow Christians that he probably led to Christ. He considered these Christians his children, since they were birthed into the family of God under his ministry.

In a broader application, what about our physical offspring? Do you have children? If so, are they walking in the truth? What is the truth that John is referring to? It is simply the truth about God as revealed in the scriptures. In other words, are your children followers of Jesus Christ? Parents, this is your top priority. Make sure your children know Jesus. Jesus Himself said that He was the truth (John 14:6). Children are often the most neglected when it comes to divorce. They are the ones who suffer the most. They are torn between two homes and two worlds battling for their allegiance. Both parents are trying to win the love and respect of the children. The devil is also trying to destroy the children too. It is tough to be a child of divorced parents.

Be that parent that loves them as Jesus would have you to love. Be that parent who is willing to set aside personal interests, and perhaps even dating, to make sure your kids are walking in the truth of Jesus. If you feel that your children have been neglected, begin to ask God for wisdom to turn the situation around.

Suggested Prayer
*Dear Lord,
I know my children are suffering. Let me put aside my personal interests to ensure that my children know You and that they are walking with You. By faith I receive that my time will come where I can be remarried and enjoy companionship. Until then let me and my children concentrate on walking with You. Amen.*

God Is Keeping Score, So Play by The Rules

2 Samuel 16:12

It may be that the LORD will look on the wrong done to me, and that the LORD will repay me with good for his cursing today.

King David had to flee from his kingdom because his son Absalom rebelled against him and took over his throne. As David fled, a man named Shimei cursed him and threw rocks at him. The warriors that were with David wanted to kill Shimei, but for some reason David would not allow it. In the end Shimei was executed by King Solomon, David's son and successor to the throne.

David felt that God would repay him with good for all the wrong that had been done to him. God does see all the wrong that has been done to us. God made our eyes, and our sight is limited; but God's perfect eyes see everything. Vengeance belongs to God and He will punish those who have wronged us. David never had to lift a finger against this rock-throwing man. We also do not need to seek revenge. If those who have wronged us deserve punishment, God will do it and He does not need our help.

David felt that God would repay him with good for having the right attitude towards his persecutors. God always blesses us when we are obedient to Him and let Him fight our battles. God is keeping a record of all our good deeds and not one of them goes unnoticed. God also sees how we respond to the evils that are hurled against us. He will bless us when we respond properly. Like David, we can believe that God is looking at those who have caused us trouble and He will repay us with good. Let us determine to live as He would have us to live, trusting Him to take care of all things, even those who are causing trouble in our lives.

Suggested Prayer ———————————————————————

Dear God,
You have seen those who have caused me trouble. Lord, I do not want You to judge them. Please bless those who have cursed me. Look upon my cause for good, and please open the windows of heaven and pour out a blessing on me as I purpose in my heart to live by Your Word. In Jesus' Name I pray, Amen.

Where Did Everyone Go?

2 Timothy 4:16-18

At my first defense no one came to stand by me, but all deserted me. May it not be charged against them! But the Lord stood by me and strengthened me, so that through me the message might be fully proclaimed and all the Gentiles might hear it. So I was rescued from the lion's mouth. The Lord will rescue me from every evil deed and bring me safely into his heavenly kingdom. To him be the glory forever and ever. Amen.

When Paul wrote 2 Timothy he was in prison. Paul wished someone would have been by his side at the trial. He longed for a friend, but everyone had deserted him. He prayed that God would not judge those who should have offered help. Obviously, there were some people who could have helped and Paul was indeed counting on them. Paul knew that there were Christian friends who were neglecting their responsibility to help him. Sometimes the help of man is all in vain.

Paul realized that God had not forsaken him, but had stood with Paul and strengthened him. God saw that Paul really needed a friend, so Jesus Himself came alongside him and helped him. Perhaps the friends forsook Paul so the apostle would realize the power and presence of God in his life. There would be no doubt that Paul knew his help came from God and God alone.

What an encouragement! When family and friends forsake us, God is that friend that sticks closer to us than a brother. As a result of God's presence Paul was able to share the message of Christ with the Gentiles. God gives us Himself, not that we might feel good, but that we might further His kingdom. What a friend we have in Jesus. He will never leave us or forsake us.

Suggested Prayer ——————————————————————————

Father,
Thank You for sending Your Son. It seems like family and friends have left me. Forgive them, Father. Jesus, please come to my rescue and be a Friend that will stand by me and strengthen me. Thank You! May all my troubles lead to an advance of Your kingdom. In the Name of Jesus I pray, Amen.

Is God Judging Me?

Revelation 6:15-17

Then the kings of the earth and the great ones and the generals and the rich and the powerful, and everyone, slave and free, hid themselves in the caves and among the rocks of the mountains, calling to the mountains and rocks, "Fall on us and hide us from the face of him who is seated on the throne, and from the wrath of the Lamb, for the great day of their wrath has come, and who can stand?"

In the end times God will send His judgments on the earth and people will wish for death because the sufferings will be so great. There will be no place to hide. Divorce makes people wish that they could also crawl into a cave and die. We honestly need to take a spiritual inventory of our lives. We should ask, "Is God judging me?" More often than not God is not judging us. He loves us and wants to help. There are many things that are byproducts of divorce: loneliness, financial difficulty, loss of friends and family, poor work performance, broken hearts, children suffering, and a bitter spirit. The list can be endless, and people misinterpret these things as the judgment of God.

A challenge would be to list all the things that you feel are against you. Once you have your list, pray over each item, dedicating it to God. The result will be that God is using these things to develop your character, and you will begin to see Him working in your life in a positive way. More importantly, you will find that God is on your side and that He is not pouring out His wrath on you. Blessed be the Name of the Lord!

Suggested Prayer ———————————————————————

Dear loving Father,
I have found some things that are happening in my life that I do not understand. These things make me feel like You are judging me. Lord, I dedicate all these things to You, asking that You take each one and let Your Name be glorified through it. Lord, take my loneliness, finances, and all these problems and do something great with them. In Jesus' Name, Amen.

Take Your Stand and God Will Bring Victory

1 Chronicles 11:12-14

And next to him among the three mighty men was Eleazar the son of Dodo, the Ahohite. He was with David at Pas-dammim when the Philistines were gathered there for battle. There was a plot of ground full of barley, and the men fled from the Philistines. But he took his stand in the midst of the plot and defended it and killed the Philistines. And the LORD saved them by a great victory.

D avid had thirty mighty warriors among his vast army. One of the top three was a man named Eleazar. The name Eleazar literally means God is my helper. The only way we will realize that God is our helper is by going through a spiritual battle and leaning on Him. Eleazar found himself surrounded by the Philistines while his fellow troops fled from the battle. Sometimes we must stand alone to realize that our help does not come from man but from God.

God allowed David's human helpers to flee so that he might realize he needed divine help. It really hurts when you look to the left, right, forward, and behind you and no one is there. It is a horrible feeling to realize that you are all alone. However, Eleazar took his stand in the middle of the barley field and God wrought a great victory. He stood his ground and the enemy was soundly defeated. He reflected on the battle and the Lord spoke in a still small voice, saying, "Eleazar." That day he realized that God was his helper.

This barley field that we are in is the world. Our enemies are not the Philistines, but the world, the flesh, and the devil. Where are our helpers? They all fled just like the Israelites fled from the battle. We are left in the battle with no help from man. However, the Lord of Hosts is with us and will fight our battles. When we take our stand and the enemy is defeated, the Holy Spirit will whisper the word "Eleazar" to our hearts.

Suggested Prayer

Dear God,
I am in a battle, not physically but spiritually. The enemy has surrounded me while friends and family have retreated. I take my stand for You and ask that You bring victory. Lord, You are my helper. I stand on You, Jesus, because You are my Rock. Amen.

It Is Time to Build Yourself Up

Jude 20-23

But you, beloved, building yourselves up in your most holy faith and praying in the Holy Spirit, keep yourselves in the love of God, waiting for the mercy of our Lord Jesus Christ that leads to eternal life. And have mercy on those who doubt; save others by snatching them out of the fire; to others show mercy with fear, hating even the garment stained by the flesh.

Jude spoke of false teachers and the need for Christians to earnestly contend for the faith or the body of truth delivered to the church. We are always one generation away from losing the faith if we do not pass it on to the next generation. In these verses he calls it a holy faith, which is based on the Word of God. We must read, meditate, and study the scriptures to experience growth. We should pray in the Holy Spirit, allowing Him to lead us and guide us in our prayers. We are to keep ourselves in the love of God by having fellowship with Him and experiencing His love poured out in our hearts.

We are also to wait on God because He is coming back for us. Patiently waiting for His return is the idea Jude has in mind in these verses. We must show compassion on those who doubt, making a difference. We must pull some out of the fire. Compassion is truly what makes the difference when we minister to others. Without compassion we cannot make a difference.

As you grow in your holy faith God will begin to put people in your path that need His help, and you will be ready to minister to their needs. Your own problems will get smaller and smaller, and God's plan for you will get bigger and bigger until your whole life will be consumed with wanting to please Him. You will then find that you are earnestly contending for the faith.

Suggested Prayer ————————————————————————
Dear Lord,
I want to grow. I commit myself to the reading of the Word and praying in the Holy Spirit. Until You come back, please put some people in my life that I can minister to. Use me to have compassion on some, and others pulling them out of the fire. In the Name above all Names I pray, Amen.

Being Effective and Fruitful

2 Peter 1:5-8

For this very reason, make every effort to supplement your faith with virtue, and virtue with knowledge, and knowledge with self-control, and self-control with stead-fastness, and steadfastness with godliness, and godliness with brotherly affection, and brotherly affection with love. For if these qualities are yours and are increasing, they keep you from being ineffective or unfruitful in the knowledge of our Lord Jesus Christ.

Peter admonishes us to add to our faith. He of all people knew that there is no standing still with God. We are either going forward or going backward with God. There is simply no middle ground with spiritual things. Peter went backward and denied the Lord Jesus three times. He wept bitterly over his sin and determined that he would march forward and never look back. He says that when we continue to go forward, we will be effective and fruitful.

He tells us to add to our faith virtue or moral excellence, then to add knowledge in the things of God. Next add self-control, which is desperately needed in this evil world. Then he says that we are to add steadfastness or patient endurance, followed by godliness or holy living worthy of sharing the gospel. Peter admonishes us to have brotherly affection or brotherly love for each other. Finally, he wants us to love sacrificially. We are to love God and each other unconditionally. If we have these eight qualities working in us, and if we develop them more and more, we will be effective and fruitful in the knowledge of God. We will know God more and do those things that He would have us to do.

Suggested Prayer

Dear Lord,
I want to be fruitful and effective for Your kingdom. Please make my life count. I dedicate myself to adding to my faith. Lord, I do not want to go backward. Please let me go forward. Teach me how to add to my faith. In Jesus' Name, Amen.

A Need for Revival

2 Chronicles 7:14

If my people who are called by my name humble themselves, and pray and seek my face and turn from their wicked ways, then I will hear from heaven and will forgive their sin and heal their land.

After Solomon dedicated the temple to God, the Lord told him that there could be restoration and forgiveness for the nation if they would cry out to Him. When a person truly wants a revival in their life God may do some strange things to bring this about. Revival is not evangelism, it is God reanimating or reenergizing His work. It is putting the Holy Spirit's power and presence in the believer's heart to carry out God's plan. As believers, we may reach a point where our life is mechanical, with no vibrant energy flowing through us. Revival unstops the dammed-up waters of our soul and the Holy Spirit begins to flow freely in our lives, reanimating His work in and through us.

This text surely lays down a path to revival. We must humble ourselves before God in prayer. Humility speaks of being honest with God. We must also pray for revival. We must seek God's face. We also must turn from our wicked ways. When we do this God forgives us and heals us and reenergizes us for His work. If we want revival more than anything, God will honor that request. Do not be surprised if He changes your life and puts you in some strange circumstances to bring about revival. God may revive you, but it may cost you everything to achieve this. God is not limited to the scope of revival so don't be surprised if He starts changing your church and workplace too.

The question is, do we really want revival? If we do, are we willing to let God do whatever He wants with us to bring about this change? Are we willing to let Him have full control of our families, jobs, finances—everything? Can we lay our all on the altar? We must surrender all if we will have any hope of revival.

Suggested Prayer

Dear God,
I want revival. I give myself to You. I humble myself and want to turn from my sins. I turn from self and turn to You. May You have Your will and way in me. In Jesus' Name, Amen.

Keep Growing!

Luke 2:52
And Jesus increased in wisdom and in stature and in favor with God and man.

We all grow in five major areas. We often think of growth in the physical sense only. As we grew up as children, our grandparents always commented on our growth and said something like, "My, you sure have grown since the last time I saw you." However, we grow mentally, physically, spiritually, socially, and emotionally. In this verse the Holy Spirit records how Jesus was growing as a boy at the age of twelve. Eventually we stop growing physically but we should never quit growing in the other four areas. Determine that you will develop into the person God wants you to be. The text says that Jesus grew in wisdom, and this speaks of intellectual development. It says that He grew in stature, or physical development. He also grew in favor with God, meaning He grew spiritually. He grew in favor with man, or social development. The text does not include the fifth way we grow, which is emotional development.

Stimulate intellectual growth by reading, learning new skills, and developing God's wisdom. Grow spiritually by reading the Bible, Christian books, going to church, serving, and praying. Grow socially by meeting new people and developing lasting friendships. Grow emotionally, perhaps by keeping a journal and tracking your feelings, thoughts, and emotions. These are only suggestions to prompt you to grow. Ask God to develop you in these areas, and before you know it you will begin to feel much better about yourself.

Soon a trusted friend will see your growth and comment on your growth. It would be nice for someone to recognize your efforts as you struggle to grow. Rest assured that God sees your efforts to grow and He will reward you. People may or may not see the growth, but God sees all.

Suggested Prayer
Dear Father,
I want to grow. Show me how to grow mentally, socially, spiritually, and emotionally. I do not want to stop developing. Make me more like Jesus. Thank You Father. Amen.

My Responsibilities Are Overwhelming

1 Corinthians 4:2
Moreover, it is required of stewards that they be found faithful.

When divorce occurs our responsibilities increase tremendously. The single parent is now some genetic freak of nature because he or she must be mom and dad fused into one person. God did not design a woman or man to be both parents fused into one; yet God requires that we be responsible for the things of our household and the people that make up our home. We should take inventory of what we are responsible for and who we are responsible for. He has entrusted us with our children and perhaps even the care of our elderly parents. Everything we possess belongs to God and He is trusting us to do a good job. If He trusts us, He will help us and provide for our needs. We need to be trustworthy and do the things that He asks of us.

We are required to function at work, home, and church. Our children need us more than ever before. Oftentimes there is simply not enough energy left in our bodies by the time the evening rolls around. Yet the kids are crying out for our attention. This is not a time in our lives to take on any new responsibilities. Learn to say no at church when people ask you to volunteer and your plate is beyond full. In time God will help you and you will feel comfortable with what you are doing. Perhaps then you will be able to do more. We should focus on God, children, work, and church. We are also very lonely, but this might not be the right time to start a new relationship. We must make sure we are good stewards of our current responsibilities before taking on new ones.

Suggested Prayer ————————————————————————
Dear Lord,
Help me realize my responsibilities and help me do a good job with all of them. Let me see these things not as a burden, but to honor You. Help me prosper at work. Help me to take good care of my children, and help me maintain my household. In Jesus Name, Amen.

A Place of Joy and Love

Song of Solomon 2:4
He brought me to the banqueting house, and his banner over me was love.

Solomon's bride was overwhelmed with him because of the love that he had for her. In this verse we see the banqueting house and the banner. Solomon brought her to the banqueting house, which means the house of wine. Wine is a picture of joy in the Bible. In a spiritual sense Solomon represents the Lord and the bride represents the church. Jesus is our bridegroom and He brings joy into our lives. Ultimately, we are going to heaven, a place of supreme joy, but until then God's desire is that we have joy in this life too. We may have a broken home and heart, but we can still have joy in the midst of sorrow.

The second thing the verse talks about is the banner, or flag. The flag over the Christian is love. We are going to a place of supreme love. The Father is love, Jesus is love, and the Holy Spirit is love. God wants us to experience His love for us each day. The colors and symbols of a flag represent something. For example, the Jamaican flag consists of three colors: black, gold, and green. The black color represents the people, the green the agriculture, and the gold represents the sun. God's flag is all about love. All the colors and symbols equate to one thing, and that is love. There is a single lady who has a picture of Jesus on her nightstand. Before she goes to bed at night, she reminds herself that Jesus loves her and that He is her husband. When she wakes up in the morning she is reminded that she is in a place of joy, and that the flag flying over her heart is love.

Suggested Prayer —————————————————————————
Dear God,
I want to come to that place where I am full of joy and overwhelmed by Your love. Lord, the most important thing is that You love me. May Your love and strength get me through the day! In the Name of Jesus I pray, Amen!

Our Message

1 Timothy 3:16

Great indeed, we confess, is the mystery of godliness: He was manifested in the flesh, vindicated by the Spirit, seen by angels, proclaimed among the nations, believed on in the world, taken up in glory.

P aul summed up the whole Christian message in this verse. First Timothy 3:16 was a hymn of the early church. This is a one-verse summary of the New Testament. This is a life-changing message if we will submit to God. We see the great mystery of God Himself in this verse. He appeared to us in the flesh. He was God and yet a man. He was born of a virgin to take on human form. He was God, but in His humanity He hungered, grew thirsty, and grew tired. As God He answered prayers, and yet in His humanity He prayed to the Father. He left His arena to come down here to redeem us. He was declared just (righteous) by the Holy Spirit. The Spirit put His stamp of approval on the work of Jesus by raising Him from the dead. He was seen by angels. The angels announced His birth, ministered to Him, and witnessed His ascension to heaven. He was proclaimed among the nations, showing that He was not just the God of the Jews but also of the whole world. He was believed on in the world, the whole Roman Empire, at the time of Paul's writing. He was received back to heaven, having obtained eternal redemption for us. Right now, He is at the right hand of the Father to intercede on our behalf.

Do you know Jesus? If you have never trusted Him, why not accept Him today? If you have already trusted Him, what is your greatest need of this hour? He is listening, and wants to plead your case to the Father.

Suggested Prayer

Dear God,
I accept Your Son Jesus as my Lord and Savior. I do not quite understand it all, but I believe He is my Savior. I turn from my sin and ask that You will save me. Thank You. In Jesus' Name, Amen.

God Is Able

Ephesians 3:20-21

Now to him who is able to do far more abundantly than all that we ask or think, according to the power at work within us, to him be glory in the church and in Christ Jesus throughout all generations, forever and ever. Amen.

Our abilities are always limited. However, God is able to do more than we can ask or think. Paul says He can "do far more abundantly than all that we ask or think," and that should really encourage us to pray. We can think of a vast number of things and we can ask for many things too. God can do much more than we can ask or even think. Paul also said there is power working in us. We have the dynamic power of God in the person of the Holy Spirit working in us. As the Spirit controls our thinking and asking in prayer, we will begin to see that God is able. In the desert Israel asked if God could furnish a table in the wilderness. They were in a desolate place with not many resources around. As they began to call on Him, manna came down from heaven. Water flowed from a rock and quenched their thirst. He sent quail to give them meat.

God can and will furnish a table in our wilderness journey. Watch God blow your mind because He will do far more than you are asking. Tune your heart to the Spirit and watch Him work. We are not trusting our abilities, we are trusting God and His abilities. It is not our resources that we are looking to but the resources of heaven. The end goal is to bring honor and glory to God. The Father is always good, and He will do more than we expect from Him. To God be the glory!

Suggested Prayer

Dear God,
I believe You are all powerful and that Your power is in me. God, help me, I have asked for so many things. Surprise me, Lord. You know my needs and desires. In Jesus' Name, Amen.

Your Lot in Life Is No Accident

Esther 4:14

For if you keep silent at this time, relief and deliverance will rise for the Jews from another place, but you and your father's house will perish. And who knows whether you have not come to the kingdom for such a time as this?

Esther was a beautiful Jewish orphan who was raised by her cousin Mordecai. The Jews were taken from Israel and were exiles in the kingdom of Persia. When the King of Persia needed a queen, Esther was taken from her cousin as a potential candidate. Esther so impressed the king that she became the new queen. In the meantime, a wicked man named Haman had plotted to kill all the Jews in the Persian Empire. In our text, cousin Mordecai pleads with Esther to go to the king to stop the planned genocide of the Jews. He tells her that she has become queen for such a time as this, meaning that she came to the position of being queen to save the Jews.

No one could approach the king's throne uninvited, and if the king did not hold out the golden scepter the person approaching the throne would be executed. Esther had not been invited to see the king, but she knew that God had her in the right place at the right time to save the Jewish people. She said she would go to the king, and explained, "if I perish, I perish." After much prayer and fasting she went before the king and she did not perish at all. In fact, the Jews were saved, and to this day the Jewish holiday of Purim is celebrated to commemorate Esther's bravery and the salvation of the Jews.

Here is a lady with no parents in a strange land and placed in the king's palace to preserve God's people. She was willing to act on the call of God in her life. Today God also has you in a place for such a time as this. He has removed some things in your life and has allowed your whole world to be turned upside down for such a time as this. Respond to the call, because your obedience will have eternal results. Amen and amen!

Suggested Prayer ——————————————

Dear Lord,
I am not sure why my life has turned upside down, but I am trusting You. Please show me what You want me to do. I know I am placed where I am at for a reason. Open my eyes and heart to see Your calling. In Jesus' Name, Amen.

Help Wanted

Matthew 9:36-38
When he saw the crowds, he had compassion for them, because they were harassed and helpless, like sheep without a shepherd. Then he said to his disciples, "The harvest is plentiful, but the laborers are few; therefore pray earnestly to the Lord of the harvest to send out laborers into his harvest."

As Jesus lived and walked on this earth, He was full of compassion for people. He saw the masses as lost sheep without a shepherd. Our Lord explained to His disciples that there is a big harvest of souls in the world, but very few laborers. Jesus asked His disciples to pray that the Father would send laborers into the harvest. There are some amazing things to ponder in these verses. One is that God had prayer requests. The One who created everything had a prayer request! He asked that earnest prayer be made for laborers because God is not willing that anybody should perish.

Another thought is that the need is great. The need is greater now than when Jesus uttered these words. People will live and die today, having never seen a Bible or read one verse of scripture. People will die without even knowing anything about Jesus. These people are doomed to an eternity without God unless they respond to the gospel call. How can these masses of people believe if no one has told them about Jesus?

Finally, the laborers are fewer and fewer because we are selfish and want to live for money and possessions. God's heart aches for the souls of men badly enough that we have a preserved prayer request from Jesus Himself, pleading that we might become laborers or join in praying for workers. Perhaps your divorce has freed you up so you may spend the rest of your days in the harvest field, reaping the souls of men.

Suggested Prayer
Dear Lord,
I give myself to You as a living sacrifice. I pray that You send me into the harvest. Please send others but send me too. I give up my desires and dreams that I might spend the rest of my days in Your harvest. In the Name of Jesus I pray, Amen.

One Reason Why We Suffer

Philippians 1:12

I want you to know, brothers, that what has happened to me has really served to advance the gospel...

Paul wrote the book of Philippians while sitting in prison. One of the major themes of the book is joy. This seems odd since his circumstances were deplorable. Paul said that what had happened to him had a purpose. One of the purposes of this trial was that the gospel might advance—so the purpose of Paul's imprisonment was to advance the gospel.

Honestly, this might be last on our list when we think of why we are suffering. We must ask ourselves why we are suffering. It is not wrong to ask God why we are suffering; on the cross, in His humanity, Jesus asked the Father why He had forsaken him. The answer to your question might be that God wants to spread His gospel through you.

Now that you are single you are free to serve Him with fewer distractions. You will also be meeting new people and acquiring new sets of friends. Some of these people will more than likely need the gospel. We might find that our suffering is being used to bring many souls into His kingdom.

When Jesus died on the cross it was for the purpose that we might live. In one way His death was an advance of the gospel. Joy comes from a right relationship with God. Paul had joy as he served. The cross of Jesus Christ was explained as the joy that was set before Him. The cross was a joy to our Lord. May the Holy Spirit fill us with joy as we serve Him.

Suggested Prayer

Dear Father,

I am suffering, and I know You have a purpose for it. Lord, why am I suffering, and what is the purpose of it all? May You use my affliction to advance the gospel and bring me joy as I serve You. In Jesus' Name, Amen.

Determination

Ezra 7:10
For Ezra had set his heart to study the Law of the LORD, and to do it and to teach his statutes and rules in Israel.

E zra was a scribe that grew up among the captives of Babylon. After seventy years the Jews were allowed to return home. Many Jews stayed behind, choosing the world over worship of Jehovah God. Ezra, as a scribe, handled the Holy Scriptures. He read them, studied them, and made copies of them. He knew the scriptures and knew that God had a future for His people. God made an unconditional covenant with Abraham and David and Ezra knew all about God's promises.

Ezra had a threefold determination. First, he would pour his heart into the studying of the scriptures. Secondly, he determined that he would live by the Word. Finally, he determined that he would teach the Word in Israel. He made the decision to teach the Word in Israel before he went back to the promised land. He predetermined in his heart that he would do this, and that is exactly what happened.

The most effective teaching is done by those who not only know the Word but live by it and have a passion for it. There is a strange presence of God that can be felt when one is listening to a teacher who lives by the Word. It seems like God Himself is talking to us as He uses His teachers. The name Ezra means aid or helper. By God's grace he was determined to live up to his name. So today, determine that you will be a student of the Word, that you will live by the Word, and that you will teach the Word. God might not want you to be a formal teacher, but there are those around us that need to hear a word from God—perhaps family, friends, or coworkers. Determine beforehand that you will teach it in your Israel.

Suggested Prayer
Dear God,
I submit to Your Word. I determine to study it, live it, and teach it wherever You want me to. Lord, let me be an Ezra in the place that You have called me. In Jesus' Name, Amen.

Reading the Bible is a Matter of Life or Death

1 Peter 2:2
Like newborn infants, long for the pure spiritual milk, that by it you may grow up into salvation.

Peter encouraged us to read the scriptures, just like a newborn baby nurses from its mother. A baby must depend on its mother's milk to survive and grow. An infant cannot eat solid food or even feed itself. The only hope a baby has is its mother's milk. Our spiritual life depends on the sincere milk of the Word of God. If we could picture ourselves as a newborn infant it would help us grow. Peter is not calling us babies, or immature; he is simply using an illustration to stress the importance of the scriptures.

The Bible is the most purchased book, and yet the most neglected, unread book. Our only hope of survival is the Word of God. We all want to grow spiritually but growth will not come without spending time in the scriptures. There is no other spiritual food out there on the market for us to consume. The psalmist said we should want God's Word more than silver or gold.

We must come to the place where we believe that God's Word is the most important thing in our lives. We have many ambitions, plans, and goals, and there is nothing wrong with that. But we need to realize that God is the most important thing. The only way to recover spiritually after the horrors of divorce is to let God's Word be your sole source of nourishment. All a newborn baby needs is its mother's milk. All we need is the Word.

Suggested Prayer ————————————————————————
Dear Lord,
I come to You brokenhearted, and realizing that I can only turn to You for help. Lord, I purpose in my heart to read my Bible so I can grow. Lord, please heal me, and then use me so that others can be healed. Amen.

Where Is Your Heart?

Colossians 3:1-2

If then you have been raised with Christ, seek the things that are above, where Christ is, seated at the right hand of God. Set your minds on things that are above, not on things that are on earth.

Paul admonishes us to set our hearts on things above, not on this earth. Our time on earth is temporary compared to all of eternity. We desperately need an eternal perspective on life because it puts the temporary in perspective. Our old lives died at Calvary with Jesus. Just as Christ was raised on the third day, we too walk in new life. We walk in resurrection power and not our own power. Our new lives are now in Christ. We are citizens of heaven and we are just passing through this world. We are strangers and pilgrims on earth. Our loneliness is temporary. Our discouragement and failures are all temporary. We are citizens of heaven. We need to seek the things that are above, where Christ is seated at the right hand of the Father. We are here to accomplish His will and not our own. Christ is now our life, and we will live with Him for all of eternity.

If we do not have an eternal perspective on life, we will be discouraged and our focus will be inward. We will be miserable, never accomplishing all that God has for us. One of the hardest things to do is to stay focused on Christ. God will help us as we focus on Christ and things above. If you want to know where your heart is, start a journal. Write down where and how you are spending your time, then write down where you are spending your money. This should help you see where your focus is. Make the necessary changes to make God the center of everything that you say and do.

Suggested Prayer

Dear Lord,
Help me have my heart and mind on things above and not on this earth. I have Your power in me; help me see that this trial is nothing compared to all of eternity. Help me stay focused on You. In Jesus' Name, Amen.

Why Are Things So Difficult?

Zechariah 3:1
Then he showed me Joshua the high priest standing before the angel of the LORD, and Satan standing at his right hand to accuse him.

When people go through tough trials, they either get bitter or better. Those that get better find themselves calling on God and getting very close to Him. God is at the center of their lives and He is beginning to use them. Then suddenly things just do not seem like they are working anymore. The good feelings go away and loneliness and depression set in again. Why? The answer lies in the fact that there is a real devil who never gives up. He is out to resist every work of God and every child of God.

The name Satan means accuser or adversary. He is God's opponent. He wants to take you out of the race. Every time you pray, he is there to put bad thoughts in your head. When you read your Bible you are always distracted. A friend drops by just as you were heading out the door for church. Where do all these distractions and negative thoughts come from? They come from Satan and his entourage as they war against your soul. At night he whispers lies to you: "It won't get better. You will always be alone. God does not have anyone for you. If God loved you, He would not have taken your husband." The lies are endless because he is the father of lies. Hang in there, because greater is He that is in you than he that is in the world. Satan might win a few battles in your life, but he will not win the war. Realize that you have an enemy that will not quit. But he is also a defeated foe.

Suggested Prayer
Dear Father,
I am really struggling. Help me get through this dry season in my life. Help me realize that I have an enemy who is out to destroy everything that You are doing in my life. Please give me a spirit of discernment as I purpose to serve You. Lead me into a deeper walk with You. In Jesus' Name I pray, Amen.

Being Confident in Prayer

Hebrews 4:14-16

Since then we have a great high priest who has passed through the heavens, Jesus, the Son of God, let us hold fast our confession. For we do not have a high priest who is unable to sympathize with our weaknesses, but one who in every respect has been tempted as we are, yet without sin. Let us then with confidence draw near to the throne of grace, that we may receive mercy and find grace to help in time of need.

God wants us to approach Him boldly with confidence. We can come boldly to the very throne room of God. The King stepped off His throne, entered our arena, and then went back to heaven. While He was here, He experienced life with all its weaknesses. He can sympathize with us because He was tempted in all areas of life. Since He was the God-man He did not sin. We can be confident, not in ourselves, but in Him as the perfect high priest who understands our shortcomings. He is on our side!

We can come to His throne, which is called a throne of grace. At this throne we find mercy and grace to help us in our time of need. We will find the help that we need as we approach the throne with confidence. We have this assurance because our God is perfect and without any sin. We can be confident because He knows how we feel.

We can come boldly because the throne is the designated place that God has established for us to get help. He is our great high priest. The priest of the Old Testament was the mediator between God and the people. Jesus is our priest and the throne of grace is the place. God has ordained that we meet Him in prayer by this prescribed way. God is not pleased when we go other places to look for help. Come to the throne with confidence, knowing that this is the will of God for your life. If you are not coming to the throne, you either do not have any needs or you are trying to do everything yourself. Stop striving to do everything in your flesh and let God be God in your life.

Suggested Prayer

Dear Lord,
I am so ashamed to come to You sometimes. My sin and pride keep me from having confidence. Lord, I believe in You and Your throne. Please let me approach with confidence. In Jesus' Name, Amen.

I Did It Again, God

---

1 John 1:9

If we confess our sins, he is faithful and just to forgive us our sins and to cleanse us from all unrighteousness.

No matter how hard we try to do good we eventually will fall short. John says a Christian will sin, but it should not be a habitual practice. To say that we do not sin or that we are without sin is a lie and a denial of the truth. We should not sin, simply presuming that God will forgive us. However, there is forgiveness with God. We should not set out to sin and to indulge in something wrong. We should fix our hearts and minds on God and His Word with the single purpose of pleasing Him. As we yield to God, we will not be sinless, but we will sin less and less.

So now we find that with all our good intentions we sinned again. What do we do? We confess our sins, meaning that we agree with God that we did something wrong and that we do not want to do it again. What does God do? He forgives us of our sin and cleanses our souls from all unrighteousness. Why? Because He is always faithful and just to His children.

You might not feel forgiven at all. With sin comes shame, sorrow, regret, and a low self-esteem because we let the God of the universe down. If you truly confess your sin, God does forgive you. Perhaps you need to forgive yourself. The bottom line is that we cannot go by feelings. God was faithful to forgive, and as you begin serving Him again you will feel His cleansing power of forgiveness. He delivered you from the guilt and shame of your sin. Like the woman taken in adultery that was forgiven, go and sin no more.

Suggested Prayer ———————————————————————

Lord,

I blew it again! I am sorry for my sin and I ask that You forgive me. My sin was wrong and I do not want to do it again. Please cleanse me from the guilt and shame and let me not only know I am forgiven, but let me also feel forgiven. I am so sorry, Lord. In the Name of Jesus I pray, Amen.

I Really Messed Things Up Yesterday

Lamentations 3:21-24

But this I call to mind, and therefore I have hope: The steadfast love of the LORD never ceases; his mercies never come to an end; they are new every morning; great is your faithfulness. "The LORD is my portion," says my soul, "therefore I will hope in him."

People going through a divorce have bad days. At first, every day is a bad day. After some time and healing the person begins to learn to live with the pain and loneliness. Then just when they think they have victory they yield to some temptation. Often it is a spirit of anger that takes over and they end up saying some harsh things to some innocent person. After they are through venting, they realize the error of their way and ask for forgiveness from God and the offended party. They feel horrible. They ask, "How did this happen?" They think to them-selves, "I thought I was over the bitterness."

Then we find hope in the fact that God's love never stops. God's mercy never ceases. We stopped being faithful, but God did not stop because He is always faithful. He gives us a fresh start every morning. He says, "I love you; let us walk through this valley together." There is not a man on earth that is willing to give you a fresh start each morning. Yet there is a man in heaven, Christ Jesus our Lord, who will give us a fresh start and a clean slate every morning. We begin to put all our hope in Him as we realize that He is our portion. Our portion could have been many things—money, fame, a nice house. But God, in His love and grace, is our portion. The world's portions do not satisfy; that is why God Himself is our portion.

Suggested Prayer

Dear God,

I messed up again. I thought I was over my anger and bitterness. Please forgive me and cleanse me. Give me a new start this morning. Thank You for Your love and mercy. Let me realize that You are my portion and that is all I need. Amen.

The Lonely Times Are for Preparation

Luke 3:1-4

In the fifteenth year of the reign of Tiberius Caesar, Pontius Pilate being governor of Judea, and Herod being tetrarch of Galilee, and his brother Philip tetrarch of the region of Ituraea and Trachonitis, and Lysanias tetrarch of Abilene, during the high priesthood of Annas and Caiaphas, the word of God came to John the son of Zechariah in the wilderness. And he went into all the region around the Jordan, proclaiming a baptism of repentance for the forgiveness of sins. As it is written in the book of the words of Isaiah the prophet, "The voice of one crying in the wilderness: 'Prepare the way of the Lord, make his paths straight.

John the Baptist lived a lonely life. He was secluded and separated from the rest of society. His diet was locusts and wild honey. He was thirty years old when he began his preaching; his ministry lasted only about six months before he was thrown into prison and then executed. From all outward appearances John's life looked like a complete and total failure, but that was not the case because God used him to introduce Jesus Christ to the world. John even baptized our Lord. His thirty lonely years on earth were years of preparation. He prepared for thirty years and preached six months. Today we would like to prepare six months and then preach thirty years.

At the right time the Word of the Lord came to John and he came out of this desolate, lonely place and began preaching. The book of Isaiah even prophesied about John's ministry. The great apostle Paul spent about eighteen months in seclusion as God prepared him for the ministry. Moses spent forty years in seclusion before he was prepared to deliver Israel from Egyptian bondage. Today realize that your lonely times are not times of punishment. This is the time that God is preparing you for some great task. The hardest note in all of music is the rest. In the Christian life the hardest thing to do is to rest and pause before the next note of your life is played. These lonely times are not times of torture—they are times of training.

Suggested Prayer

Dear Lord,

I am struggling in this lonely, desolate place. I am not in the desert physically but spiritually. Help me see that You are preparing me for some great task. When I am discouraged help me see Your perspective on things. I dedicate these lonely times to You. Amen.

The Lonely Times Are for Proving

Luke 4:1-2

And Jesus, full of the Holy Spirit, returned from the Jordan and was led by the Spirit in the wilderness for forty days, being tempted by the devil. And he ate nothing during those days. And when they were ended, he was hungry.

After Jesus was baptized the Holy Spirit led Him into the wilderness to be tempted by the devil. Jesus fasted forty days and Satan tried to tempt our Lord to sin. Satan had a threefold attack on Jesus and all three temptations failed to produce sin in the life of Jesus. The devil then left Jesus, looking for a more opportune time to tempt Him.

Our Lord's obedience to the scriptures kept Him from sinning. These lonely times were proving grounds for Jesus. He decided He would do the right thing and He did not sin. Our lives are no different—the Holy Spirit leads us to lonely places and allows us to be tested. How many people realize that the lonely times are proving grounds for their faith? We say that we love God and will obey His word, so God tests us to prove our faith. It is easy to say that we will obey God when we are in a church service, but in the lonely quiet times we see what we are really made of. Jesus always passed the test by knowing and obeying the scriptures. We too will pass the test, not by quoting scripture, but by living by the scriptures.

Do we realize the leading of the Holy Spirit in these lonely places of life? God has led us to the lonely places to test our faith, that we might learn to live for Him. Will you pass the test? God has given you the answers to the test questions in the sixty-six books of the Bible.

Suggested Prayer ———————————————————————

Dear God,
I realize that You led me to these lonely times to test me. I submit to You and Your word. Help me pass each test that you send my way. Lord, I am experiencing lone-liness and it seems like everything in my life is all in vain. Help me see that You are testing me and help me obey Your word. In Jesus' Name, Amen.

The Lonely Times Are for Prayer

Luke 5:16
But he would withdraw to desolate places and pray.

Jesus was very busy throughout His ministry. He spent many hours a day ministering, and yet He never seemed rushed or hurried. Jesus would find lonely, desolate places to pray to His Father. Jesus would withdraw from the busy places in life to pray, and sometimes He would spend the whole night in prayer.

God speaks in a still small voice, and we cannot hear Him speak to us unless we withdraw to a lonely place. With the stress of life and the pressures of the world, we need a quiet place to pray. We must come apart from the world and pray before we fall apart. We need to speak to God, and we need to listen to Him. We will never hear from Him until we carve out a place to be alone with Him. It might be difficult but ask God to give you a special place. That is one prayer He will answer.

Find a time to pray. Mornings might be beneficial, before children wake up; some are night owls and find evening prayer works for them. The point is to find a time and place where you feel comfortable, and unwind in His presence.

Perhaps the lonely time in your life is designed by God for the purpose of developing a deeper prayer life. We did not volunteer for the loneliness that has invaded our souls, but this can be a tremendous opportunity to be a man or woman of prayer. God is calling you to pray and the avenue He might be using is your loneliness. Jesus was able to handle every tough circumstance in His life because the battles were won on His knees in prayer the night before the fight took place.

Suggested Prayer
Dear Lord,
I realize that this lonely place in my life can be used to make me a person of prayer. Help me withdraw to a special place each day to hear You speak to me. Lord, I need Your presence and Your power. Teach me to pray. In the Name of Jesus I pray, Amen.

The Lonely Times Are for Provision

Luke 9:12

Now the day began to wear away, and the twelve came and said to him, "Send the crowd away to go into the surrounding villages and countryside to find lodging and get provisions, for we are here in a desolate place."

The only miracle recorded in all four gospels is the feeding of the five thousand. Jesus had taught the people all day, and the disciples asked Jesus to dismiss the crowd so they could find food and lodging for the night. Jesus told them to feed the crowd, and the twelve apostles could only come up with five loaves and two fishes. Jesus prayed and a miracle took place. Five thousand men were fed, not counting the women and children. The exact number of people fed does not matter because a miracle had taken place. There were even twelve baskets of leftovers.

What can we learn from all these facts? In our lonely place God sees exactly what we have. Just like the five loaves and two fishes, it is not enough to go around. On our own, our resources will never be enough. However, when we give what we have to God a miracle takes place and He supplies all our needs. He even gives above our needs and there will be baskets of leftovers. God puts us in the desert so that we may not rely on our resources but on His resources. When we dedicate it all to Him a miracle takes place. Bills are paid, groceries are supplied, and some money will be left over for savings. Give what you have to God in your desert place and watch a miracle take place.

Suggested Prayer

Dear Lord,
I give all my possessions to You. I do not have enough in this desert that I am wandering through. Take my things and make a miracle happen that will supply every need and even some left over. Thank You for the lonely times because I am seeing You provide. In the Name of Jesus I pray. Halleluiah, Amen.

The Lonely Times Are for Pardon

Luke 15:4

What man of you, having a hundred sheep, if he has lost one of them, does not leave the ninety-nine in the open country, and go after the one that is lost, until he finds it?

Sometimes we lose our way spiritually. We are like that lost sheep that wandered from the fold. With the wolves present, our Good Shepherd leaves the ninety-nine and seeks out that lost and lonely sheep. Jesus Himself carries the sheep back to the fold. All of heaven rejoices over one sinner who repents. What a beautiful picture of God! He loves us enough to seek us out. He is gracious enough to forgive us. He is merciful enough to restore us back to the fold.

Are you in a lonely desert because of sin? The enemy has crippled you and is moving in for the kill. But wait—the Good Shepherd is in sight and as He approaches the enemy flees. He reaches down and picks you up. He forgives you and cleanses your soul. Then He brings you back home. What a Savior! Thank God there is forgiveness and restoration with God. The Lord is persistent because He seeks us out till He finds us. God will keep calling our names when we are in the wilderness of sin until we respond to Him.

He will also keep us in the desert to accomplish His perfect work of forgiveness and restoration. If we are in the desert perhaps there is some unconfessed sin in our lives that God wants to cleanse us of. But we must realize that just because we feel like a lost sheep in the desert does not necessarily mean that we have unconfessed sin. The enemy might have won a round or two in your life, but he will not win the fight because you belong to the Good Shepherd.

Suggested Prayer ————————————————————
Dear God,
I am ashamed to admit that this is all my fault. I yielded to temptation and sinned against You. Please forgive me and bring me back into Your fold. In Jesus' Name, Amen.

My Ex-Spouse Cheated. Do I Have to Restore the Marriage?

Hosea 1:2
When the LORD first spoke through Hosea, the LORD said to Hosea, "Go, take to yourself a wife of whoredom, and have children of whoredom, for the land commits great whoredom by forsaking the LORD."

Hosea was instructed by God to marry a prostitute. The results of this marriage were horrible. She cheated on him, and he was not the father of some of their children. She left the home, leaving her kids behind to be with other men. When her lovers left her and she was in deep poverty, she sold herself as a slave. As she stood at the auction block, no one would buy her except for one man—Hosea. The name Hosea means deliverer. He delivered her from the shame of slavery and sin and degradation. She became a faithful wife and a wonderful mother as Hosea loved her each day.

God allowed this heartache to show the prophet how He felt about His people, the nation of Israel. They were spiritual harlots and had left God to be with their idols. But one day Israel will be a faithful bride for Him.

We must understand that the book of Hosea is a special case. Jesus said that if fornication was involved a person has a God-given right to divorce (Matthew 19:9). People mistakenly read the book of Hosea and think they must take the cheating spouse back. Each case is unique, and it is up to the offended party whether they will take the unfaithful one back. God gives you that choice. You should be much in prayer and seek out godly counsel before doing so. Forgiveness does not mean that you must take a person back. You can forgive and yet decide that it is not best to restore the marriage.

Suggested Prayer
*Dear God,
I do not know what to do. My spouse cheated on me and I do not know if I should take them back. Please lead me and guide me. I thought I had to restore the relationship and now I am learning that I am not obligated to do this. Please help, Lord! Clear my cloudy mind because I am confused. Amen.*

Going the Extra Mile

Matthew 5:41
And if anyone forces you to go one mile, go with him two miles.

While Jesus preached the Sermon on the Mount, He emphasized going the extra mile with people. When Jesus walked on this earth the nation of Israel was under Roman rule. A Roman soldier could ask any civilian to carry his pack a mile. Jesus said to go beyond what is required and carry the pack another mile. In terms of Christian service we should not merely do enough to get by but go the extra mile by pouring our whole heart into the endeavor. Then we will discover that the burden is not heavy at all, and the extra mile changes us.

In terms of separation and divorce we have been forced to carry a heavy backpack: child support, spousal support, feeding and clothing the kids, transportation issues, etc. All of this was forced on us and we are required by the courts of the land to go one mile. Heaven's requirement is that we go that extra mile. In other words, do not just pay child support and think your duty is done. Make sure your children are well taken care of at both homes.

Instead of grudgingly cooperating with your ex-spouse, go the extra mile and communicate well with them. Our feelings have been hurt and the last thing we want to do is go the extra mile with our ex-spouse. But we are not going the extra mile for them—we are doing it for the Lord and for the sake of our children. Our children need us to go the extra mile. The kids need to see Christ working in us and through us. Great things usually do not happen in the first mile. In that second mile, when resources are exhausted and strength is gone, God shows up on the scene and does miraculous things.

Suggested Prayer
Dear God,
Forgive me please. I confess that I have only gone one mile, and I went in a spirit of hatred and bitterness. God, please help me to go the second mile with my ex, with my children, family, co-workers, and friends. I am sorry for how I have acted and how I have represented You. In Jesus' Name I pray, Amen.

Don't Lose Your Crown

Revelation 3:8, 11

I know your works. Behold, I have set before you an open door, which no one is able to shut. I know that you have but little power, and yet you have kept my word and have not denied my name. I am coming soon. Hold fast what you have, so that no one may seize your crown.

Jesus encouraged the church at Philadelphia not to lose their crown, or reward. God had set before them an open door that no man could shut. He also said they had a little strength and had kept His Word. God opened the door, knowing that they had only a little strength. The church had endured trials patiently.

We also have an open door before us that no man can shut. Jesus is coming soon, and earthly things simply will not matter at that time. We should hold the things of God to our hearts dearly and deeply. Jesus is our most prized possession. We have a crown waiting for us, but let us beware not to let anyone or anything take that from us. What open door has God given you?

Jesus is coming soon, and the door will not always stay opened. No man can shut that door, but we can close the door by disobedience. God wants us to succeed. He has given us a little strength because He wants us to do the job in His strength. What is in the doorway that keeps you from pursuing and receiving your crown? Is self in the way? Anger? Bitterness? Hatred? Lust? We only have one life to live, it will soon be past; whatever is done for Christ is the only thing that will last.[1] The open door is the path to your crown. If you do not walk through the door you are allowing the devil to take your crown. Remove the obstacles in the doorway by confessing them and releasing them into God's hands. Ask Him to remove the obstacles so you can win your crown.

Suggested Prayer

Dear Lord,
I have a little strength and I see the open door that You have placed before me. God, I have some sins and resentments that will not let me get through the door. Please remove these things from me. In the Name of Jesus I pray, Amen.

---

[1] Phrases borrowed from lyrics "Only One Life" written by C. T. Studd, copyrighted by Tony Cooke Ministries, 2001-2019. Other songs and compositions have used similar phrases.

Is God Recruiting You?

Ezekiel 22:30

And I sought for a man among them who should build up the wall and stand in the breach before me for the land, that I should not destroy it, but I found none.

God is looking for a man or woman who will stand in the gap and make a difference in the world. God is a loving Lord and does not want to execute His wrath on anyone. God will get His will done with or without our help. His most desired method is to use men and women to perform His tasks. God will do all the work—we just need to be available for Him. It is His power that flows through us and does the task.

Moses did not deliver Israel out of Egypt. God delivered them, but He used Moses to accomplish this feat. Peter did not save anyone as he preached on the day of Pentecost. It was God who saved some three thousand souls that day. Esther did not save the Jews from destruction—God did it all. These are just a few examples of men and women that God used. They were willing to stand in the gap and make a difference. Moses, Peter, Paul, Esther, Deborah, and many others all answered a personal call from God to do a great task. He just needs one person to stand in the gap. He will do all the work.

We must respond to the call and then obey Him as He leads us along the way. All we must do is stand in the gap and He will do the rest. Notice that God said that He was looking for *a man* and not *men*. It is a personal call. God will speak to you personally, and you will know that it is Him calling you. The call will be very clear when it comes to you. God only needs one person. Is that person you?

Suggested Prayer

Dear God,
You did not find a man in Ezekiel's day to stand in the gap. Lord, I give myself to You for whatever task You have for me. I forsake all to follow You. Please make a difference in hearts and lives as I allow You to work through me. In Jesus' Name I pray, Amen.

Are You Willing to Follow Jesus?

Matthew 8:19-20

And a scribe came up and said to him, "Teacher, I will follow you wherever you go." And Jesus said to him, "Foxes have holes, and birds of the air have nests, but the Son of Man has nowhere to lay his head."

One day a scribe told Jesus that he would follow Him wherever He went. It is one thing to know the scriptures and to memorize them by heart like this scribe had done; it is quite another thing altogether to have a totally surrendered heart to the Savior. We have a Bible, but does the Bible have us? Jesus told the man that He did not have a home. Jesus would spend many nights on the Mount of Olives praying all night to the Father. He was what we would call a homeless person. Some of the most despised and neglected people are those that roam our streets, begging for food and money. These people find anywhere to sleep at night; a park bench, under an overpass, in a dark alley. Such was the living conditions of the God of the universe. Jesus said that the land animals have homes. The animals that soar the heavens have nests. Jesus had not so much as a pillow.

Are we willing to give our all to Jesus? We cannot follow until we forsake all. More than likely He will not take away our homes, but we must have a willingness to let Him have full reign of our hearts and homes. It is not until we are completely surrendered that God can use us in the way that He sees fit. Perhaps the divorce you experienced is part of God's plan to open a greater ministry for you. God wants to work in you and through you, but it may cost your time, money, possessions, family, and friends. We will not be disappointed when we go all in for Jesus.

We will be rewarded in this life and the life to come. In the end the only thing that really matters is serving God. We might give up money and gain a ministry. We might give up a home and receive heaven. We might give up possessions and receive peace. God will do awesome things, but He is waiting for you to put the for-sale sign out; not on your home but your heart. God wants your heart!

Suggested Prayer

Dear God,
I sell out today. I give You everything. My home, my heart, my money, my family and all my possessions I give to You. I surrender all to follow You. Please bless my sacrifice. In Jesus' Name.

Making the Best of Your Situation

Acts 16:25

About midnight Paul and Silas were praying and singing hymns to God, and the prisoners were listening to them.

Paul and Silas were thrown in jail at Philippi for doing the Lord's work. They were beaten with rods and had severe wounds on their backs. Their feet were secured to the wooden stocks. Battered and beaten, they did not get mad at God. Yes, they could have complained to God for their harsh treatment; after all, they were serving Him when all of this occurred. Instead, they decided to make the best of the situation.

At midnight they began to pray and sing praises to God. The other prisoners heard and marveled at how these men could praise God, even in such pain. Suddenly there was an earthquake and all the prison doors were opened. Then the jailer was on his knees, asking what he had to do to be saved. The answer to his question was to believe in the Lord Jesus Christ and he would be saved. Paul taught the jailer and his family the gospel and all of them were saved. The jailer then fed Paul and Silas and cleaned their wounds. Paul would later say that he bore the marks of the Lord Jesus through all his suffering.

The next day Paul and Silas were released from the jail. These brave men could have missed God's will by focusing on their own pain and suffering. Instead they chose to make the best of things in the worst of times by praying and praising. When they chose to honor God, the Lord did some miraculous things in their midst. We also can make the best of things and see God work wonders. If we could get our eyes off ourselves and see the Risen One, the ground would shake, the prison doors would open, and we would be free to serve Him.

Suggested Prayer

Dear Lord,
Forgive me. I have focused on my pain and sufferings and have totally missed Your will. Now, God, I chose to make the best of my situation. I choose to worship You. Let me see some people saved and lives changed as I do my very best for You. In the Name of Jesus I pray, Amen!

God Will Restore Your Losses

Joel 2:25
I will restore to you the years that the swarming locust has eaten, the hopper, the destroyer, and the cutter, my great army, which I sent among you.

God sent a horrible plague on His people, the nation of Israel. His great insect army swept through, eating all the crops and the fruit-bearing trees of the land. These pests even ate the bark off the trees, leaving nothing behind. Wave after wave of devastation occurred, leaving the land desolate and the people desperate. Without a doubt this was God's judgment for Israel's sins. But God is a loving, merciful God, and He promised to restore the years once the nation confessed their sins.

Did God send His army to your home? Perhaps the conditions you are in are because of your own sin. You might have received the desolation because of someone else's sins. The locust may have come as a combination of your sin and your ex-spouse's sin. Either way, God's army devoured everything in its path. His army did not leave one green leaf on any tree. Examine your heart and respond accordingly. Job did not sin, and God restored the years to him. Israel sinned and confessed their sin and the years were restored. Let God show you what you need to do.

Be encouraged, because at the right time the trees will begin to grow again, crops will be in the field, and the land will yield its precious fruit. God will bless you again and He will be faithful to restore the wasted years to you. Notice that He said, "I will." It is a promise. Then He said, "I will restore to you," letting us know it will happen. Highlight the verse, memorize it, and watch God restore the years. Who will help you? God said, "I will."

Suggested Prayer ——————————————————
Dear Lord,
You used your mighty army to take everything away from me. I realize that You had to do this to get my attention. I am truly sorry, God. I confess my sin and ask that You will restore the years of destruction back to me. Above all, let me honor and glorify You. Amen.

I Didn't Expect That to Grow

Galatians 6:7-8

Do not be deceived: God is not mocked, for whatever one sows, that will he also reap. For the one who sows to his own flesh will from the flesh reap corruption, but the one who sows to the Spirit will from the Spirit reap eternal life.

We all have probably heard someone say, "you reap what you sow." God said that we will reap a harvest of whatever we have planted. If we have planted good words and deeds, these things will take root and produce an awesome reward that will be harvested in this life and the life to come. If we plant bad thoughts, words, and deeds there will be a day of reckoning when the sinful fruit is ripe for harvest.

The problem is that there is a time factor involved with each thing that we plant. If we do a good deed the reward may come several years later, and the tendency is to just give up, with the thought that good works do not matter. On the other hand, it also may take years for a bad crop to come into full harvest, and it is tempting to continue doing wrong, thinking that we might have gotten away with something. Those that habitually do good are confused and angry because they do not see any punishment for those who do wrong. Those who do bad think that the good people are wasting their time because nothing good ever happens to them.

Paul warns us not to be deceived in all of this because God will not be mocked by any person. No one gets away with sin and the painful harvest that awaits them. God also sees the good and will bless in His own time. Let us all strive then to please Him.

What did you sow in your garden? Will you enjoy the fruits, or will each bite be a taste of bitterness and regret as God judges you?

Suggested Prayer

Dear Lord,
I see others doing bad things and nothing seems to happen to them. My ex-spouse caused so much trouble, but they seem very happy. Lord, help me focus on You and not on other people. Lord, I want to reap a righteous harvest, not only in this life but in the one to come. In Jesus' Name, Amen.

God, I Can't Do This Anymore

Galatians 6:9

And let us not grow weary of doing good, for in due season we will reap, if we do not give up.

The single parent is overwhelmed with duties and responsibilities. Flying solo brings one down very low. We want to please God, our bosses, co-workers, and our children. We try and try but we just do not see any good results. We cannot take another emergency room visit, a bad report card, a rude phone call, or a misunderstanding at work or church. We simply are worn out. There is not enough emotional and physical energy to deal with things anymore. God knows we will get tired or this verse would not be in our Bibles. There is an awesome promise in this verse: there will be a harvest for us if we do not give up.

Much work goes into planting and growing crops. It is hard work, but there is a harvest time when it all pays off. If we quit before the harvest the weeds of affliction will overtake the fruit of righteousness. We want to harvest godly children. We want to excel at work. We want to please God. Our intentions are good. The spirit is willing, but the flesh is weak.

If you are worn out today and about to quit, pray and ask God for divine strength. The key to the Christian life is the Holy Spirit. We must be controlled by Him and led by Him. It is His power in us that gives us the strength to carry on. The arm of flesh will eventually fail, but the Holy Spirit never grows weary and will prevail if we surrender daily to Him. God knows you need the strength of the Holy Spirit. He also sees that you are tired and He knows exactly what you need. Perhaps the finish line is closer than you imagined. The latter rains are just hours or days away. Hang in there, and rely on God's strength. The fruit is on the vine and about to be harvested, so do not quit.

Suggested Prayer

Dear God,

I am worn out and no one seems to understand what I am going through. I cannot take it anymore. I can't deal with anything else. I am really trying my best, and that is not good enough. Today I ask for divine strength because my strength is gone. Give me strength to make it. I am close to Your blessings, so strengthen my heart and mind. Put strength back into these hands and feet. God, I am desperate—please fill me with Your Spirit. In Jesus' Name, Amen.

God Does Hear Our Cries for Help

Jonah 2:7

When my life was fainting away, I remembered the LORD, and my prayer came to you, into your holy temple.

Jonah was in the belly of a great fish for three days and nights. One word that could describe Jonah is the word "down." His life went downhill when he decided not to preach to the Ninevites. We find Jonah down in the depths of the ocean in the great fish or whale. His life is slipping away fast and then he decides to repent. He remembers the LORD. His prayer comes into the LORD'S temple and into the very ear of God.

God heard Jonah's prayer. It is noteworthy that Jonah knew that God heard his prayer. God had the fish vomit Jonah up and he landed on the dry land. Jonah began preaching a simple hell-fire-and- brimstone message. He basically said, "you have forty days before God destroys this place if you do not repent." His message could be simplified to "turn or burn." The response to the message was awesome! The people repented and the biggest revival in the Old Testament took place. God did a tremendous work with the City of Nineveh, and taught Jonah a few lessons along the way.

Your pain has probably been a lot longer than Jonah's three days and three nights. Be confident that God is listening and has heard your cry for help. At the right time your captivity will end. You will be a changed person and God will do a mighty work through you. The message will be easy to preach because you have lived it.

Suggested Prayer

Dear LORD,

I am suffering and I know that You answer prayer. Help me realize that You are listening to my prayers. Change me and mold me. At the right time send me to a people that need You. In the Name of Jesus I pray, Amen.

There Is No Other Name

Acts 4:12
And there is salvation in no one else, for there is no other name under heaven given among men by which we must be saved.

P eter and John went to the temple and God used them to heal a lame man who was over forty years old. The next day the Jewish religious authorities questioned the two apostles about the incident, and Peter, filled with the Holy Spirit, began to preach the gospel to them. He explained that the Father raised Jesus from the dead and that the crippled man was healed by the resurrected Christ. Peter then explained that salvation is in no one else but Jesus Christ. There is no other person who can save. He went a little further and said that there was no other name under heaven—except Jesus—that will save us. On the eve of Jesus' crucifixion, Jesus Himself claimed that He was the only way to heaven (John 14:6). Peter said, "we must be saved."

What does it mean to believe on the name of the Lord? It means that we believe everything that His name stands for. We believe He is God, born of a virgin, sinless, perfect, and the sacrifice for our sins. We believe that He lived, died, was buried, and the third day arose for our sins.

Have you believed in Jesus? He will save you and set you free from your sins. Perhaps all your troubles were designed by God to help you become a follower of Jesus. As you look inward you know you cannot help yourself. As you look outward no one can help you. If you will look upward, you will realize Jesus is in heaven, waiting for you to call on Him so He can save you and help you. Let today be the day of salvation for you. There is no other name that can save you. Jesus is the *only* way, not one of many ways.

Suggested Prayer
Dear Lord,
I am a sinner. I believe that Jesus died for my sins. I ask that You save me today. Lord, I believe in Jesus! Thank You, Lord! In Jesus' Name I pray, Amen.

Is Jesus Welcome in Your Home?

John 12:1-2

Six days before the Passover, Jesus therefore came to Bethany, where Lazarus was, whom Jesus had raised from the dead. So they gave a dinner for him there. Martha served, and Lazarus was one of those reclining with him at table.

Jesus did not have a home, but He spent many hours in Bethany at the home of Mary, Martha, and Lazarus. These three were siblings and they all loved Jesus. It was as if there were a welcome mat at the front door that said, "Jesus, You are always welcome here!" The siblings enjoyed fellowship with Jesus. Martha was always busy serving, Mary was always at His feet learning, and Lazarus was at the table, taking it all in.

Today we cannot give Jesus a home, but we can give Him our hearts. We can have a welcome mat across our hearts that says, "Welcome, Jesus!" We must give Him our hearts, initially in salvation. Then we must open our hearts to Him daily for fellowship. Like Mary, we need to sit at His feet and worship; we need a heart of worship. Like Martha we need to serve, or have a heart of service. Like Lazarus we need a receptive heart, or a heart for fellowship. Give Jesus your heart. If Jesus is Lord of your heart, He will also be Lord of your home. Mary, Martha, and Lazarus saw one of the biggest miracles in the Bible when Lazarus was raised from the grave after being dead for four days. Their miracle started when they opened their home to Jesus and began to know Him. Our miracle will come as we open our hearts to Him.

Suggested Prayer ⸻

Dear Jesus,
I know I am saved but today, right now, I give You my heart. Be Lord of my heart, mind, and spirit. Let me have a heart of worship, service, and fellowship for You. Let me see a great moving of You in my life as I surrender to You. I love You, Jesus. Amen.

Stand Still and See the Salvation of the Lord

Exodus 14:13-14

And Moses said to the people, "Fear not, stand firm, and see the salvation of the LORD, which he will work for you today. For the Egyptians whom you see today, you shall never see again. The LORD will fight for you, and you have only to be silent."

When Israel broke away from Egypt they found themselves in a predicament almost immediately. The Red Sea was before them and Pharaoh and the Egyptian army were behind them, closing in. They were trapped, it seemed. The people were terrified, but under God's leading Moses told the people not to be afraid. He told them to stand still and see God work this great problem out for them. He even said that they did not need to fight in the battle because it was not their fight. The battle is the Lord's. It is always the Lord's battle. Moses lifted his staff over the waters and the Red Sea parted. Israel crossed through the sea as if they were on dry land. God's cloud was behind them, acting as a barrier between Israel and Egypt. Once Israel passed through the waters, God destroyed Pharaoh and his army by bringing the waters over him and all his soldiers.

God puts us in places and circumstances beyond our control to teach us that the battle is His. We do not need to fight these battles. We are to be still and watch Him work. The battle of divorce is not your battle. It is God's battle. Patiently stand still and watch Him deliver you from the darkness of Egypt. The enemy is the devil and not your ex-spouse. Watch God fight for you. There is coming a day when we will see the enemy no more.

Suggested Prayer ——————————————————————————————

Dear Lord,

I am in a tough spot. I have the old life of failure at my back. I have come to a place where there is a vast unknown before me. Lord, I choose to stand still and watch You work. The battle is Yours and I surrender it all to You. Thank You, because I anticipate You fighting my battles in the days ahead. I will be silent and watch You work. In the Name of Jesus I pray, Amen.

Oh, the Pain!

Revelation 21:4

He will wipe away every tear from their eyes, and death shall be no more, neither shall there be mourning, nor crying, nor pain anymore, for the former things have passed away.

If there is one word that aptly describes divorce, the word "pain" would be high on most people's lists. There is the initial pain, when a person finds out their soul-mate is unhappy with them and wants a divorce. One man described the pain as like someone stabbing him in the back over and over as he tossed on his bed all night, perhaps getting thirty minutes of sleep. There is also the pain of watching the family fall apart and the children suffer. The emotional pain is often unbearable as self-images are shattered.

The pain of coming home to an empty house that was once full of life is gut-wrenching. People just want the pain to stop. They ask God to take away the pain and yet it is a chronic, lingering pain. For some, alcoholism and drug abuse come into play. Anything to ease the pain seems justifiable. Some want to commit suicide. As we cry out to God, we start feeling better; then on a lonely evening, the pain comes back in full force, as if it never left. The pain a divorce brings is indescribable. Some would rather give birth or pass a kidney stone before going through the nagging, constant emotional pain they are experiencing.

Will it ever end? God says one day the pain will stop. In that day all tears will dry up, sorrow will turn to joy, death will be no more, and, praise God, there will be no more pain. By God's healing power He will take care of the pain. It will be a process but in the end God will bless you. It is always too soon to give up. God will help you work through the pain.

Suggested Prayer ────────────────────────────

Dear God,
I am so hurt. The pain is unbearable. Father, I would rather die than experience this pain. Lord, I dedicate this pain to You, trusting that You will heal me. Thank You, God, that one day all pain will be gone from all of creation. I praise You. Amen.

Help for the Hurting

2 Corinthians 1:3-6

Blessed be the God and Father of our Lord Jesus Christ, the Father of mercies and God of all comfort, who comforts us in all our affliction, so that we may be able to comfort those who are in any affliction, with the comfort with which we ourselves are comforted by God. For as we share abundantly in Christ's sufferings, so through Christ we share abundantly in comfort too. If we are afflicted, it is for your comfort and salvation; and if we are comforted, it is for your comfort, which you experience when you patiently endure the same sufferings that we suffer.

God knows how much we are hurting. No matter how hard we try to explain our hurts to others, it seems like no one really understands the pain that we are going through. We should praise God because He is a Father of mercy and a God of all comfort. God Himself comforts us in all of our affliction. God may use various means to comfort, but it all comes from Him. We cannot receive anything unless He sends it down from heaven. Praise God! He looks on our suffering, has mercy on us, and brings us comfort.

We all find comfort in something—food, hobbies etc. Nothing compares to the comfort that the Holy Spirit gives as He puts peace in our hearts. Comfort food is wonderful, but a comfortable faith is divine. God has a way of calming the storms that rage in our hearts. Now that we have received comfort, God wants us to give comfort to those who are hurting. The same amount of comfort we have received is the same amount God wants us to give to others. As we feel better and experience healing, God will send us others who are suffering just like we suffered. For example, those who have survived cancer will be able to comfort those who have been recently diagnosed with cancer.

Who does God want you to comfort? Think about all the comfort that you have received. Now give this same comfort to your hurting friend. There is a great reason to be troubled, but there is a greater reason not to be troubled as we receive and give comfort. Praise Him today, even though you are hurting.

Suggested Prayer

Dear Lord,
I am hurting, yet You have had mercy on me and given me comfort. I choose to praise Your Name. Use me to comfort my friends who are hurting. Thank You for being a loving merciful God. Amen and Amen!

God Promises to Take Care of Us

Leviticus 26:11-12

I will make my dwelling among you, and my soul shall not abhor you. And I will walk among you and will be your God, and you shall be my people.

God gave this promise to the nation of Israel. God made a promise to Abraham that He would make a great nation from his posterity and that all the nations of the world would be blessed by the Jewish people. All that God required was that they would keep His word and follow Him. All the requirements that God placed on Israel were for her own good. If Israel would honor His word, He promised to provide for them and to protect them. He also promised to give the land peace. He even said He would prosper their families and the work of their hands. He promised to be present with them. He said He would live among them and walk among them. He promised to be their God and they would be His people. He would not despise them, but develop them as He walked among them.

Today we need many things, but the most important thing we need is to focus on our relationship with God. As we honor Him by reading and practicing the Word, He begins to honor us. He gives His provision, protection, peace, prosperity, and presence. It is very important to know God is with us, especially during the tough times. Hang in there, because He so desperately wants to live among us and walk among us. In this dispensation it is the Holy Spirit who is with us and guides us. God loves us and He wants to bless us.

Suggested Prayer ———————————————————————
Dear Lord,
I see that You want to walk with me and provide for me. As I develop a relationship with You let me honor Your word. Help me love You with all of my heart. May Your presence fill my soul. In Jesus' Name, Amen.

Did I Say That?

Matthew 12:36-37

I tell you, on the day of judgment people will give account for every careless word they speak, for by your words your will be justified, and by your words you will be condemned.

The good news is that we are going to heaven to spend eternity with Jesus. The bad news is that we will give an account for everything we have said and done on earth. God will bring into account every careless word that we have spoken. Ouch!

We have the opportunity to give life-changing words to those around us. If we are careless about what we say our words will do much harm. We must be filled with the Spirit and exercise self-control or we will be sorry. We have been hurt and the tendency is to speak badly of our ex-spouse. We should never speak badly of our ex-spouse in front of our children. They have received enough damage already and do not need our words of hatred.

Confess your sin to God and ask Him to forgive you and cleanse you. Get to the root of the problem and confess the hatred, anger, and bitterness. If you have said bad things about your ex-spouse, hold a family meeting with your kids. Tell them that your actions and words have been wrong. Honesty still goes a long way, especially with your children. Find a neutral adult to talk to instead of venting on the children. Some people have sought the help of counselors or divorce groups at church.

Pray and ask God to get the help that you need. Your careless words indicate that you have some things that you need to deal with. Children are not counselors and they need peace and security. You can stop the careless talk through God's help. Be on guard—a hurtful word will damage a life and bring God's chastisement on you.

Suggested Prayer ───────────────────────────────

Dear God,

Forgive me, I have said some hurtful things and hurt many people in the process. I am hurt and I confess the hatred and bitterness. Help my kids forgive me when I talk to them about this. Lord, let life-changing words flow from my lips. Take away the anger and fill me with Your Spirit. In Jesus' Name, Amen.

Complete and Equipped

2 Timothy 3:16-17

All Scripture is breathed out by God and profitable for teaching, for reproof, for correction, and for training in righteousness, that the man of God may be competent, equipped for every good work.

In this world everyone wants to make a profit, but the most neglected resource is our Bibles. The scriptures are the most profitable commodity on earth. Paul told the young preacher Timothy that every scripture was God-breathed. The Holy Spirit used the minds and vocabularies of holy men and they wrote the scriptures. Every scripture and every book of the Bible is profitable.

It is profitable for teaching, showing us God's view of everything. It is also profitable for reproof, what God forbids us to do. Moreover, it is profitable for correction, or how to make right our wrongs. It also trains us in instruction in righteousness or how to live right and be pleasing in God's sight.

As we apply the scriptures to our hearts it does two things. The first thing it does is make us complete or mature in Christ. We begin to grow as believers. We learn what to do, what not to do, how to correct wrongs, and how to live godly. The second thing it does is equip us for good works. In other words, we will be able to help others. We will train them how they can live a godly life and fix their personal problems. Since we have received help from the scriptures, we are able to give help. God did not give us a Bible just to read it and memorize it. He gave it to us that there might be an inward transformation that will manifest itself outwardly with good works.

Suggested Prayer

Dear Lord,
I ask that You change my life through Your Word. Search my heart and show me my faults, that I might be able to mature in You. Then, Lord, equip me to do good works. Thank You for the scriptures, and let me see and understand that this is my most profitable investment on this earth. In Jesus' Name, Amen.

APRIL 6

Lest We Forget

Amos 2:10
Also it was I who brought you up out of the land of Egypt and led you forty years in the wilderness, to possess the land of the Amorite.

God had to judge the nation of Israel for its sins. If the nation would have confessed its sin, God would have shown mercy. He sent prophet after prophet to try to get Israel to repent. He had to remind them that He was the One who brought them out of the land of Egypt. He was the One who led them through the wilderness. He was the One who brought them into the promised land. He gave them the land of the Amorites, not because they were a righteous people, but because the Amorites were a very wicked people! It was all of God! God did so many things for His people.

We also seem to forget that it is all of God. God saved us and brought us into a wonderful place spiritually. He is the Great One who blesses us. Many Christians try to take credit for God's work in their lives and become clothed with arrogance instead of grace. They become holier-than-thou and feel like God and the world are obligated to fulfill their every demand. Pride will always bring us low.

There is something wrong with a salvation that makes one arrogant and judgmental. We have heard people say, "He forgot where he came from." Let us not forget that we were slaves in a spiritual Egypt and servants of the devil. It was God who brought someone greater than Moses to deliver us. God Himself came in human form to deliver us and to give us a spiritual inheritance. It is all of God, so let us beware lest we forget.

Suggested Prayer
Dear Lord,
Help me to never forget that You are the One who saved me and gave me a spiritual inheritance. It is because of my pride that I have strayed away from You. Please forgive me and cleanse me. In Jesus' Name, Amen.

Everyone Wants Your Attention

Mark 1:35-39

And rising very early in the morning, while it was still dark, he departed and went out to a desolate place, and there he prayed. And Simon and those who were with him searched for him, and they found him and said to him, "Everyone is looking for you." And he said to them, "Let us go on to the next towns, that I may preach there also, for that is why I came out." And he went throughout all Galilee, preaching in their synagogues and casting out demons.

As soon as the kids wake up your whole day changes. Now you must not only focus on yourself but on them too. The dog needs to be fed and taken out to go to the bathroom. You did it again! You slept late and now you must rush to drop the kids off at school and arrive at work on time. You arrive at work, just to find out your boss dumped a big project in your lap. As you start your work day a creditor calls. Your ex-spouse sends a horrible text to you. Your day is a mess! You finally get home from work and now the cooking begins; then you courageously do some dishes.

By the time your day ends you are too tired to fellowship with God in prayer. The most important One who wanted your attention was neglected. Jesus woke up early and went to a quiet place to talk to His Father. He received power and strength for the day to do the Father's bidding. We must realize that our relationship with God is most important. He will not play second fiddle in our lives. Everyone is seeking your attention—including God. After the rejection that you have experienced it does feel good to be wanted and needed, but the danger is that everyone that is seeking your time will keep you from the relationship that you should concentrate on the most. Decide that God is the most important thing in your life. Sacrifice and put Him first. We must sacrifice for the God we love. What do you need to do to spend more time with Him?

Suggested Prayer ————————————————————————

God,

I am guilty of talking to everyone but You. No wonder things are all out of balance in my life. Right now I want to return to You and put You first above all others. I put You above everything. Forgive me for neglecting You. In Jesus' Name, Amen.

APRIL 8

The Preacher Never Told Me That

Luke 9:23
And he said to all, "If anyone would come after me, let him deny himself and take up his cross daily and follow me."

Jesus has always wanted people to follow Him into a deep relationship. We often miss the boat by thinking everything is fine because we are Christians. We met the minimum requirement when we said yes to Jesus. But God calls us into the deep waters, and to do this we must leave the comfortable shores.

To truly have a meaningful life we must follow Him. God offers this relationship to all of His children, but the qualifications are tough, though the rewards are out of this world. We must deny ourselves. We are not our own anymore. We gave up all rights to Jesus when we were saved. We must take up our cross. In other words, we must die to self. This is a painful process but a rewarding venture. As God takes things away, He replaces them with Himself.

We must die every day. Sometimes we think of some big assignment like Peter and Paul received—our death may lead to that. However, the daily death will get us doing little things that will eventually lead to greater things. We die to self and talk to a friend about Jesus one day. The next day we die, and God leads us to an extended period of prayer. Before long we are following the Lord. By the way, the word *Lord* means owner or controller. He is the master and we are the slaves. Suddenly we are not as frustrated about our problems and loneliness. God finally has us where He wants us. We saved our lives by losing them. Your divorce got your attention. Now your daily death Has God's attention. The daily death is the path of peace.

Suggested Prayer
*Dear God,
I am saved, but I am following at a far distance. I want to come home. I deny myself and I die right now. I surrender to whatever You have for me. In Jesus' Name I pray, Amen.*

Me? Teach the Word? I Am Not the Preacher!

Malachi 2:7
For the lips of a priest should guard knowledge, and people should seek instruction from his mouth, for he is the messenger of the LORD of hosts.

The Old Testament priest was one who was to instruct the people in the Law of God. He was to guard the Law in his heart and teach its truths. The people were to receive instruction from Him because he was God's messenger to the people. He was not supposed to compromise but teach it accurately. God often punished the unfaithful priests who perverted His Law and sacrifices. With the privilege of being a priest came great responsibilities. A priest must not only teach the Word but live by the Word as well.

In the New Testament every believer is a priest (1 Peter 2:9). We all have the responsibility and privilege to live by and teach the scriptures. But no one should teach in a formal setting unless God is leading that person in that direction. God does not call everyone to be a public pastor or teacher (James 3:1). He only selects a few to be His public mouthpieces, yet all of us have people we need to share the scriptures with on a personal level.

Our children need to hear the Bible and see it working in our lives as we obey God. Coworkers and friends need to hear its precepts. God does not give us knowledge to hoard; He wants us to share its precepts with others. He wants to change our hearts and make us more like Him.

Suggested Prayer ───────────────────────────────
Dear Lord,
I might not be a preacher, but I do want to share Your Word. Lord, help me live by the Word and please put some people in my life that I can share it with. In Jesus' Name, Amen.

Rules, Rules, and More Rules

2 Timothy 2:5
An athlete is not crowned unless he competes according to the rules.

Paul told Timothy that no athlete is crowned unless he plays by the rules. Many of us are hurting because someone did not play by the rules. Our ex-spouse broke the marriage vows or the rules, running far ahead of the competition and distancing themselves from all other contenders. Don't worry about those who think they are getting away with things by not playing by the rules. When the finish line is in sight the Great Judge will render them disqualified.

No one will be rewarded who does not play by the rules. So decide that you will sell out to God on His terms. When we said yes to Jesus, we said no to ourselves. He is the Master and we are the slaves. If we try to dictate to Him what we will do and not do, we should not be surprised if He leaves us to our own devices. God's rules are not a burden but a blessing. God can only honor faithfulness. We will be rewarded according to how faithfully we followed His Word and His Spirit.

Every athlete adheres to a set of rules. We have seen many sports figures have rewards taken away because they cheated to get ahead. Not only did they lose the reward, their reputation is tarnished and the whole organization that they play for looks bad. We represent the kingdom of God, and though we are not perfect we can have a good reputation that will honor our Owner. The devil offers shortcuts. Determine today that you will run the race by honoring God as you play by His rules.

Suggested Prayer
Dear God,
It is troubling when we are surrounded by cheaters who seem to prosper. Lord, I am tempted to give in and neglect You. Right now, I submit to Your Word and the Holy Spirit's leading. I choose to do things right. In Jesus' Name, Amen.

APRIL 11

Everyone Gets a Trophy

1 Corinthians 9:24-27

Do you not know that in a race all the runners run, but only one receives the prize? So run that you may obtain it. Every athlete exercises self-control in all things. They do it to receive a perishable wreath, but we an imperishable. So I do not run aimlessly; I do not box as one beating the air. But I discipline my body and keep it under control, lest after preaching to others I myself should be disqualified.

We find it comical today that all the kids get a trophy at the end of their season. Everyone knows that there was only one winning team. Paul compared the Christian life to an athletic race. There could only be one winner. The participants went through vigorous training and self-denial to receive a perishable wreath.

Paul said he was running the Christian race like there was only one crown to win. Paul was admonishing us to do our very best. He said the key to the race was self-control in every area of life. He was afraid that after preaching God would have to disqualify him for not living the gospel. Any person can preach the gospel. But can we live the gospel?

Paul was not going through the motions. He said he was not shadow boxing, but rather was in a full arena fighting for the souls of men. Paul's opponents were the world, the flesh, and the devil. He decided that he would give it his all. How did Paul fare? (Look at 2 Timothy 4:4-8 for the answer.) The truth is that every Christian can receive a trophy, because they are on the winning team. As an athlete trains for the Olympics physically, we must train spiritually. Are we giving Jesus, the Author and Finisher of our faith, our very best?

Suggested Prayer —————————————————————————

Dear Lord,
I confess that I am not doing my best. I have no discipline in my life. Lord, I ask that You forgive me. Help me run my race like it all depends on me, but let me trust like it all depends on You. I will do my part. I want to lay a crown at Your feet when I get to heaven. In Jesus' Name, Amen.

APRIL 12

The Perfect Storm Is Brewing

Obadiah 1:15
For the day of the LORD is near upon all the nations. As you have done, it shall be done to you; your deeds shall return on your own head.

When Jesus returns, He will judge every individual from all the nations. We will give an account to God for every word, thought, and deed. Our job is to live for Him and do our best for Him. All judgment belongs to Jesus and vengeance belongs to Him too. He wants us to love Him and our neighbor. We will give an account of all our deeds.

What about that person or persons who made havoc of our lives? They will not get away with anything. They might prosper on this earth, but their end will be destruction. Let God be true and every man a liar. Fornication may have played a major part in your breakup and divorce. God said He would judge all adulterers. The man or woman that slept with your ex-spouse will be judged. It takes two to tango and God will judge them both. Do not seek revenge, because these things belong to the Almighty.

At the other home, both cheaters may be prospering as you live in misery. Blessings seem to flow at their place and outwardly God seems cruel or unfair. After all, you did not cheat. What we cannot see is that God has a perfect storm brewing out on the high seas. At the right time He will bring a quick and swift judgment that will devastate those who caused so much trouble.

So, resolve to live right lest God judge you. Also pray each day that God would be merciful to those who destroyed your home. It is a horrible thing to fall into the hands of God when He judges us. No one gets away with anything, even if the judgment comes later in the life to come.

Suggested Prayer ————————————————————————
Dear God,
Forgive me for trying to seek revenge. Vengeance belongs to You and I give it back to You. Lord, help me live for You and treat others with respect lest You judge me. I pray for my cheating ex and their partner. In Your wrath please remember mercy. In Jesus' Name, Amen.

What Is the Object of Your Love?

1 John 2:15-17

Do not love the world or the things in the world. If anyone loves the world, the love of the Father is not in him. For all that is in the world—the desires of the flesh and the desires of the eyes and pride of life—is not from the Father but is from the world. And the world is passing away along with its desires, but whoever does the will of God abides forever.

The apostle John was overwhelmed with the love of God. He refers to himself as the disciple whom Jesus loved. John also gave us the most memorized and quoted verse in the Bible, John 3:16. John saw a great enemy that would rival our love for God, and it is this present evil world's system. The philosophies and thinking of this world wages war against our hearts. This world would rob us of everything—our peace, joy, hope, and love. We cannot love God and the world. For the Christian it is an "either or" and not a "both and" relationship. We will either love God or the world.

The two worlds collide in our hearts because they are from two different sources. The lust of the flesh is strong because we want to please ourselves. The eye wants all it sees and will never be satisfied. The pride of life is a direct attack on our egos.

We must keep in mind that there are two durations in the love that we can express. The world is only temporary and is passing away. All our possessions and accomplishments will pass away. God's love is permanent. We can love Him now and throughout eternity. Love for God will be rewarded and will never fade away. So, guard your heart against the temptation of this world instead of God. Fall in love with Jesus! When we fall in love with God, we find that we really do not want what this world has to offer.

Suggested Prayer ───────────────────────────────

Dear Lord,

I struggle in this world. I want to love You with all my heart. I choose to love You today with all my heart. Help me resist the temptation to be caught up in this world. I love You, Jesus! Amen.

Lord, Open My Eyes to Your Word

Psalms 119:18
Open my eyes, that I may behold wondrous things out of your law.

Psalm 119 is the longest chapter in the Bible and its subject is the Word of God. The psalm uses about ten descriptive words for the scriptures: the law, precepts, commandments, testimonies, words, ways, statutes, rules, promise, and judgments. All but about two verses will use one of these words to describe the scriptures.

The psalmist wanted his eyes opened to the scriptures. He wanted God to reveal wonderful things to him from the Word. He wanted to know the deep things of God and the awesome truths of the scriptures. Verse 18 is in the form of a prayer, and is a good prayer to pray before we read the Bible. As we call on God to reveal His Word to us He will answer that prayer. He will begin to show you something that will help your situation. For some, words of promise will come to help them through their trials. For others, words of correction will come. Still others will receive instruction.

God's Word has the answer to our problems. Do we believe the Bible to be true? Do we believe God wants to speak to us through the Word? Do we believe it has the answers to our problems? My friend, the Bible has the answers we are looking for. May this verse be our prayer before we open its pages and begin reading it.

Suggested Prayer
Dear God,
I believe in Your Word. I believe it is the most important thing on earth. Now, Lord, please open my eyes that I might see wonderful things from Your Word. Jesus, You are the living Word, and may Your Word live in me. In Jesus' Name I pray, Amen.

The Word Gives Life to Those Who Are Depressed

Psalms 119:50

This is my comfort in my affliction, that your promise gives me life.

When we are afflicted or depressed, we are looking for something to revive us and give us strength for another day. The psalmist found great comfort in the promises of God. As his spirit dwindled through his affliction, his very life was being sucked out of him. His spirit began to dry up. Then he began to read the Word and it brought back life into his spirit. One result of this spiritual life was that he now had energy in his body. He began to live again.

God wants to send us a revival in our spirit that will totally change us and make us into something awesome that He can use for His glory. Are you depressed or downtrodden? Is your spirit dry? Do you feel like your life and energy have been drained from you? There is hope. The Word of God can give you life again. You can live again after the horrible thing you have been through. If a doctor prescribed a daily pill to change your life you would more than likely take the pill. Well, the Great Physician has written us a prescription: a daily systematic reading of His Word. The result will be life and spiritual energy. These are the doctor's orders.

Suggested Prayer —————————————————————

Dear Lord,
I now realize that a daily dose of Your Word can give me life. I ask that You give life to my dead spirit. Send a revival to my spirit that will change me. Let those around me see the difference that You are making in my life. In Jesus' Name, Amen.

What Is Your Bible Worth?

Psalms 119:72
The law of your mouth is better to me than thousands of gold and silver pieces.

We all know that money cannot buy happiness or a home in heaven. However, we also know that it is a useful tool. When we lack funds, everyday life becomes very difficult. When our outgo exceeds our income, our upkeep will be our downfall. The psalmist says that God's Word was more important to him than thousands of gold and silver pieces. The scriptures come from the very mouth of God.

What God says to us is more important than anything else on this earth. Our Bibles are our most prized possession. The value of the scriptures far exceeds the cost of the printed page. Of all the things we could buy or possess, the words from the very mouth of God are the most important. We strive and strive to get ahead and to make a name for ourselves, oftentimes to no avail. If we cared about the Word more than we cared about possessions, we would soon see that things truly do not satisfy. What is your goal? To make more money or to know God's Word more and more?

Suggested Prayer —————————————————————
Dear Lord,
My priorities are wrong. I have worried about and striven for possessions, only to fall short. I want Your Word to be the most important thing in my life. Blessed be Your Holy Book, my most valued treasure. Amen.

APRIL 17

The Word of God Fights Against Depression

Psalms 119:92

If your law had not been my delight, I would have perished in my affliction.

The psalmist was depressed and in a very low state in life. He felt like he would have perished if it were not for his enjoyment in the Word of God. When we are depressed and discouraged, it is hard to find anything that is enjoyable. Oftentimes we try to find enjoyment any place but in God's Word. The first thing we do is quit reading our Bibles. Truth be known, many of us are mad at God and we have built walls between us and Him. As each day passes, we add another layer of bricks till we have a seemingly unsurmountable wall built up between us and God.

That would have been the psalmist's fate except for one exception. He found delight in the Word. The Word then began to change his heart and mind. The love for God's Word kept him from perishing. As we delight in God's Word, He begins to change us and bring hope to our spirits. Walls come tumbling down. Little by little the depression begins to subside, and God revives our soul. How? It all begins when we open our hearts up to the Word and let it minister to our spirits.

Suggested Prayer

Dear God,
I have been depressed and it feels like I am perishing. Lord, I neglected Your Word as I became bitter. Forgive me and help me to delight in Your Word again. Help it change me and restore me. Lord, I don't want to be bitter. Please help as I look for answers in Your Word. In Jesus' Name, Amen!

Lord, Guide Me with Your Word

Psalms 119:105
Your word is a lamp to my feet and a light to my path.

Every person needs guidance and direction. Parents direct their children into a path that would be best for them. As children get older, perhaps a teacher or mentor guides them to make wise choices. We all are guided by someone or something. The psalmist plainly tells us that the Word of God should be our guide. The Word will let us see what is around us because it will be like a lamp or candle around our feet.

As we obey the Word, the path that we should take will begin to light up for us. Before we know it we are on the straight and narrow road that leads to life and brings honor and glory to God. Unfortunately, many Christians decide to follow their own way instead of God's way. We replace the wisdom of the Word with the wisdom of the world. We might have a measure of success, but one day we will realize we are on the wrong road. All our efforts without God will lead us to a dead-end street. Joy, peace, and happiness are gone, and instead we have remorse, regret, and sorrow. Our way is not the best way.

The happy successful life begins when we deny our way and embrace the Bible way. Let the Word direct your path. So many people do not know which way to go. God's Word cries out to us—it wants to show us the right path if we will read it and obey it. Our parents always had our best interests in mind as they guided us. The holy scriptures have our best interests in mind too. Are you confused as to what path to take? Begin reading systematically and prayerfully through the Bible and the confusion will be replaced with confidence.

Suggested Prayer

Dear Lord,
I have tried to live a Christian life with my own will and way. Lord, I have made a mess of things. I confess my sin and I now decide that I will live my life according to the Bible, trusting You to be a lamp to my feet and a light to my path. In Jesus' Name, Amen.

APRIL 19

Fanning the Flame

---

2 Timothy 1:6-7

For this reason I remind you to fan into flame the gift of God, which is in you through the laying on of my hands, for God gave us a spirit not of fear but of power and love and self-control.

Timothy was a pastor who was very special to the apostle Paul. Timothy had a sincere faith and was an ordained pastor that Paul had laid hands on. Timothy had a grace-gift given to him by the Holy Spirit. Paul encouraged this young preacher to fan the flame that was in him.

Many fires die out eventually if they do not have enough oxygen. When enough air is fanned over the smoldering embers, a great fire erupts that produces light and warmth. Paul evidently saw Timothy's fire starting to fade and he was concerned that Timothy would be ineffective. Paul reminded him of the great fire that resided in his heart. The Spirit in us is not a spirit of fear or timidity. We should not be afraid or hesitant or ashamed. We must get past our fears to fan the flame.

We have a Spirit of dynamic power that can change us and those around us. We also have agape love in our hearts. We can love as Jesus loved. We also have a spirit of self-control to keep our lives holy before God. Paul prayed for Timothy night and day that he would be all that God wanted him to be. We might not have been called to be pastors, but we all have a sincere faith in the Lord. With that faith He has given us gifts to glorify Him and further His kingdom. Let us put aside the fears and fan the flame so there will be a hot fire of power, love, and self-control flowing from our hearts to reach those who need God.

Suggested Prayer ———————————————————

Dear Lord,

My troubles, fears, and worries have started to extinguish the flame in me. God, I am saved and You have gifted me, so please help me to be all that You want me to be. Take away the fears and fill me with Your power and love. Help me have a spirit of self-control so I can be a good testimony to those around me. In the Name of Jesus I pray, Amen.

APRIL 20

Did You Lose Your Life?

Matthew 10:39
Whoever finds his life will lose it, and whoever loses his life for my sake will find it.

Jesus said that the person who lives for himself will one day discover that he has lived a wasted life. Perhaps your divorce has caused you to lose many things. It seems like your life has been wasted. Everything that you hoped for and dreamed about is gone. Wait! There is hope. Jesus said if we would lose our lives for His purpose, we would find them.

Everyone wants to be successful. We all want God to be pleased with us. That starts the moment we decide to lose our lives for God. When we decide that He is most important, other things do not matter as much. Dying to self is a slow, painful process but it is worth it. Soon all you will want is Jesus. You will not care if you are remarried. You will not care about fame and possessions. Your only priority will be Jesus. Now He can live through you. Now you will find the life that God designed for you. Perhaps your divorce was designed to get you to sell out completely to God.

Suggested Prayer
Lord,
You are my Lord and Savior. I give up my life now for Your sake. I have made a mess of things. Please take the remaining time I have here on earth and use it for Your sake. Today! Right now! I lose my life for Your sake! In Jesus' Name I pray, Amen and amen. Lord, I am expecting You to do great things through me. Amen.

Consider Your Ways

Haggai 1:7-9

Thus says the LORD of hosts: Consider your ways. Go up to the hills and bring wood and build the house, that I may take pleasure in it and that I may be glorified, says the LORD. You looked for much, and behold, it came to little. And when you brought it home, I blew it away. Why? declares the LORD of hosts. Because of my house that lies in ruins, while each of you busies himself with his own house.

God did not bless Israel when they came back into the land from their seventy-year captivity in Babylon. God called for a drought on the land so their produce would not be blessed. The Israelites ate but were not satisfied. They sowed crops but reaped a small harvest. God allowed their money to dwindle down to nothing. Their money was described like putting it into a bag with holes. Why did God do all of this? The answer is that the people were living for themselves and not for God. They had rebuilt their own homes and neglected His home.

God said that He would bless them if they put Him first. The main indication that God was their priority would be the reestablishment of His temple. God said that He was with them and the Spirit was with them, so they began to work on His house again.

Are things going bad in your life? Is He your number one priority? If He is, that is awesome. Just because you are struggling does not mean that you are being judged. But some who are reading this are being chastened by God because you have neglected Him. Put Him first and He will lift the curse and bring blessings. It is a good thing for all of us to consider our ways to see if we are walking with Him.

Suggested Prayer

Dear Lord,

I lay my ways before You. Please examine my heart and let me live for Your ways and not mine. You are with me and Your Spirit is with me, so please let me consider my ways, and may all my ways bring honor and glory to You. In Jesus' Name, Amen.

Can't We Just Live Together?

Hebrews 13:4
Let marriage be held in honor among all, and let the marriage bed be undefiled, for God will judge the sexually immoral and adulterous.

It is amazing to me that many "Christian" people think that it is perfectly fine to live together and have sex without the benefit of marriage. Marriage is precious to God and He created it. Marriage reflects Christ's love for the church and God's love for Israel. He created intimacy between a man and a woman to be enjoyable, and there is great peace in our lives when we follow God's principles. He punishes those who violate His principles. God said He would judge all fornicators and adulterers.

Before you begin the dating process, determine that you will wait to be intimate until marriage. God will bless you for your decision because it honors Him and His Word. Life is too short to spend our remaining days under the judgment of God. If we decide to dishonor God, we are forcing Him to act, and this never turns out well. If you begin dating, stay away from those who think it is perfectly fine to shack up. These people have a shallow commitment to you and your values. More importantly, their commitment to God is even more shallow. These are the people who will bring you down. The problem is that you might go so far down that you cannot get back up again. Loneliness is real and God can help you without compromising your convictions. If you stand for nothing, you will fall for anything.

Suggested Prayer
Dear Lord,
It is tough to be pure and holy in Your sight. I commit myself to wait till I am married to be intimate again. Please give me the strength of Your Holy Spirit to accomplish this. God, please protect me from those who would bring sin and judgment into my life. In Jesus' Name, Amen.

No Comparison

Romans 8:18

For I consider that the sufferings of this present time are not worth comparing with the glory that is to be revealed to us.

P aul says that our present sufferings do not even hold an honorable mention compared to the glory that awaits us. Now Paul was not making light of our sufferings; he went through many trials in his life and living through them was very difficult. He also was caught up into heaven and given a glimpse of what was in store for all of us. We have not been taken up to heaven, but we have the Holy Spirit, which is the first fruits of what is to come. The Holy Spirit is a little bit of heaven on earth. As we yield to the Spirit, the more we feel His presence. All of creation is crying out to God to make all things new. Creation is said to be experiencing birth pains as it awaits a new era. We will even be renewed with glorified bodies that are without sin, disease, and decay. Today might be gloomy but a glorious day is just around the corner.

Our list of sufferings may include sickness, sorrow, loneliness, and depression. The sufferings of each Christian are unique and this weighs heavy on our spirits. But we are going to a place of no sickness, no sorrow, no loneliness, and no more depressing days. Please consider your sufferings as temporary. If we do not focus on the glory, we will be consumed with grief that will suck the life right out of us. The next time you begin to feel the weight of your sufferings, stop and ask God to let you see the glory. We know in our heart that there is a glorious day coming, but in our flesh we lose focus on the prize. Ask God to keep you focused on the glory. All the troubles you are going through will soon come to an end and they will not matter anymore.

Suggested Prayer ————————————————————————

Dear Lord,

I know a glorious day is coming, but I get sidetracked and sometimes all I can think about is my problems. Help me stay focused on You and the prize. Holy Spirit, put a little of heaven on earth in my life, even now in these days of suffering. In the Name of Jesus I pray, Amen.

APRIL 24

Sin Impacts Everyone

Joshua 22:20
Did not Achan the son of Zerah break faith in the matter of the devoted things, and wrath fell upon all the congregation of Israel? And he did not perish alone for his iniquity.

Achan committed a grave sin when Israel fought against the city of Jericho. God gave clear instructions that they were not to take any personal spoils of war. Temptation got the best of Achan and he took a garment, some silver, and some gold. All seemed well till Israel tried to fight the city of Ai. Suddenly they found themselves retreating, after thirty-six Israelites lost their lives. The wrath of God fell on the Jewish camp. When Achan's sin was detected the Jews stoned him, burned his tent with the belongings inside, killed all his livestock, his wife, and even his sons and daughters. It was a horrifying scene, as sin had to be dealt with in the camp to take the curse off Israel. Achan did not perish alone for his sin.

A divorced person sees the sin of divorce and that infidelity impacts everyone. It is heartbreaking to watch children suffer because of the sins of the parents. Divorce touches every relationship we have. If, like Achan, we are at fault, may Almighty God help us find a place of repentance and restoration. If we are not the main cause of the divorce, may we determine that we will live right in the sight of God. Our children have suffered enough, and may God help us to be a people that will love Him and obey Him. May He lift the curse off our families!

Suggested Prayer
Dear God,
I confess my fault in the marriage. I realize everyone lost but the devil. I ask that from this day forward I would live for You, keeping myself from sin. Have mercy on my children. May I live for You and be a good example for my children. I pray that my ex-spouse would also honor You. Have mercy, Lord. Amen.

You Want Me to Do What?

James 1:2-3

Count it all joy, my brothers, when you meet trials of various kinds, for you know that the testing of your faith produces steadfastness.

James tells us to count it all joy when we are surrounded by trials. This seems very odd at first, then we realize that there is no use in getting mad. He did not say *if* we are surrounded by trials, but *when* we are surrounded. They are coming, so we should count it a joy because God is going to work through these trials. He allowed them and wants to teach us something through them. No trial or adversity comes our way without God allowing it to happen.

If we start out angry and bitter, we are in danger of developing a root of bitterness that will destroy us. The best way to not be a bitter old person is to not be a bitter young person. If we dedicate the trial to God initially the results will be good. The next time a trial comes, dedicate it to God with joy. We joke about patience or steadfast endurance, but we all need it. James tells us that having the right attitude in a trial will produce patience. Keep this in mind, that your trial is also for someone else. As you are suffering God is teaching those around you something.

It took the fiery furnace that the three Hebrew teens experienced for Nebuchadnezzar to see the true God. Christ's crucifixion was for Him (Hebrews 5:8) and us. Paul's imprisonments and shipwrecks were for others as well as himself. So many great things happen in our trials if we will endure with a joyful patience. We will see God's hand at work and so will others. Bite the bullet and count it a joy.

Suggested Prayer

Dear God,

I am surrounded by trials. They are too much for me. I count it a joy that I am in this situation, trusting You to work in my life and the lives of others. I dedicate this trial to You, and may Your will be done. Thank You for the trial. In Jesus' Name, Amen.

Go Grow Show

John 15:16

You did not choose me, but I chose you and appointed you that you should go and bear fruit and that your fruit should abide, so that whatever you ask the Father in my name, he may give it to you.

We must set the record straight. We did not choose God—He chose us. He has appointed us to bear fruit. Your horrible situation is a divine appointment for you to go, grow, and show. God has chosen us to go into this world and help those who are hurting. Many lives have been destroyed and God has chosen us to go help them. He wants to love them through us.

He has also chosen us to grow. He wants us to bear fruit. As we yield to Him, we begin to bear fruit. We will have the fruit of the Spirit manifested in our lives as we abide in Him. This fruit will help us, but ultimately it is for others to experience God's love. God has chosen us to show the world the love of Jesus. The world needs to see that Jesus is the Savior, sent from a God of love.

How will you know if you are bearing fruit? The answer is that it will manifest itself. One manifestation is that the fruit will remain. It will not be hit or miss. A constant walk with Jesus will show itself with fruit that will last. The other way to know that you are bearing fruit is by answered prayer. As you abide in Him you will have a deep prayer life, and God will answer your prayers because you are praying for the right things. If you abide in Him you will go, grow, and it will show.

Suggested Prayer ———————————————————————

Dear Lord,

I want to go to those who are hurting. Lord, I want to be fruitful. I want people to see Jesus in me. I want an awesome prayer life. Thank You for choosing me. I decide right now that I will follow you. In Jesus' Name, Amen.

I Can't Eat Another Frozen Pizza

Daniel 1:8
But Daniel resolved that he would not defile himself with the king's food, or with the wine that he drank. Therefore he asked the chief of the eunuchs to allow him not to defile himself.

Nutrition plays a major part in our wellbeing. It is so beneficial to eat well and to drink at least eight glasses of water each day. Now Daniel purposed in his heart that he would honor God's Word by not defiling himself with the meats on the king's table, so he requested only to eat vegetables. The result was that he was in better health than those who ate the king's meats.

We are not trying to suggest that a person eat only vegetables, but rather, that they would eat healthy. A single person is often too tired to cook a healthy meal, so they eat fast food or frozen prepared foods all the time. Some people are not used to cooking anything because their spouse did all the cooking. Some people do not like to cook. The problem is that our health suffers and so does the health of our children.

We are never too old to learn how to cook and eat healthy foods. Like Daniel, purpose in your heart that your diet will honor God. Take the time to learn how to cook some simple, healthy meals. Eventually you and your children will feel and look better as you eat properly.

Daniel lived a long life, and part of the reason was his diet. Our bodies are often neglected in Christian circles because so much emphasis is placed on our spirits. Yet, Paul wrote that our bodies are the temple of the Holy Spirit (1 Corinthians 6:19). In our older years we will not be able to serve God if we do not take care of our bodies in our younger years. Years of neglect will shorten our life span and quality of life.

Suggested Prayer
Dear Lord,
I realize this body houses Your Spirit. Help me and my children eat properly so we can honor You. Help us to look and feel better, and may You give me many precious years to serve You. In the Name of Jesus I pray, Amen.

Jesus, Our Treasure

Matthew 13:44
The kingdom of heaven is like treasure hidden in a field, which a man found and covered up. Then in his joy he goes and sells all that he has and buys that field.

In this parable a man finds a hidden treasure in a field. He wisely covers up the treasure, sells all that he owns, and purchases the field. It costs him everything he has to make the purchase, but in the end the rewards are worth it. In a card game a person will go all in. He thinks his hand is good enough to win the pot so he places all of his money on that hand, hoping to win the prize. If he wins, his move was worth it. But there is a chance he could be wrong.

When we go all in for Jesus we will always win. What will it cost us? The simple answer is—*everything*. The treasure will open up in this life and the life to come. Going all in is not easy with God. Now that you are starting life over as a single person, why not go all in for the Lord? Give up everything for the treasure. Jesus is the treasure. God will honor you as you honor Him. Believe that He will work it all out.

Some two thousand years ago our Savior went all in at the cross. What was His treasure? The church, His bride of believers, is His treasure. You are His treasure! Decide today that He will be your treasure and go all in for Him.

Suggested Prayer ————————————————————————
Lord,
Thank You for Your commitment to me. Today, right now, I go all in. I give up everything that I may obtain You. Lord, I expect You to bless me as I honor You. Lord, I am nervous about this decision so please give me peace about all of this. In Jesus' Name, Amen.

You Expect Me to Love Them?

Hebrews 13:1

Let brotherly love continue.

The writer of Hebrews was concerned that our love for each other would continue. There is a great danger if we stop loving our brothers and sisters in Christ. We focus on the rejection. Many people whom we thought were our friends sided with our ex-spouse. Some have avoided us, trying their best to stay neutral. Honestly, those who have hurt us do not deserve to be loved.

Wait a minute! *We* do not deserve the love of God because of the way all of us have rebelled against Him. *We* have all sided with the enemy from time to time, breaking God's heart. The Lord is saddened when we sin. He loves us so much. Just think, the God of the universe weeps over our souls.

We are not completely innocent in the matter of divorce. If we choose not to love our brother, we will soon find ourselves out of God's will and a spirit of bitterness will settle in our hearts.

Love those who have hurt you. Ask God to give you wisdom and insight on how to love them. Resist the temptation to fight back. Vengeance and judgment belong to God. If you are not willing, ask God to make you willing. The world will know that we are Christians and that God is real by the love that we have for one another. Some two thousand years ago the writer of Hebrews saw, through the Holy Spirit, that there is a danger of not loving our brother. Decide that you will let brotherly love continue.

Suggested Prayer

Lord,

I am mad at those who turned their backs on me. They supposedly claim to be Christians but are full of hatred. Lord, make me willing to love my brothers who have hurt me. Use me as a channel for Your love. In Jesus' Name, Amen.

God Goes Before Us and Makes a Way

Judges 4:14
And Deborah said to Barak, "Up! For this is the day in which the LORD has given Sisera into your hand. Does not the LORD go out before you?" So Barak went down from Mount Tabor with 10,000 men following him.

In the days of the Judges the nation of Israel had a female judge named Deborah. She asked Barak to lead Israel's army into battle against the forces of the Canaanites. She told Barak the Lord would bring victory to Israel that very day. She also said that God had already gone out before them on the battlefield. God had already won the victory for them and now all they had to do was go. God was true to His Word and Israel obtained victory that day.

God always goes before His children. Before you were ever born, or even married, God knew you would go through a divorce. Now He has gone before you again so that you will get the victory over this present battle. He has already put people in place to help you. He has provided the finances and all the resources you need to get you through. So, rest in the fact that He always goes before you. Your battle might not be won in a day, but rest assured, victory is ahead.

Suggested Prayer
Dear Father,
I know You have gone before me to help me obtain victory. Lord, I trust that You have paved my way for this victory. I rest in Your providence and provision. Thank You, Lord, for making a way for me in my wilderness wanderings. In Jesus' Name, Amen.

When Is God's Day Off?

John 5:17

But Jesus answered them, "My Father is working until now, and I am working."

We all enjoy our days off from work. However, a day off for someone struggling with divorce can be a nightmare. Now we have all day to think about all of our problems, and wish we were back at work. If you are blessed to have a job, it is still nice to have a day or weekend off.

Jesus said that His Father has always been working, and that the Father is working now. Jesus then said that He Himself is also working. It is true that God rested after six creation days. It is also true that He instituted a sabbath day of rest for the Jewish people. Our lives would be richer and fuller if we could take a day of rest each week.

Ultimately, God never takes a day off! If He took a day off this world and all of our lives would crumble instantly. God is always working on our behalf. Jesus is always interceding on our behalf. The Holy Spirit is always working too. Can you imagine trying to pray in a time of need, and God saying, "I can't answer you today, this is my day off." That sounds absurd, doesn't it? Thank God that He is always there for us. Furthermore, God never sleeps. We can come to Him anywhere and at any moment. He is always working for us. Praise God for His faithfulness to us.

Suggested Prayer

Lord,
I realize You are always working for me and that You never take a day off from me. You are always here for me, and so now I ask that I can be all that You want me to be. I want to always be available for You like You are for me. Help me be available to those who are hurting. In Jesus' Name, Amen.

Don't Compare Yourself With Others

2 Corinthians 10:12
Not that we dare to classify or compare ourselves with some of those who are commending themselves. But when they measure themselves by one another and compare themselves with one another, they are without understanding.

One thing that often brings discouragement is when we compare ourselves to others. Our standard is Jesus Christ, not other people. How do I measure up to Jesus? Is He pleased with me? When we compare ourselves with others it is not hard to find someone in much worse shape than ourselves. Then in self-righteous pride we feel that we are better than they. It is not hard to find someone better off and then we become discouraged.

In matters of divorce we see some who have defied God and His Word, and yet they seem to prosper. Others do not struggle financially like we are struggling. Still others find a new partner very quickly. Then the discouragement sets in as we struggle to pay our bills. As we spend every weekend alone while others are having a great time, we are even more discouraged. What can we do?

First, quit comparing yourself to other people. Paul says that we are not wise when we do this. Secondly, do not judge anyone. Jesus is the judge and does not need our help. Finally, yield to the Lord. He has a unique plan for you. In due time He will send you a new partner. In His time, He will turn your finances around. Do not look around at your brother, look up to the One who sticks closer to you than a brother.

Suggested Prayer
Lord, forgive me. I see those who are sinning, and they seem to prosper. I also see others being blessed and it seems like You are passing me by. Lord, I decide not to compare myself with others. I want to quit being jealous and judgmental. I submit to Your plan for my life. I yield to You now, trusting You will bless me in due season. In Jesus' Name, Amen.

A Biblical Pattern for Investing

Ecclesiastes 11:1-2

Cast your bread upon the waters, for you will find it after many days. Give a portion to seven, or even to eight, for you know not what disaster may happen on earth.

Solomon encouraged people to invest. People should first establish an emergency fund. Then they can concentrate on getting out of debt. Once that has been accomplished, a person can follow Solomon's counsel in these verses. Solomon suggests that a person invest in seven or even eight ventures. In other words, diversification is encouraged.

Solomon said that we do not know what kind of disasters will happen on the earth. If a person's investment is in just one area and that area does badly, he will lose all that he has worked for. The biblical balance is given to safeguard your investments. How many do you have right now? What are some possible ventures you could invest in? Giving to God is one investment that may or may not be rewarded in this life; however, in the life to come there will be rewards in heaven for your investments in God's kingdom.

The possibilities are endless when it comes to investing. Pray and ask God to lead you into seven or eight investments. Ask for wisdom, insight, and perception in this area. Watch God work it all out for you as you follow His leading. God wants you to be in a position to be used any time and any way He chooses. Many honest seeking Christians are not blessed in this area because they never took the time to follow God's principles on finances: giving, saving, and investing.

Suggested Prayer ————————————————————————————————
Dear Lord,
I want to be a good steward of my finances. Help me get out of debt and have an emergency fund. Then help me learn how to save and invest. Lord, I am not asking for a get-rich-quick scheme, but I ask for wisdom and leading into seven or eight ventures that will honor You. Please teach me, Lord. In Your Name I pray, Amen.

MAY 4

God's Peace and Presence

2 Thessalonians 3:16
Now may the Lord of peace himself give you peace at all times in every way. The Lord be with you all.

Two things our souls long for is peace and a sense of the presence of God. When we experience peace, we realize that God is in control, and that He approves of us. We also know our hearts are right and that we are pleasing in His sight. Peace is an awesome thing, and it can only come from God. He is the God of peace, and only He gives peace. Paul wanted the Thessalonian church to experience the peace of God all the time and in every circumstance, and to feel His presence.

His presence lets us know He is there with us in life's storms. His presence brings this desired peace in our hearts. The presence of God lets us know that He has not forgotten us and is working everything out for our good. The peace and presence of God go hand and hand to give us comfort in this wearisome world.

How do we obtain such peace and His presence? It can only come from Him. It only comes when we are walking with Him day by day. As we pray, read the Word, and submit to Him the peace will follow. It might not happen immediately but one day your cup will overflow with His peace and presence. Then others will be attracted to the God of peace.

Suggested Prayer
Now Lord,
I praise You that You are the God of peace. Lord, I want peace and I want to sense Your presence. I commit myself to a living, loving relationship with You. Please send peace soon. In Jesus' Name I pray, Amen and Amen!

God's Promises

Romans 4:18

In hope he believed against hope, that he should become the father of many nations, as he had been told, "So shall your offspring be."

Abraham was the father of the Jewish people. God called him out of Ur and told him that He would make a great nation from him. He also said that all families of the earth would be blessed through him. His name at that time was Abram, which meant *father*. But Abram had no children. He was too old and his wife was way past the age of childbearing. Can you picture it? People would meet him and ask him his name. He would say, "Abram." Then the next question would be, "How many children do you have?" He would have to answer, "none." Well, God keeps his promises, and at age one hundred Abram became a father. God changed his name to Abraham, which means *father of a multitude*. Ultimately, all families would be blessed because our Savior, Jesus Christ, would come from Abraham's descendants.

Abraham believed God and did not look at the circumstances. He was, as Paul wrote in Romans 4:21, "fully convinced that God was able to do what he had promised." God may not have given us a promise like this, but He has promised all of us some things. For example, He has promised to take care of all our needs. So, we must believe Him at His Word. We cannot look at the circumstances or even look to our own ability. It is God who will carry out these promises as we look to Christ and not at our circumstances.

Suggested Prayer

Dear Lord,
I am trying to do everything by myself. I quit, and now I look to You for help. I will trust Your Word and quit looking at the discouraging circumstances. You can perform what You have promised to me. Hallelujah, Amen!

God Supplies Our Needs in Miraculous Ways

1 Kings 17:6
And the ravens brought him bread and meat in the morning, and bread and meat in the evening, and he drank from the brook.

The sin of the nation of Israel was so great that God called for a three-and-a-half-year drought on the land. The prophet Elijah told King Ahab that the heavens would dry up. God told Elijah to flee to the brook Cherith; there God would send ravens to feed him morning and evening, and he could drink from the brook. Eventually the brook would dry up and Elijah would be fed by a widow. This widow had just enough oil and flour to bake a cake for herself and her son, but Elijah asked her to make his meal first. She did, and through the drought there would always be enough oil and flour for all three to eat.

God provided for His people in a miraculous way. He still performs miracles today. We do not see miracles all the time, because they would then cease to be miracles and we would call them ordinaries. God is going to take care of your needs in a miraculous way. He is not bound to your finances. He can call the ravens to feed you if He chooses. Pray about your needs and watch God supply them. He knows the struggles you are going through, and He is aware of your limited resources. God's resources are not limited, and He can and will supply all your needs.

Suggested Prayer
Lord,
I have a great need and I cannot supply it on my own. I need Your help. Lord, I need a miracle. I believe You will help me. Please show me the way that I need to take. My resources are dried up and I need You. Thank You, Lord. Amen.

The Patience of Job! Really, Lord?

James 5:10-11

As an example of suffering and patience, brothers, take the prophets who spoke in the name of the Lord. Behold, we consider those blessed who remain steadfast. You have heard of the steadfastness of Job, and you have seen the purpose of the Lord, how the Lord is compassionate and merciful.

Sometimes we read about the Old Testament prophets or Job, and we do not think that these scriptures apply to us. James reminds us that God works in our lives, just like He worked in their lives. They were God's mouthpieces and suffered dearly for it. Yet God had a purpose in it all. Job patiently waited on God and the Lord was merciful to him and He was compassionate.

God wants us to be His mouthpieces to this world. God has never used anyone that He did not deeply hurt. Job's testimony is preserved in the Word of God forever. Everyone that knew him saw how God blessed him. The people that knew Job came face to face with the Living God.

God wants to bless us, and sometimes the path of blessing is extreme suffering. God has a desired end so we must, like those prophets of old, endure patiently. He is coming back soon, and He requires that we trust Him. Our part is to trust. He will do His part on His time, not ours.

As we try to open our own doors, we become frustrated; but when we wait on God the walls fall down and doors swing wide open. Then we hear a voice saying, "this is the way, walk in it." Those around us will see the true God as a result of His working in our lives. Some will even come into the kingdom as a direct result of your steadfast endurance. "How long must I wait?" This is getting old to you, I know! Remember, He is the Lord, which means owner or controller. Let's let Him be Lord. We are on His time and not ours. How long? Long enough for the Lord to accomplish His purpose in us.

Suggested Prayer ————————————————————————

Lord,

Be Lord of my life. Let Your purpose be accomplished and give me the strength to patiently endure. Help me see that You are working in my life. Use my trials to bring others into Your kingdom. Lord, I am patiently waiting on You. Amen.

Finish Well

---

2 Timothy 4:6-8
For I am already being poured out as a drink offering, and the time of my departure has come. I have fought a good fight, I have finished the race, I have kept the faith. Henceforth there is laid up for me the crown of righteousness, which the Lord, the righteous judge, will award to me on that day, and not only to me but also to all who have loved his appearing.

When Paul wrote 2nd Timothy he was in prison and about to be executed. The Lord had shown Paul that there was no getting out of this one. Years earlier, Peter had a miraculous deliverance from jail, but not so with Paul. Paul, the great apostle, would soon be in heaven with Jesus. In his parting words we see that God had a race for him to run, and by God's grace he finished it. He completely did everything God wanted, and rewards and glory awaited him. He fought a good fight as a contender in the race. He finished the race on top. Soon the awards ceremony would take place. Now Paul had many distractions: the devil, his own flesh, physical illness, shipwrecks, beatings, imprisonments, hunger, Jews, Gentiles, and the list goes on. He had so many distractions, but with God's help he finished on top.

You have had many distractions with the pain of divorce. Determine today that you will finish well. Chalk up your losses and get back in the race. So many people along your race course need God. With His help you can finish well. Perhaps today needs to be a time of recommitment and dedication to the Lord. Don't allow your distractions and difficulties to keep you out of the race. You might have to do some retraining and rehabilitation before you are healed enough to get back in the race. Let your coach, Jesus Himself, assign the necessary steps to allow you to finish on top. You are the only one who can run your race, so fight a good fight.

Suggested Prayer
*Dear Lord,
I have allowed this divorce and all the depressing things that come with it to overwhelm me. Now Lord, I want to finish well. I confess my sins and I want to run again. I recommit myself to You and the race that You gave me. In Jesus' Name I pray, Amen.*

A Double Portion of God's Spirit

2 Kings 2:9-10

When they had crossed, Elijah said to Elisha, "Ask what I shall do for you, before I am taken from you." And Elisha said, "Please let there be a double portion of your spirit on me." And he said, "You have asked a hard thing; yet, if you see me as I am being taken from you, it shall be so for you, but if you do not see me, it shall not be so."

In the days of Israel's apostasies God always had prophets to warn the people of their sins. Elijah was a remarkable, miracle-performing prophet. His apprentice was a man named Elisha. The men were complete opposites, but their common bond was Jehovah God. God took Elijah to heaven one day in a chariot of fire. Before he departed, he said he would fill any request that Elisha had. Elisha asked for a double portion of Elijah's spirit. He could have requested many things, but he wanted God in all of His fullness. We have heard over and over that material things will not satisfy us. We also know that our relationship with God is the only thing that will last.

By now you have probably experienced great losses and realize that God wants to give Himself to you. He wants to pour out a double portion of His Spirit on you. He wants to do miraculous things through you like He did with Elijah and Elisha. God wants to use you! So, use this time of singleness to focus completely on God. Determine that above all you want a double portion. If you remarry, your devotion will be divided between your spouse and God. So, take advantage of every moment to get closer to Him. Instead of being depressed and lonely determine to be devoted and full of Living water.

Suggested Prayer

Dear Lord,
Please give me a double portion of Your Spirit. Help me use this time to draw closer to You. Use this time to place me into Your service. Let this double portion be for Your service. I realize it is not just to make me feel good. By faith I receive this. Amen.

MAY 10

Calling on God

Romans 10:13
For "everyone who calls on the name of the Lord will be saved."

Paul's Epistle to the Romans is a literary masterpiece concerning salvation. He writes this letter by answering one question: "how can a man be right with God?" Paul explains that man is not right because of sin. He also tells us that Jesus died for our sins. We have a problem, and it is that we are sinners by nature and by choice. God has a solution—Jesus Christ. Paul explains that if we will believe in our heart that Christ died for our sins, we can ask the Lord to save us.

He admonishes us to call on Him. Everyone who calls on the Lord will be saved. When we call on the name of the Lord, we are calling on what Jesus stands for. He is God who left heaven and came to earth. He lived a sinless life, died, was buried, and rose again for my sins. He is the way to heaven as He died in my place.

Have you called? If you have not, why not? Whatever is holding you back is not worth the price you will pay if you die without God. Call on Him while He is near. Don't delay. Today is the day for you to call. We are not promised tomorrow so do not gamble your life away. Tomorrow may never come. The only way to be saved is to call on the Lord; there is no other way. This is one call you cannot afford not to make. God will answer your call for help. When you call on Him you are acknowledging your need. You are turning from sin and turning to Him. If you have called on God, tell someone about your commitment. Find a church that teaches the Bible and that believes that Jesus is God.

Suggested Prayer ────────────────────────────────
Dear Lord,
I am a sinner and in great need of salvation. I admit that I am lost. I turn from my sins and call on You to save me. Thanks for saving me. Help me now to learn how to walk with You. Amen.

Your Friends and Family Need Your Testimony

Mark 5:18-20

As he was getting into the boat, the man who had been possessed with demons begged him that he might be with him. And he did not permit him but said to him, "Go home to your friends and tell them how much the Lord has done for you, and how he has had mercy on you." And he went away and began to proclaim in the Decapolis how much Jesus had done for him, and everyone marveled.

Jesus cast many demons out of this man who lived among the tombs. His name was Legion because he had many demons inside of him. He even had some great demonic powers because he could break any shackles and chains put on him. The demons were no match for Jesus, so He cast them out of the man. The healed man wanted to depart from his region to be with Jesus.

Salvation makes us want to be with Jesus. It also makes us want to obey Him. We also want to share Him with others. Our Lord did not grant this man's request, but told him to declare to his friends what great things God had done for him. The man was obedient and began to tell people in the Decapolis what Jesus had done. The Decapolis was a ten-region city, and all the people marveled at what had taken place.

Sometimes we beg and plead to be somewhere else. We want a change of scenery or a fresh start. However, God has us exactly where He wants us. We are where we are supposed to be. Our friends and family have watched our lives and now we must also tell them of the Wonderful Savior who changed us. We are only human, and we are not perfect. Yet, God still wants us to tell others what happened to us. People need to know that there is a Savior and One who helps us get through the tough times. It would be nice to sail away with Jesus, but our mission field is right where God has us.

Suggested Prayer

Dear Lord,
I so desperately want to sail away to another place because of all my troubles. Lord, help me realize I am where You want me to be. Help me tell my story to others. May these people get saved, and may they receive encouragement from You. In Your Name I pray, Amen.

God Is Good!

Nahum 1:7
The LORD is good, a stronghold in the day of trouble; he knows those who take refuge in him.

Our God is a good God! Our circumstances may not seem very good, but God is still good. We should not look at our bad situation and come to the false conclusion that we have a bad God. God is good all the time to everyone. He is our fortress that we run to in the day of trouble. Sooner or later we will have trouble, and at that time we have a good God to go to. He is our fortress, and we can run into His everlasting arms. We can find refuge for our souls in the fortress of His goodness and love.

God also notices those who are trusting Him in the day of trouble. God notices us! He sees our day of trouble. He sees how we run to His fortress. He sees that we are trusting Him. He is not obligated to help anyone at all. Since He is good, He decides to honor our faith and help us in our affliction. God sees our faith and that honors Him. David said no one cared for his soul. God cares! We must rid our minds of the type of thinking that sees God as a tyrant.

Are you in a day of trouble? Are you trusting Him? Did you run to His fortress? Can you honestly say, "God is good," or is there a problem with your faith? Perhaps you quit trusting. If you are feeling that God is not good, this is an indication that you are not trusting Him.

Suggested Prayer ———————————————————————
Dear Lord,
Through my divorce and loneliness, I feel that You are a cruel God. I am sorry, Lord. I realize that I am not trusting You and I am trying to do it all by myself. Help me trust in Your goodness. Thank You, Lord. Amen.

Prevailing Prayer

Mark 11:24

Therefore I tell you, whatever you ask in prayer, believe that you have received it, and it will be yours.

Prayer can be defined and discussed in various ways. We can talk about how to pray, when to pray, what posture, etc. Jesus said pray in such a way that you are already receiving the answer to your prayer. We can pray about anything and everything. Yet we must pray believing and expecting God to work on our behalf. One of the preachers of old said you can pout and do without or you can believe and receive.

At our church we have a prayer meeting every Sunday night. In the meetings there is a young lady who attends, and she prays like Jesus would have all of us to pray. She prayed for her brother's salvation in such a way that she already received the answer. She prayed for the sick already receiving their healing. Her prayers encouraged me to pray in faith. I greatly admired the faith that she displayed in her prayers.

Now this is no secret magical formula to get God to do your bidding. However, this type of praying gets heaven's attention as we pray in faith. God honors faith. Without faith we cannot please God. Jesus said to have faith in God (Mark 11:22). So let us exercise our faith by believing that we have already received the things we are praying for.

Suggested Prayer ───────────────────

Dear Lord,
I receive healing and restoration for me and my children. I receive my needs being met by Your gracious hand. I receive a new spouse that I can serve You with. I receive restored finances from the great cost of this divorce. I receive new friends. In Jesus' Name I pray, Amen.

MAY 14

A Time of Suffering

John 5:6
When Jesus saw him lying there and knew that he had already been there a long time, he said to him, "Do you want to be healed?"

The man that Jesus healed was an invalid for thirty-eight years. As he lay at the Pool of Bethesda, he felt that if someone would put him in the water, he would be healed. He had no ability to heal himself and he could not rely on others for healing. His situation was hopeless. However, King Jesus came by and healed him. At Jesus' word he was instantly healed and began walking. His suffering turned to a celebration as God met him at his deepest need. The suffering became a testimony to the power of God.

In all our suffering we realize by now that no man can help us; only the Lord can help. We also know that we cannot heal ourselves. No matter how hard we try we always come up a little short. Today God is asking, "Do you want to be healed?" By faith we can be healed from our sufferings as we trust Him and obey His commands. This man was to rise, take up his bed, and walk. Your prescription may be different, but rest assured you will be healed as you follow the doctor's orders. Your prescription may be to "read your Bible, pray, and volunteer at the local nursing home and you will be healed." Then your testimony will bring glory to God because you will tell others about how God healed you. Thank God we have a God who sees our suffering and helps us.

Suggested Prayer
Dear God,
I want to be healed. I cannot do it and no one else can help me. You are the only one who can help. I will trust You and do whatever You want me to do. By faith I receive the healing from this horrible divorce. In Jesus' Name, Amen.

A Time of Separation

John 6:66-69

After this many of his disciples turned back and no longer walked with him. So Jesus said to the Twelve, "Do you want to go away as well?" Simon Peter answered him, "Lord, to whom shall we go? You have the words of eternal life, and we have believed, and have come to know, that you are the Holy One of God."

Jesus had many followers but lost several after His sermon. Many were offended at the truths He taught and went back to their old ways of life. When He asked the Twelve if they would leave too, Peter said there was no turning back. They believed that Jesus was the Son of God and there was no other system or person to follow. Peter realized that all they could do was trust Jesus.

Sometimes a circumstance comes in our life and we allow it to separate us from Christ, and we no longer follow Him. For example, there was a faithful Christian lady who attended church regularly. Then tragedy struck and her husband died. Through this tough time, she separated herself from Christ. She quit going to church and quit growing as a Christian. Instead of getting closer to Christ she ran away.

The text says, "after this many of his disciples turned back..." After what _____? In this particular circumstance it was Jesus' sermon. We can fill in the blank with several things. After a divorce, a death of a child, a job loss, etc. The tragedy is that we permit this thing that God allowed in our lives to keep us from Him. God brought this circumstance to draw us closer to Him, and if we are not careful, we will push Him away. Peter knew there was no other place to go. Today do not let your tragedy be a separation. Instead, let this trial be a time of dedication. Draw closer to Him and let Him use you. Peter did this and when he preached his first sermon three thousand souls were saved. We will either consecrate or separate.

Suggested Prayer ——————————————————————————————
Dear Lord,
I have been deeply hurt and I am mad at You for allowing this to happen to me. You could have prevented this, Lord. Today I choose to dedicate this trial to You. Lord, do not let this separate me from You. Let this trial get me closer to You and may I be a blessing to others. In Jesus' Name, Amen.

A Time of Saving

John 7:6
Jesus said to them, "My time has not yet come, but your time is always here."

Jesus said that His time had not yet come. What He meant was that it was not quite time for Him to go to the cross. Jesus came to die on the cross as the sacrifice for our sins. In eternity past, before the world was created, Jesus decided to redeem us from our sins. Before Adam was created, Jesus would come to die for us. So, Jesus told His family that His time was not here just yet. The time would be soon.

Then Jesus said, "your time is always here." Jesus was essentially saying that they could be saved right now by believing in Him. Paul wrote in 2 Corinthians 6:2, "…In a favorable time I listened to you, and in a day of salvation I have helped you." "Behold, now is the favorable time, behold, now is the day of salvation." In penning those words, Paul was quoting Isaiah 49:8.

Jesus gives us an open invitation to be saved. This invitation is based on the Old Testament, the words of Jesus, and the New Testament. In fact, the Bible is a 'hymn' book: it is all about Him. The Old Testament describes how Jesus will come and die on a cross. The gospels[2] show the birth, life, death, burial, and the resurrection of Jesus. The book of Acts shows us the ascension of Jesus. The epistles[3] look back to the cross. The book of Revelation shows us how Jesus will come again.

Are you ready to meet God? If you are not, let today be the day of salvation. This is your time to make the most important decision of your life. Your time is here, so trust Christ today.

Suggested Prayer
Dear Lord,
Today I realize that I am lost. I thought I was a Christian but I am not. I believe You died for me and rose again for me. I turn from sin and turn to You. I ask that You be my Savior. Thank You for saving me today. In Jesus' Name I pray, Amen.

---

[2] Gospels: the books of Matthew, Mark, Luke and John in the New Testament.

[3] Epistles: the books of Romans through Jude in the New Testament.

A Time of Seeing

John 11:39

Jesus said, "Take away the stone." Martha, the sister of the dead man, said to him, "Lord, by this time there will be an odor, for he has been dead four days."

John chapter 11 is one of the richest chapters in the entire Bible. Lazarus, brother of Mary and Martha, had died. Jesus had told the disciples that his illness would not result in death but would be for the glory of God. But Lazarus had been dead four days when Jesus came to the tomb. He told the people to take the stone out of the way. Martha told Jesus that he had been dead four days and that there would be an awful stench. Jesus reminded her that she would see the glory of God if she would exercise her faith. When the stone was removed from the tomb she believed, and Jesus brought Lazarus from the dead.

By faith we too can see the glory of God. The Father's desire is that Jesus be magnified in our lives. This trial of yours is for a time of seeing the glory of God. God asks us to have faith. Then He wants us to exercise our faith. There are some things we can do, like rolling away the stone. There are some things we cannot do, like raise the dead. The Father's desire is that you would show the glory of God in your life.

People that know you see the desperate situation you are facing. They are watching you. If you decide to trust Him the miraculous will take place. Bills will be paid, and transportation will be supplied. Food will come the table. You will see the glory of God. Your friends will also see the glory of God and the Holy Spirit will encourage them to trust Jesus. This rough time in your life is where you will see the resurrection power of our Lord Jesus Christ.

Suggested Prayer

Dear Lord,

I am in a bad situation. I want to see Your glory as You work in my life. I want others to see You too. I decide that I will trust You. I also decide that I will give you all the honor and glory by taking no credit for myself. In Jesus' Name, Amen.

MAY 18

A Time of Showing

John 21:14
This was now the third time that Jesus was revealed to the disciples after he was raised from the dead.

There were forty days between Jesus' resurrection and ascension. During that time He appeared to His disciples on different occasions. He commissioned them to preach and gave them some final instructions. Peter decided to go fishing; he felt the past three years were a waste as they followed Jesus. After fishing all night Jesus was already on the shore to greet them with breakfast.

The great thing about God is that He never leaves us. God in the person of the Holy Spirit decides to show up in our lives. These appearances are always for a purpose. Peter and the disciples needed reassurance for the journey of faith they were about to embark on. During the Lord's crucifixion Peter denied Him three times. At this breakfast Peter confessed his sins and confirmed his commitment to Jesus. Jesus told him to feed His sheep. These apostles were about to turn the world upside down, but God let them catch 153 marvelous fish and fed them breakfast.

You see, God is interested in our physical needs and our spiritual needs. Praise God that He still passes by. He still calls out from the shore. He still calls, commissions, and equips His children. So, hang in there. Jesus is going to show up and meet your physical and spiritual needs. There will be no doubts in your mind when Jesus arrives. John heard a voice and said it is the Lord. He did not have to wonder if it was God or not. He knew immediately that it was Jesus. You too will hear His voice. He has not left you.

Suggested Prayer
Dear Lord,
I feel abandoned by everyone, including You. Please surprise me like You did Peter and the other apostles. Please show up and supply my needs and fill me with Your presence. Lord, I realize that Your visit will be a divine appointment for a desired purpose that You have for me. So, help me be obedient. Amen.

He Is in the Midst and He Will Help

Zephaniah 3:17

The LORD your God is in your midst, a mighty one who will save; he will rejoice over you with gladness; he will quiet you by his love; he will exult over you with loud singing.

Zephaniah speaks of a time when Jehovah will be in the midst of the City of Jerusalem. God is always in the midst or middle of our lives. Jesus is always in the midst of His followers. He wants us to put Him in the center of everything we do. So be encouraged, because God is in the middle of everything that is happening with you. He is right there with you.

The verse also uses the word "will" four times. He is the mighty Warrior in our midst that will save us and protect us. The text says, "he will rejoice" over us with joy. It is His pleasure to find joy in us. The world might not see any good in us, but God is glad to take notice of us. He will calm our spirits with His love. When we realize and feel the love that He has for us our problems become small. He will also sing over us. The singing is described as *loud* singing. Jesus loves me! Jesus is in my midst! Jesus rejoices over me! Jesus sings to me!

God is here and is in control. Let us reciprocate by putting Him first, by loving Him, by rejoicing in Him, by singing to Him. Invite Jesus to be in the center of your life today. Let your life revolve around Him, and do not try to fit Him into your busy schedule. In our solar system everything revolves around the sun. Without the sun life simply could not exist. As it is in the physical world, so it is in the spiritual world. Everything must revolve around the Son.

Suggested Prayer ——————————————————————————
Dear Lord,
I did not realize how much You care. Help me to love You and to praise You. Help me to put You first in everything I do. I love You and rejoice in You. Amen.

I Need Someone to Encourage Me

Romans 15:4

For whatever was written in former days was written for our instruction, that through endurance and through the encouragement of the Scriptures we might have hope.

Good news! There is an encourager in your house already. Divorced people are some of the loneliest people. They have lost a spouse, family, and friends. Sometimes they have trouble trusting people, and this is quite understandable. We all need a friend and you cannot put a price on a great friend. A friend encourages us and gives us hope in the tough times.

We do have a Friend who has written sixty-six books to us. Paul says that the things that are written are for our instruction. He goes on to say, as we patiently endure, our hearts can receive comfort through the scriptures. We will have hope as we allow the scriptures to work in our lives. God is the lover of our soul and our true friend. He wants to speak to us and instruct us. He wants our hearts to be comforted and He wants us to have hope. The scriptures provide the help that we need. Without a regular, systematic reading of the Word there will be no comfort or hope. There will be no patient endurance without the scriptures.

King Jesus is the Great Physician and He has prescribed us some medicine that will comfort our pain. His prescription will bring hope and steadfast endurance. "Where is this prescription?" you ask. It is in your house already in the form of the Holy Scriptures. You need it, so begin to read it and above all heed it. You will find your personal prescription within its pages.

Suggested Prayer ——————————————————————————
Lord,
I have had enough! It is tough-going through this trial, trying to stay positive. Lord, I need encouragement and I need a glimmer of hope. I will read Your Word daily. I ask that it comfort me and bring me hope. In Jesus' Name I pray, Amen.

Feuding Families

Romans 12:18
If possible, so far as it depends on you, live peaceably with all.

The Holy Spirit directed Paul to write this very interesting verse concerning our relationships with others. We must all come to grips with the fact that there will be some people that we just cannot get along with. It may not be possible to live at peace with these people, especially those who have hurt us so deeply. But the Lord does not let us off the hook. He tells us as much as we have in us, we are to pursue peace with everyone. So, we must do our very best.

It must be a one-hundred-percent effort on our part. If we cannot live peaceably, let the problem lie on the shoulders of the other person. It may not be possible to live peaceably but it is possible to try your very best. Many of us do not want to try to live in a state of peace with these people. In our flesh and our hurt pride, we want to take vengeance on these people.

But as we grow closer with Christ and fellowship in His sufferings the hurts are healed. Then we do not care about the hurts, we just want to serve our Master in heaven. We must do this for the Lord's sake. We represent Jesus Christ and we do not want to mar His reputation with an unforgiving spirit. We must also do it for the children's sake. Their entire world has been destroyed and they are the true sufferers. We must also do it for an example to believers so they will see that they can serve God even when there is hatred towards them. We must do it as a testimony to this lost world so they can see the love of Christ. We must also do it for ourselves.

Suggested Prayer
Lord,
I do not want to live at peace with those who have hurt me. I know you want me to, so I am willing to give it my best shot. I am trusting that You will work all things out. Let me glorify You, and may I be a testimony to my children, the church, and other people. In Jesus' Name, Amen.

No One Can Compare to Our God

Micah 7:18-20

Who is a God like you, pardoning iniquity and passing over transgression for the remnant of his inheritance? He does not retain his anger forever, because he delights in steadfast love. He will again have compassion on us; he will tread our iniquities underfoot. You will cast all our sins into the depths of the sea. You will show faithfulness to Jacob and steadfast love to Abraham, as you have sworn to our fathers from the days of old.

Micah said that no one compares to our God. We have an awesome, compassionate God who delights in love. His love is steadfast because it never changes, and He never stops loving us. We who have experienced a divorce arrived at the day when our spouse said, "I don't love you anymore." Their steadfast love came to a screeching halt and left us feeling less than human.

But God! Who is like Him? He is the One who loves us with an everlasting love. Praise God! Mankind's love will fade away, but God's love is forever. He also forgives our sin and pardons our transgressions. He casts our sins into the depths of the sea to surface no more. No other "deity" can forgive. There is only forgiveness with our God—the One True God. He will not always be angry with us because of His love. He is a compassionate God who comforts us in our afflictions. He shows us His faithfulness by redeeming us and supplying all of our needs.

The same God that made a covenant with Abraham has committed Himself to us. He said that He would never leave us or forsake us. What a friend we have in Jesus! May you be overwhelmed by His steadfast love today.

Suggested Prayer ———————————————————————————

Father,

I praise You! There is no one like You! You love, forgive, and remain true to us. May we be overpowered by Your love and presence. I choose to praise and worship You today. Hallelujah! Amen!

Contenders, Not Contentious

Jude 3

Beloved, although I was very eager to write to you about our common salvation, I found it necessary to write appealing to you to contend for the faith that was once for all delivered to the saints.

Jude set out to write about the salvation that all Christians have in common. However, he found it necessary to exhort the believers to earnestly contend for the faith. Sometimes we, like Jude, have eager plans, but God changes our plans to line up with His plans for us. What is the faith? The faith can be defined as the body of truth entrusted to all believers. This would include the essential doctrines of our faith: the virgin birth and the deity of Christ, the Holy Spirit, etc. The reason why we must contend is because God is under attack by false teachers, satanically inspired to undermine the Word of God. Our foundation is Jesus Christ as revealed in the Holy Scriptures. The apostle John calls Him the Word of God (John 1:1). The Bible is our measuring stick to see if things are right or wrong.

We are always just one generation away from losing the faith. It is critically important that we pass the torch to the next generation. The world is shaping its culture and mannerisms from sinful desires inspired by Satan. Contend—we must! Instead of concentrating on how bad things are in your life, why not decide that you will be an earnest contender of the faith. It will be the salvation of your soul and it will save your family too. You also will pull others out of the fire as you contend. Jesus will come soon, so let's contend for the faith. How do you do this? Know and live the truth, then share it with others.

Suggested Prayer —————————————————————

Dear Father,

Please use me to contend for the faith. There is a great cause, and I want to do my part. You have a role for me, and I submit to this in my life. Teach me to be a contender. Give me courage and boldness to be a contender. In Jesus' Name I pray, Amen.

Be Careful, There Are Children Listening

Mark 9:42
Whoever causes one of these little ones who believe in me to sin, it would be better for him if a great millstone were hung around his neck and he were thrown into the sea.

veryone loses when a divorce takes place. Most people feel that the lawyers are the only winners and the children are the biggest losers. No child deserves to go through life with a broken home. However, God uses this to mold our children into His special vessels to carry the gospel to a new generation. Jesus had a special love for children while He was here on earth. He always had time for them and blessed them. They did not bother him.

How do we compare? Ouch, that hurt! Jesus even said that if we do not become like little children, we would not inherit the kingdom of God. He meant that we must exercise a childlike faith in Him to be saved and admitted into the kingdom. Today let us recommit ourselves to our children. Besides God, they are our most important priority.

Let us no longer talk badly about our ex-spouse. If you feel that you have offended your kids, confess your sins to God. Then sit down and apologize to them. Then live out your faith by trusting God and not becoming bitter at your ex-spouse. The idea in the text is that we do not put a stumbling block in our children's way. We do not want them to trip up and fall. We also need to trust God in this most diffi-cult time. Meet your children's needs and then trust God to meet your own needs.

Suggested Prayer
Dear Lord,
I have messed this all up! I have talked badly about my ex and I put a wall between my children and my ex. Forgive me, Lord! God, help me to ask their forgiveness. Help me to trust You, and may You bless my children. Lord, I dedicate myself to You and my children. I also have needs and I am trusting You to supply them. In the Name above all Names I pray, Amen.

Living Alone

Genesis 2:18

Then the LORD God said, "It is not good that the man should be alone; I will make him a helper fit for him."

One of the worst feelings is being alone. Loneliness is hard to bear. A quiet, empty home is nothing to look forward to after a hard day's work. If we knew that our loneliness was only temporary it would not be as hard to endure. God said that it is not good for people to be alone. God has the answer to our loneliness. God created for Adam a beautiful wife named Eve. God did not give Adam a slave, but created a perfect counterpart. Eve was someone he would love, laugh with and serve God with. Adam and Eve were one in body and spirit.

No wonder intense loneliness has invaded your soul. So, will God give you another spouse? This is the question that all single people want answered. The next question we want answered is, "When? How long must I suffer and be alone, God?" From this verse we see that God does not want us to be alone. We can also see that He has a solution for our problem. God saw Adam's loneliness and made provision for him. God does see our loneliness and help is on the way.

Many people are looking for the perfect mate. They are looking to solve their loneliness in their own power. Guess what? It is doomed to fail. We must allow God to send us His choice in His time. Perhaps you are still single because God is working on your character so your new marriage will last. If He wants you to remain single, He will give you peace and surround you with awesome friends. Today, dedicate your loneliness to God and ask Him to supply your need.

Suggested Prayer ————————————————————

Dear Lord,
I have tried and tried to find a new spouse, to no avail. I dedicate myself to You and ask that You will bring Your choice for me in Your time. In the meantime, please send me some great friends so I don't have to be alone. Thank You, Lord, that You see my loneliness. You see my need and I trust You are working on my behalf. Amen.

MAY 26

Rejoice Always. Really, Lord?

1 Thessalonians 5:16
Rejoice always.

In this verse Paul is commanding us to always rejoice. It seems like a simple task to be joyful, but it is not an easy task at all. We do not rejoice because of the circumstances that we find ourselves in. We do not rejoice because of past failures. We also cannot seem to rejoice because we do not see anything great for us in the future. In short, our past, the present, and the future keep us from rejoicing in the Lord.

Probably the biggest cause of our not being able to rejoice is our own personal sins that we commit. We have an enemy that will do everything in his power to keep us from rejoicing. The next time your spirit is down, focus on Christ. Think about how He saved you. It was with great love that He left heaven and came to die for your sins. Begin to think of the riches that you have in Christ. You possess eternal life in your soul. You are preserved and kept by His power. You have an awesome inheritance awaiting you. There is a mansion prepared for you. There will be no more sin or disappointments. The worries and cares of this life will be gone. We can rejoice that our names are written in the Lamb's Book of Life.

An old-time preacher, Tom Hayes, said, "The worst day of a believer is better than the best day of a non-believer." Tom's statement is so true, and we must allow God to show us the reality of his statement. Another preacher who is with the Lord now, Harold Sightler, said that we are saved, but we are not saved from suffering, sorrow, and shame. Thank God he went on to say that we are saved from sin, ourselves, and Satan. Moses endured all the onslaught of Pharaoh because he saw Him who was invisible.

Trials abound, but the calm assurance of our Savior brings peace and joy. The next time you feel down, look into the eyes of Jesus, and you will find that your joy will return. You will also receive divine strength for the journey.

Suggested Prayer
Dear Lord,
I don't feel like there is anything to rejoice about. Everything I have worked for is gone. Lord, let me see what I have in You. Lord, I always want to rejoice, especially in my sufferings, sorrow, and shame. Let me see things as You see them. In Jesus' Name, Amen.

Keep on Praying

1 Thessalonians 5:17
Pray without ceasing.

Paul commands us to pray without ceasing. Prayer is the real power to the walk of faith. We should have times of prayer when we are in our prayer closet, away from all distractions. However, Paul describes a oneness with Jesus so that we can pray at any moment. An attitude of prayer like this is an example of unbroken fellowship. To have this we must confess our sins. We must also actively seek the Lord. Prayer pleases God and we will be rewarded for our faithful prayer life. Before the apostles went out to preach, Jesus taught them how to pray. A preacher who does not have a good prayer life will not have any power in his preaching.

People that are in the nursing homes always want their children to come by and visit them. Some of the residents are depressed because their children do not come by to visit or call. These poor people feel all alone and neglected. How do you think God feels when we neglect to pray? We are His adopted children. He died on the cross for us. He wants to hear our voice. He is saddened when we do not talk to Him.

Prayer like Paul describes here pleases God because this means that we are in constant fellowship with Him. As we pray, our temptations become less tempting because we now have the divine strength to say no. The spirit of depression is lifted, and we can hear His still small voice. The voice will lead us and guide us and even provide for us. So, begin to start praying without ceasing.

Suggested Prayer ———————————————————————
Lord,
Forgive me for not praying like I should. I now realize You are seeking a deeper relationship with me. I ask that You help me to be in an attitude of prayer each day. Help me see the benefit of prayer. Help me see how a lack of prayer hurts Your feelings. In Jesus' Name I pray, Amen.

It's Time to Make A Choice

1 Kings 18:21

And Elijah came near to all the people and said, "How long will you go limping between two different opinions? If the LORD is God, follow him; but if Baal, then follow him." And the people did not answer him a word.

The prophet Elijah lived in dark times with Ahab and Jezebel ruling the country. The people gave lip service to Jehovah while serving the god Baal. Elijah asked how long they would go back and forth with their loyalties. He said if Baal is God then serve him, or if Jehovah is God then serve Him. He asked that they make a clear choice to serve the true God.

A showdown at Mt. Carmel took place. The God who answered by fire would be the true God and the people were to serve the right God. The 450 prophets of Baal placed their sacrifice on the altar, to no avail. They prayed and cut themselves, but nothing happened. Baal did not answer their prayers. Then Elijah had his turn. They poured so much water on the sacrifice that the trenches were filled with water. At the time of the evening sacrifice Elijah called on Jehovah. God sent fire down and consumed the offering, the wood, the stones around it, and all the water vaporized.

Jesus died on the cross at the time of the evening offering. As believers we have the power of the resurrected Christ in us. We do not need to see fire come down from heaven. We have the fire in our hearts. If you believe in Christ it is time to make a choice. You cannot serve God and something else. Decide today that God is your God and then serve Him with all your being. Are you limping along between two choices? No man can serve two masters, so decide to serve Him.

Suggested Prayer

Lord,
I have been limping along through life, trying to serve You and myself. Today I acknowledge You as God and I decide to serve You unconditionally. Let the fire in my heart consume any desire that is unholy or that would keep me from serving You. In Jesus' Name, Amen.

Giving Thanks

---

1 Thessalonians 5:18

Give thanks in all circumstances; for this is the will of God in Christ Jesus for you.

Paul, through the Holy Spirit, commands us to give thanks in all circumstances. It is easy to be thankful when things are going well, but when things go wrong it becomes very difficult to offer thanks. Paul, in Romans 8:28, says that God is using everything for our good. So, there is no negative circumstance in God's eyes. Our thoughts are not God's thoughts, so we do see negative circumstances. The key is the will of God. Paul says that it is God's will that we be thankful in every situation. To be in the will of God is to recognize a sovereign God who is in control and does as He pleases. So, a thankful heart is one that acknowledges Jesus, not only as Savior but also as Lord. No circumstance comes our way that the Lord did not allow. If He allows it then He is going to do something good in our lives. Submit to Him and be thankful that He is at work.

The situation you find yourself in my be tough, but God is there with you. He is working out something for His purpose. By thanking Him for the trial, you are submitting to Him and His purpose for you. He will not harm you and you will be more like Him. One of the biggest problems that we have is that we simply do not like the suffering that we are going through. We must somehow look at the bigger picture.

Perhaps the biggest pain of divorce is loneliness. We pray and beg God to send us someone and yet nothing happens. So, we pray and pray some more, and nothing happens. We go out on dates and they end up in disaster. Finally, we realize that we are not on the same page with God and so we must be thankful that we are single. This is very difficult. However, as we thank God, we are submitting to Him. Perhaps He will send someone in His time. He might have a plan for you that does not include marriage. These are things that only God can show you. However, as we become thankful, He will give us the grace to go through the ordeal of loneliness.

Suggested Prayer —————————————————————————

Lord,

I admit I have not been thankful. I do not like these trials You have sent my way. But today I acknowledge You as my Lord, so I submit to You. Thank You that You are working in my life. I believe You are doing something good, so I submit to You. In Jesus' Name, Amen.

Don't Put Out the Fire

1 Thessalonians 5:19
Do not quench the Spirit.

Paul commands us not to quench the Holy Spirit. The Spirit is a Person. He can be thought of as a fire that is burning in our hearts. The Holy Spirit lives in the heart of every believer. The Spirit's fire gives us light or understanding. He helps us understand the scriptures, and helps us learn God's will. He leads us and guides us into all truth. He gives us the heat or energy to serve God. However, He can be quenched.

Quenching the Spirit is like putting a wet blanket over the fire of our hearts. By very nature God is holy, so any sin in our lives will quench His work. God is working in us and through us to accomplish His purpose. If we quench the Spirit, we do not lose our salvation, but we miss out on all that He has planned for us. We can quench the Spirit by refusing to be led by Him. He is sovereign and He wants to do great things in our lives. If you have quenched Him, there is still hope. Confess your sin and yield to Him. Then He will become dominent and not dormant in your life. As we allow Him to be Lord His presence will be stronger and we will do His will.

One thing that may be hindering your walk is an unforgiving spirit. After all of the hurt that you went through it is very easy to come away with a spirit of bitterness. Today do not quench the Spirit. Choose to forgive those who have harmed you. It will release an outpouring of the Spirit of God in your life. You will feel the burden of sin lifted. God will now have you in a place where He can work again.

Many things quench the Spirit. All unrighteousness is sin. Ask God today to show you if you are quenching Him. Get in your prayer closet and spend some time confessing sin and asking God to reveal anything to you that may be displeasing Him.

Suggested Prayer

Lord, I have quenched You. Forgive me. I now yield to You and ask that You would cleanse me. Show me where I have failed You. I do not want to go another moment with my sins unconfessed. Show me every sin so I can yield to You. Help me hear Your still small voice. In Jesus' Name, Amen.

We Are His Possession and His Passion

Song of Solomon 7:10
I am my beloved's, and his desire is for me.

The Shunamite woman was overwhelmed with Solomon's claim on her life. She was the King of Israel's possession. Solomon had married this country girl, and now she was the king's wife. She had access to everything the king had as they became one. Not only was she overwhelmed with being the king's possession, she was enthralled by his passion. The king's desire was toward her.

We also have a beloved in the Lord Jesus Christ. We are His possession. He found us in the wilderness of sin and brought us to a heavenly kingdom not made with human hands. We now have access to all the King's possessions as we are joint heirs with Christ. At our conversion there was a union that took place and we became one with Him. Praise God that we are His possession.

Not only are we His possession, we are His passion. His desire is toward us because we are His bride. His thoughts are toward us. He wants to take care of us, pamper us, and protect us. He desires intimate fellowship with us. We are not deserving of such love. In God's grace and love we are His possession and His passion.

Suggested Prayer
Dear Lord,
It feels good to be Your possession. Lord, it is awesome to know that I am also Your passion. Let me draw strength from You and let me begin to realize the oneness that I have with You. May You be my possession and my passion. Praise the Lord! Amen.

Something New Is on the Horizon

Revelation 21:5
And he who was seated on the throne said, "Behold, I am making all things new." Also he said, "Write this down, for these words are trustworthy and true."

We get discouraged with this evil world's system, but God promised that a new day is coming. He will make everything new again, and there will be a new heaven and a new earth. You might be thinking to yourself, "Well, that's fine and dandy, but what about now? I am not feeling anything new at all." Do not be discouraged. God is going to make something totally new out of you.

Just as John was told to write down the true and trustworthy words of God, we can write them down in our hearts. At the time of this writing, June 1 would have been my twenty-sixth wedding anniversary. As I woke up, I felt absolutely horrible. I started thinking about the loneliness and how much my children have suffered. With no real hope in sight, the Holy Spirit led me to this verse. At that moment I realized that God was doing something totally new in my life. I received divine strength in my spirit as I realized that God had not forgotten me. I began to see that something new and big was just over the horizon.

Take comfort in the fact that God is doing a great work in you and for you. Something great and glorious is going to come out of your situation. It will be way beyond your wildest dreams. God has been there all the time. He has not left you at all! He has been devising something that will blow your mind. It will cause your friends, neighbors, family, and coworkers to see that God is a God of love. It will transform you from the inside out.

God's plan will be done on earth as it is in heaven. If you are discouraged today, realize that God is making something new in your life. Your life story does not end with defeat. No, no! There is a new chapter about to unfold that will change you and change the world. God says, "I am making all things new, so just trust Me."

Suggested Prayer
Dear Lord,
I must admit I am discouraged and disappointed. How long do I have to suffer? Lord, I believe deep down that You are doing something. By faith I choose to believe that something new is on the horizon and I receive it in Jesus' Name. Amen.

But It Was on Sale

Luke 12:15

And he said to them, "Take care, and be on your guard against all covetousness, for one's life does not consist in the abundance of his possessions."

Buying things brings temporary satisfaction to the pain and loneliness you are experiencing. Many people go out and buy a new car after a divorce, a bad choice if one cannot afford the vehicle. That person has now placed him or herself under a great debt. Jesus said to beware of covetousness because it can take on so many forms. Jesus said life is way more than physical possessions; life can be good with or without possessions. Only a life in the will of God truly satisfies.

We must guard our heart against all covetousness. It is not wrong to possess nice things, but it is wrong for things to possess you. A professor at Baptist Bible College, Dr. Hollis Cook, used to say, "purge the urge to splurge." He was so right! Those in debt cannot tithe. Debt adds so much stress. If you are a single parent, you have enough stress and do not need any more. Covetousness can simply be defined as an itch for more. We will never be satisfied until we are content with Jesus.

There are so many practical ways to break those bonds of covetousness. One way is to find a set amount that you can save from each paycheck that will not harm your budget. Begin saving for that desired item. When you have saved the money, ask yourself if you really need it. Then ask yourself if it will enhance your life. Can the money be used elsewhere for something more practical? Are you buying the item to fill the void in your life? Remember that things do not satisfy, so be content with Jesus.

Suggested Prayer —————————————————————————

Lord,

I find myself buying things to ease the pain in my heart. Lord, I give this pain to You. Let me be satisfied with You. May You lead me into wise decisions when it comes to material things. Purge me from all covetousness. In Jesus' Name, Amen.

JUNE 3

Don't Give Up Hope

Proverbs 13:12
Hope deferred makes the heart sick, but a desire fulfilled is a tree of life.

We all have longings and expectations in our hearts that come from God Himself. We pray and pray and pray and pray some more, but nothing seems to happen. I have been praying for seven years for a godly wife. After seven long years He answered my prayer, or so I thought. During those years I got depressed and discouraged because nothing was happening. I began to think I was crazy because it seemed like heaven was silent.

I had prayed for God to send me a lady from a far land with a different language and culture. I wanted a lady who would love me just for me and not what I could do for her. Well, I live in Texas—and to some that is a far, distant land with its own language and culture. As I was praying one night for a wife, a dear sister in Christ told me of her friend who lives in Hong Kong. I conversed with the lady from Hong Kong for about a year. One day she sent me a message that she would have a business conference in Orlando, Florida. I made arrangements and flew to Florida to meet her. It was the strangest thing that I could imagine! It was like I had known her my whole life! I fell in love with her instantly. Later I discovered that her intentions were only to meet me and see what I was all about. In my state of loneliness I really thought she was the one for me.

The whole experience taught me two things. One is that I needed to be controlled by the Spirit of God and not a spirit of loneliness. The result is that I became closer to God and He has more of my heart. The loneliness subsided. The other thing I learned was more of an encouragement. If God can send someone to me from the other side of the world, surely He has someone out there for me. Even though this lady was not the one, it made me realize that the right one is coming. Do not be discouraged, perhaps God has a lesson or two for you before the right person arrives.

Suggested Prayer
Dear Lord,
I have prayed and nothing seems to work. Right now, I choose to trust You and not look at my circumstances. Forgive me for getting discouraged. I receive by faith the spouse that You have for me. In Jesus' Name, Amen.

You Have a Unique Perspective

Mark 16:15
And he said to them, "Go into all the world and proclaim the gospel to the whole creation.

J ust before Jesus' ascension He issued a charge to the eleven apostles. They were to go into all the world and preach the gospel. Who could be better equipped for the task? After all, Jesus had handpicked them. They had spent three years with Him. They knew His teachings and His miracles. They had even performed miracles in His Name. With the experience they had gained, these eleven were ready to take on the world. These men had a unique perspective that other men did not have.

Guess what. You also have a unique perspective and God wants to use you to share the gospel. Your experiences in life, the success and setbacks, will equip you to teach the gospel. Your divorce will further God's kingdom because there are hurting people that will listen to you and the message. You know what it is like to hit rock bottom and have the Lord restore you. You know what it is like to struggle financially and emotionally. Yes, your perspective on life is unique, so let God use it to further His kingdom. Your suffering and pain will be worth it when you are able to use it for the glory of God. God changed your life and now He can change other lives through you. Do not be upset—you are uniquely equipped and divinely enabled to carry the gospel to a hurting, dying world.

Suggested Prayer
Lord,
I have suffered tremendously! It is truly more than I can bear! Lord, use my pain to further Your cause on earth. Help me bring the good news to a lost world. Do not let my suffering be in vain! In Jesus' Name, Amen.

JUNE 5

The Good Life

Philippians 1:21
For to me to live is Christ, and to die is gain.

When we think of living the good life we often think of money or success or fame. All of us want to prosper in some way or form. Paul summed up his life in one word—Christ. To the apostle this was the good life. Paul had a living, loving relationship that took him all over the Roman Empire. This relationship caused him to establish churches and write most of the epistles of the New Testament. It even brought him before kings and paupers. Oh, yes! This was the good life to Paul.

What one word would summarize your concept of the good life? Some would say money or fame, others might say sex. There is nothing wrong with money or fame or sex in their right contexts. All these things could be considered good. However, for the serious Christian the good life can only be summed up in one word—Christ. Paul said death itself would be a gain because he would spend eternity with his treasure—Jesus Christ. As you are struggling through the pain of your divorce you are beginning to see what is truly important in life. Jesus is still the answer to life's problems. The good life is found in Christ.

Suggested Prayer
Dear Lord,
I want to be like Paul. I want to be able to say my life is Christ. If You should take me home, I realize this is gain. Lord, I am asking that You change my heart so I can truly and honestly say my life is Christ. In Jesus' Name I pray, Amen.

You Can't Hold It All In

Job 32:18-20

For I am full of words; the spirit within me constrains me. Behold, my belly is like wine that has no vent; like new wineskins ready to burst. I must speak, that I may find relief; I must open my lips and answer.

Job's three friends had no answers for him. Elihu was the fourth man present, but he was quite a bit younger that Job's three friends. Elihu listened to these three men interact with Job and thought that their wisdom and experience would help Job. He wanted to say something, but he held back. Now he was about to burst. He had to speak.

In many industries various pieces of equipment have PSVs (pressure safety valves), sometimes called PRVs (pressure relief valves). These valves are safety devices, needed to keep something like a tank from exploding. If the tank pressures up, the valve will open to keep the vessel from exploding.

With all that you have been through you have built up an amazing amount of emotional pressure. You need to vent, or it will destroy you. Please do not vent to your children. They do not need to hear anything negative about their mother or father. Find a good counselor or a godly friend that you can talk to. Ask God to help you find someone to talk to. The key is to not let the pressure build up to the point of an emergency. If this happens you will say and do some things that will cause irreversible damage. Find a safe, healthy outlet for the pressure that is built up inside.

Suggested Prayer

Dear God,

Forgive me. I have yelled at my kids and told them some things that they should never have heard. I also yelled at my ex-spouse. Forgive me, Lord, please. Let me talk to you about all my troubles. You are my counselor. I also ask that You give me someone to talk to so this bad situation does not happen again. In Jesus' Name, Amen.

And His Righteousness

Matthew 6:33
But seek first the kingdom of God and his righteousness, and all these things will be added to you.

This verse has been a favorite for many Christians. The promise is that if we put God first, He will take care of our needs. As we seek His kingdom or His welfare, He takes care of us or our welfare. One phrase that is often overlooked is "and his righteousness." Jesus was emphasizing that we should seek to be holy people. It is not enough to just seek the kingdom. We must also seek to be like the King. We must strive to be holy. It seems like a holy life does not matter to this world. We often think, "What is the use in striving for something that we will never achieve?" It matters to God! Be holy for Christ's sake.

There are two sides to every coin. One side of the coin is to seek the King's will; the other side is to seek the King's way. The apostle Paul confirms this fact in Romans 12:1 when he says to give our bodies as a sacrifice, and he says we must be holy. Paul also told Timothy to take heed to himself and the doctrine. We must strive to do both if we expect God to bless us.

Suggested Prayer
Dear Lord,
I have done a good job at seeking Your Kingdom. Lord, I have done a poor job in seeking Your righteousness. Forgive me for my shortcomings. I will not be sinless, but I hope to sin less. God, help me to seek You and Your righteousness. In Jesus' Name, Amen.

How Can I Get Out of This?

John 2:2
Jesus also was invited to the wedding with his disciples.

Weddings, birthdays, sporting events, graduations—it never seems to end. It seems like you can never get away from your ex. The last person you want to see is him or her. Yet life goes on. Your children did not deserve this divorce, so please be sensitive to their needs as you consider all the big events in their lives. Believe it or not, as your healing takes place you will be able to be in the same room with your ex. Right now, they might be the last person you want to see.

The day arrives for your son's soccer game. He wants his mom and dad to see him play. You want to go to the game, but you somehow want to avoid the whole awkward situation. What can help you in this difficult situation?

The answer is not *what* can help but *Who* can help. Jesus was invited to a wedding and a miracle took place. Invite Jesus to whatever event it is that is taking place. You ask Him to take control of the situation, and guess what! A miracle takes place. He might not turn water into wine, but He will give you the grace to get through the situation. He might even allow some healing to take place in your heart and in your ex-spouse's heart. Do not try to get out of the invitation and avoid the situation. Instead, invite Jesus to go with you and watch Him turn it around for your good and His glory.

Suggested Prayer
Dear Lord,
I don't want to be around my ex, but I know my kids deserve a decent life. We ruined their childhood and I feel so bad for them. Now I invite You to take full control of the situation and ask that You would be glorified through all of this. Give me grace and let the event be a positive situation for everyone. In the Name of Jesus I pray, Amen.

160 | PRESSING ON

Can We Believe the First Verse?

Genesis 1:1
In the beginning, God created the heavens and the earth.

Genesis 1:1 explains so much about the origins of all things. God created everything! He spoke all things into existence. The word for God in this verse is *Elohiym*, which speaks of a plurality. The Father, the Son, and the Holy Spirit were all active in creation. If God is our creator, then He is also in control of all things. He is surprised by absolutely nothing. He is never caught off guard. He is working out His purpose through the ages of time.

If we can believe Genesis 1:1 we should not have any problem believing the rest of the Bible. We should be able to embrace Jesus Christ, realizing that He is our Savior. We should also be able to trust God for our daily lives, knowing that He is in control. In time past there was the old creation, as described in this verse. Right now, God is making new creations called Christians (2 Corinthians 5:17). Soon He will make a new heaven and a new earth (Revelation 21:1).

Can you believe Genesis 1:1? If you can, then you can start to believe that there is a purpose for your sufferings. He is in control and actively making you more like Him. If He has the whole universe in His hand, He surely has your best interests in mind. Allow Him to create something good in you.

Suggested Prayer
Lord,
I am quick to believe that You are the Creator and my Savior. Lord, I am also quick to doubt when I look at my circumstances. Help me realize that You are in control and that You are doing a great work in me. In Jesus' Name, Amen.

The World Needs God

Matthew 10:16

Behold, I am sending you out as sheep in the midst of wolves, so be wise as serpents and innocent as doves.

When Jesus sent the twelve disciples out to preach the gospel, He told them to be wise as serpents and harmless as doves. What great advice for witnessing to a world that hates God, yet needs God. When we are dealing with this world it is good to remember that we are the lights of this world. Our job is to be salt and light to this dark, evil world.

But you have been through a divorce and life is not so easy for you. The tendency is to talk about our problems to anyone who will listen. Quite frankly, the world does not care about our problems. Find a faithful Christian or go to a good counselor if you need to talk to someone. When we are giving our testimony to the lost, we always want to put God in a positive light and not come across as a complainer. We are the counselors for this world. We are God's mouthpiece for our generation.

This verse is also good advice when dealing with our children. Do not bash your ex-spouse in front of your children. Be harmless as a dove. Do you realize that you are talking bad about your child's mother or father? This is simply wrong and never justifiable. With each relationship we must use wisdom and we must be harmless. There is a right way to talk about our problems that will honor God. There is a right way to talk about the divorce and the ex-spouse. We do not want to be the reason why our family or friends did not make it to heaven. Let God use you to bring them into the kingdom.

Suggested Prayer ——————————————————————

Dear Lord,

Please give me wisdom to be a good witness. Teach me how to talk about my problems without bringing reproach to Your Name. Give me a gentle and understanding spirit. Give me a heart of compassion. Help me not be offensive, and use me to bring people into Your kingdom. It is in the Name of Jesus that I pray, Amen and Amen.

Is It Ever Going to Get Better?

2 Thessalonians 3:3
But the Lord is faithful. He will establish you and guard you against the evil one.

We are familiar with the saying, "when it rains it pours." Sometimes the trials and difficulties are too hard to bear. The divorce was bad enough, next the car won't start. A month later the refrigerator goes out. Next it is the hot water heater. As we look around at all the repairs that we need to do, with no available funds, we begin to wonder if God is with us or not.

Rest assured that He is with us. The text says that He is faithful. Beloved, He is faithful and will provide a way for you. It may seem like He has forgotten you, but He has not. He will be with you each step of the way. The text also says that He will establish you. He will set you on a solid rock foundation because He is the Rock. It may seem like chaos now, but He will establish you firmly so that you may be able to live and thrive again. This time it will be in His power and not your ability.

He will also guard you from the evil one. The devil may influence you and harass you, but he cannot do anything to you unless God allows it. God is faithful! He is establishing you! He is guarding you! Brethren, take heart; it will get better as you are being established more and more in Him.

Suggested Prayer
Dear Lord,
I am tired and weary. I have not always been faithful, but you are always faithful. Help me see that You are faithful and that You are establishing me and guarding me. Lord, give me the faith to trust You. In Jesus' Name I pray, Amen.

What Does God Get?

Deuteronomy 32:9

But the LORD'S portion is his people, Jacob his allotted heritage.

We all want our fair share of the pie. We want the portion allotted to us whether it be wages, discounts, or health benefits. It is a strange thing that God's portion is His people. The verse before us clearly teaches us that His allotment is Jacob, meaning the nation of Israel. The United States is nice place to live in and it has a rich Christian heritage. The country was founded on Christian principles, but Israel is God's portion, not the United States.

There is one primary interpretation of scriptures but many applications. This verse can be applied to Christians. Every child of God is the Lord's portion. Of all the things God could desire He chose us. This fact lets us know that He loves us and will never leave us. He will nurture and take care of us. He has our best interests in mind. He is all in for us. What a great privilege to be His portion. With great privileges comes great responsibilities. We must determine that we will be the best for Him. He has so much invested in us! It is time to be our very best for Him—we are His portion.

Suggested Prayer ————————————————————————

Dear Lord,

Thank You that I am Your portion. Help me realize that You are for me. Now Lord, I give myself to You and I want to be my very best for You. I want You to be proud that I am Your portion. Amen.

Think God Thoughts

Philippians 4:8
Finally, brothers, whatever is true, whatever is honorable, whatever is just, whatever is pure, whatever is lovely, whatever is commendable, if there is any excellence, if there is anything worthy of praise, think about these things.

Your divorce has caused many strange thoughts to enter your mind. What did I do wrong? Will they give me another chance to prove myself? Will God give me another spouse? Does God hate me? Why do I hate him/her? Doesn't God care that I am raising these kids by myself? I would like to harm my ex-spouse's new partner. Why am I lusting? Why am I so jealous? Why do I want to die? The list could go on and on.

Paul wants our thoughts to line up with this verse. Is it true to God's character? Is it honorable? It is right? Is it pleasant? Is it commendable? Is it praiseworthy? If the answer is yes, then think or meditate on these things. If the answer is no, then do not meditate on these thoughts because they will lead to sin and depression. These are the thoughts that come from the evil one. They are earthly, sensual, and devilish. They are not worthy of our time. Ultimately these negative thoughts will be our downfall.

We must give our minds to God. Then we must yield our mind to the Holy Spirit and let Him control our thoughts. At salvation we obtained the mind of Christ, but we must yield to Him or our minds will be the devil's playground.

Suggested Prayer
Dear Lord,
Forgive me. I have had some horrible thoughts lately. I give my mind to You. Holy Spirit, I give my mind to You. Jesus, let me think as You would have me to think. In Jesus' Name, Amen.

Waiting for Direction

Psalms 25:5

Lead me in your truth and teach me, for you are the God of my salvation; for you I wait all the day long.

It is very difficult to wait on the Lord! We live our lives in an instant society, and we do not know what it truly means to wait. Now we are single and we want a new spouse, and nothing is happening. Our friends get on our nerves by telling us to wait on God. No one seems to understand our loneliness and our needs. We pray, and nothing happens. Yet we must wait!

We need to let God lead us into His truth. Perhaps there are some things we need to learn or unlearn before we can be a good partner. Let us allow God to be our teacher. With so many people giving us advice who apparently know God's plan for us, we need to be taught from the Lord. What do your married friends know about the loneliness of divorce? Yet they are going to explain God's will to you. Oh, how we need to be taught from God! Your best friend is not named Holy Spirit, even though they think they know what is best for you.

God is our Savior. Our new life in Christ began with Him. He is the author and finisher of our faith. We need to let Him lead us and teach us. So, let us learn to wait for Him to give us direction. Jesus said He was the truth. He was also called a teacher. In fact, He is our Truth and Teacher. Let us wait for Him to give us direction.

Now, about that well-meaning best friend—patiently endure. He/she is not a prophet and does not know God's will for you. They do love you and are only trying to help. Jesus is the Great Prophet who will direct you. Patiently wait to hear from Him.

Suggested Prayer ———————————————————————

Lord,

I am tired of waiting. I am also tired of hearing nonsense from my friends. Lord, my problem is that I am trying to figure this all out myself. I am relying on my wisdom and not your wisdom. So today I want You to direct me and teach me. Mold me into the person You want me to be. In Jesus' Name, Amen.

Ok, I Got It Already!

Psalms 27:14
Wait for the LORD; be strong, and let your heart take courage; wait for the LORD!

The Lord mentions the word "wait" twice in this verse. Whenever God uses the same word twice we should take note, because what He is saying is very important. Jesus Himself would say, "truly, truly I say to you," stressing the importance of the subject (John 3:3). God often spoke a person's name twice to get their attention (Acts 9:4). God is stressing to us the importance of waiting in this verse.

It seems like waiting is the hardest thing to do. When we wait on God it strengthens our inner person. Waiting produces divine strength. Waiting also increases our faith because we become dependent on Him. As we wait on God, we become one with Him in fellowship. Our hearts knit with His heart and we become one. If we decide that we are tired of waiting, the outcome will not be good. Abraham and Sarah grew tired of waiting, and Ishmael was born. We settle for something worse than second best when we do things on our time and not His time.

God wants to bless us in His time and in His way. He wants the glory. The world needs to see God at work in your situation. You have already suffered a great loss; now God is stressing to you the importance of waiting on Him. He is working out a marvelous plan to give you His very best. Do not grow impatient and settle for less than the best—unite with Him and wait. Waiting implies that you believe God is in control and is working on your behalf.

Suggested Prayer
Now, Lord, in my mind I have waited long enough. I can't seem to wait another day. However, Lord, I want Your best, so I am deciding to unite my heart with Your heart and to wait on You. Help me to trust You enough to wait on You to work it all out. In Jesus' Name I pray, Amen.

They Seem to Be Doing Good

Psalms 37:7
Be still before the LORD and wait patiently for him; fret not yourself over the one who prospers in his way, over the man who carries out evil devices!

It must be our fallen natures to get all worked up when we see the wicked prospering. By now you have seen the guy who divorced his wife and married another lady. His business is prospering too. It seems like everything is going great in his life. Then you look in the mirror. You see yourself all alone, and yet you are faithful to the Lord. You are struggling week to week, living paycheck to paycheck. Your Friday night is a walk in the park alone. You don't have the funds for a dinner and a movie. You have also seen people divorce and get remarried very soon. Yet here you are all alone. No wonder we fret as we see those who do not know God prospering.

We need to get still before the Lord. We need to stop striving and realize that He is our God. Then we need not only to wait for Him, but to patiently wait. Patiently waiting implies that you are trusting God. The wicked have a judgment day. There is a day of reckoning. Remember that your situation is only temporary. There is coming a day when you will be able to do things again. There could also be a day when there is a companion in your life again. God is sovereign and is working out His purpose in your life. He is also working out His purpose in the wicked too. In your lonely time realize God is at work, so be still and wait patiently.

By the way, as you are walking in the park there might be someone that you need to witness to or encourage. Maybe, just maybe your future spouse is also walking there. Do not limit God!

Suggested Prayer ————————————————————————
Lord,
It is hard to be still when I see the wicked prospering and I am suffering. It is hard to wait patiently. By faith I give myself to You and Your Sovereignty. Work out Your purpose in me. In the Name of Jesus I pray, Amen.

I Don't Know How Much Longer I Can Hold On

Psalms 69:3

I am weary with my crying out; my throat is parched. My eyes grow dim with waiting for my God.

King David was up to his neck in troubles. He felt like the waters were about to go over his head. He felt like his feet were in the miry clay with no sure footing. However, he knew that his help came from God. So as a man of prayer, David prayed. He prayed till his eyes grew dim because of weariness. He had cried so much that he was tired of crying. His throat was even sore from his continual crying out to God. He was wearing out, but he knew God would show up on the scene and deliver him. God had helped him in the past and he knew that he would soon receive help. Yet, it was a painful process, this waiting on God to help him.

Perhaps today you are neck deep in problems with no sure footing. Maybe you have cried and cried to the point that your throat is dry, and your eyes are dim. Do not give up. God sees your pain and your tears. He will help you. Be like David and pray and cry out to Him. Like David, tell Him how you feel. God will answer and restore your soul. We serve a God who can change our circumstances very quickly. He will help you and deliver you. Be encouraged because He will never leave you or forsake you. He can dry every tear and heal every hurt.

Suggested Prayer ———————————————————————

Lord,
Help! I am up to my neck in sorrow. Unless You help me, I will faint along the way. Please help me and deliver me. Give me the strength and faith to wait on You. In Jesus' Name, Amen.

Will God Heal My Broken Heart?

Psalms 147:3
He heals the brokenhearted and binds up their wounds.

What a tremendous word from God: "He heals the brokenhearted and binds up their wounds." Separation and divorce leave people with a broken heart and gaping wounds. It is like divorce fatally wounds her victims and leaves them for dead. There are several wounds involved: adultery, lies, deception, betrayal, etc. Each person's wounds are unique to that particular individual.

Because of the uniqueness of our wounds our case requires the Great Physician to bind our wounds and heal our hearts. The psalmist said *He* heals. God must do the healing because we cannot heal ourselves. Healing is a process. Many people try to speed up their healing, only to be divorced again. We must let the Lord heal us on His timetable. If we wait on the Lord, He will bring healing and restore us to our former state.

You will be better than before. You will also be able to minister as a good soldier of Jesus Christ. Oh, how I wish it was a fast process, but it is not. Can you trust God to heal your broken heart? Can you surrender all your wounds and hurts to Him? You have a choice—you can try to heal yourself, or you can trust God to heal you. I think you get the picture.

Suggested Prayer
Dear Lord,
You are the Great Physician. I have a broken heart and unbound wounds. I give myself to You. Here is my heart and here are my wounds! These are my hurts! Lord, I cry out to You! There is a Balm in Gilead. Please heal me and restore me so I can live and love again. Amen.

JUNE 19

Holy Ground

Acts 7:33-34
Then the Lord said to him, 'Take off the sandals from your feet, for the place where you are standing is holy ground. I have surely seen the affliction of my people who are in Egypt, and have heard their groaning, and I have come down to deliver them. And now come, I will send you to Egypt.'

When Moses saw the burning bush, God told him to take off his sandals because he was on holy ground. It was truly a sacred moment when God shared what was on His heart with Moses. God had seen the affliction of His people while they were slaves in Egypt. He had heard their cries, and now it was time to do something about it. He called Moses to go deliver the people out of Egypt.

You too are on holy ground, so take off those Adidas or Nike shoes. God has seen the affliction of the divorced people all around you. He has heard their cries. Now God is sending you out into this world to help those who are suffering. Before this holy ground experience Moses received forty years of academic training in Egypt in the finest of schools. Then Moses received forty years of spiritual training in the desert. Now, after eighty years of training, he is ready for the task at hand. You have received healing from God from your divorce and now it is time for God to send you out. Tell the Lord that you will do it. Ask Him to break your heart for those who are hurting.

Suggested Prayer
*Dear Lord,
I now see that my divorce can be used for good. I feel that You are calling me to help the hurting. Lord, You saw my affliction and pain, so send me to those going through similar pains. I surrender all. Thank You for calling me.*

Responsibility Results in Rewards

2 John 4

I rejoiced greatly to find some of your children walking in the truth, just as we were commanded by the Father.

Every minister has the responsibility to have his congregation walk in the truth. As parents we also have this same command to make sure our children walk in the truth. We are commanded by God to bring our children up in the nurture and admonition of the Lord. We might be tired and exhausted at the end of the day, but we should do what we can to instruct our children in the ways of God. We will see the results, that our children are walking in the truth.

What does it mean to walk in the truth? It simply means to obey and follow the body of truth that God has given us. Jesus Himself said He is the truth (John 14:6). Our starting point is Jesus Christ. We must make sure our children know Jesus as their Lord and Savior. Once they are Christians they can be instructed in further truths as explained in the scriptures. Our goal and responsibility is that our children become followers of Jesus Christ.

So what about the rewards? There is great rejoicing on our part, knowing our children are following Jesus. Many parents worry all their lives over their children. They have no rest in their spirits because of the worry they have for their kids. Their own children became a source of heartache and pain. Why? They did not heed the command to show them the truth. Other parents do not worry about their adult children. They are a source of joy because they are responsible adults. Why? Because the parents took the time to teach them the truth.

There are exceptions. There are those children who were taught the truth, but rejected God. And there are those children, with sorry excuses for parents, who are now preachers and missionaries. These are the exceptions and not the rule. Keep in mind that God can do anything.

Suggested Prayer

Lord,

I have a responsibility to teach my children the truth. Please give me wisdom and knowledge to do this. Give me courage and divine strength to carry out this command. Lord, I want my children to follow You. I want to rejoice over my kids instead of living a life of regret. Lord, I dedicate all of this to You and ask for Your help and strength. In Jesus' Name, Amen.

Renewal from The Lord

Judges 16:22
But the hair of his head began to grow again after it had been shaved.

Sampson's great strength was a gift from God. He also had a Nazarite vow, which meant he abstained from grapes, raisins, wine, and any other products made from grapes. He was not to cut his hair when under this vow. Delilah, after several attempts, finally got Sampson to reveal the truth to her about the secret of his great strength. When she had cut Sampson's hair, his strength departed because he had violated the vow he made to the Lord. Yet, our text for today says his hair began to grow again.

This is a very significant statement. The vow was renewed before God and his great supernatural strength was restored to him once again. Sampson would accomplish one more feat in his life before he died. So what is the point? Sampson played around with the call of God, the holiness of God, and did not take the things of God seriously. However, when he repented and recommitted himself, God began to restore and renew him to his former state.

The outward growth of hair was a token of an inward transformation that was taking place in his heart. Today God wants to renew you from the inside. If you have not taken God seriously, repent and let Him renew your spirit. Perhaps God has one more great feat or even several things He wants you to do. Get this renewal from the Lord and go in the spirit of Sampson to do the will of the Lord.

Suggested Prayer ────────────────────────────────
Dear Lord,
I ask that You forgive me. I have played around with the holiness of God and the things of God. Please forgive me and restore me. Renew my spirit, and please use me again. In Jesus' Name, Amen.

JUNE 22

Most Things Work Together for Good

Romans 8:28
And we know that for those who love God all things work together for good, for those who are called according to his purpose.

T his is one of my favorite scriptures. I can still remember the first time I heard this verse—I was blown away with the power of it. So much has been written and said about this verse that it makes it difficult to comment on. If I could say one thing about it I would say *believe it.* We quote the verse, but we do not believe it. Why?

First, it is for those who love God and are committed to Him. This verse is for the Christian who is trusting God, loving Christ, and believing in the God of the Bible.

Next, we must talk about those circumstances. The circumstance can be good or bad. We get discouraged because we tend to walk by sight and not by faith. Peter was able to walk on water until he looked at his circumstances. John the Baptist was full of faith until he looked at the circumstances. The circumstances are supposed to look contrary to our reasoning because we walk by faith, not sight.

Then, there is a calling. This calling is according to His purpose and not ours. We get upset with God because we are living for our purpose, not for His purpose. So if *most* things are working for good and not *all* things, re-examine your commitment. Don't fall prey to circumstances, and consider your calling. *Most* things, or *all* things?

Suggested Prayer ————————————————————————
Dear Lord,
Forgive me! I know this verse, but I have not believed it. Help me to be committed to You. Help me to quit looking at circumstances and start looking at You. Lord, help me see that I am called for Your purpose and not my own. Lord, help me believe that all things work together for good. In Jesus' Name I pray, Amen.

Strange Happenings

---

1 Peter 4:12
Beloved, do not be surprised at the fiery trial when it comes upon you to test you, as though some something strange were happening to you.

Some surprises are welcomed, like a surprise birthday party or a pay raise. But some surprises are not welcome—like your divorce. Trials often catch us off guard and we begin to question our relationship with God. Peter tells us that we sometimes go through trials. The Holy Spirit calls these fiery trials. Indeed, they are! These trials do not happen every day but they do happen from time to time. The verse says *when*, letting the reader know that they *will* happen. Please do not think some strange thing is happening to you.

Fire is a purifying agent, and that is what God does in our lives with these difficulties. He purifies us that we might become vessels of honor in His sight. Why not think it strange? Well, Jesus said we would go through much tribulation before entering the kingdom. He also said that we are not above Him. In His humanity He suffered, and so we must also suffer to enter the fellowship of His sufferings. What we need to understand is that God is in control.

When we go through trials we feel like Cain; that we are cast out of God's presence and from God's people. We feel like we are under a curse. But in reality God is for us, with us, and controlling us. He wants Christians that can go through the fire. These are the people He can count on to do His will. The trial may seem strange to you, but it is not strange to God. Start trusting instead of resisting His plan for you.

Suggested Prayer ——————————————————————
*Dear Lord,
This divorce caught me by surprise. Help me see that You are in control and that You are doing something good through this trial. By faith I receive this trial, knowing that it will purify me, make me more like You, and better equip me to serve You. In Jesus' Name I pray, Amen.*

In for the Long Haul

Exodus 5:22-23

Then Moses turned to the LORD and said, "O Lord, why have you done evil to this people? Why did you ever send me? For since I came to Pharaoh to speak in your name, he has done evil to this people, and you have not delivered your people at all."

Moses thought his encounter with Pharaoh would be a cakewalk. God had called him to bring the people of Israel out of Egypt. Moses was endued with power and his brother Aaron was his spokesperson. All seemed well until they encountered Pharaoh. Pharaoh did not let Israel go and would not let them leave. In fact, Pharaoh made their work harder and the oppression grew stronger.

Moses was astonished, thinking God had failed him. He did not quite fully understand the plan of God and all that our Lord wanted to accomplish in Egypt. Moses thought the deliverance would be quick and simple. Little did he realize what was in store; a great epic battle between God and Satan was about to take place. In the Bible, Pharaoh is a type of Satan and Egypt is a type of the world. Satan does not ever go down without a fight. His mission is to destroy the work of God.

I remember thinking my trial would end very soon. I figured God would send me a bride very quickly; after all, the divorce was not my fault and I was innocent. I felt entitled to a new wife. But at the time I am writing this I am still single, and over eight lonely years have passed. I must admit I am like Moses, because I thought there would be a quick deliverance. However, God is still working out His purpose in my life.

At the right time you and I will receive deliverance. Perhaps you are like me and Moses—you are in it for the long haul until God fulfills His purpose. We know the end of the story. God delivered the children of Israel. We know our end, too—victory in Jesus! Amen and amen!

Suggested Prayer ───────────────────────────────

Lord,
We do not understand Your will sometimes. What we think would be a simple task turns out to be something very difficult. Lord, Your ways are not our ways, so let us have wisdom to know Your will. Lord, work out Your plan and purpose in this trial. In Jesus Name, Amen.

My Table Has Been Turned Upside Down

John 2:14-15

In the temple he found those who were selling oxen and sheep and pigeons, and the money-changers sitting there. And making a whip of cords, he drove them all out of the temple, with the sheep and oxen. And he poured out the coins of the money-changers and overturned their tables.

When Jesus came to the temple the place looked more like a swap-meet than a place of worship. In divine power He cleaned house. He made a thorough cleansing of the Father's house. The whole Jewish sacrificial system had become a big business. Religion was a for-profit organization. The path to degradation was slow, subtle, and steady.

In our lives, sometimes, Jesus overthrows our tables. Slowly and steadily we get far away from God. We hear a sermon and it convicts our hearts, but we do not change. A Bible verse speaks to us and we do not allow it to change us. God is steadily trying to grab our undivided attention. Our Christian brothers and sisters warn us that we are slipping. All of God's mercy, love, and grace are not changing our hearts, so Jesus cracks the whip in our lives. He overthrows our tables and cleans house.

Our bodies are the temple of the Holy Spirit. Sound familiar? The overturned tables are an act of love to get us where we need to be. God's chastening can be difficult. However, when He finishes His perfect will in our lives, we will be where we need to be. Once God cleanses us we need to remain true to Him. Jesus overturned the tables at the beginning of His ministry, only to have to do it again some three years later at the end of His earthly ministry (Matthew 21:12). Let us decide today that we will serve God. Let us decide to let Him cleanse us. Let us decide that we will allow Him to be Lord of our lives. Let us confess our sins and serve Him. His chastening hand is a loving hand.

Suggested Prayer ———————————————————————————

Lord,

I have slipped. You have had to disrupt every area of my life. You overthrew my tables and disrupted everything I was trying to accomplish. Today I see this as Your love, and I confess my sins. Help me live for You. May I be faithful, so this does not have to happen to me again. In the Name of Jesus I pray, Amen.

Can You Go Out to Dinner with Your Ex?

Revelation 3:20

Behold, I stand at the door and knock. If anyone hears my voice and opens the door, I will come in to him and eat with him, and he with me.

This scripture has been interpreted many ways, some good and some not so good. The actual meaning is that Jesus is knocking at the door of the Church, hoping that someone will respond to Him and fellowship with Him. He is not knocking on a physical door but a spiritual door. He is knocking on our hearts in a spiritual sense.

To share a meal together meant that you and those involved were in harmony together. You could not sit down with your enemy and enjoy a meal together. Jesus is wanting us to adjust our lives so we can fellowship with Him. He does not need to make the adjustments because He is sinless. It is you and I who need to make the adjustments. We meet God on His terms, not on our terms. We must confess our sins and actively seek Him to enjoy His fellowship.

One thing that hinders our relationship with Christ is bitterness towards our ex-spouse. Could you sit down and enjoy a meal with him or her? If the answer is no, there must be resentment on one or both sides. It takes time to heal and to confess our hatred and bitterness. One great sign that you are healing is when you can completely forgive them. You will then be able to communicate with them in a natural way without all the awkwardness and anxiety. You will be able to discuss the future of your children and concerns about them. You will even be able to discuss things over a meal together. Does this seem farfetched to you? It can be a reality to those who can let go of the hatred and bitterness. It took about six years for this to take place in my heart. May God grant you restoration and healing in a timelier fashion!

Suggested Prayer ——————————————————————————
Dear Lord,
I want to be set free from the past so I can enjoy the present and the future that You have for me. Lord, I confess all the hatred and bitterness and right now I am asking for a complete cleansing. Lord, I am asking for a working relationship with my ex,_____. Lord, let this relationship benefit our personal walks with You and let it help our children. In Jesus' Name, Amen.

What Is Too Difficult for God?

Genesis 18:14
Is anything too hard for the LORD? At the appointed time I will return to you, about this time next year, and Sarah shall have a son.

Abraham and Sarah were promised a son by God. No big deal, right? Well, it is a big deal when the prospective parents are way too old to have children. God performed a miracle and Abraham was a proud father at the age of 100. The new mother, Sarah, was 90 years old when she had Isaac—the child of promise. Can you imagine the newspaper headlines? **90-YEAR-OLD WOMAN GIVES BIRTH! 100-YEAR-OLD MAN IS A PROUD FATHER!** This all seems crazy, but it is a reality. What is impossible with men and women is possible with God. There is nothing too difficult for God!

Our Lord and Savior Jesus Christ would come through this lineage of Abraham. The world would be saved through the child God promised to Abraham and Sarah. The whole concept is too deep to comprehend fully. The God of the universe did something that was impossible. Was the task of giving Abraham a son a difficult thing for God? Absolutely not! What was the role of Abraham and Sarah in all of this? They were called to believe in the God who promised them this child. "Now that's a great story," you say, "and it makes for some interesting reading. It is neat to see how God worked in the past." No, friends, it is much more than that.

Your situation is not too hard for God. He desires to carry out some great purpose in your life. It is easy for Him to give you a new spouse. It is easy for Him to restore your finances. It is easy for Him to give you the things that you lost in your divorce. What is your requirement for God to work on your behalf? The requirement is the same for us as it was for Abraham and Sarah. Believe God! It is time for us to not just read about the God of the Bible, but it is time for us to believe in the God of the Bible.

Suggested Prayer
Dear Lord,
Nothing is too hard for You. Lord, I am in a difficult place in life. It is not too difficult for You. Lord, I choose to place my complete faith in You. Just like Abraham, I am expecting a miracle to take place. Lord, I believe, help my unbelief.

God Answers Your "If" With His Own "If"

Mark 9:22-24

"...And it has often cast him into fire and into water, to destroy him. But if you can do anything, have compassion on us and help us." And Jesus said to him, "'If you can'! All things are possible for one who believes." Immediately the father of the child cried out and said, "I believe; help my unbelief!"

The scene is desperate. Sound familiar? A man's son is desperately tormented by apparent demonic activity. The man calls on the big twelve for help and receives none. Sometimes people cannot help us, but there is a Person who can help. We need a touch from the Master. So here is the first *if* in the narrative. The man tells Jesus, "*if* you can do anything, have compassion on us." Now the second *if* comes into play. Jesus tells the man *if* he can believe, all things are possible for those who believe.

The man's *if* stems from a lack of truly knowing who God really is and what He can do. God is the all-knowing, all powerful God who is in control of everything. It seems crazy to ask God *if* He can do anything. He can do everything.

Hence the second *if*. If we could just believe in His Person, all things are possible. The man's response is awesome. He said, "I believe; help my unbelief!" What happened? Jesus healed the boy. God did something that was impossible for men to accomplish. Dear friend, is your plight desperate? Have people let you down? Perhaps your circumstances have caused you to see God as something less than the Almighty. *If* you can just believe, all things are possible.

Suggested Prayer

Lord,

I have allowed circumstances to make me see You in a lesser light. I have grown desperate and tried to get help from others. It all failed, Lord. At this moment I believe that You can help me, so I am asking You to help me. My situation is easy for You to fix. Please come to my rescue. I believe...help my unbelief.

What If?

John 11:21, 32, 40

*Martha said to Jesus, "Lord, if you had been here, my brother would not have died...
Now when Mary came to where Jesus was and saw him, she fell at his feet, saying to
him, "Lord, if you had been here, my brother would not have died...Jesus said to her,
"Did I not tell you that if you believed you would see the glory of God?"*

It is interesting that both of Lazarus' sisters hit Jesus with the big "IF." "If You
would have been here, our brother would not have died." Jesus responded to
Mary and Martha with His own *if*. Jesus' *if* was centered around faith: *if* these sisters could only believe, they would see the glory of God.

Both ladies were devoted Christians. Martha was a great servant and Mary
was a great worshiper. Yet both women misunderstood what God was doing. Jesus
gave the challenge to believe. And what happened? Jesus raised Lazarus from the
grave, showing that shortly He, Himself, would rise from the grave. Ultimately, we
too will rise from the grave.

There was a much bigger work going on here that the sisters could not see. The
big picture is the glory of God. We, like the sisters, are full of "ifs." *If* I had spent
more time with my wife/husband. *If* I had never divorced. *If* I didn't have to pay
child support. *If* my kids lived with me. The list could be endless. Like Martha and
Mary, we miss the big picture and do not know what God is doing.

Jesus is telling us today that *if* we can trust Him, we too will see the glory of
God. Do you want to see God glorified in your tragedy? The solution is simple;
start trusting and stop wondering *if*. The ultimate purpose is the glory of God. The
purpose has not changed. Today, decide that you will believe that your divorce will
bring glory to God. Please, please allow this to happen! The devil has had enough
victories. It is time to see the glory of God manifested in Jesus Christ.

Suggested Prayer

Lord,
I admit I do not understand my divorce. A thousand "ifs" have crossed my mind. Now,
Lord, I want to see Your glory, so I choose to trust You and trust that my trials will
ultimately bring You glory. To God be the glory! Amen.

Burn Out

Leviticus 6:13
Fire shall be kept burning on the altar continually; it shall not go out.

As we walk through life, we grow tired and weary. We sit down in our chair long enough to pause from our busy schedule and we realize that we are burned out. We have no energy physically, mentally, emotionally, or spiritually. We are exhausted. In the Old Testament economy, the fire was to never go out. The priests would add wood to keep a perpetual fire. We do not have a physical fire in our bodies, but we do have the Holy Spirit. He will keep a fire burning in our hearts.

Not only does the Holy Spirit reside in our hearts, the Father and Jesus are there too. Scriptures tell us that we have the Blessed Trinity residing in our very being. Even with God in us we still grow tired and feel stagnant in our walk. The pain and misery of divorce brings much against the fire of God in our hearts. At times it feels like we cannot make it through another day.

What can we do? God Himself started the fire in our hearts when we were first saved. We cannot extinguish the fire, but we can smother it with sin and worry. So how do we fan the flame? We must force ourselves to put some fresh wood on the altar. The priests put wood on the altar daily. This chore was probably monotonous at times, but it was essential to keep the fire burning.

So how do we add wood to our hearts? We add this wood by daily reading the scriptures and by prayer. It may seem monotonous, but these acts of worship are essential. Force yourself to do it and ask God to renew the fire in you.

Suggested Prayer ————————————————
Dear Lord,
I am tired and burned out. I know I need to keep the fire burning in my heart. Help me to read and pray, and please use these things to revive my spirit. Let me burn for You that others may receive the light of the knowledge of Jesus Christ. I pray this in the Name of Jesus, Amen.

In God We Trust

Proverbs 3:5-6
Trust in the LORD with all your heart, and do not lean on your own understanding. In all your ways acknowledge him, and he will make straight your paths.

I n the United States the phrase "In God We Trust" is on our money, but it needs to be in our hearts. Solomon tells us to trust in the Lord with all our being. When we trust God with all our hearts we are surrendering to His sovereignty. We are saying, in essence, "God, You are in control of my life and circumstances." We are not to lean on our own understanding. God gives us a mind, and we are to reason with our minds. As humans we try to do things that make the most sense to us. However, we must trust when circumstances do not make sense. As we acknowledge God in everything, we know that He will lead, guide, and direct us.

Your whole world was rocked when the divorce happened. Now you must trust God more than ever before. Trust that He is in control and working on your behalf. Begin to put God first in all your decisions. Soon the path will be less cluttered. Soon the path will make sense. Soon you will discover the path that leads you closer to Him.

A preacher once said we should look at trials as an opportunity to die. In other words, our difficulties are an opportunity to die to self and to yield to Christ. So trust Him today, even if it does not make sense. Look at your circumstances as a chance to die to self and live for Christ. This is a pivotal verse to help bring about the desired change that God is trying to orchestrate in our lives. We are at the halfway mark of the year—wouldn't it be great if this verse could be a reality to us? Decide today to trust Him with all your being.

Suggested Prayer ───────────────────────────────

Dear Lord,
I choose to trust You with all my heart. I choose to seek Your will and not mine in all my decisions. I choose to lean on You instead of my own understanding. I give my problem to You, seeing it as an opportunity to die to myself and to live for You. In Jesus' Name I pray, Amen.

Are We Having Fun Yet?

Psalms 1:1-3

Blessed is the man who walks not in the counsel of the wicked, nor stands in the way of sinners, nor sits in the seat of scoffers; but his delight is in the law of the LORD, and on his law he meditates day and night. He is like a tree planted by streams of water that yields its fruit in its season, and its leaf does not wither. In all that he does, he prospers.

The answer is probably yes and no. At times we feel happy and everything seems fine. Some days are filled with sorrow and intense loneliness. King David, who wrote this psalm, had his ups and downs too. He describes the happy man in this psalm.

The happy person does two things. He avoids sin: He does not walk in the path of sinners; He does not pull up a chair with sin and fellowship with it. He chooses not to stand in sin's path. The thing he *does* is saturate his heart and mind in the Word of God. He spends time, not only reading it, but also heeding it. He meditates on the scriptures throughout the day. He delights in the Word.

The results of these two actions are the blessing of God. One result is true happiness. Another is a promise that you will prosper in whatever endeavor you pursue. You might be saying to yourself that you tried all that and nothing happened. Verse 3 describes the season of blessing. If nothing has happened, then it is not the season of blessing yet. Rest assured the season of blessing will come. Do these two things, and in the proper season you will be blessed. Run away from sin and run to the Savior. God will bless you and you will be happy.

Suggested Prayer

Dear Lord,

I have seasons of sorrow. I see the wicked prospering, and I am suffering. Please help me run away from all sin. Help me read and meditate on Your Word. Please bring happiness and times of blessing again. I love You, Lord. Amen.

184 | PRESSING ON

JULY 3

Hard-Hearted

Mark 6:52
...for they did not understand about the loaves, but their hearts were hardened.

N o, I am not talking about your ex-wife or husband, though perhaps they are hard-hearted. In this verse it is the twelve disciples who have the hard hearts. Earlier that day Jesus fed 5,000 with five loaves and two fishes. Then Jesus sent the disciples away in their boat while He Himself went to pray. As the disciples struggled in the boat during a storm, Jesus walked on the water to where they were and stilled the storm for them. The miracle that they saw earlier that day (the feeding of the 5,000) should have given them faith to believe God in the middle of their storm. The disciples did not make the faith connection because their hearts were hard.

When God has miraculously supplied your needs, it should build up your faith to trust Him for your present need. Israel of the Old Testament had the same problem. They thought they would die of thirst, and God sent water from a rock. They thought they would starve to death, so God sent manna and quails. These people never made the faith connection and they died in the wilderness. You and I, if we are not careful, will be guilty of the same thing. The God who helped Israel will help you. The God who fed 5,000 will feed you. The God who stilled the storm will calm your storm. Jesus Christ is the same yesterday, today, and forever (Hebrews 13:8). We must make the faith connection when we read these events in our Bibles. We must also make the faith connection in our own lives. If God has helped you in the past, He will help you in the present and in the future. How is your heart? Is it full of faith or is it hard?

Suggested Prayer ─────────────────────────────
Dear Lord,
I am guilty of a hard heart and I have not made the faith connection. Lord, I am asking that You would soften my heart and make it pliable. Help me believe that You will help me. Forgive me for my unbelief. Give me a clean, new heart that is full of faith. In Jesus' Name I pray, Amen.

It Will Get Better

Psalms 27:13

I believe that I shall look upon the goodness of the LORD in the land of the living!

The psalmist believed that he would see the goodness of God in the land of the living. The phrase "land of the living" refers to the earth. This is the land of the living. Notice that the verse ends with an exclamation point. The psalmist wrote this verse with anticipation. He really believed he would see the goodness of the Lord.

We know God has great things in store for us in the future. We draw great strength from the fact that we have a mansion in heaven. We are going to a place of love and a place that is sinless. We rejoice over the bright future that we have. Yet, we have experienced so much heartache here that we do not see any good in this earth or our present circumstances. Sometimes all we can do is focus on our true riches in heaven.

Despite all the evil that the psalmist had endured, he still expected to see the goodness of God in this life. We too should expect and anticipate God's goodness in this life. There will be showers of blessing in this life. Expect God to restore the things that you have lost. Expect God to bring you a husband or a wife. Expect God to restore your finances. Expect to see His goodness in this life. All of this and heaven too. Amen and amen.

Suggested Prayer ———————————————————————

Lord,
I have been so discouraged with this life. I have gazed on heaven's shore and not expected You to bless me here anymore. Lord, forgive me and help me see Your goodness in this life. In Jesus' Name, Amen.

JULY 5

One Day the Nightmare Will End

Ecclesiastes 7:8
Better is the end of a thing than its beginning, and the patient in spirit is better than the proud in spirit.

S olomon tells us that the end of a matter is better than its beginning. How awesome is this? At the beginning of your trial you were hurt and rejected. Perhaps your health dwindled as you were in complete shock. Perhaps everything you worked for disappeared. Whatever happened, it was a horrible experience.

The end result is that we become one with our Lord. Between the beginning and the end, a whole lot of living takes place. There is suffering and sorrow, but there is a sweet peace that only Jesus can give us. There is regret, yet there is restoration. There is cruelty, yet there is comfort. There is betrayal, but there are blessings. The whole process is overwhelming.

However, at the end God has done His perfect work. You are now closer to Him. Perhaps God will restore your losses, like He did for Job. Whatever your case may be, God is doing a wonderful work in you. Maybe you are at the beginning. Perhaps you are at the end. Maybe you are in the midpoint of the trial. What is the secret of success? The key is being "patient in spirit" and not proud. As we submit to God and allow Him to work, we patiently endure and adjust till He works everything out. God cannot work with someone who is proud in spirit. The nightmare will end, and a new day will dawn, full of grace, peace, love, and hope.

Suggested Prayer
Dear Lord,
I long for the day when everything is put right in my life. Until then I surrender to Your will and ask that You would take full control. I want a patient spirit that waits and relies on You. It is in the Name of Jesus I pray, Amen.

There Is an End

Luke 22:37

For I tell you that this Scripture must be fulfilled in me: 'And he was numbered with the transgressors.' For what is written about me has its fulfillment.

When going through the tough trials that you are experiencing, you begin to think that it will never end. The financial problems do not seem to ever end. The intense severe loneliness seems like it will never end. When will it all end? You might be thinking, "I can't seem to take it anymore." In this chapter of Luke, Judas betrays Jesus. Jesus tells Peter that he will deny Him. Jesus even asks the Father to take away the coming crucifixion. In our text Jesus says the scriptures have a fulfillment or an end. The end for our Lord Jesus was death on a cross, crucified between two vile criminals. That would mark the end of His suffering. Three days later Jesus rose from the grave. The scriptures tell of the end or the last trial that Jesus would face.

Thank God our trials have and end! The end will happen when God accomplishes His complete and perfect will for our lives. For some the great lesson is patience. For Jesus it was complete obedience, even the death on the cross. The end is unique for everyone. Again, thank God there is an end. Be encouraged by the fact that there is an end. Find God's will for your life so He can accomplish His purpose in you. Once His will is accomplished, the end will come. Like Job of old, there will be renewal and restoration.

Suggested Prayer

Dear Lord,
It seems like it will never end. Trials come wave after wave. Thank You that there is an end. Let me be obedient to the very last wave. Let me delight in Your will. You hold the blueprints and You are the Master Builder. Build a work in me till the end. In the Name of Jesus I pray, Amen.

A Diadem or Decay

Proverbs 12:4
An excellent wife is the crown of her husband, but she who brings shame is like rottenness in his bones.

An excellent wife is a crown to her husband. Wait a minute! Why does Proverbs always talk about the woman and not the man? Well, this book is a father-to-son talk. Read the book of Proverbs and notice how many times Solomon says "my son." The truths of this book can be applied to either a man or a woman. You could say that an excellent husband is a crown to a wife.

Here is a man or woman who looks *great*, physically and spiritually. All they are missing is a crown. One day the crown comes, and they are complete. What a thing of beauty! On the other hand, here is a man or woman that looks *good*. They marry the wrong person, and now they are a living corpse. The English rock band Iron Maiden has a mascot for all their albums and concerts; its name is Eddie (don't let the preacher know that I have seen them four times in concert). Eddie is a living corpse; he is decayed but he also appears to have life. This world is full of Eddies. Who are the Eddies? Those who are alive, yet rotting away. Why? In some cases, it is those who got in a hurry and married outside the will of God. They married a spouse that brought shame and decay to their body and soul.

You do have a choice. You can get ahead of God and settle for someone who will bring about your decay and destruction. You can also wait on God and receive your crown. It is better to live and die alone than marry someone that will be your demise. Determine that you will be that crown for your future spouse. Decide that you will be the right person so God can send you that right person. Diadem or death. You decide.

Suggested Prayer
Lord,
I am so lonely. Please send me someone who will be a crown for me. By faith I am trusting that You will send the right person at the right time. I rest in Your will, patiently waiting for You to send me the right person. Lord, let it be someone whom I can serve You with. Lord, help me to be that crown for them. In Jesus' Name I pray, Amen.

JULY 8

It Seemed Right at the Time

Judges 21:25

In those days there was no king in Israel. Everyone did what was right in his own eyes.

God was faithful to Israel and would send them a leader to bring back the nation to Himself. The problem with Israel is that everyone did what they felt was right. They did not check with God to see if He thought it was right. This led to a vicious cycle in the nation that lasted some 400 years. First there would be a rebellion against God. Then God would send an enemy their way to oppress them. Then Israel would cry out to God in repentance. God would respond by sending them a judge that would deliver them from the oppression of the enemy. There would then be a time of restoration and peace. Before long the nation would do what they felt was right, and then the vicious cycle would begin all over again. Rebellion, oppression, repentance, deliverance, restoration and on and on it went.

So, what is the point of all of this? As we ignore God's principles and let our own wisdom rule our lives, we end up rebelling against God and the vicious cycle begins in our lives. Today determine that you will allow God to rule your thoughts and decisions. Things may seem right at the time but if they do not line up with God's will, disaster will occur. Let your divorce be the wake-up call to get you back to the ways of God.

Suggested Prayer

Dear Father,

I have done many things that seemed right at the time. Lord, the results were a rejection of You and Your Word. Please forgive me and cleanse me. Let me live according to Your principles and not my own. Let me live underneath Your will. In Jesus' Name I pray, Amen.

All Sufficient Grace

2 Corinthians 12:8-10
Three times I pleaded with the Lord about this, that it should leave me. But he said to me, "My grace is sufficient for you, for my power is made perfect in weakness." Therefore I will boast all the more gladly of my weaknesses, so that the power of Christ may rest upon me. For the sake of Christ, then, I am content with weaknesses, insults, hardships, persecutions, and calamities. For when I am weak, then I am strong.

Tonight as I am writing, my heart is overwhelmed with the pain of loneliness. I have a dear sister in Hong Kong who just sent me a text, and it was verse nine: *"My grace is sufficient for you, for my power is made perfect in weakness."* I needed that!

Paul asked God to remove a thorn in his flesh three times, and the answer was not what the apostle expected. Instead of a removal, there was a replacement. God told him that He would not remove the thorn, but instead, would give him grace to endure the pain. God even said that His strength would be made perfect in our weakness. The glory belongs to God, so when things are done in His power, He receives all the honor.

Like Paul, I have asked God to take away my thorn in the flesh. God did not take it away, but like Paul, He gave me enough grace. Grace for every need. Grace for every hour. Grace that is all His power. Perhaps we should pray for grace instead of asking God to remove us from a situation. The thorns help us draw closer to God. God gets the glory through our thorns. When we receive grace, God is then able to do mighty things through our weakness as we depend on Him.

Suggested Prayer
Lord,
Please give me grace to get through this evening. Lord, help me to rely on You and to trust You. May Your power rest on my spirit to do great things. In the Name of Jesus I pray, Amen.

A Time to Heal

Ecclesiastes 3:1-3

For everything there is a season, and a time for every matter under heaven: a time to be born, and a time to die; a time to plant, and a time to pluck up what is planted; a time to kill, and a time to heal; a time to break down, and a time to build up.

There is a time to kill, and a time to break down. We must put to death our sins of hatred, bitterness, and those things that are holding us back. There is a time to break down the walls of resentment and doubt. Thank God there is a time to heal and buildup. We must build up our faith. We must buildup what remains of our family.

There is a time of healing. In other words, healing takes time. Embrace the process because God is doing a great work. Encourage yourself in the Lord with this verse. Say to yourself, "God is healing me." As you wonder why God is not using you in His service, perhaps the answer is that you are still healing and that you simply need more time to heal. As you wonder why God has not sent that special someone in your life, perhaps you still need more time to heal.

Some try to heal themselves and end up in a worse condition. I think I speak for all of us when I say that we do not like to wait on God. But when God's healing takes place, you will be used in the right way for His kingdom. You will also have that special someone in your life. Reread that last sentence and believe that it is true. Yes, brothers and sisters, there is indeed a time to heal. Why aren't things transpiring like you want them to? Perhaps you need to take the time to heal.

Suggested Prayer

Dear Lord,
Kill and breakdown those things in my life that are keeping me from serving You. Take those things away that are holding back Your blessings. Lord, heal me and build me up. I am on Your time so do a mighty work in my life. Lord, when I am healed place me in Your service and bring me a godly spouse. In Jesus' Name I pray, Amen.

I Can't Seem to Make Ends Meet

Ecclesiastes 3:6
...a time to seek, and a time to lose; a time to keep, and a time to cast away;

I met a truck driver that could not make ends meet; he said that he would like them to at least get close enough where they could wave at each other. Those of us struggling with finances can certainly relate. Solomon says there is a time to seek and a time to lose. There is also a time to keep and a time to cast away. Take a good, hard, long, prayerful look at your possessions. Are there some things that you can do without? Are there some things you can lose or cast away? You might have some items that you can sell to pay off your debts and lighten the load.

Many people have thousands of dollars' worth of things that they can sell to get out of debt. Some people have an extra car, unused hunting and fishing gear, and collections of various kinds. Some have that Michael Kors purse and those brand-new shoes in the box that were never worn. How often do you use that boat? Look around and see what you can lose or cast away. You will be surprised at the number of things that you can part with to make some money.

A missionary said, "you never lose when you lose for Jesus." This process of losing is good for the soul. It helps us see what is important in life. It can be part of the cure for covetousness. It helps relieve the financial strain. It will make you feel better as you get rid of the clutter. It will strengthen your relationship with God. Yes, there is a time to lose and a time to cast away. May God help us see where our true riches lie.

Suggested Prayer
Dear Lord,
I have tried and tried and tried to pay my bills and I just can't do it. Lord, take me through the process of losing and casting away. Help it get me closer to You and to pay my debts. In Jesus' Name I pray, Amen.

Are You Really Alone?

John 16:32

Behold, the hour is coming, indeed it has come, when you will be scattered, each to his own home, and will leave me alone. Yet I am not alone, for the Father is with me.

On the eve of the crucifixion, Jesus said the disciples would desert Him and leave Him all alone to face Calvary by Himself. Then He said that He was not actually alone, because the Father was with Him. Where does this put you and me as we struggle each day with the dreaded disease of loneliness? We must embrace the fact that God is always with us and we are never alone. People come and go but God is always there for us.

In think loneliness is the greatest pain in the world. I had a kidney stone that was so large that it had to be surgically removed. I went through tremendous pain. My urologist performed the surgery and a week later it was business as usual. But loneliness has been a nagging pain in my heart that has never completely gone away. People make hasty decisions because they are lonely. Normally they would never marry a non-believer or fall into sin, but people will do anything to quench the fire of loneliness.

Jesus tells us that we are never alone. We must devote all of our love and affection to the God who loves us. We must cultivate that relationship and focus on the Lord, not on our loneliness. For some, Jesus is the only Friend that they have.

Does this relationship with Christ take away the pain? For me the answer is an emphatic no, not completely; but my relationship with God is stronger and the pain has lessened. There is a cross to bear that only you and Jesus can carry. There is no room for others on your silent journey to your Golgotha. Tell Jesus that you are lonely. In the meantime devote all your heart to the One who is altogether lovely. Look for others who are lonely and minister to them.

Suggested Prayer ———————————————————————————

Lord,

I am alone and I do not like it. The lonely hours have turned to days, then weeks, then months, and now, Lord, it has been years. Lord, I am still lonely. Please let me be content with You, and if it is Your will, please send someone. In the Name of Jesus I pray, Amen.

Death Brings Revival

Isaiah 6:1
In the year that King Uzziah died I saw the Lord sitting upon a throne, high and lifted up; and the train of his robe filled the temple.

I saiah chapter 6 is one of the richest chapters in the Bible. The Holy Spirit tells us that the prophet saw a vision of God in the year that King Uzziah died. The vision was so strong that Isaiah answered a divine call to serve the Lord. Before the great vision a death occurred, and this is a very important key to this chapter. The same key is true for us today. A death must take place if we are to hear from God.

You might ask, "Who needs to die?" The answer is that you and I must die to ourselves if we are going to hear from God. We must die to our plans and our goals. We must die to every ambition that we may have. Once we have surrendered everything to God, we are at a place where He can speak to us and show us His plan for our lives.

A friend of mine owned a nice home on forty acres. He had plenty of money, cars (in Texas it's trucks), big savings and retirement. He could purchase whatever he wanted, within reason. He had made some great plans, but they were not God's plans. He was a miserable person and hard to be around at times until he surrendered everything to God. Once a death took place, he received God's plan for his life. He sold everything he had and moved to the Philippines to do missionary work. Now he is happy because he is in God's will and not in his own. Death before direction. Death before duty. The way to truly live starts with a death.

Suggested Prayer

Dear Lord,
I die to my plans and myself. Now, Lord, let me find Your will. Call me into Your service and direct my paths. I die to myself that I might live for You. In the wonderful Name of Jesus I pray, Amen.

Temptation

1 Corinthians 7:1-2

Now concerning the matters about which you wrote: "It is good for a man not to have sexual relations with a woman." But because of the temptation to sexual immorality, each man should have his own wife and each woman her own husband.

P aul says that it is great if a man or woman stays single. However, Paul also knew that every person would be tempted to do immoral things, so he says that every man and every woman has a God-given right to be married. The problem is that many people are out of control when it comes to their sexuality. They do not have self-control, and they are not strong enough in their walk to be controlled by the Holy Spirit. As a result they get married, thinking that marriage will be a cure-all to their lack of discipline. After a while the man is looking at porn or cheats on his new wife. The wife has an affair.

Marriage is not a cure-all for unbridled passions. Every man and woman must be controlled by the Holy Spirit. Anything short of this is an open invitation to allow sin and Satan to ruin another marriage. Married people will always be tempted. A marriage ceremony does not end sexual temptation. A divorced person is in a win-win situation. If they can control themselves and stay single, they can serve God without distractions. If they choose to marry, they have not sinned, but their loyalties will be divided between God and their new spouse. They do have this right to marry and it is an opportunity to show the world what a true marriage is all about.

God has set an open door before you, so honor Him by abstaining from fornication. Seek professional help for any sexual addictions.

Suggested Prayer —————————————————

Dear Lord,
I give myself to You. I do not want to sin against You. Help me exercise self-control. Holy Spirit, please control my thoughts and actions. Give me wisdom to know if I should remarry. In Jesus' Name, Amen.

I Got Lonely and Married a Non-Believer

1 Corinthians 7:12-16

To the rest I say (I, not the Lord) that if any brother has a wife who is an unbeliever, and she consents to live with him, he should not divorce her. If any woman has a husband who is an unbeliever, and he consents to live with her, she should not divorce him. For the unbelieving husband is made holy because of his wife, and the unbelieving wife is made holy because of her husband. Otherwise your children would be unclean, but as it is, they are holy. But if the unbelieving partner separates, let it be so. In such cases the brother or sister is not enslaved. God has called you to peace. For how do you know, wife, whether you will save your husband? Or how do you know, husband, whether you will save your wife?

If this describes your marriage, you are not alone. Many people are lonely and marry unbelievers. They know they made a mistake, but now what do they do? Paul says to remain married to the person as long as they are willing to stay married. Your decision could result in their salvation. Paul is telling us that something positive can come out of our mistakes. The marriage is great for the children. They are under God's protection and have a stable home.

Be faithful to God. Let your spouse see that there is something different about you. Wives, you can win your husband without nagging at him. (Read 1 Peter chapter 3; Peter also addresses this issue.) Paul says let the unbeliever be the one to break the marriage covenant and not the believer. If the unbeliever does not want to stay with you, allow them to go. You will not be bound in such cases.

God can take any bad situation and make it turn out for your good and His glory. Whatever you do, decide to honor the Lord in all your choices. Your actions are a matter of heaven or hell for your unbelieving spouse. The key is to wait on God and let Him work everything out. Dedicate the situation to God and watch Him work.

Suggested Prayer —————————————————————————

Lord,
I willingly married an unbeliever. I was so lonely. Please forgive me. Now I give myself to You. I give my spouse to You. I ask that You save my spouse and that we could serve You together. In Jesus' Name I pray, Amen.

Divided Interests

1 Corinthians 7:32-35

I want you to be free from anxieties. The unmarried man is anxious about the things of the Lord, how to please the Lord. But the married man is anxious about worldly things, how to please his wife, and his interests are divided. And the unmarried or betrothed woman is anxious about the things of the Lord, how to be holy in body and spirit. But the married woman is anxious about worldly things, how to please her husband. I say this for your own benefit, not to lay any restraint upon you, but to promote good order and to secure your undivided devotion to the Lord.

When contemplating remarriage, one must consider their relation-ship with God. Paul explains that a single man or woman can devote him or herself totally to the Lord. A married man by nature is a divided man. He must put God first in everything that he does. Yet he must also devote time to his wife to have a proper relationship with her. A married woman is also divided between her husband and her Lord Jesus Christ. Paul wrote these things for our benefit. He is not trying to restrain anyone from staying single or marrying. Paul's main concern is that men and women serve the Lord.

Our devotion to God is the most important thing in our lives. Marriage will divide our attention and bring anxiety in our lives. This is one reason why Paul promoted singleness. Ask yourself if you can be devoted to God *and* a spouse. Also ask if a new spouse will help or hinder your relationship with God. Find out what God wants you to do: for some, a new marriage will hinder His plans; for others a spouse will further His plans. The gift is not singleness. The gift is the plan God has for you. Singleness just helps you carry out His plan. Paul was an example of this truth; Jeremiah was also an Old Testament example of this truth.

A husband or a wife is a great blessing from God. If you remarry, make sure it is someone that you can serve Him with. If you choose to stay single, serve Him with undivided interests.

Suggested Prayer ————————————————————
Dear Lord,
I understand that a married person has divided interests. Today, Lord, I devote myself to You. Help me understand Your plan for my life. Help me serve You and be devoted to You. Help me know if I should remarry or not. In Jesus' Name I pray, Amen.

Only in The Lord

1 Corinthians 7:39
A wife is bound to her husband as long as he lives. But if her husband dies, she is free to be married to whom she wishes, only in the Lord.

These four words, "only in the Lord" are very important when it comes to remarriage. Paul is letting us know that Christians are to only marry other Christians. There is great freedom in this portion of scripture because it teaches us that she can marry whomever she wishes as long as he is saved. Any person who is not a Christian is not marriage material and certainly not dating material. It is not *altar* then *alter*. In other words, you do not go to the marriage altar expecting to make them a Christian later. In some cases this has worked, but why take the chance?

The Kingdom of Light has no fellowship with the Kingdom of Darkness. Most sensible Christians understand this concept. However, when intense loneliness invades our souls we will compromise if we are not careful. We want the loneliness to end and are even willing to compromise the Word of God to end the pain. It is a big recipe for disaster. This is Satan's plan for you and not God's plan.

We must guard our hearts into the ways of God. We must also use wisdom in our freedom. *Any* Christian will not do; most of us are just thankful to meet a Christian. However, we must not compromise for a backslider or a bitter Christian. You want a person that loves God and serves Him. Do not settle for second best. It is better to live and die alone than to be married to a lost person; better to be alone than marry a Christian who does not have a desire to serve God.

Suggested Prayer ───────────────────────────────
Lord,
I am struggling. I am lonely and I just can't find a person who is saved that loves You. Lord, I have compromised, and I know I am wrong. Help me to wait on You. Give me wisdom and an understanding heart. In Jesus Name I pray, Amen.

Be Yourself

1 Corinthians 7:6-9

Now as a concession, not a command, I say this. I wish that all were as I myself am. But each has his own gift from God, one of one kind and one of another. To the unmarried and the widows I say that it is good for them to remain single, as I am. But if they cannot exercise self-control, they should marry. For it is better to marry than to burn with passion.

Be that man or woman that God has called you to be and do not worry about what other people may think. It is fine to be a single person; it is also fine to be married. The Bible does not command us to be married. Paul really wanted widows to stay single if they could; he felt that they would be happier remaining single. I recently met a widow who said she would never remarry; there was nothing wrong with her decision. My sister died of breast cancer at the age of 53. It has been nine years since her death; my brother-in-law has decided to remain single. There is nothing wrong with his decision. I know another lady whose husband, a preacher, committed suicide. She was lonely and married an unbeliever very quickly. She regretted her decision and wished she could change it.

God, in His infinite grace, has given you a grace-gift to serve Him. Be yourself. Follow the leading of the Lord. If you feel like you want to be single, that is fine. Much of our society is geared around the family, especially the church. Paul was not saying that you must stay single. Paul's main concern was that people serve the Lord. He felt he could do more for God as a single person. If you change your mind and want to marry, that is fine. God is on your side. Do not think He will be mad at you if you cannot stay single.

God will bless you either way. You are in a win-win situation. What is the desire of your heart? If you are single and content, then this is a good indication of the Lord's leading in your life. If you are restless all the time and have a desire to have a companion, then you probably need to be married. If you are just not happy by yourself and discontented, you need a spouse. Do not be ashamed to be yourself.

Suggested Prayer ————————————————————————

Dear Lord,
I want to be the person You want me to be. I want to be myself and be true to myself. I want to do Your will and I submit to You. If You want me to be single, give me grace. If You want me to be married give me grace to wait for the right person. In the Name of Jesus I pray, Amen.

JULY 19

The God of Second Chances

Jonah 3:1
Then the word of the LORD came to Jonah the second time, saying...

Jonah is an interesting man, to say the least. He was a prophet and a godly man. When God called him to go to Nineveh he rebelled and tried to hide from God. His rebellion got him thrown overboard and a great fish swallowed him alive. Yes, I believe this event is true because my Lord believed it was true. In the depths of the ocean Jonah repented of his sin. God, in His mercy, forgave him and restored him, then caused the fish to vomit Jonah up onto the land.

He was placed in the right spot where he needed to be. Then the word of the Lord came to him a second time. This time he responded with obedience, and revival broke out as the people of Nineveh repented of their sins. The people listened to the preaching and repented. It was an awesome event.

What has God called you to do? God's purpose does not change. Perhaps you responded with rebellion the first time, like Jonah. Repent and let God restore you. Then listen for Him to speak to you a second time. Do not tempt God by pushing for a third time. Respond in faith. Do you need a second chance today? God will give it to you if you are serious. A dear friend of mine once told me this: "Don't play with God, because He is not playing with you." Get serious with God. Let Him give you a second chance. Let Him use you in a mighty way. Just when you think it is all over, God will grant you a second chance.

Suggested Prayer
Lord,
Today I need a second chance. I repent of my sins. God, You have called me, and I ask that this time I would respond in faith. Lord, please use me. Place me where I need to be. Then let me give the people Your message. In Jesus' Name I pray, Amen.

Out of The Mouth of Babes

Psalms 8:2

Out of the mouth of babes and infants, you have established strength because of your foes, to still the enemy and the avenger.

Most of us have heard the saying, "out of the mouths of babes." We always associate the saying with the innocence of a child. Children will say and do things out of innocence that an adult just will not do. Well, out of the mouth of a dear sweet little four-year-old girl came a strong rebuke to my spirit. When my wife first left me, I lost 45 pounds. I exercised every day, ate less, and did some major praying and fasting. The added stress in my life also caused me to lose weight.

Well, there came a day when I quit exercising. As depression put down its roots, I was back to my old eating habits. Before long I had regained 28 of the 45 pounds that I lost. I was so depressed I just did not care about my weight anymore. A dear friend of mine invited some friends over to make sushi. One of the visiting families had a dear, sweet girl named Alisa. She and her parents are from China. Each night Elisa prays for a baby brother because she is an only child. Alisa and I made sushi together as the rest of the adults seemed to ignore her. She gave me a hug, and as she put her arms around me, she asked me if I was having a baby. Those words were funny to me and to all the guests. Suddenly the words began to convict me. I thought I must start exercising and eating right again. I thought to myself; "why did you lose all that weight, only to gain it back?" Out of the mouths of babes came this little rebuke from the Lord. I began exercising and watching my food intake once again. I began to care again.

Why am I sharing this? Because it so easy to give up and just let go. For me it was my body that I neglected. What have you given up on? Church? Your health? Family? I totally understand your perspective even though it is wrong. You have two choices before you. One, you can ask God to forgive you and start making the right decisions. The second choice is that Alisa can come over and say something that will get you inline.

Suggested Prayer ────────────────────────────────
Dear Lord,
Forgive me for not caring. I let some things go. I ask that You get me out of my depression, and that I would not neglect You, myself, or those around me. I commit myself to following You. In Jesus' Name I pray, Amen.

God Hates Me

Romans 8:31

What then shall we say to these things? If God is for us, who can be against us?

Preacher, you can't say that "God hates me." Well, I know it is not the right thing to say, but this is my book. This thought has crossed my mind on several occasions, and probably yours too. Why would we think such nonsense? The biggest reason is that we do not realize that God is indeed for us. He is on our side. Do you realize God is on your side today? He is our coach and we are on His team. We are His first-round draft pick. Ask the Holy Spirit to open your heart up to the truth that God is for you.

The second biggest reason that we think God hates us is because of what is against us. The world, our own flesh, and the devil are all against us. Not only that; our circumstances are against us. The biggest circumstances to me are the financial strain, the loneliness, and the dismal hope of the future. When circumstances look bad, we feel like our owns sins have caused the problem. This is usually not the case. Wait a minute! You are saying, "I bought this book to be encouraged." I know you did. So, what are we to do?

We must get our eyes off the circumstances and on the Risen Christ. As we ask God to show us that He is on our side, an inward transformation begins to take place. He gives us hope and we realize that He is for us. As we realize that God is for us, we begin to trust Him and to realize that He is in control. Since God is for us, there is no person or circumstance that will take us over. Things might look bleak, but God is on your side and you are going to have victory. Once God has done a work in your heart, you and I will realize that my title for today is utter nonsense.

Suggested Prayer

Dear Lord,
I have often felt like You hated me. Forgive me for this. Holy Spirit, make the truth of this verse a reality. Also help me get my eyes on You and not on circumstances. Lord, give me hope. In the Name of Jesus I pray, Amen.

Consecrated for Sympathy

Exodus 29:20

...and you shall kill the ram and take part of its blood and put it on the tip of the right ear of Aaron and on the tips of the right ears of his sons, and on the thumbs of their right hands and on the great toes of their right feet, and throw the rest of the blood against the sides of the altar.

Aaron and his sons were consecrated (set apart) to be priests to God. They could not serve as priests until they were anointed with oil. They also had to wear priestly garments. They were consecrated with blood, having blood applied to their right ear, right thumb, and right big toe. The late great Dr. Harold Sightler, a Baptist preacher in Greenville, South Carolina, said that when we go through some tragic event, God consecrates us to the ministry of sympathy. He consecrates our ear that we might listen to others who are suffering. Then He consecrates our hands to help. He even consecrates our feet so we can go to those who are suffering.[4]

His statements are profound. To think that God has consecrated us to a ministry of sympathy puts our sufferings into a totally different perspective. God has chosen you and set you aside to be sympathetic ears, hands, and feet to those who are divorced. How will this happen? Just as the priests were anointed with oil, you are anointed with the Holy Spirit. It is the Holy Spirit that will give you a sympathetic ear and hands and feet to help.

Your divorce consecrated you into a ministry of sympathy. You may be divorced but you are consecrated to serve. Congratulations on your new ministry. You might help more people than your pastor because you have gone through some deep waters and can help others. So be praying for wisdom on how to fulfill your new ministry. God bless you!

Suggested Prayer

Dear Lord,
I believe that You have consecrated me to a ministry of sympathy to those who are divorced. Lord, this new purpose for my life encourages me. Thank You for entrusting me with this ministry. Now, Lord, I want to fulfill this ministry. Put people in my life that I can lend a sympathetic ear to, lend a hand to, and people I can go visit. In the Name of Jesus I pray, Amen.

---

[4] Harold Sightler, *The Ministry of Tears* (The Brightspot Hour: Greenville, SC, 1977)

The Best Plan for Your Troubles

Proverbs 12:13
An evil man is ensnared by the transgression of his lips, but the righteous escapes from trouble.

It is no secret that you are in a time of deep trouble. You know it. Those around you know it. It is not a pleasant experience. No doubt you have devised several plans on how to get out of this mess. Did you ever think that living right would be your best strategy? There is a promise in this verse that we should not dismiss: *those who are living right will come out of trouble.* There is a promise for the wicked too. They will be trapped in their messes. Their very words will ensnare them. Wickedness leads to entrapment, and ultimately death. Righteousness leads to freedom.

Begin each day yielding to God. Read and apply your Bible. Pray and pray and pray some more. Force yourself to go to church if you do not feel like going. Go by yourself if no one will go with you. Find a place of service in the church. Be that godly person that He has called you to be. Treat your ex-spouse with respect. Be that parent you are supposed to be. This is the path to freedom. This is the path that will eventually lead you out of the trouble that you are in. The Kingdom way is a narrow way, but it is the path that leads to freedom. Decide to do right and live for Jesus. No one ever regrets living right. Regrets and sorrow are marked by those on the broad way that ultimately leads to destruction. Get right! Be right! Stay right! God will do what is right!

Suggested Prayer
Lord,
Forgive me for sinning against You. I have chosen the easy way and now I am paying for it. Lord, I want to do right and be right, so I give myself to You anew and afresh. Please use me for Your service. In Jesus' Name I pray, Amen.

Are You Doing All You Can Do?

Mark 14:8
She has done what she could; she has anointed my body beforehand for burial.

Here is a lady who anointed the feet of Jesus prior to His crucifixion. Her deed was ridiculed and scorned. The pure nard (used to make the spikenard ointment) cost almost a year's salary, and yet she poured it on Jesus' feet. The consensus was that the lady was crazy. However, Jesus said she did a good deed that would be remembered long after her death. This lady knew that our Lord would die for our sins. She had a vision of the plan and purpose of the Son of God. She did what she could, which was to pour out her most treasured perfume on the feet of Jesus. Would you give a year's wages to the cause of Christ?

Pastor Gary Grey said, "do what you can do and let God do what you cannot do." This statement is so true. As we do what we can do, God will do what we cannot do. The lady gave her very best for Jesus. Are we doing what we can do? If not, why not? One reason is that we have given up hope. The work that this lady did was based on faith. She believed God and responded accordingly. God is still on our side! God still cares! God is answering your prayers. God is going to work miracles through your tragedy. Perhaps today you need a fresh vision of who your God is and what He will do for you. Do not lose hope. God is going to do a miracle. It is always darkest before the dawn. A bright new day is coming, so do what you can do.

Suggested Prayer ————————————————————
Dear Lord,
I have given up hope and quit doing my part. Lord, I lost sight of who You are. Restore my hope and help me do everything I can do to further Your Kingdom. Let it be said of me, "he did what he could." In Jesus' Name I pray, Amen.

Ashamed

Psalms 25:1-3

To you, O LORD, I lift up my soul. O my God, in you I trust; let me not be put to shame; let not my enemies exult over me. Indeed, none who wait for you shall be put to shame; they shall be ashamed who are wantonly treacherous.

Have you ever felt shame or been ashamed? I have! When my wife left me, I was ashamed. At work most of my coworkers congregate in a central control room. For months I would go to a different room to be alone. I was ashamed to be around others. The rejection and pain were so bad that I could not be in the same room with my colleagues. Several of my coworkers would come to the room that I was in and would try to comfort me. They knew I was hurting.

My lawn was another major issue for me. My work schedule is such that I have days off during the week. I would not mow my lawn on weekends because of the shame that I felt. I would wait to mow on a weekday when everyone else was at work. I was too ashamed to be outside in public view, and I did not want to talk to the neighbors. The reality is that most of my neighbors are good Christians and could feel and sense my pain and sorrow. The front yard was off limits to me in daylight hours. I would even check my mailbox at night.

Like the psalmist, I did lift up my soul to God. I began to trust Him more and more. I also learned that I must wait on Him. After some time, I was healed enough to be around my coworkers. I can now mow my yard if the neighbors are at home, but this took a whole lot of time. Recently a friend of mine lost her husband. She mows her backyard because it is fenced, and she will not have to see any neighbors. She pays someone to mow her front yard. When she and I swapped lawnmower stories my heart was comforted, and I developed a burden to start praying for her. So you are not alone if you are too ashamed to be around others. Lift up your soul to God, and He will rise with healing in His wings. He will restore you and bear your shame and sorrow.

Suggested Prayer

Dear Lord,
I am so ashamed. Lord, I have good neighbors and coworkers. I thank You for these people You have put in my life. The problem is with me, though, and not my friends. Heal me and take away my shame. In Jesus' Name I pray, Amen.

Have You Ever Thought About Playing an Instrument?

Psalms 33:2-3

Give thanks to the LORD with the lyre; make melody to him with the harp of ten strings! Sing to him a new song; play skillfully on the strings, with loud shouts.

Some of us had piano or guitar lessons as a child, and somewhere down the road we lost interest in playing the instrument. The instrument became a dust collector and was eventually given away. Well, here you are with nothing but time on your hands. You are living in a prison, yet you are not behind bars. There is time to reflect and regret. There is too much time.

You need something to occupy your time, something that you can invest your time in. A friend of mine soaked his mind in woodworking and made nice furniture that he gave as Christmas gifts to his children. The singer, songwriter, actor, and producer Phil Collins wrote his biggest hits when he was coping with the pain of divorce. He used that time to saturate his whole being into music. The results are phenomenal even to this day. His songs are still touching people.

Perhaps you need a hobby that can supplement your income. You could have a hobby that could benefit your church. The possibilities are endless. Find something to do to occupy your time. The healing process takes time and it may be a while before God sends you another spouse. You might endure years of loneliness. Spend time with God in Bible study and prayer, but you should also pick up a hobby.

Suggested Prayer ───────────────────────────

Dear Lord,
This spare time is driving me crazy. I am reading and praying, but still, I am going nuts. Please give me a hobby that will help me and glorify You. In the Name of Jesus I pray, Amen.

How to Die as a Bachelor Or as an Old Maid

1 Corinthians 11:8-9

For man was not made from woman, but woman from man. Neither was man created for woman, but woman for man.

We must understand that God created a woman to be a suitable helper and companion for the man. Mister, can I help you? Quit trying to make a woman fit into a certain mold. There are a lot of nice ladies out there, but you need one that will help you serve God. If she is not a good fit for what God is doing in your life, quit trying to force her to fit. God has someone else that will compliment you and will help you along life's journey. Let her go! Quit compromising and trying to accommodate a woman that is not suitable for you.

Ma'am, can I help you? Throw your list in the trash and find a man that you can serve God with. Your list says he must be rich, have a nice home, and nice cars. He must also be able to take you places and buy you the nicest things. Instead of placing so many demands out there, begin to pray differently. Ask God to send you a true man of God that you can be a good wife to. Pray for someone that you can complement in God's service. It is not what he can do for you but what you can do for him.

Mister, keep trying to make a lady fit your mold and you will be rewarded with heartache and disappointment. Ma'am, hold onto your list and hold it tight, because at the end of your days you will discover that no one could meet your standards.

Suggested Prayer ———————————————————————

For the man:
Dear Lord,
I have tried to make a woman fit my mold and it did not work. Now, Lord, I ask that You send me someone that I can serve You with. Let us serve You together. Send the lady that You want me to have. Amen.

For the woman:
Dear Lord,
My list is all about me and what I want. The list is all about what a man can do for me. Now, Lord, I am sorry. I ask that You send me a man that I can be a blessing to. Help me compliment him as we serve You together. Amen.

How Does Your House Look?

Proverbs 31:27
She looks well to the ways of her household and does not eat the bread of idleness.

I was hoping you would not ask about my house. If I had to make a confession, I would have to say I have been guilty of having a messy house. Dirty floors, dishes—you name it, I have neglected it and am guilty as charged. I have thought to myself, "Why clean? No one is coming over anyway. It does not matter, if I don't have a girlfriend or even a remote possibility of one." I realized that I just did not care anymore.

The Proverbs 31 woman's house was spotless. One is quick to add that she was not divorced either. But I must admit that running a household is a two-person job, and God never intended it to be a solo act. I found myself getting more and more depressed and the house looking worse and worse. Then one day I decided that I must make a change. I began to care about myself and my surroundings. Is my house spotless? Absolutely not, but I am making more of a conscious effort to clean.

I also understand that if you are paying child support and giving to your church you do not have the money to fix things that are broken. Take care of what you have. One day the money will come in and you can make the needed repairs or upgrades.

When my Proverbs 31 woman enters my house, I want her to see a man who looks "well to the ways of her (his) household." Decide to give your house ten minutes a day. The idea is to get into the habit of cleaning. The greater need is to start caring again. The dirty home is a sign that you are depressed. The issue is not the carpet, it's the heart.

Suggested Prayer ————————————————————
Lord,
I admit that my home looks bad and that I am not a good steward of what You have given me. Lord, my problem is not a physical one. It is my heart. I just do not care. Lord, I am depressed and do not want to live like this anymore. Something needs to change and that something is me. Lord, change me even now. In Jesus' Name I pray, Amen.

Does God Want Me to Stay Single?

Jeremiah 16:1-2
The word of the LORD came to me: "You shall not take a wife, nor shall you have sons or daughters in this place."

This is a tough question that only God can answer for you. Jeremiah was the weeping prophet. He warned Judah that God would send the Babylonians to judge them if they would not repent. Instead of heeding God's warning, they kept on sinning and even threw Jeremiah in prison. The Babylonians came and destroyed the city of Jerusalem. God's plan for Jeremiah was to stay in Jerusalem and prophesy amidst the devastation. God told him not to have a wife or children because poverty and disease would be rampant. The will of God led him to a muddy pit of a dungeon and a life of suffering among the survivors.

Thank God we will probably never suffer like this. The fact is that God has great plans for us. For some, God will send a spouse and they will serve Him together. Others will remain single and serve God. The singleness helps them accomplish the will of God for their lives. The big question is not to marry or stay single. The bigger question is what God's will for my life is. Once we begin to see His plan unfold, we will begin to see if a new marriage is a part of His plan. So ask God the bigger question: "What is Your plan for my life, God?"

Suggested Prayer ————————————————————————
Lord,
My focus has been wrong. I have concentrated on my loneliness and a desire for a new spouse. I now realize my focus should be doing Your will. Lord, show me Your plan and let me accept it. I purpose to do Your will, either single or remarried. Your will be done; I want You to be my main priority. Thank You for working in my life. In Jesus' Name, Amen.

Thankful for Everything? Give Me a Break!

Ephesians 5:20
...giving thanks always and for everything to God the Father in the name of our Lord Jesus Christ...

Paul told us that we must be thankful all the time to the Lord. He also said to be thankful in everything. The words "always" and "everything" mean always and everything. Yes, the previous statement is filled with a little sarcasm, but I am trying to make a point, so bear with me. The point is that in our flesh it is difficult to be thankful all the time for every situation. Thankful for a divorce? Abandonment? Heartache? Poverty? The loss of family and friends? This seems impossible.

Thankful always? Well, that is easy when the "always" means that things are always going well. If God wants us to always be thankful for everything, how do we do this? The key is submitting our lives to God. As we submit to Him, we are trusting Him, knowing that He has our best interests in mind. If we truly believe that God is working in our lives, we will submit to Him. The result is that we will be filled with or controlled by the Holy Spirit. As the Holy Spirit controls our thoughts and actions, He will help us respond to difficulties in a spiritual manner.

At this point you might need to confess your sins, and get a bigger view of a God who is in control of everything and working out His purpose in you. It may take some time and a whole lot of prayer, but one day you will be thankful for the trials you are going through.

Suggested Prayer —————————————————————————
Lord,
It is tough to always be thankful for everything. I confess that my view of You has been very small. I have allowed misfortunes to make me bitter. Lord, I confess the bitterness and resentment. I surrender to You. Fill me with Your Spirit, and let me be controlled by You and not my own fallen nature. In Jesus' Name I pray, Amen.

I Can't Figure It Out

Isaiah 55:8-9

For my thoughts are not your thoughts, neither are your ways my ways, declares the LORD. For as the heavens are higher than the earth, so are my ways higher than your ways and my thoughts than your thoughts.

God is on a totally different level than we are on. We can think our way through some things because we have limited knowledge; we can figure some things out—but not all. People have used their minds to invent some awesome things. What makes sense to us might not make sense to God. Our thoughts and actions are simply not like God's thoughts and actions.

We become frustrated because we cannot figure out what is happening in our lives. Why do I suffer, and others live at ease? Why am I alone while others are surrounded with friends? Why did I have to go through a divorce? When will things get better? There is a frustration level building in our hearts because we cannot figure things out. So, what are we to do?

There is a key in this verse that will help us. God's thoughts are on a much higher plane than ours. As the heavens are higher than the ground, so are God's thoughts much higher than ours. God is seated in heaven, and we are on earth. He has an eternal perspective; we have an earthly perspective. He is The Most High God. Instead of trying to figure it all out, it is time to start trusting the Almighty. Since He is greater than we are, we must trust Him—even if things do not make sense. We must trust that He is using all our problems to bring about a desired end. When we respond to God in faith, the frustrations seem to dissipate. We have a choice today: we can stay frustrated or we can start trusting Him.

Suggested Prayer ———————————————————————————

Lord,
I have been frustrated and discouraged. I can't figure this all out and it bothers me. I am looking for answers and receiving none. Lord, I believe You are The Most High God. Today I die to my thoughts and place my life into Your hands, whether answers come or not. In Jesus' Name I pray, Amen.

AUGUST 1

We Need Godly Advice

Proverbs 19:20
Listen to advice and accept instruction, that you may gain wisdom in the future.

As our minds and emotions are consumed with the divorce, it becomes more and more apparent that we are not thinking properly. We need the godly advice and instruction of friends. Sometimes we even need them to do our thinking for us. I can remember going outside and seeing each neighbor's trash can out on the curb for trash pick-up. Then I would suddenly realize that it was trash day. Normally I would know what day the trash is picked up. My mind was so spent that I did not even know something as simple as trash day.

At that point I realized I would just have to trust some godly friends to watch over me and help me with some of my decision making. At times I simply could not think. I would pray and say something like the following, "Lord, I cannot think. I trust that you sent this person in my life to tell me what to do. So, by faith I am doing it, knowing that they are walking with You. I receive this instruction, believing it came from You."

God's goal is healing and restoration, but in our weakness we can make some poor decisions. Today, right now if this is your case, pick out a few friends that can help you make wise choices. If you do not know anyone who can help, then ask God to send you someone. There are probably people at your work that can help. There are surely some at your church that can help. If your church has a program for divorced people, sign up and get some godly advice. God wants to send you some godly counselors to help you. This would also be a great time for an accountability partner.

Suggested Prayer —————————————————————
Dear Father,
Please send some people who can help me go through this tough time. Lord, I can't think straight and I need a godly counselor to help me. Lord, I need a friend who is following You. In Jesus' Name I pray, Amen.

AUGUST 2

I Lost Everything

Philippians 3:8
Indeed, I count everything as loss because of the surpassing worth of knowing Christ Jesus my Lord. For his sake I have suffered the loss of all things and count them as rubbish, in order that I may gain Christ...

For some of us the title of today's devotion is a stark reality. Many people have lost their homes through divorce. Others have lost vehicles, jobs, savings, 401Ks, and the list can go on and on, even including the family pet. The biggest loss is the breakup of the family. It is a shame that a woman can be a devoted faithful wife and now she has nothing. A man works all his life to be reduced to nothing.

Paul said he lost everything, so we can relate. He also said that he counted his losses as mere rubbish that he might have a closer walk with Christ. There is a difference. Paul lost everything, yet he did not care because he gained Christ. He was satisfied with knowing Jesus.

We are angry because we lost everything, and now all we have is Jesus. We look at our losses and become bitter and angry. We must count our losses as rubbish and see Jesus as our greatest treasure if we ever hope to have victory. Some of us (me) needed to lose everything to realize what we have in Jesus Christ.

Everything in this life can be taken away from us at any time. In fact, we will not take one single item or even one penny with us when we die. On the other hand, no one can take Jesus away from you. Let's accept our losses and embrace Christ Jesus our Lord. Who knows? He might even restore your losses.

Suggested Prayer
Dear Lord,
I lost everything and it hurts so bad. I am angry and bitter about the whole thing. Forgive me of my anger. Let me see that things are not important and let me see You as my treasure. Let me have a deep relationship with You. Whether You restore my losses or not, I choose to love and serve You. In Jesus' Name I pray, Amen and Amen.

A New Start

Psalms 92:10
But you have exalted my horn like that of the wild ox; you have poured over me fresh oil.

Ever need a new start? Who doesn't? Thank God that He forgives sin and restores us. The psalmist spoke of fresh oil being poured on him. When a person was appointed by God to a special office they were anointed with oil. For example, when God chose David to be Israel's new king, the Lord sent Samuel the priest to the house of Jesse. Samuel watched as each of Jesse's sons passed by, except one. Finally God told Samuel that David was the chosen one. Samuel then poured oil over David, anointing him for the great task that lay ahead. This anointing would guide David in the affairs of the Greater King—Jesus.

The oil was a consecration to God's service. In the scriptures oil is a type of the Holy Spirit. Every Christian has the Holy Spirit. We can ask ourselves this question, "You have the Holy Spirit, but does the Holy Spirit have you?" The Holy Spirit is with us to lead, guide, and direct us in the things of God. The Holy Spirit is the real power behind the Christian life. If we allow Him, the Holy Spirit will accomplish the will of God in our lives.

Perhaps you have sinned and need a touch from God. Perhaps all your hopes and dreams were shattered through your divorce. Maybe you feel like you are miles and miles away from God. There is something great about this verse. God pours fresh oil on His servants.

Today ask God to pour fresh oil on your spirit. The fresh oil will help you confess your sins. The oil will give you a new vision for the future. The oil will get you back in the will of God. The oil will get you back in the race. Spirit of the Living God, fall on me, and please pour fresh oil on my spirit. Revive my old broken heart and fill me with new life to serve You.

Suggested Prayer
Lord,
I lost my hope and purpose through my grief and sorrow. Today I am asking that You will pour fresh oil on me. Let this new anointing change my life and those around me. Let it allow me to do Your will. In Jesus' Name, Amen.

I Am Too Tired to Discipline My Kids

Proverbs 29:17
Discipline your son, and he will give you rest; he will give delight to your heart.

Solomon said a wise parent will discipline his or her children. Discipline can take many forms; some parents spank and others do not. The key to parenting is consistency. Set clear boundaries and explain the consequences of disobedience. Be consistent! As children get older discipline takes on more of the form of instruction. We must instruct and teach our children. We never stop instructing our kids.

Two byproducts of good discipline are rest and rejoicing. We find rest or peace in our homes as we discipline. Today many homes are chaotic and the parents are worn out. The kids rule the home and there is no rest for the parents. What is the problem? Lack of instruction. The other byproduct is rejoicing in your heart. We are proud of our children and their accomplishments. We rejoice that they are becoming respectable children of God. We all want to be proud of our children, and it starts with proper discipline.

Too tired to discipline? Do you need rest? If you choose not to discipline, there will be no rest for your soul, especially when they reach the teenage years. Do not let your divorce keep you from instructing your children. Many parents fall into the trap of not disciplining, fearing that they will lose their children. Some feel their children will reject them. The rejection of your ex-spouse can be so strong that you will not discipline your kids, thinking they will leave too. The truth is that if you choose not to instruct your children and set boundaries, you *will* lose them. You have lost enough already, so be a consistent parent and you will find rest and rejoicing with your kids.

Suggested Prayer
Lord,
I am tired and I have trouble disciplining my kids. Help me bring them up right. Let me reject the fears and receive the faith to be a good parent. Lord, I need the rest this verse speaks of. I want to be proud of my children. Please give me the wisdom and courage to instruct my children. Help me be patient with them like You are with me. In Jesus' Name I pray, Amen.

An Open Door

1 Corinthians 16:9
...for a wide door for effective work has opened to me, and there are many adversaries.

God has a way of opening doors for us. God opens *wide* doors, which seems strange since we are walking on the straight and narrow path of His ways. We are on the narrow road and not the broad road that leads to destruction. Yet, God opens a wide door. What for? For effective ministry. After explaining my situation to Tom Hayes, an extraordinary evangelist, he told me to walk through each door God opens and to enjoy His plan for my life. That is sound advice for me and for you.

Notice that there are many adversaries to each door that God opens. As soon as the door opens, everything that opposes God and the ministry comes storming through like a flash flood. The great thing is that God has open doors for us. Paul said that his was opened up "to me..." So, God personally opens up doors for each and every one of His children. It is your personal door. It is a wide door; it is an effective door. The enemy lurks behind the door.

When God calls He also enables us. He will help you accomplish His will. If you have children, this is a wide door for effective ministry. The door may be shut on your marriage, but as God heals your spirit a door for effective ministry will fling wide open. Going through the door will not be easy for two reasons. One is that it is a personal door and you alone must go through it. The other reason is that all the forces of hell will try to keep you from going through. When you go through the door a ministry and a new purpose for your life will open. Jesus said, "Behold, I have set before you an open door, which no one is able to shut" (Revelation 3:8).

Suggested Prayer ———————————————————————
Dear Lord,
Thank You that You have a wide door for me. Give me the courage to walk through the door. Help me have an effective ministry. I ask that You show me the door. Let the ministry change my life and those around me. In the Name above every Name I pray, Amen.

AUGUST 6

Sin's Destructive Path

Ecclesiastes 9:18
Wisdom is better than weapons of war, but one sinner destroys much good.

Solomon tells us that one sinner can destroy much good. It does not take long to see this truth at all. We only make it to Genesis chapter three when we read about the fall of man. The whole world fell under a curse. All our sins, heartaches, sufferings, diseases, and death can all be traced back to Genesis chapter three. One single act did so much harm. The sin was so bad that God Himself left His throne to die for our sins to reverse the effects of man's sin. All our modern-day problems, like war, cancer, AIDS, and starvation have their origins in Adam's transgression.

Your divorce was a result of someone's sin. The effects go way beyond all human comprehension. My son liked Legos when he was young. At Disneyworld he had four special Legos made with our names on them. There were four Legos, one for me, one for his mom, one for his brother, and another for himself. Each Lego had our names on them and a special symbol that represented something that we liked. He fastened all four together and they represented our family. When he realized that his mother was not coming home, he separated the Legos and gave each person their individual brick. We were no longer a family but four separate individuals. Sin had destroyed our home, never to be put back together again. The Lego that I possess is a vivid reminder of sin's destructive path.

You will continue to live with the consequences of the sin of divorce the rest of your life. Thank God we will one day go to meet God in heaven, where all sin and sorrow will be eradicated. May we all do the right thing and do our best to live for Christ.

Suggested Prayer
Lord,
I keep feeling the effects of this divorce. It is tough to bear. Please forgive me for my faults in the divorce. Please give me grace to live through this tough time. In Jesus' Name, Amen.

Get the Proper Rest That You Need

Psalms 127:2

It is vain that you rise up early and go late to rest, eating the bread of anxious toil; for he gives to his beloved sleep.

God created sleep and He intends for all His creation to get proper rest. God rested on the seventh day after creating the world and everything in it in six days. He even instituted a sabbath day of rest. He wants every person to get their proper rest each night.

Why can't we sleep? One reason is that we are trying to work out our problems in our own strength instead of trusting Him. The bedroom is a dark, lonely place when you are used to having a companion sleeping by your side. No one wants to be alone. Your mattress can feel like a morgue. Another reason is that we do not recognize that He is in control of our lives. Still another reason is that we are trying to do too much. One single person cannot do it all. It is too difficult to work, take care of children, cook, maintain a household, and serve God. We must learn to prioritize. We must also learn to let some things go.

Our bodies are drained when we are going through this difficult season. We desperately need proper rest. The devil attacks us when we are tired. Determine today that your body is a temple for the Holy Spirit and that you will get the proper rest. Realize that God is in control and He will help see you through the tough times. Learn to let some things go.

Suggested Prayer

Dear Father,
I have been a nervous wreck, trying to get everything done. Lord, I believe You want me to rest. Help me trust You for the rest. Help me to let go of the less important things so I can rest. In the Name of Jesus I pray, Amen.

Gifts of The Spirit

Romans 12:6-8

Having gifts that differ according to the grace given to us, let us use them: if prophecy, in proportion to our faith; if service, in our serving; the one who teaches, in his teaching; the one who exhorts, in his exhortation; the one who contributes, in generosity; the one who leads, with zeal; the one who does acts of mercy, with cheerfulness.

Every Christian has a gift or gifts from the Holy Spirit. A gift is different from a talent or a natural ability. The hurt of divorce is so intense that God may put on hold some of our gifts so we can take time to heal. God does not take our gifts away. When you have achieved healing God will open doors again to use your gift. The only difference now is that your gift will be used in a greater capacity for God.

In this list, one gift is teaching. Perhaps you had to resign your teaching position due to your divorce. First, God is not finished with you, so keep studying and praying. Secondly, at the right time a teaching opportunity will present itself. A person cannot effectively teach who is overwhelmed with trouble; all lessons will eventually be a discussion of his or her own problems.

However, when God heals a man or woman and the Lord opens doors to teach—look out! Now the teacher is full of the Lord and the power of His might. He is now relying on God and not himself. God is making mighty warriors out of us. He is making champions for His service. Just like David was a shepherd before a king, God is preparing you. Just like Moses, who spent forty years in desolation in the wilderness, God has you in a special place where He can mold you. Do not be discouraged if doors are not opening. A closed door simply means that you need a little more time to heal.

Suggested Prayer

Dear Lord,
I feel so bad because I used to exercise my gift each week at church. Now I feel like I am out on a shelf left to rot. Lord, I realize You did not take away the gift. So, heal me so I can use my gift again. In Jesus' Name I pray, Amen.

God Is in Hot Pursuit

Proverbs 13:21
Disaster pursues sinners, but the righteous are rewarded with good.

We have all watched a show where the police are chasing a criminal. The officer comes on the radio and says, "I am in hot pursuit." What does this mean? It means they are in a fresh pursuit; it is live and happening right now. This is an emergency that requires the officer's and other authorities' undivided attention. We sometimes see the police in hot pursuit, trying to catch a bank robber as he is getting away with the money.

Do you ever think God is in hot pursuit? Well, He is in hot pursuit, but there is no nervousness on His part. For the sinner, evil and disaster are pursuing him. Rest assured, no one gets away with anything. On the surface it may look like the ungodly are prospering. But rest assured, God is in hot pursuit.

How about those of us who are doing good? God is also in hot pursuit to repay us with good. Be confident that God is watching you and sees the good you are doing. He will repay you with good. When? Where? How? We do not know, but it will happen. Can you imagine the heavenly SWAT team surrounding your house? A call comes on the megaphone, "we are here to bless you." Instead of a trip to jail it is a divine visitation of the Holy Spirit blessing you.

Suggested Prayer
Dear Lord,
This seems so weird to me, but Your Word says You will bless me. Lord, help me to do good, not expecting You to bless me. When I least expect it, pour out a blessing. In Jesus' Name I pray, Amen. Thank You, God. Hallelujah!

No One Cares

Psalms 142:4
Look to the right and see: there is none who takes notice of me; no refuge remains to me; no one cares for my soul.

D o you ever feel that way? The psalmist felt like no one cared. It is easy to feel this way if we are not careful. People whom you thought were your friends no longer associate with you. No one at church will stop long enough to listen to you. Coworkers look at you as a complainer. Even family and neighbors seem to isolate themselves from you. Just like the psalmist we feel like no one even notices that we exist.

Friends, God cares! If we could grasp the fact that God is doing a great work in our lives it would help tremendously. Perhaps we trusted friends and family more than God. God wants us to totally depend on Him. Life seems easier when we have friends that care. More than likely, there are some who care about you but just do not know how to minister to you.

Today, dedicate your heart and time to the One who takes notice of you and cares for your soul. Choose to draw closer to God by spending more time in prayer and the reading of His Word. Yes, it is a lonely time; yes, it seems no one cares. So, spend more time with the One who truly cares. Now is the time to grow stronger in your walk with the Lord. At the right time caring friends and a new spouse will come into your life. Who cares? God cares, even to the point of death on a cross.

Suggested Prayer ————————————————————
Dear Lord,
It seems like no one notices or cares, but you notice me and care for me. So, let me grow deeper spiritually. Help me walk with You. Please send some friends and a godly spouse. In Jesus' Name, Amen.

God Will Take Care of You

Philippians 4:19
And my God will supply every need of yours according to his riches in glory in Christ Jesus.

P aul told the Philippians that his God would supply all their needs. The church at Philippi had supplied the needs of Paul, and God would honor their giving by supplying all their needs. Our needs are not supplied with our riches, but with His riches in glory. We must do our part. Decide that you will be a giver and a supplier of other people's needs.

You are probably going through great financial difficulty but that does not mean you are useless or helpless. Now would be a good time to dedicate everything you have to God, especially your finances. Paul did not give this promise to just anyone. The recipients of this promise were those who were supplying the needs of others. Paul used the possessive pronoun "my" in this verse. If you can say He is *my* God, then you should have no problem trusting Him to supply your needs. God will supply your needs! Our needs are met in Christ Jesus. He is our biggest need. Fall in love with Jesus afresh! Begin to tithe. Begin to look for ways to supply the needs of others. Soon you will find all your needs supplied.

You might be thinking your financial situation is impossible. We have a God who specializes in the impossible. The things that are impossible with man are possible with Him, so He can receive the glory and not us. Pray about your needs and reach out in practical ways to supply the needs of others. If you see a need and you can help, do not hesitate to supply that need.

Suggested Prayer
Dear Lord,
I give my life and possessions to You. Lord, I give my finances to You. Help me to tithe. Help me to meet the needs of others. You are my God and You will supply my needs. In Jesus' Name I pray, Amen.

Go to His House and Beat Him Up

1 Samuel 26:10
And David said, "As the LORD lives, the LORD will strike him, or his day will come to die, or he will go down into battle and perish."

King Saul wanted David dead because God had chosen him to be the new king. Saul knew this and was trying to prevent this from happening. One night while Saul and his army slept, David and his nephew Abishai came across Saul and his army. Saul was fast asleep and his spear lay by his side. Abishai told David that he could go down and strike him dead and relieve David of his foe. But David had a high respect for the office of the king and realized that God would not be happy if they killed Saul. David said, "the LORD will strike him, or his day will come to die…" David realized God was in control, and that he did not need to do anything. God would take care of Saul in His own way. Either God would kill Saul, or he would die in battle, or he might grow old and die. David knew God had a plan to make him the new king and He would work it all out.

When my ex cheated on me someone told me to go over to the man's house and beat him up. Part of me laughed inside and part of me said that's not a bad idea. We must, like David, realize that our weapons are not physical but spiritual. I was not in a physical battle but a spiritual war. Getting in a fight would not solve anything. In fact, it is a good way to get shot (everyone has a gun in Texas).

When there is a third party involved it is almost impossible to reconcile a marriage. It there is just a husband and wife involved there is a great chance that with proper counseling things will work out. Experience proves that if a man has a girlfriend or a woman has a boyfriend, it will be almost impossible to reconcile the marriage. A fist fight or worse is a very bad idea. We must, like David, realize God is in control and He will handle it. If we try to handle it we will sin against God. The Lord will take care of the culprits in His own way, like He took care of Saul for David.

Suggested Prayer
Lord,
It is hard to be still when I see what has happened to me. Lord, keep me from revenge and sinning against You. I dedicate the whole situation to You, knowing that You will take care of it. In Jesus' Name, Amen.

Plenty or Poverty

Proverbs 21:5
The plans of the diligent lead surely to abundance, but everyone who is hasty comes only to poverty.

I f we had to vote I think we would all chose plenty. The Bible does not teach us that we will all be rich with material blessings. It is a wonderful idea, but it is just not taught in the pages of the Holy Scriptures. However, God does bless diligent efforts. Those who plan and diligently think things through will be blessed. Those who make quick decisions without really thinking about the consequences will suffer for it.

Some of us never had to think much about finances until the divorce happened. Now we are forced to think about money and to be diligent with it. Some go hastily out and buy things for themselves to fill a void in their lives. The new car, new clothes, boat, etc. are all nice until we find ourselves in insurmountable debt. When we accumulate debt, we are not free to serve God. God cannot give us a new spouse because we cannot take care of him or her. Hasty decisions are deadly.

My divorce was a blessing in disguise. The divorce put me in a very difficult financial situation. My finances were so bad that I had to really make some wise money decisions. I found out what coupons, online surveys, rebates, and sales were all about. I also discovered the difference between a want and a need. The road was rough, but those decisions helped me get through the tough times. I developed a mindset that will help me for the rest of my life. If my divorce would not have happened, I would probably still be making hasty decisions.

Suggested Prayer —————————————————————————————
Dear Lord,
Help all of us to make diligent decisions with our finances. Give us wisdom. Help us have a mindset that will lead to abundance. Bless us financially, that we might be a blessing to others. In Jesus Name I pray, Amen.

God's Hand Is a Lifting Hand

Isaiah 41:10
Fear not, for I am with you; be not dismayed, for I am your God; I will strengthen you, I will help you, I will uphold you with my righteous right hand.

God's hands are very interesting. Jesus touched Peter's mother-in-law, and she was healed. God brought the children of Israel out of Egyptian bondage with His strong right hand. In the scriptures the right hand is always a symbol of power. Most people are stronger in their right hand. Even some left-handed people are stronger in their right hand. A hand can be a source of power, and it can be very gentle. Some Christians speak of just holding on a little longer as they go through some trial. The text tells us not to fear because the One True God is our God. We do not serve an idol fashioned with the hands of men. We worship the Lord whose hands were pierced for our salvation.

God also said that He would strengthen us. He will replace our strength with His strength. When we have no strength, His hand touches us and we receive strength. He said, "I will help you." Read that again. Is it true? Yes, it is true. God will help us in His time and in His way. He said he would uphold us, lift us up, with His right hand. It is not just any hand. It is the right hand which tells us of His power. Not only is it a right hand, it is a righteous right hand. He will do what is right.

We do not always do right, but God does. We can picture someone falling farther and farther into the depths of despair. There is no hope on the horizon. Suddenly God's righteous right hand comes and lifts them up. He lifts them out of the pit of despair and places them in His kingdom. He holds them now and throughout eternity. His right hand never grows tired or weary. As He keeps them lifted, He takes away the fear, He strengthens them, and He helps them. Brethren, fear not! The righteous right hand of God will lift you up and sustain you through this season in your life.

Suggested Prayer
Dear Father,
Lift me up today. I am full of fear and there seems to be no hope. God, Your hand is a powerful hand, so lift me up and strengthen me. Lord, please help me. I wait for your help; hold on to me with Your hand. In Jesus' Name I pray, Amen.

AUGUST 15

God's Hand Is A Loving Hand

Isaiah 41:13
For I, the LORD your God, hold your right hand; it is I who say to you, "Fear not, I am the one who helps you."

God's hands are awesome and beyond all human comprehension. Jesus touched the blind and they received their sight. He touched a coffin with a dead person in it and raised him from the dead. He touched the deaf and they were able to hear. He touched the lepers and they were cleansed of their leprosy. Yes, it is a loving gentle hand that our God possesses.

This text says that He is holding onto our right hand. The right hand, as we have seen, is the hand of strength. We could say the Lord is our strength. As the Almighty holds our hand He whispers into our ears, "Fear not, I am the one who helps you." There is nothing to fear because God is holding onto us. As we walk through the valley of the shadow of death, He is holding our hand. As your world crumbles around you He is holding your hand. When bad news hits He is holding your hand.

When my ex-wife told me that she was leaving I was devastated, but God was there holding my hand. I went to the park to try to find some sort of peace. As I sat on a picnic table, I cried out to God and told Him that I needed someone to talk to. About thirty minutes later an older couple from India came and sat beside me. The man began to share the gospel with me, and I told him that I was already a Christian. Then I could not keep back the tears and they began to flow as I shared my story with him. At this point he took me by my hand and began to pray for me and my sons. He gave me his phone number and email address, and told me that his home was open to me 24 hours a day. As he held my hand, I pictured my heavenly Father holding my hand. To me, this was a miracle from God, and a day that I will never forget.

By the way, the man's name is Abraham John. He is named after the missionaries that brought the gospel to India and were instrumental in his salvation. Friends it is a loving hand that reaches around this world, touching lives and changing hearts. So, when you are all alone close your eyes and see that God is holding your hand too.

Suggested Prayer
Dear Lord, thank You that You are holding my hand. Thank You for the still small voice that says, "Fear not, I am the one who helps you." God, take away the fear and strengthen my weak hands. Thank You for Your loving hands. In Jesus Name I pray, Amen.

The Lord's Hand Is a Long Hand

Isaiah 59:1

Behold, the LORD'S hand is not shortened, that it cannot save, or his ear dull, that it cannot hear...

You and I are limited in what we can do with our hands. This is not the case with God. I remember a commercial where some friends are out to eat, and the check comes. One man offers to pay the bill for everyone, then he suddenly turns into an alligator and his hands just can't seem to reach the check. God does not have alligator arms. Sometimes we withhold our hand from helping others for some reason. At times we are dull of hearing and we do not listen to people or God. God said that He would hear us unless we willfully rebel against Him and refuse to confess our sins.

God's hand is a long hand, attached to a long arm. On the cross Jesus' arms were spread wide and His hands were pierced. Those hands have reached the world with the good news that Jesus saves. God is all powerful and can save anyone. He is also able to deliver us from any situation. Oh, that we would see our God as the all-powerful God who is working on our behalf! God hears the honest prayers and cries of His children. He made the ear, and He hears.

Do not be discouraged today. There is a God who has heard your cries. He also has a long hand that will bring about a change in your life. God is going to do something great for You. The same God that brought Israel out of Egypt with a mighty hand will bring you out. God can save, He can sustain, and He can satisfy. Do not give up, because the long hand of God is going to save you. He is going to do something for you! It will be so great a deliverance that You will praise Him the rest of your life. Amen and Amen.

Suggested Prayer

Dear Lord,
I have fallen short so many times and given up. Today let me see You high and lifted up. Let me see that You have heard my cries and are working on my behalf. Let me see that Your powerful hand is about to bring deliverance in my life. I give You all the praise for what You are about to do. In Jesus' Name I pray, Hallelujah!

The Lord's Hand Is a Laboring Hand

Isaiah 64:8

But now, O LORD, you are our Father; we are the clay, and you are our potter; we are all the work of your hand.

God is always working everywhere. The hand of God is at work in a sunset as well as a Sunday service. What an encouragement to know that the hand of God is working in our hearts and orchestrating something great for all of us. Our verse is quick to point out that He is our parent as well as our potter. We are the children as well as the clay.

As a Father to His child, His hand is working for our good. He is working to bring about a nice life for His children. His hand is giving good gifts to His children. As a potter, He is constantly working to make us vessels of honor.

So much goes into making a clay pot. The clay must be pliable so the potter can work with it. If it is not pliable the potter will soak the clay in water to make it pliable. God works our hearts over with His Word to make us pliable clay. All the air bubbles must be removed from the clay before it can be placed in a kiln. If the air bubbles are not removed the pot will explode in the oven. God is working diligently to get these air bubbles out of our lives so we can stand the heat of the furnace. If we work ahead of God and try to do it ourselves, the result will be a shattered life.

When the potter makes a jar he always starts on the inside. He works from the inside out, just like our Father. God takes His time; let Him take His time. If we rush things, we will not be effective for His service. The clay does not have a voice in the potter's plan. We must completely surrender to God if He is to be our potter. If we allow God to work, He can proceed to put us in the fire. Out of the fire comes a vessel that God can use.

God is a laboring God. He is working diligently with His hand to make you a vessel that He can use and that He can bless. His hand will be working on you until He takes you home to heaven. Why not submit to Him and allow Him to make you a vessel of honor?

Suggested Prayer

Lord,
You are my Father and I am the child. Lord, I submit to Your authority as my Heavenly Father. Lord, You are the Potter and I am the clay, so I surrender to You. Comfort my heart. I know that You are constantly working in my life. Thank You, Lord, Amen.

The Lord's Hand Is a Lasting Hand

Isaiah 49:16
Behold, I have engraved you on the palms of my hands; your walls are continually before me.

God put the names of Israel on the palms of His hands, and this speaks of permanence. Their names were engraved like someone chiseling them in stone. In the Old Testament the high priest would bear the names of Israel on his priestly garment. There were jewels engraved that were on his shoulders and over his heart.

God's engraving is everlasting because it is in the palms of His hand. The mention of walls in this verse means that God has not forgotten His people; He will protect them and be with them. He loves the nation of Israel with an everlasting love. The lasting hand of the Lord will never expire or change because their names are etched into His very being.

The good news also applies to the Christian. We are engraved in the palms of Jesus. He engraved our names into His everlasting palms at Calvary. There He gave His hands to the Roman soldiers who drove the stakes into His palms. If you ever doubt God's love for you, just gaze into those nail-pierced hands. Even in heaven we will see the prints in His palms.

God gave us everlasting life when He saved us. Our walls are not physical walls around a city. Our walls are the Holy Spirit who sealed us to the day of redemption. Friends, the everlasting hand of our Savior has brought about everlasting life for you and me. Sorrow may come in the night, but joy comes in the morning.

The disciple Thomas said he would not believe in the resurrection unless he could put his fingers through the palms of Jesus' hands. When Jesus appeared to him Thomas said, "My Lord and my God," and he forgot all about the palms. God has you in the palms of His hands, etched forever with your name written in the Lamb's Book of Life. Your suffering is temporary—your salvation is eternal.

Suggested Prayer

Lord,
Thank You that my salvation is eternal. My suffering seems hard to bear, but I know You have a purpose. Thank You that I am sealed with the Holy Spirit. Lord, I can't wait to see You and thank You for all that You have done for me. Thank You for Your everlasting hand that brought about my eternal salvation. In Jesus' Name I pray, Amen.

I Had to Give Up Too Much

Romans 8:32

He who did not spare his own Son but gave him up for us all, how will he not also with him graciously give us all things?

I must admit that I have often felt like I had to give up too much because of the divorce. We all have some sad stories to tell about the things that we lost. I had a big collection of Star Wars items that I had collected over the past thirty-eight years. I tried and tried to hold onto the collection, but it eventually had to go. Perhaps Luke Skywalker found a better home —who knows. This might not mean much to you, but that collection was my pride and joy. I had spaceships, action figures, light sabers, and even cups. I might have had more toys than all the children on my city block combined. Go ahead and laugh at me, it is alright and justifiable. Did I give up too much? No, because my divorce has brought me into a deeper relationship with Christ.

What did God have to give up when we divorced ourselves from Him by sinning against Him? We do not stop to think about the cost God had to pay to redeem us. Well, the Father did not have to give up His collection. He had to give up His Son. He could have held onto His Son and let us all perish, but He decided that we were too valuable to just let go. So, He did not spare Jesus but gave Him up for us. We are saved because the Father gave the Son as our sacrifice.

Not only are we saved, we are satisfied, because God our Father and the Lord Jesus Christ are both freely and graciously giving us the things that we need. God can and does supply our needs. How? It is through Christ that my needs are supplied. Notice that word "all" in this verse. The word "all" is used two times. The sacrifice of Jesus was for all people. It is a gift available for all. The second "all" shows that "all things" will be given to us. God wants to save and satisfy all people. Did you give up too much?

Suggested Prayer ————————————————————————————————

Dear Lord,
Forgive me! I have complained about all the things I had to give up. I realize now that You had to lose everything too. Lord, thank You that I am saved. Thank you for satisfying me by supplying my needs. Lord, help me to be more like You. In Jesus' Name I pray, Amen.

God Is My Portion

Psalms 142:5

I cry to you, O LORD; I say, "You are my refuge, my portion in the land of the living."

We all want our portion. When parents die the siblings fight and bicker over what is left in the home. Everyone wants their fair share. The Bible tells us that *we* are God's portion. We are what God is investing in. Of all the things God could invest in, He chose us.

In this verse we see that He is *our* portion. He is a God that we can cry out to because He hears our cries and sees our pain. He is also our refuge. He is our shelter in this land. He is our portion in this life or "the land of the living," as described in the text. He is our portion in this life and in the life to come. When we come to the end of life the only thing we will take with us is God. He truly is our portion and there is no other allotment. We will not take any money, houses or lands with us.

Since He is our portion our prayers should be that we possess Him in all His fulness. Our focus should be solely on Him. What is your portion? What are you striving for? Are we striving for temporary things or for the Eternal One? He is my portion right now and through eternity. I want all of Him. Let the things of earth lose their grip on us as we pursue our God. May our hearts and minds be consumed with Jesus and His Kingdom. May we receive all that He has for us. Our fair share is Jesus Christ. Amen.

Suggested Prayer

Lord,
You are my portion. I can cry out to You. You are my refuge. Lord, I commit myself to You. May my soul be entirely focused on You. May I have a double portion of You. In Jesus' Name, Amen.

The Lord Loves You and Will Lead the Way

Psalms 143:8

Let me hear in the morning of your steadfast love, for in you I trust. Make me know the way I should go, for to you I lift up my soul.

The psalmist placed his complete trust in God and wanted to know of the Lord's great love for him. He wanted to hear of this love in the morning as he started out the day. Too many times our day is gone and we never once thought that God loves us. No wonder our day was horrible! We have placed our trust in a loving God. We need to wake up, knowing He loves us.

A dear sister in Christ sent me a message in Mandarin. The message came from Hong Kong, about 8,354 miles away from my home. Actually, the message came from the very throne of God to reach my poor soul. I translated the message in great anticipation, wondering what the message said. The translation was simple: "Jesus loves you." The results were indescribable. I had goosebumps all over me as the Holy Spirit made that word real in my heart. She has sent that same message to me several times and it never gets old. It is the most profound truth in the whole Bible.

Not only did the psalmist want to know of God's love, he also wanted to know the way to go. He had given his soul to God and was expecting Him to lead the way. God will show us the way to go in His time and not ours. What a comfort! The God of the universe loves me and will show me the way to go. What is our job in all of this? We must really trust Him and give ourselves to Him daily.

Suggested Prayer

Dear Lord,

Forgive me. I have doubted Your love and leading. It seems like You do not love me and that You are punishing me. I realize now that You do love me and will lead me through the trial. Forgive me for doubting. In the Name of Jesus I pray, Amen.

The Need for Trials

1 Peter 1:6-7

In this you rejoice, though now for a little while, if necessary, you have been grieved by various trials, so that the tested genuineness of your faith—more precious than gold that perishes though it is tested by fire—may be found to result in praise and glory and honor at the revelation of Jesus Christ.

Did you ever think you would come to the place where you would see the great need for trials in your life? Can you say, "God, I needed a divorce. I needed the financial struggles. I needed the loneliness, heartache, and suffering?" Does it sound crazy? When God does His perfect work in you it will change your perspective. What you thought was the end was just the beginning. God allowed the divorce and all that goes with it to get you closer to Him. You now know what is important in life.

We have a salvation in Him that is reserved for us in heaven. We are kept by His great power. He is working in us and through us to accomplish His great will. Peter does not deny that these things are painful and weigh our spirits down. In fact, without God they are horrible. Yet the day is coming when you will be able to say you needed these trials. When you reach that point, look out! God has healed your heart. When you are healed, He will open up a new chapter in your life. God does not hate you and He is not cruel. He is a God of love and mercy and grace. He loves you with an everlasting love. Do not try to fake your feelings; be real with God. One day you will say, "I needed that." If it is not now that is fine. Let God continue to heal your broken spirit. God bless you.

Suggested Prayer

God,
I want a complete healing so I can realize I needed the trials that came my way. Lord, I have never seen pain or difficulty as a need for my development. Help me see my need because of all the pain that I am going through. In Jesus' Name I pray, Amen.

The Bears Come Home to Roost

Proverbs 17:12
Let a man meet a she-bear robbed of her cubs rather than a fool in his folly.

W hen our spirits are defeated, we are tempted to do some foolish things. Before your divorce you would never dream of going out and doing something crazy. You were able to see the consequences miles away. You could see the potential damage, so you chose to do the right thing. We know and believe that we will reap what we sow. It would be better to meet an enraged she-bear robbed of her cubs, ready to shred someone to bits, than to meet up with our sin. Sin devastates and assassinates.

So why do we want to go out and sin, knowing the consequences? It is because we hurt so bad that we do not care anymore. We feel so low that we do not care. We are looking for satisfaction in life. We think it cannot possibly get any worse. It can get a lot worse and will get worse if we deliberately choose to sin.

What is the solution? We must begin to care again. How? Why? It all starts with our relationship with God. He still loves and cares for you. Just because we feel bad and things look bad does not mean that God doesn't care anymore. Actually, His love for us has never changed. Meditate on what you possess in Christ. Then see your worth in Christ and see that your children need you too. When the bears come home to roost it will be deadly. Sin always brings death. Ask God to help you, right here, right now.

Suggested Prayer ————————————————————
Lord,
I must admit I don't care, and I ask not that You will help me. Make me see Your great love for me. Lord, it seems like You don't care. Help me care again. Amen.

What Does God Take Pleasure In?

Psalms 147:10-11

His delight is not in the strength of the horse, nor his pleasure in the legs of a man, but the LORD takes pleasure in those who fear him, in those who hope in his steadfast love.

People find enjoyment in various things. Some things are good, some are not so good. What does God take pleasure in? He does not take pleasure in the strength of the horse or the legs of a person. In other words, the person who is trusting his own abilities and resources is pleasing himself and not God. Our loving Savior must wear us down to let us see that our own strength will not get the job done. He also dwindles our resources to let us see that our resources will not get the job done. Hopefully by now we have realized that our strength and abilities are useless in a spiritual battle. If the battle were physical our "horse" and "legs" would be awesome assets in the fight. However, we are in a spiritual battle and we need spiritual weapons.

How can we please God? We can please Him by having a fear of Him. This does not mean that He is some cosmic bully and that I should hide from Him. What it means is that I have a reverent respect for Him, recognizing that He oversees everything, including me. Along with this fear we must patiently wait for His loving mercy. We often become impatient and rely on "horse" and "leg." The results are defeat, depression, and frustration. When we fear Him and wait on His mercy there is spiritual victory. The results please God and it brings peace in our lives.

Suggested Prayer ———————————————————————

Dear Lord,
I grew impatient and tried to do it all myself. Now I am frustrated and mad. Lord, forgive me. Let me realize my strength comes from You. Let me please You by having a fear of You, and patiently waiting for You to act on my behalf. In Jesus Name I pray, Amen.

Is Your House in Order?

1 Corinthians 14:40
But all things should be done decently and in order.

When writing to the church at Corinth, Paul wanted them to conduct their services honorably and orderly. He wanted the church to use the gift of tongues and prophesy in an orderly fashion. We must have order to be effective.

My home was not in order. Household chores were neglected, simply because I did not care. I lost all hope that things would get better. Then God gave me a change of heart and I began to have hope again. I made a list of responsibilities for the home and we began to clean the house again. Before long we were thinking of creative ways to make the home look better. We even felt better about ourselves when we came home to an orderly house.

Every member of the house should get involved. The cleaning of the home should be a team effort. Chores should be age appropriate. I remember driving home one evening thinking I needed to take down the Christmas tree and the lights off the house. When I arrived home all the lights were off the house. The tree was in the backyard and all the ornaments and decorations were in the attic. My two sons did all this while I was at work. The only problem with this is that my boys were ten and twelve at the time. They were too young to be on extension ladders and climbing in the attic. I did not yell at them but asked them to check with me before doing any special projects. Where do you start with cleaning your home? It all starts when your hope is renewed.

Suggested Prayer
Dear Lord,
My home is a mess because I am a mess. Lord, restore my hope so I can live again. My house is a direct reflection of my heart. Give me hope and help me come up with an orderly plan to maintain the home. In Jesus' Name I pray, Amen.

A Wife or a Husband Is a Good Thing

Proverbs 18:22
He who finds a wife finds a good thing and obtains favor from the LORD.

Please keep in mind that Solomon is writing the book of Proverbs to his son. If he had written to his daughter he would have said, "She who finds a husband finds a good thing and obtains favor from the LORD." So, for a man or a woman to find a spouse is a good thing. Why? Because the person God wants you to have is a good person. It is also not good to be alone. Marriage also brings God's favor. God also shows favor to the single person; so do not be discouraged. God blesses married people in a special way.

If it is good to be married and we obtain God's favor if we are married, where do we find him or her? First of all, make sure that you are healed and ready. This is vital. Secondly, let God do it. There is nothing wrong with dating sites if you like that sort of thing. I tried them and met some very nice people. A friend of mine says that you must know your ABP's meaning: "always be playing." He does not mean this in an immoral sense. He means to be friendly wherever you go because you never know when you will meet the right one. I told him I liked that and told him about my ABP's meaning: "always be praying." He liked that too and we both became the laughingstock of our coworkers as they overheard our conversations.

I was praying at my house, and as soon as I said Amen, a sister at a nearby church sent me a text and told me about her friend that I should meet. Put God first, let Him lead you, and He will direct your path. If He can create heaven and earth and number the stars and the sand on the beaches, surely He can send you an awesome spouse. God wants to bless you! If it has not happened for you yet, perhaps He is still healing you and preparing you.

Suggested Prayer
Lord,
I want to be a good spouse and I want a good spouse. I do not want to live alone any more than I must. I do not know where to start so I give myself to You. Please lead, guide, and direct me. In Jesus' Name I pray, Amen.

We Need to Be Taught

Psalms 143:10

Teach me to do your will, for you are my God! Let your good Spirit lead me on level ground!

The psalmist asked God to teach him to do the Lord's will. We must be taught to do His bidding; that is why He gave us the Holy Spirit. Notice that the Spirit is a *good* Spirit. There are other spirits in this world, and they are not good. The good Spirit will lead us to level ground. When we realize that God is our Lord and we yield to His Spirit, we begin to do His will.

Perhaps your divorce has shown you that you are not doing God's will. Perhaps you have been listening to the wrong spirit. By now, hopefully you have come to realize that God's will is the most important thing for you. Sometimes we must be stripped down to nothing before we decide that we need to serve God. Thank God for the good Spirit who comforts our souls.

Our lives have been shaken down to its very core. Our foundations have all crumbled. Wait! At the point of surrender God puts us on a solid foundation. That foundation is Christ Himself. As we daily yield to Him we find ourselves in the middle of God's will, being led by the good Holy Spirit. Look at your divorce as a recommissioning of God's will for your life. There is a great plan out there for you and the good Spirit will lead you into this plan.

Suggested Prayer ———————————————————————

Dear Lord,

I have listened to some spirits that were not from You. Lord, it brought about anger and hatred and depression in my life. Lord, I confess these things and ask that You will lead me from this day forth. I give up my will to do Your will. In Jesus' Name, Amen.

Denying Christ

Mark 14:72
And immediately the rooster crowed a second time. And Peter remembered how Jesus had said to him, "Before the rooster crows twice, you will deny me three times." And he broke down and wept.

We tend to beat up on poor Peter, but we are guilty of the same faults and failures. Peter had good intentions but when Jesus was arrested, he denied any association with Him. Peter would later feel sorry for his sins and confess them. He would become a shining light for God. He would write two New Testament books and become a pillar of the Jerusalem church. He would preach a sermon and 3,000 people would be saved. What was the difference? Previously, Peter tried to serve God in his own power and eventually denied ever knowing Jesus. When he repented, he began to rely on God, and the Lord worked through him in a mighty way.

We must guard our hearts against denying our Lord. If we are relying on our own power, there is coming a day when we will deny Him. We are at a crossroad in life. We can denounce our old life and begin to walk with God, or we can go the path of self and walk the road of bitter tears. We are all sinners and it is impossible to be sinless in this life. But we can lean on God and let Him use us, even though we may commit an occasional sin. We should never intentionally sin.

Have you ever cut a person's ear off? Peter did. Have you ever denied any and all affiliation with Jesus? Peter did. However, Peter had such an inward transformation that God was able to use him in miraculous ways. Are you depending on yourself or God? If the answer is self, you too are denying the Lord.

Suggested Prayer
*Dear Lord,
Like Peter, I have tried to do it all myself. Lord, I failed. Now, God, I ask that You teach me how to rely on You. Lord, use me in a mighty way. In the Name of Jesus I pray, Amen.*

AUGUST 29

Defuse the Dynamite

Proverbs 15:1
A soft answer turns away wrath, but a harsh word stirs up anger.

W hat happens when two bitter people begin to argue? Well, I do not have to tell you because you have probably yelled at your ex-spouse or he or she has yelled at you. More than likely both of you have yelled at each other. The kids heard it too. Unfortunately, this is where we live. In a perfect world there are no divorces or arguments.

I can personally recall saying some hurtful things to my ex-wife. Yes, the kids heard too. Harsh words stir up anger. You answer their question loudly and roughly and it stirs their spirit to answer in a similar manner. Before you know it, each person is yelling at the other. Who knows what kind of damage this is doing to the kids if they are around?

You be the one to defuse the argument. When your ex comes at you in full force, take the advice of Solomon. Answer back with a tender, kind word. When they come at you the second time, answer with a kind word. Keep this up. Eventually you will defuse the explosion that was about to take place. Now the two of you can discuss things. Now the children see their parents acting like adults instead of kids themselves. Do your part to defuse the dynamite. If the dynamite explodes the results will be fatal. Ask God to help you answer with kind words. Realize that you will be tested, but with His help you can do it.

Suggested Prayer
Lord,
I have said some rough things and I am sorry. Forgive me. Lord, I know I will be tested in this area so help me learn to answer with tender words. Let my conversations with my ex be God-honoring and let my children see that I am trying to do the right thing. In Jesus' Name, Amen.

Use Good Sense to Overlook the Offense

Proverbs 19:11
Good sense makes one slow to anger, and it is his glory to overlook an offense.

If anyone has the right to hold a grudge or not forgive someone, it is probably you. The hurt you have been through is great and might be the worst hurt that you will ever go through. There are the so-called friends that do not even talk to you now. There are those church members who distance themselves from you. How could your husband or wife do this to you? How could you have deserved all of this? You did not deserve any of it, but it fell into your lap and now you must deal with it.

Exercise some good old-fashioned common sense when dealing with all of this. Look at all the angles. We tend to only see our angle. Our angle is something like, "I am hurt, and it is all their fault." Forgive the person or persons that have hurt you. We know that God is always faithful to forgive us when we sin. We must confess our own sins. He might not take away the consequences of our sin, but he always forgives us.

Let there be honor or glory in forgiving those who have caused us the most harm. It seems strange but there is great honor in forgiving. This act brings healing to us and others. It glorifies our Lord and Savior. There are great things that happen when we forgive; there is great power in forgiveness. There is honor and glory in forgiveness. God will use your testimony to help others. Exercise common sense against the offense and watch God work a miracle in your life.

Suggested Prayer
Now, Lord, I want to honor You. I want to bring glory to Your name. I want to see Your power. Lord, I want to experience a miracle. I want to testify about Your love and forgiveness. Lord, give me good sense and a forgiving spirit. In Jesus' Name I pray, Amen.

Stay the Course

Colossians 4:17

And say to Archippus, "See that you fulfill the ministry that you have received in the Lord."

We have all received a ministry in the Lord. As we read the Bible we see that some were apostles, deacons, missionaries, prophets, and teachers. God had specific men and women that He chose to fulfill a certain aspect of ministry. Sometimes we think that ministry does not apply to us today or we think the pastoral staff are the ministers.

Every person has a ministry that God wants them to carry out or fulfill. Look at your divorce as a crucial turning point in your life to fulfill the ministry that God has called you to do. If you are already involved in ministry, stay the course. If you are not involved, begin to ask God what He would have you do with the rest of your time on earth. We all need to be spurred on in this idea of ministry or this verse would not be in the Bible. Archippus needed to be reminded to fulfill the ministry; we also need to be reminded. It is so easy to fall into self-pity and bitterness that we forget all about our service in the Lord. It is also easy to fall into sin and be ineffective for the Lord.

Today decide that You will live for the Lord. Get on the right course, then stay the course. God still uses and gives ministries to divorced people. If you do not know where to start call your pastor. His insight into your situation and his knowledge in the Word will help you find a place of service. Most churches have a whole lot of need and very little help. Along with talking with the pastor, pray and pray some more. The Holy Spirit will speak to you in your prayer time and show you a path to take. Read the scriptures too. Some people have been led into a ministry because a particular verse spoke to them. A seeking heart will find a ministry that is from God. Whatever door God opens, walk through it and stay the course. When you are faithful with one task God will give you a bigger task. Oh, that God would raise up a mighty army of men and women that will fulfill their ministries in the Lord. My friends, stay the course.

Suggested Prayer

Dear Lord, I have gotten sidetracked with the ministry and what my purpose is on earth. Lord, I recommit myself to You. I ask that You use me in a mighty way. Lord, let the temporary things of this world fade away in my life and may I be caught up in Your service. Let me find the course You have for me and then give me the grace to stay the course. In the Name of Jesus I pray, Amen.

SEPTEMBER 1

God Knows Our Sorrows

Exodus 3:7
Then the LORD said, "I have surely seen the affliction of my people who are in Egypt and have heard their cry because of their taskmasters. I know their sufferings…"

God is not an inactive force in the universe. In this passage God is calling Moses to deliver the children of Israel out of Egypt. God has seen their affliction all along. He has heard every cry for help. God saw the Egyptians treating His people poorly. They were all slaves in Egypt. God knew their sorrow. It is not the fact that God sees, hears, and knows, it is that He is about to do something about it. He is about to bring Israel out of Egypt, by His power through His servant Moses. These people suffered tremendously. God knew all their troubles intimately. They were born as slaves, lived as slaves, and would have died as slaves if God did not intervene.

This is also a picture of our human condition. We are born sinners, live as sinners, and will die as sinners unless God intervenes. God did intervene by sending a Deliverer in Jesus Christ. God does not want us to die in our sins. The slavery was harsh, and they were truly suffering because of the sins of others. Today you might be suffering due to no fault of your own. Rest assured, God has seen your affliction and your sorrow and He has heard your cries. He also is bringing deliverance. At the right time you are coming out of this bitter bondage.

Suggested Prayer
*Dear Lord,
I cry out to You. I am suffering and sorrowful. Lord, I feel that I am suffering because of the sins of others. Lord, I know You have heard and seen my sorrow. By faith I believe You are sending a deliverer. Lord, help me hold on until my deliverance comes. By faith I also believe You have heard and are sending deliverance. Thank You, Lord, Amen.*

Deliverance Is Coming

Exodus 3:8

...and I have come down to deliver them out of the hand of the Egyptians and to bring them up out of that land to a good and broad land, a land flowing with milk and honey, to the place of the Canaanites...

God, seeing the afflictions of Israel, hearing their cries and knowing their sorrow, decided that He Himself would come down to deliver Israel out of Egypt. He chose Moses to be the deliverer, but it was God working in and through Moses that got the job done. Moses was a conduit for God. God Himself came down to help through His servant Moses. God was bringing them out of Egypt and bringing them into a good, spacious land. The land would flow with goodness. They would inherit houses that they did not build. Even today the nation of Israel supplies Europe with fruits and vegetables.

God knew your trouble long before it ever happened to you. God cares and sees your sorrows. The great news is that God is bringing deliverance to you. He Himself is coming down to help you. He is bringing you out of your bondage and bringing you to a place of blessing. God is going to bless you in such a way that you will be a blessing to others.

When will my deliverance come? I do not know but I do know that it is coming. He loves you and sees your pain. Someday soon, suddenly, unexpectedly your deliverance will come. God will sweep down like an eagle and change your situation instantly. Just as there was a day that Israel left Egypt, there is coming a day of deliverance for you. Continue to cry out to God. Continue to be faithful. Deliverance is in the forecast.

Suggested Prayer

Dear Lord,
I know You have seen my sorrow. I also believe You are coming to deliver me. Thank You that You are going to deliver me from my afflictions. Amen.

All Things Are Possible with God

Mark 10:27

Jesus looked at them and said, "With man it is impossible, but not with God. For all things are possible with God."

J esus had told the disciples that is difficult for a rich person to enter heaven. There is nothing wrong with being rich, but when our faith is in riches and we can do everything in our own power, it becomes difficult to be saved or trust God. Peter asked Jesus, "Who can be saved?" Jesus said that it is impossible for a man to save himself. Each person who tries to enter heaven on his or her own merits will always fall short of the prize. Salvation is impossible with man's power or ability.

Do you know how many people are in heaven that saved themselves or entered by some great work that they did? Zero! There is no one in heaven who made it there on their own efforts. We cannot do anything without God. However, God says all things are possible with God. He can do anything, anytime, and anywhere. There are no limits to God's power. Everything is possible with God.

Friend, do you need a Savior? It is impossible for you to save yourself, but God can save you. What do you need today? It is impossible for you or else you would not have this tremendous need. Come to God today and give Him your need. Believe that He will help you. There is nothing too hard for Him. If you have prayed and the need is still not supplied, then pray for wisdom so God can show you why the need is not being met. God wants to help! He is able to help, and He will help! He specializes in impossibilities. This is where faith and obedience come in. God will do the impossible for you.

Suggested Prayer ─────────────────────────────

Dear Lord,
My situation has been impossible! I acknowledge that I cannot do it without You. Lord, I prayed and nothing happened. So today I ask for wisdom to know what I need to do. I believe You will show me the way. In Jesus' Name I pray, Amen.

Temptation

Job 31:1

I have made a covenant with my eyes; how then could I gaze at a virgin?

Job had already decided that whatever happened to him, he was going to live right. His wife was disconnected from him emotionally and physically. His wealth, health, and children were all gone. His friends were used by Satan to crush his spirit. Job's ego and manhood were at a zero. Job could have gone into town to find someone to give his manhood a boost and to relieve some of his pain; after all, didn't he deserve to have some young lady boost his ego? Job's response was proper in the eyes of God. He placed his trust in God and relied on the Savior to help him. In the end Job's marriage was renewed. He and his wife were intimate once again and had more children. Job's life turned out well.

What if he had made that trip into town and had visited places that are forbidden for the Christian? What if he would have started sleeping around with other women? The results would have been completely different. Perhaps Job himself would have gone through a divorce or worse. We know Job's response was right.

The question is not how Job responded, but how are we going to respond? We are weak and lonely, but when we give this area over to God, He will bless us and help us. Any area not surrendered to God is open prey for the enemy and he will attack you there until you are defeated. No matter what happens in life, choose to live a pure life.

Suggested Prayer

Lord,
I am so tempted to sin against You to relieve this pain that I am experiencing. Lord, I surrender my body, soul, and spirit to You. I surrender all areas of my life to You the best way I know how. Lord, reveal to me the areas that are not surrendered to You because I do not want the Devil to have a stronghold in my life. Lord, no matter what happens I decide to trust in You. In the Name above all Names I pray, Amen.

It's a Lonely Time

Ecclesiastes 4:11
Again, if two lie together, they keep warm, but how can one keep warm alone?

The day was busy with work, kids, chores, bills to pay, and now it is time to go to sleep. You are tired but you cannot sleep. Why? There is an overwhelming loneliness that invades your soul every night. No matter how you try to ease the pain it simply will not go away. When it is silent and the day is done, loneliness invades your soul along with a whole host of other emotions: anger, tears, bitterness, resentment, and even lust. There seems to be no cure for the cancer of loneliness.

In my loneliness I dated a lady soon after my divorce. We dated for three months, but it did not work because I was not healed up. In my loneliness I went on match.com (there is nothing wrong with dating sites) and dated a lady for a year. I bought her a ring and paid for a honeymoon cruise. We were all set to get married till she dumped me. I was stuck with a ring and no one to go on the cruise with. In my loneliness I began buying clothes and shoes. In my loneliness I flew 1,000 miles to Orlando, Florida to meet a Christian lady; of course it did not workout. In my loneliness I looked at things that were inappropriate.

One day I realized that I was wasting God's time and money trying to cure the cancer of loneliness. I also saw that the enemy was having a field day with me because I was holding on and trying to solve the problem by myself. After a seven-year battle with my flesh, I surrendered this area completely to God, trusting Him. What happened? Did a nice Christian lady come into my life? Not at all! Instead, I felt that God began helping my lonely spirit. The cure for the cancer of loneliness was beginning to work. He began to fill me with Himself and the loneliness began to leave. Temptations were manageable and I now had spiritual discernment to see when the enemy was attacking me. My restless soul found peace. The tide began to turn when I surrendered the loneliness to Him. I still feel lonely from time to time, but it is now manageable.

Suggested Prayer
Dear Lord,
I am in this battle of loneliness. I realize that it is not my battle; it is Your battle.
Forgive me for trying to fight Your battle. Today I surrender the loneliness to You,
trusting You for whatever or whoever You have for me. In Jesus' Name I pray, Amen.

SEPTEMBER 6

Walking Through the Devastation

Revelation 3:2
Wake up, and strengthen what remains and is about to die, for I have not found your works complete in the sight of God.

When Satan destroyed your family, it was like a war took place. There you lay, wounded and barely breathing. Your children lay wounded in a nearby trench. Even your ex was hurting. We need to wake up and see what is left from the aftermath. Whatever is left needs to be strengthened because it is about to die.

You were severely wounded, so you must strengthen yourself in the Lord. As you devote time to God, He begins to heal you. Your children are battered too, so strengthen them. Love on them! Be there for them! Pray with them! Read the scriptures to them! Encourage them! Let them know that you love them and accept them. As you look further and see your ex, who seems to be the root cause of all of this, pray for him or her too. Eventually you will even be able to help your ex-spouse. Look further! Family and friends are hurt too. Strengthen those family members and friends who are receptive to your ministry. Ask God to show you how to strengthen what remains. Eventually you and your family will be healed. So much was ruined by the enemy, but God can do all things and heal all hurts.

Living on the Gulf Coast, we experience hurricanes from time to time. Our most recent devastating hurricane was Hurricane Harvey. Many lost so much in this area. So many had to rebuild and are still in the rebuilding process. Experience tells us that another hurricane will come and cause more destruction. A divorce is like a category 5 hurricane. Once the storm dissipates, wake up and strengthen what remains. If you choose to do nothing you will die and so will your children.

Suggested Prayer
Lord,
We were hit hard as we received this deathblow from Satan. I am wounded and so are my children. Lord, show me my condition and that of my family. Give me wisdom to strengthen what remains. Lord, thank You that You did not leave us to die. Give me courage as I step out by faith to strengthen my children. In Jesus' Name I pray, Amen.

Wilderness and Drought

Hosea 13:5
It was I who knew you in the wilderness, in the land of drought...

When the scriptures speak of the wilderness it refers to a desert land. In this verse it is speaking about Israel's journey from Egypt to Canaan. It was a barren land with no water. It was not the ideal situation to be in, and some even preferred slavery in Egypt compared to the wilderness experience.

Do you see yourself in a barren land, characterized by drought? Divorce is a land of emotional, financial, spiritual, social, and relational drought. The heat of divorce emotionally drains a person, much like dehydrating in the desert. One becomes delusional and desperate in the desert. Once we realize that God is with us in the wilderness, we begin to see our situation differently. We realize that He loves us and that He cares for us. He is supplying all our needs. It is in this season of our lives that our relationship becomes stronger with Him. He restores us and heals us. Soon you will be out of this barrenness. Soon the Jordan River will dry up and you will enter a rest in the Lord. Soon the walls of Jericho will fall flat for you. Soon you will be allowed your portion in the land of promise. There is victory in the days ahead! Friend, do not be discouraged or depressed, because God has a purpose for your drought in the wilderness.

Suggested Prayer
Dear Lord,
As I travel through the dry barren times, let me know that You are shaping and forming me into the person that I need to be for You. Lord, let me see the victory that lies ahead. In Jesus' Name, Amen.

I Am Suffering Because of Their Sin

Numbers 14:33
And your children shall be shepherds in the wilderness forty years and shall suffer for your faithlessness, until the last of your dead bodies lies in the wilderness.

When Israel sent out the twelve spies to survey the promised land, most of them brought back a bad report and decided that they could not possess the land. God said that all the men of the population of Israel that were twenty years and older would die in the wilderness except Joshua and Caleb, because these two spies believed that with God's help they could conquer the land. The spies had a forty-day mission and God said they would stay in the wilderness forty years. Each day of disobedience brought about a year of punishment. The people had no faith and trusted in their own ways. The verse tells us that the children of these parents would suffer because of the parents' lack of faith. The poor children received the fruits of the parents' disobedience.

Sound familiar? Our children are suffering because of our sins. Divorce is horrible and the worst part is the suffering that the children experience. Mom and Dad refused to work things out and the children will suffer for it the rest of their lives. There are no easy answers to this dilemma. Judgment belongs to God. As a single parent the best choice that you can make is to have a right relationship with God. Make sure you have repented of your sins. Walk with God and do His will. Perhaps God, in His mercy, will give you and your children a good life. Perhaps He will ease the suffering that your children are going through. It is never wrong to be right with Jesus.

Suggested Prayer ───────────────────────────
Dear Lord,
I have suffered so much. My children have suffered for my bad choices and lack of faith. Lord, I confess my sins and ask that You lead me into a deeper relationship with You. Lord, please have mercy on me and my children. In the Name of Jesus I pray, Amen.

God Is with Us

Acts 7:9
And the patriarchs, jealous of Joseph, sold him into Egypt; but God was with him...

I s God with us when everything looks bleak? The answer is an emphatic yes. Joseph suffered so much but God was with him the whole time. Joseph's brothers were jealous of him and sold him as a slave instead of murdering him. God had given Joseph some awesome dreams about the future that he did not fully understand at the time. Joseph's brothers despised him and all his dreams. Joseph later went to prison for a crime that he did not commit. God was still with him in the prison. At the right time God changed his circumstances and he was made second in command in all of Egypt. God was still with him! God gave him dreams that would save all of Egypt and Israel. Joseph reunited with his father and brothers and restoration and healing took place. God was with him during the good times and the bad times.

God is with you too. He is with you in these dark days that you are experiencing. In the bad times we often feel forsaken by God. Some have even felt that God hated them because of all the suffering that they were experiencing. However, in the good times it is easy for us to forsake God. When everything is going our way, and if we are not careful, we will forget God. We don't need to depend on God when our pockets are overflowing with money. When our health is good, we do not rely on God. In the good times rejoice in the Lord and do not forget Him. In the bad times rely on God. In fact, we should depend on God for everything, regardless of our circumstances. Without Him we can do nothing. Let us recognize that through the bad times God is working out a great purpose in our lives. Today, realize that God is with you. May the Holy Spirit make this truth real in your heart today.

Suggested Prayer
Dear Father,
It seems like You abandoned me! Holy Spirit, open my eyes to let me know that You are with me. Help me see that You are working out a great plan. Thank You, Lord, that You did not forsake me. I surrender to You; please lead, guide, and direct me into Your paths. In Jesus' Name I pray, Amen.

A Shrub in The Desert

Jeremiah 17:5-6

Thus says the LORD: "Cursed is the man who trusts in man and makes flesh his strength, whose heart turns away from the LORD. He is like a shrub in the desert, and shall not see any good come. He shall dwell in the parched places of the wilderness, in an uninhabited salt land.

If we place our trust in ourselves our souls will be like a shrub in the desert. When we are trusting our own abilities, we are turning our hearts away from God. We will rely on ourselves to supply our needs. Who supplies your needs? Is it self or the Savior? We will be cursed when we decide to live life in our own strength. God also says no good will come to us. We will dwell in a parched land that is uninhabited in a spiritual sense. God paints a dim picture for those whose strength is the arm of flesh. Jeremiah says the heart is deceitful and desperately wicked. We must beware, because we all have wicked hearts.

We must have a heart that relies on God if we are going to have a blessed life. A blessed life is characterized by relying on God and seeing Him work in you and through you. A cursed life is marked by trusting in self. God has so much for those who will simply trust Him. A self-life is a lonely life, marked with pain and suffering. God wants to bless you. He does not want your life to be cursed. Since our hearts are sinful, we need the Holy Spirit to control them. Who is on the throne of your heart? You cannot have two kings sitting on the same throne. Determine that you will have a blessed life by trusting Him.

Suggested Prayer

Dear Lord,
My life is an isolated, cursed life because I am trusting myself. Lord, I confess my sin of rejecting You. I determine now to start living by faith in You. In Jesus' Name I pray, Amen.

A Tree Planted by the Water

Jeremiah 17:7-8
"Blessed is the man who trusts in the LORD, whose trust is the LORD. He is like a tree planted by water, that sends out its roots by the stream, and does not fear when heat comes, for its leaves remain green, and is not anxious in the year of drought, for it does not cease to bear fruit."

The shrub in the desert describes the person whose trust is not in the Lord. One who trusts in the Lord is described as one who is a tree planted by the waters. The blessed life is marked by one who is trusting God; it is compared to a well-nourished tree. This tree has deep roots that find water.

Ultimately our strength and nourishment come from God as we obey His Word. When things are rough the blessed man is deeply rooted in the Lord. When the heat of life comes his leaves are still green. Trials challenge the tree, but the tree remains green because of the rich supply of Jesus Christ. He is not afraid because he is faithful to the Lord. The Holy Spirit is this deep well that we draw from as we rely on God. His trust "is the Lord" and nothing else.

When the drought comes, he is not worried because he is still bearing fruit. Jeremiah describes a year of drought. Perhaps it has been two or three or seven or ten years of drought for you. Rest assured, dear friend, the showers will come. God keeps us fruitful in the heat and drought because our trust is in Him. Do you want to be a shrub in the desert, or a tree planted by the water? It all depends on you. Where is your heart? Who are you trusting?

Suggested Prayer
Dear Lord,
I do not want to be a shrub in the desert. Lord, I want to be a tree planted by the waters. I place my trust in You so when the heat and drought come, I will be healthy and fruitful. Amen.

SEPTEMBER 12

A Faith That Pleases God

Hebrews 11:5-6

By faith Enoch was taken up so that he should not see death, and he was not found, because God had taken him. Now before he was taken he was commended as having pleased God. And without faith it is impossible to please him, for whoever would draw near to God must believe that he exists and that he rewards those who seek him.

Can our faith please God? Enoch's faith pleased God. Enoch's faith pleased God because he was right with God. In other words, Enoch was the right person. He was a believer, he was called to be a prophet, he was committed, and he was consistent. Enoch's faith pleased God because he lived by the right principle. It is possible to be a Christian and to live by the wrong principles.

His principle in life was twofold. First, he believed in the Person of God. He believed in everything that the Bible says about God. However, he did not have a Bible. All his knowledge came from walking with God. Secondly, he believed God would reward him as he diligently sought Him. Enoch's faith also pleased God because he lived by the right promise. He knew that God would return one day and usher in a new kingdom. Enoch saw the end times when Jesus would come back to rule and reign over the earth. He also saw that a worldwide flood was coming soon.

Today the promise is still the same. Jesus is coming back for us personally. His coming might be when we die and go to heaven or when He comes to setup His kingdom. Either way Jesus is coming. We should live our lives in view of the soon return of Jesus Christ. Enoch was a righteous man who lived by a right principle and a great promise. The result was that he pleased God. If we would follow Enoch's pattern, we can please God too.

Suggested Prayer

Dear Lord,
I want a faith that pleases You. I believe in You and believe that You will reward me as I diligently seek You. Lord, I also believe that You are coming for me so let me live like it could be at any moment. In Jesus' Name I pray, Amen. Maranatha!

The Loss Is Great

Ezekiel 24:15-18
The word of the LORD came to me: "Son of man, behold, I am about to take the delight of your eyes away from you at a stroke; yet you shall not mourn or weep, nor shall your tears run down. Sigh, but not aloud; make no mourning for the dead. Bind on your turban, and put your shoes on your feet; do not cover your lips, nor eat the bread of men." So I spoke to the people in the morning, and at evening my wife died. And on the next morning I did as I was commanded.

The books of Isaiah, Jeremiah, Lamentations, Ezekiel, and Daniel make up the Major Prophets of the Old Testament. Isaiah was married to a prophetess. Jeremiah and Daniel remained single. Ezekiel was married, but suddenly his wife died. Ezekiel was a faithful man and he obeyed the Lord, yet tragedy came his way. The text says that God took away his wife. We cannot comprehend why God chooses to do certain things. We might not like what God is doing in our lives, but rest assured, God is in control.

Ezekiel responded to the Lord with humble obedience. The loss was great and the pain was unbearable, but Ezekiel knew God was in control. With this knowledge he submitted to the Lord. People respond to trials in various ways. Some go through the grieving process trusting God, while others become very bitter. Some move on after the grieving process and some never get over the loss and simply cannot move on. Today, see your trial as coming from the hand of God. Your spouse is gone because God took him or her away. God sometimes brings tragedy to strengthen His servants for a mighty task. Like Ezekiel, humbly submit to God, realizing that He is in control.

Suggested Prayer ——————————————————————
Dear Lord,
I have this hurt in my heart that will not go away. My loss is great. By faith I accept that You took away my spouse. I humbly submit to You, Lord. Let Your will be done in my life. I do not understand what is happening, but I am trusting You. Amen.

I Forgot About the Children

1 Timothy 3:4
He must manage his own household well, with all dignity keeping his children submissive...

When Paul wrote to Timothy about potential elders for the church, he set some qualifications or guidelines to go by (1 Timothy 3:1-7). One qualification is that the minister must have respectful, submissive children. Some people want to look at the preacher's kids and make excuses for their own lack of good parenting. But you and I are not responsible for raising the preacher's children. We will stand before God and give an account on how we raised our own children.

God has given all of us the duty to rule or manage our households well. Take time for your kids! Yes, you are hurting; yes, the pressures of life are great; but begin managing your household. Your children are your greatest asset. Lead, guide, and direct them. Get them involved in your life and be involved in their lives. Let them see that your family is a team and that you are the head coach.

Not only must you rule them well, but respect them regularly. Treat them with honor. If you initiate respect, they will eventually respond with respect. Look at your past mistakes and show your children how not to repeat those same mistakes. You do not need to be perfect to do this.

You need to start managing your house today. As you begin to manage your household, the job will get easier as you gain more experience. You will also get your eyes off yourself and all of your problems. Your kids need a leader. Determine that *you* will be the leader, not some musician or Hollywood celebrity. God has chosen you for the job!

Suggested Prayer ⸻
Dear Lord,
I have neglected my kids. Lord, I am sorry. Help me begin to manage my kids for Your glory. Give me wisdom and courage for this great task. In Jesus' Name, Amen.

Do a Good Job with Your Kids

1 Timothy 3:12
Let deacons each be the husband of one wife, managing their children and their own households well.

In 1 Timothy 3:8-13 Paul gives the qualifications for church deacons. Just like the elder, the deacon must run his household well. In this verse Paul mentions the wife as well as the children. Two words stick out in this verse that we need to understand. One is the word "deacon," which means servant. The very nature of a deacon is that of a person who serves the people for a need or needs.

The first church in the Bible developed deacons to take some of the burdens off the elders (see Acts 6). The deacons were to be filled with the Holy Spirit (Acts 6:3). Determine that you will be a Spirit-filled servant for your household. Jesus said that the greatest person would be servant of all.

The home has no room for a dictatorship or for a person who will not lead. Some parents complain that their kids are walking all over them. Why? Because they have taken control of the home.

The other word is that little word "well." In other words, do a good job. Do not just have a household and go through the motions. Do it well. With a divorce comes discouragement and depression. When these two twins invade our hearts, we just go through the motions. What happens? We do not run our households well and our children suffer the consequences. Determine that you will be that Spirit-filled servant. Then decide that you are going to run your household well.

Suggested Prayer
Dear Father,
Help me be that Spirit-filled servant of God. Lord, I cannot fill myself with Your Spirit, so I am asking that You fill me. Lord, I want to rule my home well. Please give me the wisdom and energy to rule it well. In the Name of Jesus I pray, Amen.

Will Your Children Take Care of You?

1 Timothy 5:4

But if a widow has children or grandchildren, let them first learn to show godliness to their own household and to make some return to their parents, for this is pleasing in the sight of God.

When does the church step in and help its widows? Paul speaks to this issue in 1 Timothy 5:1-17. In our time some churches have widow's apartments to house those who meet the biblical qualifications. In this verse Paul is saying that the children and grandchildren should take care of the widows instead of the church.

Herein lies a great problem in America. Many children resent their parents for ruining their childhood with a divorce. The children went without proper food and clothing because of their parents. They did not have the opportunity to go to college like their friends. They made the lives of our children a living hell.

The children have become angry and resentful adults. Some are simply not going to help a deadbeat mom or dad who made stupid choices in their lives. When that parent decided to leave the family for another man or woman, they had moments of pleasure but sent poverty and broken lives to the home that they abandoned. Should your child help you? Mom or dad, you have ruined your family. Your children are not going to help you unless God does a miracle in your heart and their hearts.

Today is the day to get your heart right with God. Quit playing games with God because He is not playing games with you, then work to mend the broken relationships with your children. Perhaps God, in His mercy, will heal the broken relationships. I hope that your children will help you, but some are not going to help. Start today by helping them. Today's message is not a feel-good message. It is a reminder that we reap what we sow. When your children needed you the most you were sleeping around. In your old age when you need them the most, will they be around? Will they be there for you?

Suggested Prayer ——————————————————

Dear Lord,

I have made a wreck of my life. I dedicate the broken pieces to You. Lord, my children suffered because of me. Forgive me. Heal my relationship with my children. In Jesus' Name I pray, Amen.

It Can Be Done

1 Timothy 5:10
...and having a reputation for good works: if she has brought up children, has shown hospitality, has washed the feet of the saints, has cared for the afflicted, and has devoted herself to every good work.

As Paul continues to talk about widows he says, "if she has brought up children." You can raise your children without a husband or a wife to help you. It can be done, but it is not easy. There are many single parents raising good, successful children. God's perfect design is that a mom and dad raise a child. A child needs both parents. I have watched single moms struggle and my heart goes out to them. Everything seemed bleak and hopeless in their lives. My neighbor worked long hours and had no energy, but she raised two successful boys. Then, at the right time God sent her a new husband.

Sometimes God takes away a spouse and the parent is left all alone to raise the children. The message for today is that it can be done. God gives grace and favor to the single parent. The result is children who love God and who excel in life. Single mom or dad, do not be discouraged. God has this. The battle is the Lord's. It has always been His battle—it was never your battle. God knew you would be single before you ever went on your first date. He is going to help you. He will supply your needs. He will bless your children.

Soon after my divorce I realized that all vacations, going out to eat, and all other activities were simply not in the budget. My two boys still got to do many things. They were invited by other families to go on vacation with them and my boys still enjoyed their summers. My youngest son went on three vacations with two different families. Help is on the way, dear friend. Give it your best and pray and seek God. Can you raise a family by yourself? It can be done.

Suggested Prayer —————————————————————————
Lord,
I am struggling to raise my family by myself. I need Your help. I dedicate my parenting to You. Help everything to turn out right. Have mercy on us and bless us. Help me see that it can be done through You. In Jesus' Name I pray, Amen.

Should I Have Another Child?

1 Timothy 5:14

So I would have younger widows marry, bear children, manage their households, and give the adversary no occasion for slander.

Paul is still addressing widows in this verse. He says that young widows are perfectly fine to remarry and have more children with their new husband. Blended families are tough. The number one cause of divorce in second marriages is the children. Some remarried couples want a child together. She has her children from a previous marriage and so does he, and now they want a child together in this new marriage. This is perfectly fine in the eyes of God. The opposite also holds true because it is fine not to have children in your new marriage.

The key is to be realistic and practical. Look at your ages, health, incomes, and most importantly, is it fair to the other children. Some feel a new baby would cement the second marriage, but that is not what makes a new marriage work. It actually may be the thing that makes it not work. The Lord is the One who makes a second marriage work. If a couple would love God and each other, it will work with or without children. If you decide you want more children, do not waste your time dating someone who does not want more kids. Don't waste their time either. If you get married and your new spouse has children, love them and treat them like your kids. Do not get into this his kids or her kids debate. When you say "I do" you also say "I do" to their children.

The key to remarriage and children is not to rush into anything. Let the Holy Spirit lead you. I personally decided not to have any new children because of my age, my financial situation (child support is not cheap), and I felt it would be disrespectful to my two boys who have stood by me through the years. May the Lord lead you to a new spouse who has a similar outlook on children that you have! May you share the same beliefs about God and the Bible! May your new marriage be successful!

Suggested Prayer ———————————————————————

Dear Lord,
Help me figure out what kind of family You want me to have. Lead me to a person who has the same philosophy about children that I have. May our new home honor and glorify You. In Jesus' Name I pray, Amen.

The Word of the Lord

Jeremiah 22:29
O land, land, land, hear the word of the LORD!

Anytime the Scriptures repeat a word there is an expressed importance on what will be communicated. God spoke to Samuel by calling his name twice (1 Samuel 3:4-6). Throughout the scriptures God has called people's names twice to get their undivided attention. Anytime the Bible uses a word three times it really stresses the importance of the message. When the seraphim talked of God's holiness they said, "holy, holy, holy is the Lord of hosts" (Isaiah 6:3). God's holiness cannot be fully expressed or comprehended so there was a threefold usage of the word "holy."

In this text there is a threefold usage of the word "land." Jeremiah is desperately trying to get the land of Israel to hear God's word. The hour is desperate. Jeremiah has warned of the Babylonian invasion. The people had turned their backs on God and there was a dire need for God's people to hear the Word of God before His judgment would come. The idea of hearing the Word implies obedience to the Word. Jeremiah ends the sentence with an exclamation point. Words cannot fully describe how important it was for the Jews to do God's Word.

Today God wants us to hear and obey His Word. It is a matter of heaven or hell. A life of peace or a life of peril is at stake. A life of blessing versus a life of curses. Comfort or chastisement? Reward or regret? The Christian life is not easy, but one thing that makes it easier is responding to the Word. We need to hear with hearts of obedience. James tells us not to just listen to the Word but to do the Word (James 1:25). May God help us to do the Word of God.

Suggested Prayer
Dear Lord,
Please give us ears to hear and hearts that will understand Your Word. Lord, may You give us understanding and give us hearts that will obey Your Word. Lord, may we honor Your Word and obey it in our hearts and in our homes. In Jesus' Name I pray, Amen.

The Purpose of Life

Ecclesiastes 12:13-14

The end of the matter; all has been heard. Fear God and keep his commandments, for this is the whole duty of man. For God will bring every deed into judgment, with every secret thing, whether good or evil.

Solomon tried so many things in life and summarized life's purpose in these two verses. Solomon experimented with just about everything in his day. You name it and he tried it. He occupied his mind with great building projects, alcohol, prostitutes, and a whole host of other things. Perhaps you too have tried many things and feel empty inside. Things do not satisfy us. God is good and He wants us to have good things. The problem is not that we have things, but things have us. When our focus is on this life and possessions, we will not be happy.

Solomon said we are to fear God and keep His commandments. The fear of God means that we know our proper place in our relationship with Him. We are to respect His Person, authority, His Word, and His Son who died for us. It means that we have a reverential fear of Him, and we submit to Him in all areas. The interesting thing is that God will bring everything into the light. He will reward us for every good thing that we have done in His Name.

Today I would encourage you to let this world go. Come back to God and begin to fear Him. Get into the Word and submit to the Word. Soon you will find yourself in God's will and fulfilling His purpose for your life. You will be rewarded in this life and the life to come.

Suggested Prayer

Dear Lord,
I want Your purpose for my life. I submit to You and Your Word in all areas. I ask that I fulfill Your purpose for my life. Lord, I leave all the blessings of this life into Your hands. Let me fear You and serve You the rest of my days. In Jesus' Name, Amen.

What Is Your Life?

Colossians 3:4
When Christ who is your life appears, then you also will appear with him in glory.

Paul clearly states that Christ is our life. People's lives are strange and complex. Some lives revolve around making money. Some are wrapped up in possessions. Some are wrapped up in helping people. Our lives are Jesus Christ—period, exclamation point!

Divorce is such an eye-opening experience. Before your divorce your life might have been various things. The tough nature of this trial will eventually bring you to a place where you will realize that your life is Jesus Christ. One day He will appear, and you will be with Him forever. As we think about heaven it is all centered around Jesus Christ. We will sing to Him, worship Him, and learn of Him throughout eternity. Jesus wants us to worship Him long before we get to heaven.

He is the originator of life. He gives eternal life and this life begins when we are saved. When we are first converted, all we think about is Christ because He is our new life. Slowly but surely our hearts grow cold towards Him. Eventually we do not even have time to spend with Him. Sound familiar? Then a tragedy hits and we realize that Christ is all that we have. He is all we need. He is sufficient. Today, realize that He is your life. Make adjustments accordingly. Nothing else truly matters. "On Christ the solid Rock I stand; All other ground is sinking sand."[5]

Suggested Prayer
Father,
Forgive me for trying to make a life without You. Lord, my world fell apart. I am asking that You renew me by being my all in all. Lord, You are first, second, and third. I recommit myself to You and Your kingdom. Let everything else fall by the wayside. In Jesus' Name I pray, Amen.

---

[5] "The Solid Rock." Edward Mote. 1863.

I Let Them Have It!

Proverbs 29:11

A fool gives full vent to his spirit, but a wise man quietly holds it back.

Did you ever fly off the handle and say some things you should not have said? We drop our guards— it all comes out and we say things that we cannot take back. These words go out like shrapnel from an exploding grenade. The words kill and wound those in its path. Well, I am glad this has never happened to me (just joking). Seriously, we are foolish when we act this way. We become fools and instruments of the enemy as we talk about our ex-spouses and their partners in crime who we thought were our friends. Or maybe you are mad at your family.

Solomon says the wise person holds back and does not vent all his mind. Hold back and hold on! Ask God to give you a trusted neutral friend that you can talk to. A program at your church, like Divorce Care, may be a neutral spot where you can vent and receive help. It is not wrong to feel hurt and want to vent. Just make sure it is in a loving, helpful environment that will get positive results. We all have said some things that we should not have said. We must quit acting foolishly and start living and practicing wisdom in our lives.

Suggested Prayer

Dear Lord,

I am so angry. I have said some things that were not right for me to say. Lord, help me to be that wise person that Solomon writes about. Give me a person or group that I can talk to that will bring about healing and not harm. Lord, I have suffered so much, and I just want it to stop. Send someone to help me. In Jesus' Name I pray, Amen.

Win the Daily Battle

Ezekiel 18:24

But when a righteous person turns away from his righteousness and does injustice and does the same abominations that the wicked person does, shall he live? None of the righteous deeds that he has done shall be remembered; for the treachery of which he is guilty and the sin he has committed, for them he shall die.

We are in a daily spiritual battle. What makes this battle tougher is this sinful flesh that we possess. We have the Spirit in us as well as our sinful flesh, and they fight against each other every day. When we are stressed out and discouraged, we are even more tempted to do evil. After all, divorce is the ultimate form of rejection in human relationships. Your spouse that you made vows with has rejected you. This is not an old friend, this is your soul mate that has rejected you. Now you feel very low. Now your flesh wants to do something to feel important and boost its ego.

Friends, we are in a dangerous position. We are in danger of losing our reputation, our witness, and our testimony. We will not lose our souls, but we will lose everything that we have accomplished in our spiritual lives. You may feel horrible today. You might want to sin to release the pain in your heart. It is not worth it. Your family, friends, and even your foes need you to stay the course.

Today find your worth in Jesus. He is still in your midst. He is still for you. He still accepts you. You are still complete in Him. He still loves you. He will take you by the hand and lead you through this horrible trial. Say no to your flesh and say yes to Jesus. You will never regret doing the right thing. However, you will regret losing your testimony. So, "Stand up, stand up for Jesus, ye soldiers of the cross."[6]

Suggested Prayer

Dear Lord,
I have been rejected and I do feel horrible. I do want to satisfy my flesh to ease this pain. Forgive me and cleanse me. Let me see that my true worth is in You, Jesus. Holy Spirit, please open my eyes. In Jesus' Name, Amen.

---

[6] "Stand Up for Jesus." G. Duffield, Jr. 1858

John the Baptist

John 1:6
There was a man sent from God, whose name was John.

John had the special privilege of introducing Jesus to the world. In Isaiah 40:3 the prophet spoke of the coming of John. There are three interesting points about John in this text. The first is that he was just a man. The text says, "there was a man." At the end of the day we are mere men and women. We have our strengths and weaknesses, but we are just human. John was just a man with some great strengths and some weaknesses. The second thing about John is that he had a mission. The Bible says, "he was sent from God." We too have a mission to fulfill. The third thing is that he had a specific message. He was to pave the way for Israel's King, Jesus. He was to tell the people to repent of their sins and to trust the Messiah.

This verse gives us insight to the ministry that God would have us to fulfill. It is a Christ-centered message and ministry. We are to introduce Jesus to a lost and dying world of humanity. Wherever God leads you these three elements are vitally important. You are just a man or woman. It is not your power or ability that will get the job done. You will fail, but you will also have victories.

You too have a mission to fulfill. You have been sent from God. Your message is the gospel—the death, burial, and resurrection of our Lord and Savior Jesus Christ. Jesus is the answer to a lost and dying world. Jesus is also the answer to the struggling Christian. Enjoy the mission that God has for you and remember that you are human and will make mistakes along the way.

Suggested Prayer
Dear Lord,
I am a mere man, but I believe I have a mission to fulfill. Lord, whatever Your will is let me find it and fulfill it. Lord, let me introduce Jesus to this lost and dying world. In His Name, Amen.

Seek and Ye Shall Find

Proverbs 11:27
Whoever diligently seeks good seeks favor, but evil comes to him who searches for it.

This verse lays before us good and evil, blessing and cursing, righteousness and unrighteousness. There is a great contrast that is penned in this verse. Whenever you see the word "but" it signifies a contrast. The second thought is a complete contrast of the first thought. So, if we diligently seek to do good and please God, we will receive His favor. God will recognize our desire to please Him, and He will reward us in a special way. Jesus said that He always did the things that pleased His Father (John 8:29).

We are not perfect, and God knows all about our imperfections. God is looking at our hearts. May we have hearts that diligently seek His acceptance. In contrast, if we seek evil it will find us. If we set our hearts on sinning it will find us, capture us, and destroy us. Sin is always knocking at our door. God is pursuing us with His goodness. Satan is pursuing us with sin. No matter how hard we try to avoid sinning, it is looking for us and it comes in various forms. Satan still desires to sift us like wheat. It is not enough just to seek good; we must also shun the evil. We must watch and pray and look for the enemy's traps.

Temptation is everywhere. It is around us in this world and also in our hearts. With the internet the whole world of sin and degradation is in your home, on your phone, and in the workplace. Enough is enough! It is time to put away sin and diligently pursue the things that God is pleased with.

Suggested Prayer —————————————————————
Dear Father,
I am not perfect, but I want to please You and have favor with You. Forgive me for the times that I have sought out evil. Lord, put a hedge of protection about me and keep me from the evil that is around me and within me. In Jesus' Name I pray, Amen and amen.

The Drought Is Coming

Genesis 41:29-31

There will come seven years of great plenty throughout all the land of Egypt, but after them there will arise seven years of famine, and all the plenty will be forgotten in the land of Egypt. The famine will consume the land, and the plenty will be unknown in the land by reason of the famine that will follow, for it will be very severe.

In Genesis we have an interesting fourteen-year period. There would be seven years of great prosperity followed by seven years of famine and drought. God, in His mercy, allowed Pharaoh to have two dreams about these fourteen years. Pharaoh was very disturbed by these dreams because he did not know the dreams' meanings. As Joseph was confined in prison, the chief butler suddenly remembered that Joseph could interpret dreams. Joseph was taken from prison to the palace of Pharaoh where he interpreted the dreams for the ruler. Pharaoh made him Prime Minister of Egypt because Joseph had a plan for the next fourteen years for this famine. During the seven prosperous years the nation would save 20% of its harvest each year. When the seven lean years hit there was enough food to sustain the nation and some of the surrounding territories. Joseph devised a plan, and God blessed it.

Today you need a plan. It does not matter how prosperous you have been because a divorce is costly. Take inventory of your life and decide when you will retire and plan. You have a drought coming. It would be a shame not to plan for your future and suffer for it the rest of your life. God will honor your plan. Get out of debt, save, and invest so the divorce does not bring about your financial downfall. After reading this chapter I knew I would need a new roof and air conditioner in the next few years. I saved a certain amount with each paycheck till I had $12,000 for these purchases. The roof had to be replaced and three months later the air went out. I replaced all this debt-free because I planned. Begin to make a plan that will lead you to financial freedom.

Suggested Prayer

Lord,
I have received a major setback in my finances. Lord, let me see the big picture and give me a plan so this divorce will not ruin my finances. Give me a plan that leads to financial freedom and help me be able to give more to You. In Jesus' Name I pray, Amen.

The Secret to Success

Philippians 4:11-13
Not that I am speaking of being in need, for I have learned in whatever situation I am to be content. I know how to be brought low, and I know how to abound. In any and every circumstance, I have learned the secret of facing plenty and hunger, abundance and need. I can do all things through him who strengthens me.

Paul knew the secret to successful living. The secret is Christ. We can get through any situation with Christ. Paul knew what it was like to have abundance. He also knew what it was like to be in desperate need. He learned to be content through Christ. Notice that the great apostle had to learn how to be content. He also learned the secret of success by trusting Christ. He learned that through Christ he could go through any and every circumstance. He also learned that God would give him the strength to endure. It sounds so easy, but this is a very difficult lesson to learn. Paul himself had to learn this, and so we must also learn this lesson.

When faced with difficulties we tend to focus on the circumstance and not on Christ. We tend to look to our own power instead of His power. Paul had to be brought down very low to learn this lesson. There is coming a day when our strength and abilities will fail. There is coming a day when our dollars will run out. There is coming a day when everything that we depend on will crumble. There is coming a day when we will suffer great needs. Why does this happen to us? Because God wants us to learn the secret to success. That Secret is Christ. It is His strength and not ours that will get us through the difficult times.

Suggested Prayer
Dear Lord,
I see that through my losses there was nothing I could do in my own power. Lord, I have no strength. My resources ran out. So today I choose to rely on You and Your strength. I want my life to be summed up in one word—Christ. In Jesus Name I pray, Amen.

What Kind of Fruit Do You Want to Eat?

Isaiah 3:10-11

Tell the righteous that it shall be well with them, for they shall eat the fruit of their deeds. Woe to the wicked! It shall be ill with him, for what his hands have dealt out shall be done to him.

I have a grapefruit tree in my front yard. In December the fruit is ready to be picked. My neighbors take an active interest in the tree as the fruit begins to ripen. The neighbors also know that one day soon I will be knocking on their door to give them some grapefruits. I enjoy giving them away because the fruit that it produces it not just for me. Fruit is meant to be shared with others.

Isaiah tells us that a righteous person that goes around doing good will receive good in return from the hand of the Lord. They will eat the fruit of their labors. In other words, God will see their good deeds and reward them. It is awesome to see God blessing His people for their faithfulness. Like fruit, the blessing will also be a blessing to others. On the other hand, the wicked will also eat the fruit of their deeds. This time it will be a bitter fruit that will seem unbearable. God is not unrighteous to forget our good deeds (Hebrews 6:10). God is also just, and He sees every evil deed.

Some have hurt you through all your trials. Do not let these people bother you. Keep serving God and He will bless you. You will eat the fruits of your labors. As for those who have troubled you, they will eat a bitter fruit that will consume their health and their wealth. God will bring justice to you in His time. Keep on keeping on, because God is on your side. God wants to bless you! God will bless you!

Suggested Prayer ————————————————————————
Lord,
Some have troubled me, and it upsets me. Lord, I can't control them, so I give them to You. I want to do good and to be right before Your eyes. Help me do good and let me see a harvest of righteousness in my life, my children, and those around me. Let me be a blessing to others. In Jesus' Name I pray, Amen.

Come Out with Your Hands Up

Exodus 17:11
Whenever Moses held up his hand, Israel prevailed, and whenever he lowered his hand, Amalek prevailed.

As Moses and the Israelites left Egypt they encountered a whole host of problems. The people were hungry, so God sent manna and quails. Then the people were thirsty, and Moses struck a rock and water gushed out from great depths. Then what? The nation of Amalek arrived to destroy them. Moses sent Israel into battle under Joshua's command to fight this nation. Meanwhile, Moses, Aaron, and Hur went up to the top of a hill to watch the battle. Moses lifted his hands to Jehovah and Israel began to win the battle. As his hands grew weary he let them down, and Amalek began to win the battle. Worn out, Moses sat on a stone and Aaron and Hur held up his hands. Israel won the battle.

Our hands are an extension of our hearts. When we lift up our hands to God, we are lifting our heart up to Him in dependence on Him. Get a visual picture of this scene in your mind. If you want victory over your flesh, lift up your hands to God. Thank God for good friends like Aaron and Hur. When Moses could no longer lift his hands these two men did it for him. You see, we need a godly family and church members who can lift us up when we are weak. We are in this together and we need each other. It is a simple concept but hard to follow. Keep your hands lifted to God and you will win. Drop your hands and your flesh will prevail. You will be defeated if you do not have an Aaron and a Hur in your life.

Suggested Prayer
God,
I lift both hands to You, looking to You for victory. Now, Lord, please send an Aaron and a Hur who will help hold my hands when I am weary. Lord, strengthen me so I can lift others up. In the Name above all names I pray, Amen.

I Don't Know How to Pray About This

Romans 8:26

Likewise the Spirit helps us in our weakness. For we do not know what to pray for as we ought, but the Spirit himself intercedes for us with groanings too deep for words.

We just do not know how to pray about certain things. The great apostle Paul included himself in this verse. Paul was weak in his flesh and did not know how to pray. We too are weak in our flesh and do not know how to pray. The things we see and hear and experience in our flesh make us weak and without the wisdom to know how to pray for certain things.

Thank God we have the Holy Spirit who helps us pray. He is all powerful and we are weak. He is our Helper because we are helpless. In our flesh we may perceive our situation the wrong way or ask for the wrong things. We do not know how to pray, but the Holy Spirit knows how our prayers should be worded. Our job is to pray. The Holy Spirit prays for us according to the will of God. Our prayers are not based on our abilities, eloquence, or our own power. Our prayers are based on His power and wisdom. The truth of this verse should encourage us to pray. He is our Helper and will take our prayers to the very throne of God. At this throne Jesus Himself presents our case to our Heavenly Father.

We need to humble ourselves and pray with a sincere heart. The Spirit prays in groanings too deep for words. When we pray, all three Persons of the Godhead are active and working on our behalf. There is supernatural power in prayer. No wonder Jesus said that men ought always to pray and not to faint (Luke 18:1).

Suggested Prayer ————————————————————————

Dear Lord,
Help me to have a good prayer life. Lord, I give You my heart and I humble myself before You. Lord, help me learn how to pray according to Your will. In Jesus' Name, Amen.

OCTOBER 1

He (or She) Just Came into My Life

Ruth 2:2-3
And Ruth the Moabite said to Naomi, "Let me go to the field and glean among the ears of grain after him in whose sight I shall find favor." And she said to her, "Go, my daughter." So she set out and went and gleaned in the field after the reapers, and she happened to come to the part of the field belonging to Boaz, who was of the clan of Elimelech.

Have you wondered how you will meet your future spouse? Times have definitely changed with social media and various television programs that are constantly reshaping our minds and our culture. It is not wrong to use social media and various dating websites. Our pastor said that 50% of all the weddings he performs are from couples who met online. That percentage may increase in the next few years.

Enter our text about Boaz and Ruth. Boaz was an old Jewish bachelor and Ruth was a young lady who was a new believer from the pagan land of Moab. Providence brought these two unlikely candidates together. They did not have a dating site or even a singles group at the church. There were no churches and no social media, much less electricity. One day Ruth suddenly showed up in Boaz's life. God moved her from another country and culture so their paths could meet. Boaz was just a faithful servant of the Lord and this lovely bride came his way.

In the book of Genesis Rebekah was brought to Isaac by the providence of God. A pastor friend of mine met his wife at a gas station. Imagine meeting a lady with enough character to be a pastor's wife simply getting gas! If you have been online and nothing seems to happen, or if you cannot seem to meet the right person, why not let God work the old-fashioned way by sending you the right person at the right time. Boaz was not searching for a wife and Ruth was not looking for a husband. Why not let Providence bring you the right person? God will send you the right person and He may use a dating website; God can use any method He chooses. Give the matter over to Him. Someday in the near future your spouse may suddenly appear.

Suggested Prayer
Dear Lord, I am frustrated because I have waited for the right person to come and nothing happened. Lord, I went online, and every relationship ended in a disaster. I surrender this matter to You. May Your perfect will be done! By faith I trust that the right person will suddenly appear in my life. Forgive me, Lord, for making this my priority over You. It is in the Name of Jesus I pray, Amen.

It Came Out of Left Field

Judges 3:20-22

And Ehud came to him as he was sitting alone in his cool roof chamber. And Ehud said, "I have a message from God for you." And he arose from his seat. And Ehud reached with his left hand, took the sword from his right thigh, and thrust it into his belly. And the hilt also went in after the blade, and the fat closed over the blade, for he did not pull the sword out of his belly; and the dung came out.

It was the time of Israel's judges. Moses and Joshua were both dead. Everyone was doing what they thought was right. Israel had been captured by Eglon, the King of Moab. The Jewish people cried out to God and repented of all their sins. God then raised up Ehud (a judge) who would bring peace to the land for 80 years. Ehud brought Israel's tribute money to Eglon. Ehud informed Eglon that he had a special message from God for the king. Ehud then reached for his dagger and killed the King of Moab. Ehud escaped for his life and brought Israel into battle where they defeated the Moabites.

How did Ehud sneak a weapon past the guards to kill the king? The Holy Spirit records that he was lefthanded and had his sword on the right side of his body under his garment. The guards had never encountered lefthanded people before, so they always checked for weapons on the left side. A simple oversight killed a king and eventually his army. A simple oversight or two in the United States caused the 9/11 tragedy.

A simple oversight on your part could also cause your downfall. The devil is bringing all sorts of fiery darts at you—they may come out of left field or from nowhere. It could be finances or trouble with your children or many other things. Be proactive and not reactive. The Moabites were reactive and lost to Israel. The United States was reactive and had to make several changes to try to stop terrorism. What are we to do? Every day something comes at us that we were not expecting. It is time to get close to God and to rely totally on Him. There is a spiritual war going on and you do not want a slight oversight to be your downfall.

Suggested Prayer

Lord,
The enemy is too strong for me. I have been bombarded by several things. Lord, I want to walk close to You. Please give me spiritual discernment, so I do not become a casualty. Help me to watch and pray. Please put a hedge of protection around me. In Jesus' Name I pray, Amen.

OCTOBER 3

No Shortcuts

Matthew 4:8-9
Again, the devil took him to a very high mountain and showed him all the kingdoms of the world and their glory. And he said to him, "All these I will give you, if you will fall down and worship me."

When it comes to trials in our lives, we seem to want to take any shortcuts that are possible. The pain is tough and so we want out of the pain in the quickest way possible. God's plan was for Jesus to die for our sins, be buried, rise the third day, and then to ascend to heaven. At the right time Jesus will come back again and rule and reign over all the kingdoms of this world. Satan offered Jesus a shortcut by giving Him the kingdom without the cross. The Father's plan was the cross then the crown.

If Jesus would have taken the shortcut, several things would have happened. One thing is that Jesus would have sinned. Another important thing is that we all would have perished in our sins because we would have no Savior. Instead of enjoying a kingdom we would be in hell with the devil himself. It was vitally important for Jesus to follow the Father's plan. The sufferings, the beatings, and the cross were all part of the Father's plan. There were simply not any shortcuts. We too cannot take any shortcuts. We must follow the Father's perfect plan for our lives.

We have the potential to mess up the rest of our lives in many ways. We might marry the wrong person. We might fall into sin or further financial difficulties. Our children might suffer more. The possibilities for failure are endless when we decide to take a shortcut. So, determine today that you will not take a shortcut but follow the Father's perfect will. Let God teach you all that you need to learn from the trial. The pain that you are going through is tough, but a greater pain awaits if you decide to cut corners. Dedicate the trial to God and realize that He is in control. Stop worrying and start worshiping with full assurance of His control.

Suggested Prayer
Dear Lord,
My pain seems unbearable and I want out of this trial. I am so tempted to take the shortcut. Lord, I give it all to You. Let Your will be done and teach me what I need to learn. May You be glorified in my life. Lord, I submit to Your perfect will. It is in the Name of Jesus I pray. Amen.

I Will Meet You in The Morning

Psalms 5:3

O LORD, in the morning you hear my voice; in the morning I prepare a sacrifice for you and watch.

K ing David got up early each morning to spend time with God in prayer. This must be our habit if we are to expect a vibrant relationship with the Lord. David mentions the phrase "in the morning" twice in this short song. The emphasis that David is making is that God was his first priority—He should be ours too.

The king not only prayed, he knew that God heard his voice. God still answers prayer! You do not have to be of nobility for God to answer you. God hears poor people's cries too. It may not seem like God is listening, but He is very attentive to our prayers, especially when we seek Him first thing in the morning. David directed his prayer and devotion to God every morning. David's prayers were not a one-day-a-week seeking; no, it was a daily ritual with the king.

Not only was there supplication on David's part, there was also anticipation. He was watching and waiting on God to work on his behalf. When we get serious about our relationship with God, our Lord will also be serious. When we begin to see prayers answered, we begin to anticipate God doing something more for us. It is one thing to pray, it is quite another thing when we pray expecting God to hear and answer our prayers.

Many times we are guilty of praying just to be praying. We are merely going through the motions and we are not expecting God to do anything. The sweet psalmist of Israel was looking up to the throne of God and expecting Him to work. Change your prayer life. Seek Him early. Seek Him knowing that He is listening. Seek Him expecting Him to work on your behalf.

Suggested Prayer ———————————————————————

Dear Lord,
I confess that I am just praying and not expecting You to do anything. I want to seek You first. Teach me to have an effective prayer life. Let me realize that You are listening. Let me anticipate that You are going to work on my behalf. In Jesus' Name, Amen! Maranatha!

Good and Bad from The Lord

Job 2:9-10

Then his wife said to him, "Do you still hold fast your integrity? Curse God and die." But he said to her, "You speak as one of the foolish women would speak. Shall we receive good from God, and shall we not receive evil?" In all this Job did not sin with his lips.

The spiritual war raged on between God and Satan. Job was in the midst of a battle that he knew nothing about. God allowed Satan to kill Job's children, take away his wealth and his health. Job's wife seemed to think the best thing for him to do was curse God and die. Let us be kind to her because she did not know what was happening or perhaps she would have responded differently. I can see that her response was a natural human response. She simply could not take anymore.

Let us pause a minute and consider that we too are caught in the middle of a battle between God and Satan, and we really do not understand what is going on. Job's response was a little better than his wife's; perhaps he was the calm one in the relationship. Job realized that we receive good and bad things from God. Job was the richest man at the time and realized that his wealth came from the blessings of God. When Job lost everything, he realized that this came from God too. Make no mistakes about it; God allowed Satan to do this to Job. Job did not sin when all of this came upon him.

Honestly speaking, there are several who are mad at God because of the things that He has allowed in their lives. These angry people have taken it a step further and now they live and dwell in sin. Friends, it would do our souls some good to realize that God is sovereign, meaning that He is in complete control of everything. Ultimately, God allowed your divorce, the breakup of the home, the depression of the children, the financial problems, and even the health problems. When we can see God's sovereignty our trials take on new form. Our attitudes begin to change. Please read the last chapter of the book of Job. Job was restored double. God brought the good back, but it was only after God had done His perfect work. Once your trial has run its full course and you learn every lesson that God wants you to learn, look out—a blessing is coming your way.

Suggested Prayer

Lord, I want to respond right. Let me see that You are in control and have allowed all the heartaches and troubles. Forgive me for sinning and getting mad. Today I accept the good and the bad that comes from You. Amen and amen! Praise the LORD!

Something to Rejoice In

Luke 10:19-20

Behold, I have given you authority to tread on serpents and scorpions, and over all power of the enemy, and nothing shall hurt you. Nevertheless, do not rejoice in this, that the spirits are subject to you, but rejoice that your names are written in heaven.

It seems like many things can be taken away from us. Job lost everything. Some of us have experienced extreme failures and setbacks. However, some have had some great victories and successes. Jesus sent out seventy-two disciples in pairs to the places He would visit in the near future. Jesus gave them all power and authority over the enemy. These thirty-six pairs of evangelists could heal the sick, raise the dead, and even cast out demons. When they came back to Jesus they were so excited about their accomplishments; even the demons were subject to them. Jesus told them not to rejoice in this new-found power but to rejoice that their names were written in heaven.

No matter what our earthly successes may be, the greatest thing is that we have a home in heaven. On the other hand, everything can be taken away from us. We can lose it all, and this would be very disappointing. However, at our lowest point we can rejoice that our names are written in the Lamb's Book of Life. If you find yourself feeling depressed and there seems to be no good coming your way, start rejoicing that your name is written in heaven. You are saved and no one or any circumstance can take your salvation from you. Begin to rejoice in the Lord who delivered you out of darkness. This simple act of daily rejoicing in the Lord will begin to renew your spirit and start to put hope in your day. As you begin to focus on the Lord and start rejoicing in Him, your burdens will seem lighter. Soon you will have new strength for the day.

Everything can be taken away, but your salvation and your joy can never be taken away. Is your name written in heaven? If it is, rejoice in the Lord. Jesus rejoiced in the Holy Spirit and so should we.

Suggested Prayer

Dear Lord,
I have had many things taken away. My family is gone. My finances are gone. My future seems to be gone. Yet, Lord, I see that my name is in heaven. I choose to rejoice in You and my future home. Lord, I rejoice in You for giving me eternal salvation. Praise the Lord!

My Spirit Remains in Your Midst

Haggai 2:4-5

Yet now be strong, O Zerubbabel, declares the LORD. Be strong, O Joshua, son of Jehozadak, the high priest. Be strong, all you people of the land, declares the LORD. Work, for I am with you, declares the LORD of hosts, according to the covenant that I made with you when you came out of Egypt. My Spirit remains in your midst. Fear not.

When the returning Jews came from Babylonian exile to resettle in the land and build the City of Jerusalem there was much discouragement. There were many enemies and obstacles along the way. Zerubbabel led the first return from Babylon. God told him, the high priest, and the returning people to be strong. God also told them to work at rebuilding because He was with them. He had made a covenant with them to give them the land. He told them not to be afraid because His Spirit was in their midst.

God also made a covenant with you when you trusted Jesus Christ as Savior. His Spirit remains in your midst. He has a work for you to do, so do not be afraid. The walls of your life may be broken down. Maybe you are discouraged. Today God is with you! Israel was promised a land, and we are promised the Lord. Do not fear, no matter how bad things look today. God is coming back for you one day. He gave you a promise of His return for you by giving you the Holy Spirit. The Spirit is your earnest money or your down payment that He is coming back for you, His purchased possession.

The Holy Spirit is many things to you: He is your Comforter, Guide, Teacher, and your Peace. God's Spirit remains in your midst to accomplish His will in your life. The Holy Spirit will get you through all the difficulties you are presently facing. Today decide that you will adjust your life so you can be filled with the Holy Spirit. Spirit-filling simply means that you are controlled by Him. How can you be filled with the Spirit? Confess all known sin in your life, develop a devotional life to God that includes Bible study and prayer, and yield to Him daily. As you confess sin, pray, and yield, you will be controlled by Him. What a wonderful thought—"*My Spirit remains in your midst.*"

Suggested Prayer

Dear Lord,
I am afraid and discouraged. Help me realize that You are with me. Holy Spirit, I ask that You fill me so I can accomplish Your will. In Jesus' Name I pray, Amen.

A Revival in Your Future

Psalms 71:20-21

You who have made me see many troubles and calamities will revive me again; from the depths of the earth you will bring me up again. You will increase my greatness and comfort me again.

These verses are packed with encouragement and precious promises. There was a recognition on the psalmist's part. He realized that God had allowed many troubles and calamities to come his way. Most of the battle is realizing that God allowed the difficulty, and that He has a purpose for the ordeal. When we come to this realization, we are at least seeing the problem in its proper perspective.

Not only was there a recognition, there was an expectation on his part. He was expecting God to revive him again. He knew that God could raise him up again even if it was the lowest point he was experiencing in life. What does revival look like? Revival is when God reanimates and restores the Christian. The person is now filled with the Holy Spirit, with peace, joy, power, and new-found energy, and with a new zeal to serve God. What was dead and dormant is now full of energy and has soared to new heights.

Not only was there a recognition and an expectation, there was also an anticipation. He felt that God would bring him back to the place of honor. He could visualize God restoring the things that were taken away. He foresaw great comfort from the Holy Ghost. Friends, if you are struggling today, please recognize that God has allowed it and that there is a higher purpose involved. Then expect God to send you a personal revival. Anticipate God restoring your losses.

Suggested Prayer —————————————————————————

Dear Lord,

I see that the things that have happened to me were from You. Lord, it is hard for me to grasp that You allowed these things, but I accept it as from Your hand. Lord, please revive my spirit so I can serve you again. Bring comfort and restore my losses. In Jesus' Name I pray, Amen.

OCTOBER 9

Why Doesn't God Supply My Needs?

Luke 15:13-14
Not many days later, the younger son gathered all he had and took a journey into a far country, and there he squandered his property in reckless living. And when he had spent everything, a severe famine arose in the country, and he began to be in need.

This is a very good question to ask ourselves: "Why doesn't God supply my needs?" The prodigal son spent all his inheritance on the wrong things. The word "prodigal" means wasteful. His desire to have a good time overruled his common sense. As a result, his needs were no longer being met. He saw the error of his way and repented of his sin. He took full ownership of his mistake and told his father all about his error. God, in His mercy, forgave him of his sins and restored him.

Take an inventory of your life. Why are you in dire straits? Perhaps God has already given you the money, but you spent it on something else. For whatever reason, you purchased some things that you absolutely did not need. Divorced people tend to spend money on things for an emotional high to make them feel better about themselves. The first step is to take full responsibility for your mistakes. Confess all these mistakes to God.

Secondly, do your part. Perhaps you can sell these items that you do not need. Bring that car back to the dealership and get a nice used car. Those car payments are killing you. Begin to handle your finances in a biblical way. There are many Christian-based organizations that teach biblical finances, like Financial Peace University by Dave Ramsey and crown.org.

Thirdly, watch God honor you as you honor Him and His Word. God is not obligated to help anyone. However, when we begin to live by His principles He chooses to help us. It is a tough lesson to learn but we must learn it. The story of the prodigal son has a good ending for him. The turning point was when he assumed full responsibility for his actions and repented. Your story can end the same way when you decide to take full responsibility for your actions.

Suggested Prayer
Dear Lord, I feel badly that my needs are not being met, and I have grown resentful toward You. As I look around my house, I see that I spent Your money on the wrong things. I ask that You forgive me and cleanse me. Help me understand why I am making poor choices. Open my eyes to my situation. Help me sell the things that I purchased and did not need. Have mercy on me and let me live by Your principles. In Jesus Name, Amen.

October 10

The Last Supper

1 Kings 17:13-14

And Elijah said to her, "Do not fear; go and do as you have said. But first make me a little cake of it and bring it to me, and afterward make something for yourself and your son. For thus says the LORD, the God of Israel, 'The jar of flour shall not be spent, and the jug of oil shall not be empty, until the day the LORD sends rain upon the earth.'"

The situation was bad! Here was a widow and her son living in a severe drought because of the nation of Israel's sins. It was bad enough that she had no husband, but this drought would last three and a half years. The poor lady had just enough flour and oil to make one last little cake. After she and her son shared the cake there would be nothing left. She was preparing to starve to death.

Enter Jehovah God into the situation! God sent the prophet Elijah into town and he asked the lady for some food and water. She honestly explained the situation to the prophet. Elijah told her to make him a cake first. He said if she would do this that the oil and flour would not run out during the drought. By faith she trusted Elijah's words as coming from God Himself. Jehovah was true to His word and the jug of oil never went dry. There was always flour in the jar until the drought was over. From a human perspective it was truly the last supper. From the divine perspective, God wanted to do a miracle to show Himself strong in the lives of the people of Israel.

Perhaps your situation looks impossible. Maybe you are a single person with children. Perhaps your pantry is bare. Perhaps you are in a financial drought. God has not changed; Jesus Christ [is] the same yesterday, today, and forever (Hebrews 13:8). God wants to show Himself strong in your life and in the lives of your children. Trust God for a miracle and there will be many more suppers to come. When your drought has ended, you and your children will have a testimony to share about how God supplied your needs.

Suggested Prayer

Lord,

It seems like I am all alone and there is nothing left. I need a miracle. Lord, I am down to nothing. I am in a desperate situation. Please send some help my way today. By faith I receive my miracle. It is in the Name of Jesus I ask this, Amen.

Feast or Famine

Ecclesiastes 7:14
In the day of prosperity be joyful, and in the day of adversity consider: God has made the one as well as the other, so that man may not find out anything that will be after him.

My mother is an interesting lady to me. She and my dad worked very hard to provide for us kids. They both went without many things in life to make sure we were fed and clothed. Now mom would have an awesome meal one day and the next day it would be something mediocre, just thrown together quickly. The "just average" meals were there for two reasons: lack of money and exhaustion on her part. One day I commented on her cooking to her and she said it's feast or famine around here. I never forgot those words and it took several years to see the sacrifices that she and Dad made for us. They have been married for sixty-one years, by the way.

The days of prosperity come from God, so rejoice and enjoy those days. God allows us to prosper, so enjoy it and be thankful, realizing it came from His hand. Also consider that the days of adversity come from God too. God has made both prosperity and adversity for us, feast or famine. In the days of adversity remember how God has blessed you in the past. Be encouraged that you will not always have days of adversity. There are some prosperous days coming your way too. In the days of prosperity thank God from where He has brought you. It will help our spiritual walk with God if we can grasp the concept that prosperity and adversity both come from Him. Thank God for the bad days. Rejoice in the Lord in the bad days. Then when the good days come, they will be that much sweeter. God bless you!

Suggested Prayer
Dear Lord,
I have had some bad days and it seems like the goods days will never come around. Today I thank You for the bad days. I choose to serve You in these days, even if You never send me any more good days. Lord, You are good, and I thank You for the good days that are coming my way. In Jesus' Name, Amen.

What Is Your Main Goal?

2 Corinthians 5:9

So whether we are at home or away, we make it our aim to please him.

A little bit of honesty needs to be applied to our hearts as we ask ourselves what is our main goal. Paul said we would appear before the judgment seat of Christ and that he would love to be in heaven with Jesus. He even said that while we are here on this earth we are to walk by faith and not by sight or what we perceive with our senses. Paul's main goal was to please Christ. That is it—period, exclamation point, end of story! That was Paul's goal.

For many of us our main goal is to get remarried. There is nothing wrong with having a goal to get remarried, if it is not the main goal. If you are not happy by yourself, a new spouse is not going to make you happy. I know of a lady who felt like she needed a man to make her happy. Today she is on her fourth marriage, and putting it nicely, all her children are a mess. Here is a thought: put God first and make it your main goal to please Him. Then see what happens to your lesser goals.

You will find that some goals are not important and they are distracting you from serving God. Some goals will line up with God's will and He will help you develop those goals. Any goal that is placed above the Lord is doomed to fail. You might experience early victories and successes, but in the end it will fail. Matthew 6:33 is still in the Bible and God will supply your needs as you put Him first. Plan a goal of financial freedom. Plan various activities and trips. Plan to remarry if that is your goal. However, plan on seeking God and pleasing Him first. Any goal that puts Jesus second place is an unworthy goal.

Suggested Prayer

Lord,

Today I am honest with You, and I have been consumed with trying to find a new spouse. Everything I have tried has crumbled. I have walked by sight and not faith. Lord, I confess this and put all other goals in my life in second place. I want to please You first and foremost. Forgive me Lord! Give me wisdom to know which goals to drop and which ones to pursue. In Jesus' Name, Amen.

Don't Jump to Conclusions

Proverbs 18:17
The one who states his case first seems right, until the other comes and examines him.

People are funny creatures. Many people are quick to throw their side of the story out there. They present their case in court, to a family, church members, and friends. But when their case is cross-examined, we find that they were not telling the truth. Many times they have a hidden agenda or are simply trying to justify their sinful actions. Remember that there are two sides to every story.

One thing that amazed me during my separation and divorce was how many people sided with my ex-wife and never considered hearing my side of the story. I was talking to my ex one day and she was telling me how amazed she was at people who will not talk to her or even make eye contact with her when she sees them in public. In the end it simply does not matter—God gives new friends.

Broken relationships are some of the unfortunate things that we must go through. When you go through a divorce you will discover who your true friends really are. My ex-wife's best friend knew she was having an affair. She and her husband went as far as to tell their four children that I was evil and to stay away from me. One day I made a big pot of chili, and guess who came over to help me eat it. You guessed it—the children of this man and lady who said I was evil. Looking back at the situation I had to laugh. They had told their children horrible things about me, having never heard my side of the story.

Why am I sharing all of this? Because we need to quit taking sides with people. This is a trap of the enemy that we must recognize and avoid at all costs. We are destroying friends, family, and innocent children when we fall into this trap. God will reveal the truth of a situation if He so chooses. When the truth comes out, my job and your job is to love all parties involved. Avoid taking sides at work, in the church, and with those going through a divorce. On a lighter note, I think a bowl of chili sounds good.

Suggested Prayer ————————————————————
Dear Lord, forgive me for falling into the trap of taking sides. Lord, forgive those who have taken sides with my divorce. Cleanse me, Lord, and let me be one who loves all parties involved. Let me offer solutions to those who are at odds with each other. Use me to be a peacemaker. In Jesus' Name I pray, Amen.

He Swept Me Off My Feet

Song of Solomon 2:10
My beloved speaks and says to me: "Arise, my love, my beautiful one, and come away..."

The Jewish custom of the day was that a couple would first get engaged; that was considered a marriage. Then the bridegroom would prepare a place for the bride in his father's house. When all things were ready, he would come and get his bride (John 14:1-6). Solomon's bride was swept off her feet and longed for him to come and take her away. She was excited because she was confident that Solomon loved her. Solomon had told her that he loved her on several occasions and his actions lined up with his words. He also complimented her on her beauty. Solomon had cultivated an atmosphere of love. Each day she anticipated being with him. A day away from Solomon was a disappointing and a discouraging day.

A true love like this is possible for you. Many men are more concerned about football and playing golf (nothing wrong with this in moderation) than spending time with their wives. Many women surround themselves with church activities or being with their girlfriends because they do not want to be home. Why does this happen? It is because people have not cultivated an atmosphere of love.

It is better to live and die alone than to be with a person who does not truly love you. Be much in prayer and do not settle for second best. Lady, find a man that will sweep you off your feet. Sir, find a woman that will love and respect you. With God all things are possible. He will send you someone who will sweep you off your feet. This new relationship will be an atmosphere of love and respect. The love will be so strong that you will say the divorce was worth it to spend time with this person.

Suggested Prayer ————————————————————————————
Dear Lord,
Please send me someone who will sweep me off my feet. In the meantime, let me be overwhelmed by Your love for me. Love others through me. Let my home be a place of love and acceptance. In the Name of Jesus, I pray, Amen.

OCTOBER 15

Mutual Love

Song of Solomon 2:16
My beloved is mine, and I am his; he grazes among the lilies.

The Beatles have a song titled "All You Need Is Love." I cannot disagree with these men on this point. This verse explains how the young maiden realized that her husband exclusively belonged to her. The King of Israel, depicted as a shepherd, belonged to this lowly, undeserving lady. She found acceptance in Solomon's love. She did not have to win or keep his favor because he chose her. He loved her and he belonged to her. She also acknowledged that she totally belonged to Solomon. She was his and her aim was to please him. She accepted him and respected him.

Many divorced people long for the day when they can have love and mutual acceptance again. There seems to be nothing better than belonging to someone who loves and accepts you for who you are. If you need more money or better looks or anything else to satisfy your partner, then this is not the love that God has for you. The love described in this verse is what God meant when He said that two would become one flesh.

If you are truly a Christian, you belong totally and exclusively to The Lord Jesus Christ. He loves you and accepts you. He also belongs to you, so love and accept Him no matter what He sends your way in the form of trials. Just as two become one at marriage, you and Jesus have become one. Be content with Jesus. Love Jesus, and at the right time He will send you another spouse that will love you and accept you. Instead of concentrating all your efforts on a love that you do not have, cultivate your relationship with the One who loves you and accepts you right now. "Oh, how I love Jesus, because He first loved me."[7]

Suggested Prayer —————————————————————————
Dear Lord,
I have tried to find love and acceptance, forgetting that I already have it in You. Lord, You are mine and I am Yours. May we become one in thought, love, and action. Thank You for Your unconditional love for me. I love You Jesus. Amen.

---

[7] "Oh How I Love Jesus." Frederick Whitfield. 1855.

She Stole My Heart

Song of Solomon 4:9

You have captivated my heart, my sister, my bride; you have captivated my heart with one glance of your eyes, with one jewel of your necklace.

Solomon was captivated by his young bride. Just one glance toward her and his heart began to race. As he looked at a jewel on her necklace his heart was taken away with her love. She was truly a special girl. She had a close bond with Solomon, the King of Israel. He called her "sister," indicating a close relationship. He had a fellowship love for her like a sister. He also had a romantic love for her. Here was a man who could have any woman that he wanted, and just one glance from this shepherd girl melted the heart of a king. This was a special relationship, and perhaps you had this at one time.

Friends, we serve the same God that Solomon served. God is still able to put a nice lady or a wonderful Christian man in your path. God is working on sending you someone who will captivate your heart. This person will be someone that you can have fellowship with and be romantic with. God is able and willing to send someone your way. Wait on God!

The devil also has someone who can capture your heart for a short season. I know that you are probably lonely, and you so desperately want someone to look your way. You miss the romance and fellowship. I understand. I also know that right now you already possess this relationship if you are truly saved. Let Jesus captivate your heart again. Just one look from Him or one touch from the Blessed Holy Spirit should steal your heart away from the cares and troubles of this life. Today rekindle your relationship and wait on Him to send you the right person. Be much in prayer, because the devil has a person picked out for you too. Wait, watch, worship, and win the victory.

Suggested Prayer

Dear Lord,
Sometimes I just want a person I can talk to and be with. Lord, I realize that my heart should be captivated by You. Draw me into a deeper relationship with You and let me wait on You to work in my behalf. Let me also see the traps of the enemy. Lord, steal my heart away for You. Send a glance my way through the Holy Spirit. Amen!

Lover and Friend

Song of Solomon 5:16

His mouth is most sweet, and he is altogether desirable. This is my beloved and this is my friend, O daughters of Jerusalem.

Solomon's bride really loved him, and Solomon was a lover to her. His romantic plots to win her heart worked. Solomon was also her friend. Unfortunately, to be both lovers *and* friends is a rare combination. There is nothing more frustrating than pouring your life into someone who does not feel the same way about you.

Some people get married and they cannot be friends. Other couples marry and there is no romantic spark anymore. I know of a couple that both like to cook. They have all the latest gadgets and the best utensils. However, they cannot share their passion together. He criticizes her cooking, and she scrutinizes his techniques. It is sad that they cannot be friends. What kind of example does this set for the children in the home?

Solomon's wife not only had a lover and a friend, she bragged about him to all her female acquaintances. She lifted him up in front of others. She did not belittle him privately or publicly. Solomon also had nothing but good things to say about her. Solomon viewed her as a lover and a best friend. I see so many divorced people longing to have a friend of the opposite sex. They have come to realize there is more to a relationship than sex. They want a best friend. It is not wrong to be praying for God to send you someone who is a Christian, one that can be both a lover and friend. God, in His time, will send you someone that you will be proud of. You will love him or her so much that you will brag about this person to all your friends. Keep praying and keep seeking God. When God acts on your behalf, he or she will come suddenly and unexpectedly.

Suggested Prayer ————————————————————

Dear Lord,
I long for a spouse that will be my lover and best friend. Please send someone soon. I want to pray about it, but I do not want to be consumed by it. Lord, send me a circle of friends till my spouse comes into my life. In the Name of Jesus I pray, Amen.

Can't Buy Me Love

Song of Solomon 8:7

Many waters cannot quench love, neither can floods drown it. If a man offered for love all the wealth of his house, he would be utterly despised.

One of my favorite Beatles' songs is "Can't Buy Me Love." It is a rather short song with a big message. You simply cannot buy love. On a divine scale God loved us enough to come and die for us. He did not need to redeem us, but His love compelled Him to save us. Love must be the most powerful source in the universe. You cannot stop the love that God has for us, His children.

When there is love between a couple, there is acceptance and many other great things going on in the relationship. Men and women can purchase many things and have many possessions. These purchases may or may not make us happy. We cannot purchase love with all our human resources. We can get a date or find a spouse who only wants our money, but we cannot buy true love.

Divorce is the ultimate rejection. A loving marriage is the antithesis of divorce. Do not waste God's time trying to buy the love and affection of a person who does not truly love you. You will exhaust your resources and at the end of the day you will not find true love. Many schemers are out there to take your money from you, so be careful. We will be shrouded with shame and disgrace when we try to buy love or try to make someone like us.

I hope that all deserving divorced people will find true love again. In the meantime, fall in love anew with Jesus. Experience His love again. Ask Him to refresh your spirit and send you someone. May God protect you from the money-hungry schemers who prey on your weaknesses. May God send you someone that you can truly love. Ask God to give you a new love for your family and friends. Determine to show the love of Christ to some lost person today. Hey, it is quite alright to admit that you like the Beatles too. The truth is the truth whether sung by the Beatles or found recorded in God's Holy Word. You deserve the best, so don't settle for someone who won't pass the test.

Suggested Prayer ⸻

Dear Lord, I admit that I have tried to force some relationships and tried to buy my way into having a new spouse. Forgive me. Let me fall in love with You again, dear Lord. Protect me from the enemy. May Your love flow through me! In Jesus' Name I pray, Amen. I love You, Lord!

OCTOBER 19

Abstract Life
Abundant Life

John 10:10

The thief comes only to steal and kill and destroy. I came that they may have life and have it abundantly.

W e long for the day when we will experience abundant life. Jesus came to give us life—not only life, but abundant life. This means that God wants our life to be special right now. We know we will have this great, everlasting, abundant, sinless life when we reach heaven, but God wants our earthly life to be great too. Someone has said, "all this and heaven too," meaning this life should be good too. How do we experience this life? This sort of life only comes through a deep relationship with Jesus Christ.

The problem is clearly stated in this verse—we have an enemy. He is on a threefold mission: to steal, to kill, and destroy. Satan has already stolen our homes through the divorce. He killed our families. He has destroyed everything that we hoped for and dreamed about. The aftermath of his destructive path is devastating. As you sit amid the ashes and rubble, remember that "greater is He that is in you, than he that is in the world" (1 John 4:4). God lives in your soul, and He brings you peace during your storm. More importantly, He gives abundant life.

Today realize that you have an enemy who tried to destroy you. Recognize that God wants to give you an abundant life. Then by faith recommit yourself to Him, trusting Him to give you an abundant life as you walk in His steps. Finally, commit to love Him with all your heart, having fellowship with Him through daily prayer and Bible study. Submit to everything that the Holy Spirit leads you to do. This deep relationship with Him will weather any storm and give you an abundant life. Focus on Christ and not circumstances.

Suggested Prayer ————————————————————

Dear Lord,
I have suffered tremendously. My joy is gone. I have no hope. Today I want this abundant life. I recommit myself to You and ask that You will lead me into a deeper relationship with You. Lord, let my life count for You and Your kingdom. In Jesus' Name I pray, Amen.

OCTOBER 19 | 293

Shelter in the Shadow of Egypt

Isaiah 30:1-3

"Ah, stubborn children," declares the LORD, "who carry out a plan, but not mine, and who make an alliance, but not of my Spirit, that they may add sin to sin; who set out to go down to Egypt, without asking for my direction, to take refuge in the protection of Pharaoh and to seek shelter in the shadow of Egypt! Therefore shall the protection of Pharaoh turn to your shame, and the shelter in the shadow of Egypt to your humiliation."

In the Bible, Egypt is always a type of this world's evil system, controlled by the devil (Pharaoh) himself. As humans it is very natural to rely on this world instead of God. This world appears to offer a shadow of protection. We are in the world, but we are not of the world, so it is very difficult to walk by faith.

When a need arises, what is our first response? Do we pray about it and ask God for guidance, or do we look to our own power and the shadow of Egypt? Earthly wealth, human ability, and human wisdom are merely shadows when compared to the Holy Spirit. The result of trusting in the shadow of Egypt is sin against God and we are humiliated in the process. Egypt no longer furnishes the needs of a Christian. We are no longer fit for Egypt and Egypt is no longer fit for us. Why do we fail so much? It is because we are like stubborn children having our own way without consulting God. We stubbornly want to rely on the arm of flesh.

God says that there is a better way. It is through His Spirit. As we seek the direction of the Spirit, we draw closer to Jesus. We will begin to ask God what is the right path. We will be led out of Egypt and into a deeper fellowship with God. We will have our needs met (Matthew 6:33). We will not be humiliated or ashamed. We will sin less and less against God. We will come out of the shadow of Egypt and into the Light of our glorious Lord and Savior.

Suggested Prayer

Dear Father,

I am like a stubborn child. I have looked to the world without consulting You. I am humiliated and ashamed. Lord, I surrender to the Holy Spirit. Lead me and guide me in paths of righteousness. In the Name of Jesus I pray, Amen.

I Just Want to Die

Job 6:4, 8-9

For the arrows of the Almighty are in me; my spirit drinks their poison; the terrors of God are arrayed against me. Oh that I might have my request, and that God would fulfill my hope, that it would please God to crush me, that he would let loose his hand and cut me off!

Do you ever feel like you just wanted to die? Job did, and perhaps some of us feel that way too. Job felt like God had reached back His bow at full strength and shot him with poisonous arrows. The poison was attacking Job's nervous system and slowly killing him. I never thought about killing myself, but I did feel like if there was a cave that I could go into and never come out of, that would be fine with me. I, like Job, have felt like the poison of God's arrows were slowly killing me. Job was down to his last request, that God would kill him and put him out of his misery. Job could not see the light at the end of the tunnel or what God was trying to accomplish through him. All that Job knew was that God had sent him a death blow and he just wanted to die. I totally get this because I lived it.

Dear reader, if you are having suicidal thoughts, do not be ashamed to seek professional help. In fact, put this book down and call for help right now. God loves you and wants you to seek help. Do not be too proud or ashamed to get help.

Today I want us to see the whole picture. The big picture is that God has a purpose for you and wants to do something great for you. Do not focus on the pain; focus on the purpose of God. By faith ask Him what you need to learn. Sometimes God's arrows come our way, but if we allow Him to work, we will be blessed in the end. There is coming a day when you will see the hand of God in all of your pain. You will see that He is doing great things. Job's request was to die. Perhaps our request should be for the Lord to teach us through the trial so we can be more like Him. May the Lord give your heart a hug today. May the Holy Spirit refresh your soul and give you peace.

Suggested Prayer

Lord,
All I can see is my pain. Like Job, I am ready for this pain to stop, even if it means death. Lord, let me see the purpose of all of this. Let me see that You have a plan. Lord, deep down I know that You will help me and bless me. Give me faith to believe. In Jesus' Name, Amen.

Refreshing Company

Romans 15:32

...so that by God's will I may come to you with joy and be refreshed in your company.

Paul wanted to visit Rome as the great evangelist and preacher. When he finally arrived, he was Paul the prisoner. Paul wanted to visit in the will of God and to be filled with joy. He wanted to refresh the saints at Rome. He also knew that his spirit would be refreshed by the Christians at Rome. Their meeting would bring mutual fellowship, renewal, and refreshment.

I encourage you to find a group that you will be a blessing to and they in turn will bless you. Our church has a twelve-week program called Divorce Care. Perhaps your church has the same program or a similar one. If your church does not have a divorce program, find one in your area. These programs are confidential so you can express how you really feel. Unloading all your hurts on your children is not the right place to share a burden. Many parents do this because they do not have any adult friends to talk to. These programs are a place of mutual fellowship. If you are too nervous to go by yourself, ask a friend to go with you at first.

If you cannot find a Divorce Care class, find a Bible study to attend. God has a group of people out there for you to receive encouragement from, and they also need your encouragement. Every day ask God to use you to be a blessing to someone. Purpose to be filled with joy to do the ministry that God has called you to do.

These groups also get you out of the prison of your own home. There is life after divorce. There is a whole world out there that needs your help. It is a great feeling to be refreshed by some person when you are down. It is even greater to be a blessing to someone else. Find your group! God never wanted you to bear this heavy burden alone. There is some refreshing company out there for you. God has a group for you, and He has some people that He wants you to encourage.

Suggested Prayer ———————————————————————————
Lord,
I am lonely and I need a group to encourage me. I also want to encourage others. Lord, help me find a care group where I can share my burdens. Amen.

God Pays Back His Loans

Proverbs 19:17
Whoever is generous to the poor lends to the LORD, and he will repay him for his deed.

It is interesting that God owns everything. We are mere stewards of all that He possesses. Yet this scripture points out that when we are helping the poor we are lending to the Lord. The Lord always pays back with interest. I am not advocating helping someone just to get something; I am saying that you will be blessed every time you serve the Lord.

Think about a ministry to help those who are less fortunate. See what ministries your church has and pray about joining one. If your church does not have any outreaches into your community, pray about starting one. Our church has several well-established ministries, but we still had a man that started his own ministry. He prepares meals for the homeless and gives personal care packages to those taking shelter under the overpasses. His motivation is not so God will pay him back; he had once fallen on hard times, and when God brought him out of it, he wanted to be a blessing to others. Armed with a heart of thankfulness and a love for Christ, he began ministering to these homeless people.

Perhaps ministering to the homeless is not your cup of tea. What about those kids at your church who need a Sunday school teacher? The music minister may need some help. Perhaps the church needs help with cleaning or maintaining the building. The idea is to get our hearts and minds off our problems and on the kingdom of God. We will be blessed as we serve others.

Christian service may be the therapy that you need for your own problem. Let God lead you into some kind of service. All are not meant to be teachers. Some are too nervous to talk to the homeless. God will show you what you need to do. As you set out to save a life this may be the very thing that saves your life.

Suggested Prayer ——————————————————————
Dear Lord,
I want to serve, not to get something but to further Your kingdom. Give me a heart of love and compassion for others. Lord, You know my strengths and weaknesses, so lead me into the ministry that You want me to have. In Jesus' Name, Amen.

OCTOBER 24

This Will Not Destroy Me

Psalms 118:17-18

I shall not die, but I shall live, and recount the deeds of the LORD. The LORD has disciplined me severely, but he has not given me over to death.

The psalmist must have thought that he was going to die. Many a Christian has felt that God was going to take their life. Maybe we get cancer or experience severe depression, and we think it is all over. No, folks, we are not going to die, but live. We are not going to just exist, we are going to have life again. We are going to have life and have it more abundantly. We are going to experience the joy and power of the Holy Spirit again.

With this newly found energy we are going to declare the works of the Lord. We need a second touch from God that will bring life back to our deadness and indifference. Through the Holy Spirit we will tell others about Christ. Like the psalmist, we too can say that the Lord disciplined me severely, but it did not kill me. The discipline is the pruning process that removes the deadness of our lives and replaces it with new life from above. We then will be excited to tell others about the great God that we serve. We will help those that are just starting the divorce process. More than anything I find they just need someone to lend a sympathetic ear. We can tell them that Jesus loves them and that He died for them. Are you going to die? You are not going to die. You will live and declare the works of the Lord.

Suggested Prayer

O Lord,
Remove all the dead parts of my life that are not productive for You. Lord, at one time I just wanted to die, but now I sense that You are about to do great things in my life. Cleanse me and give me a second touch so I can proclaim to others how great You are. In Jesus' Name I pray, Amen.

I Think God Overlooked Me

Hebrews 6:10
For God is not unjust so as to overlook your work and the love that you have shown for his name in serving the saints, as you still do.

We sometimes think that God has forgotten about us. Even when the Apostle John was exiled on the Isle of Patmos he was not alone. Jesus appeared to him there, and he wrote the book of The Revelation. First, God is not unrighteous. There is no sin in Him at all. He is not treating us unfairly. It may seem like He is unfair, but He is not. Second, God did not overlook you or forget about you. It may not seem like He is active in your life, but He is there for you. Third, He sees your work. He sees you struggling to support your family. He sees you volunteering for church ministries. He sees you praying and reading your Bible. He saw you give a tithe when you probably could not afford to give. Finally, He sees the love that you have shown in ministering to other people.

Some of the love that you have shown for others is quite amazing. It is the living God loving people through you. Whether it be a word of encouragement or bringing food to a needy saint, these labors of love are recorded in heaven. The rewards may or may not be seen on earth immediately, but rest assured, you will be rewarded in this life and the life to come. Perhaps you are going through a dry season in your life—do not lose heart. God has not overlooked you. He has not forgotten about you. God is not unrighteous. He sees everything that you have done in His name. Friends, there are blessings in the days and months ahead, so rest in the fact that He is working out something great in your life.

Suggested Prayer ——————————————————————————
Lord,
It seems like I am overlooked. It seems like things are not fair and that You have forgotten me. Lord, I am going to keep on ministering and working for You. Love Your people through me. Please bless me in Your time and in Your way. In Jesus' Name I pray, Amen.

A Lost Multitude

Joel 3:14
Multitudes, multitudes, in the valley of decision! For the day of the LORD is near in the valley of decision.

The Day of the LORD describes the time when Jesus will come back and set up His kingdom on earth. There will be multitudes upon multitudes that will be caught off guard. The symbolism in this verse is that of people in the valley, needing to decide for or against Christ. The text tells us that the Day of the LORD is near. Jesus will soon return and catch many people unprepared.

Today there is a deep valley with people from across the globe who are lost. Perhaps your family and friends are in this valley. Take a long, hard look at those around you—your coworkers, your family, and your neighbors. Is there someone you know that is in the valley of decision? To me, the valley of decision describes people whose minds are cloudy. They cannot clearly see Jesus as their Lord and Savior. They need someone to share the gospel with them. The Holy Spirit is the only One who can clear their minds and open their hearts to the gospel. Our job is to share the Word of God with them.

One of Satan's biggest tactics is to get our minds so involved in our own problems that we do not consider our neighbor. Today ask God to open your spiritual eyes to see those who are in the valley of decision. Ask God to break your heart for those who need Him. It would be awesome for God to use you to pull people out of the valley. When the Day of the LORD comes those caught in the valley will perish. May God use us to rescue those in darkness!

Suggested Prayer
Dear Lord,
I am sorry. I have worried about my own problems and have fallen asleep spiritually. Lord, open my eyes to see lost people. Break my heart for those who need You. Lead me to those who need to hear Your Word. In the Name of our Lord I pray, Amen.

There Is No Other Savior

Isaiah 43:11

I, I am the LORD, and besides me there is no savior.

Apart from God there is no other Savior! Here in the United States we are almost in a post-Christian era. The kingdom of darkness has invaded our land and seems to have taken over. Our enemy is not a foreign country or any one terrorist organization. Our enemy is the devil. The devil has infiltrated our schools, churches, government, and workplaces. Many people think that we evolved and will just perish one day.

Then there are those who believe that there is a God out there somewhere. Most of this group of people seem to think they can save themselves. There is not one person in heaven who arrived there by his own effort. The only people in heaven are those who have been saved by the sacrifice of God Himself on the cross. There are others who think a particular religious institution saves them. They think that if they just follow the teachings of the church they will be saved. Today there are no people in heaven who followed a religious code to get there.

Everyone in heaven today has been born again by the Holy Spirit. Being born again is not a physical baptism. It is a spiritual transformation that happens when a person repents of his sins and trusts Christ as his Savior. If you have never been saved, let me say that there is no other Savior than Jesus. If you are a Christian, take time out of your busy schedule today to thank God for your salvation. God is all powerful and He still saves. He still leads, guides, and directs His children. He still supplies our needs. He is still the only Savior. Commit to Him or recommit to Him today.

Suggested Prayer ——————————————————————————

Lord,
I confess that I am a sinner. I believe that You died for me and rose again. I surrender my heart to You. I accept You today as my Savior. Thank You for saving me. Amen! Hallelujah!

It Is Christ Alone

Romans 10:1-4

Brothers, my heart's desire and prayer to God for them is that they may be saved. For I bear them witness that they have a zeal for God, but not according to knowledge. For, being ignorant of the righteousness of God, and seeking to establish their own, they did not submit to God's righteousness. For Christ is the end of the law for righteousness to everyone who believes.

Paul's heart was with his fellow countrymen, the Jewish people. The Jewish people were very religious. They had a great zeal for God, and even tried to keep all the laws of the Old Testament. Paul points out their flaw as a nation in these verses. They were trying to be right with God by trying to observe the Mosaic Law. Paul said that they were ignorant to the truth of the gospel of Jesus Christ and had not submitted themselves to Him.

The gospel is still good enough to save an individual, a family, a town, or a nation. The gospel is the death, burial, and resurrection of Jesus Christ. When people confess their sins and place their trust in the God of the gospel, they are saved. Afterward they might do some good works. They now work because they are saved, they are not working to *get* saved. They are working because they are going to heaven, and not working to try to get an entrance into heaven.

There are basically two theories to salvation. One is a salvation based on works and the other is based on faith. The Bible tells us that the faith-based method is the one that God approves of and the works-based method is not acceptable to God. If you are trusting in your baptism, church membership, good deeds, or even trying to follow the ten commandments, you are following a works-based system. One day you will perish, and God will tell you to depart from His presence because He never knew you. You will go to hell. God never wanted any person to go to hell. Hell was prepared for the devil and the fallen angels. The righteousness that God accepts is based on faith in Jesus Christ. There is no other way to be saved but to trust Christ. What are you trusting, or who are your trusting for your salvation?

Suggested Prayer ⸻

Dear Father, I admit that I am a sinner. I have tried to be good and tried to work my way to heaven. I confess my sins and ask You to save me. I accept that Jesus died, was buried, and arose the third day for my sins. I ask You to save me. In Jesus' Name I pray, Amen. Thank You, Lord.

A Spiritual Famine

Amos 8:11

"Behold, the days are coming," declares the LORD GOD, "when I will send a famine on the land—not a famine of bread, not a thirst for water, but of hearing the words of the LORD.

God said that He would send a famine on the land, but not one where people starve for food or die of thirst. This famine would be a spiritual famine where people are dying because of a lack of revelation from God. Living in the United States, we as a country do not know much about physical famines. We have poor people who are starving, but for the most part we do not know much about famine. We have droughts, but for the most part we have abundant water sources.

However, we seem to be living in a spiritual drought in the United States. I was twenty years old before someone explained the gospel to me. Thank God someone cared enough to share the Word of God with me. In our country most of our hotels have Bibles in them. Our cities have churches, Christian radio, and Christian television programs, yet we are in darkness. Europe was once a spiritual powerhouse, but now the continent sits in darkness. The United States is not far behind.

A spiritual famine that has taken over the whole world. God has allowed this because of our sins collectively. Men love darkness more than the light because their deeds are evil (John 3:19). I recently attended a church service where a false gospel was preached. It was sad to see a whole congregation of people in darkness, thinking that they are Christians. This is becoming the norm in our land. Multitudes who are in church will perish because they are lost.

The world is experiencing a spiritual famine far worse than lack of food and water. Will we sit by idly and do nothing or will we send spiritual relief? People need food and water but they also need bread from heaven (Jesus). This world needs Jesus! Start sharing the gospel with your children and family members, then go tell your neighbors and friends. Form a habit of sharing the gospel with others. You have the spiritual food that the world needs. Will you share with them or let them perish? God has called us to share. This is His method and plan.

Suggested Prayer

Dear Lord, I give myself to You. I ask that You open my eyes and heart to my own spiritual condition, and then let me see the condition of this world. Lord, burden my heart for lost people and let me begin to share the gospel. Use me to make a difference in someone's life today. Use me every day. In Jesus' Name I pray, Amen.

Work Smarter, Not Harder

Ecclesiastes 10:10
If the iron is blunt, and one does not sharpen the edge, he must use more strength, but wisdom helps one to succeed.

I think most of us have heard the saying, "work smarter, not harder" and that is basically what Solomon is saying in this verse. If someone has a dull ax he will have to work a lot harder to succeed in chopping wood. However, if one takes the time to sharpen the ax he will not have to work as long or exert as much effort for the same results. The principle is to use wisdom before starting the task. Some managers get frustrated with lazy employees. A wise manager gave his hardest task to his laziest employee. The lazy person figured out a shortcut on how to do the job quicker.

We need God's wisdom for our lives in every area. One blessing from my divorce is that it has caused me to rethink every area of my life. I have developed spiritually and branched out in many areas. This would not have happened if I was not forced to cry out to God for wisdom and understanding.

God has some great things for you to learn in many areas of life. What are the areas you are struggling with? Ask God to give you wisdom and to lead and guide you. As you use this wisdom you will begin to work smarter and not harder. God is going to give you practical solutions to your problems. One big problem divorced people face is finances. Ask God for wisdom. He will show you how to pay those bills and recoup your losses. He will also give you wisdom to pay off your debts. He will give you the wisdom to have those retirement funds that were depleted. Finances are just one example.

Perhaps your problem is with housing or transportation. It could be an emotional or physical issue. God is going to give you the wisdom to help you. You will work smarter and not harder, leaving more time to spend with Him. You will also find more time for your children and friends. God is for us! We just need to acquire and follow His wisdom.

Suggested Prayer —————————————————————————
Dear Lord,
I need Your wisdom. I am working hard, and I am willing to work more. Lord, the more I work the further I get behind. So today I want to be one with the Holy Spirit to know Your will. I also ask for wisdom for the things that are troubling me. In the Name of Jesus I pray, Amen.

Jesus Christ, The Ark of Our Salvation

Hebrews 11:7
By faith Noah, being warned by God concerning events as yet unseen, in reverent fear constructed an ark for the saving of his household. By this he condemned the world and became an heir of the righteousness that comes by faith.

God still speaks to people today to accomplish His will. The name "Noah" means rest. God wanted to bring rest on the earth. God would bring about a flood, and start the human race over again with Noah and his family. When God speaks, we must respond in faith. God revealed His plan to destroy the world and yet preserve the world. God always warns before He judges. Noah responded in faith. He also responded in worship and works.

When God speaks, we must rise to the occasion. Noah had to adjust his whole life to respond. He began building this massive ark which represents Jesus Christ. There was only one door on this ark, and all who entered through that door were saved (John 10:9). There was only one plan in Noah's day, and there is only one plan in our day—faith in God.

When God speaks we must reach out with the message. Noah began to cry out to the world (2 Peter 2:5) and his only converts were his own family. The message seemed very foolish to the people who heard Noah preach. Noah condemned the world because the people were either converted or they confirmed their wickedness by rejecting the message.

Noah also recognized the blessing. His response of faith saved his own soul. He saved his family and ultimately the entire world. What is God asking you to do? Respond in faith. Rise to the occasion. Reach out with the message. Recognize the blessing.

Suggested Prayer
Dear Lord,
I ask that You reveal Your will to me. Help me respond in faith. Let me rise to the occasion. Let me reach out with the message. Let me see that it will be worth it as You send Your blessings. In the Name of Jesus I pray, Amen.

A Wedding Blessing

Numbers 6:22-27

The LORD spoke to Moses, saying, "Speak to Aaron and his sons, saying, Thus you shall bless the people of Israel: you shall say to them, The LORD bless you and keep you; the LORD make his face to shine upon you and be gracious to you; the LORD lift up his countenance upon you and give you peace. "So shall they put my name upon the people of Israel, and I will bless them."

As you read today's verses, you probably remember hearing them before. You probably heard them at a wedding. They are marvelous wedding verses. These verses were addressed to all the people of Israel, and not just for those on their wedding day. As a bride and groom start a new life together it is appropriate to invoke a blessing on them.

The nation of Israel was the Father's bride. He did not choose them because they were a great nation or something special; He chose them because of the great love that He had for them. He wanted to bless, protect, and give peace to His special bride. Fast forward in time and we see that the church is Jesus' bride, called out by the Holy Spirit. The church is not a building, it is the individual believers that make up the bride of Christ. In a spiritual sense these are wedding verses for Christians as well as the Jewish people.

We must rid our minds of the idea of a mean God who is out to get us for every little thing we do wrong. There is no doubt that God is love and that He is also just. He must chasten His children when they are disobedient. However, He also sees us as His bride. He wants to look on us with favor. He wants to pamper us and protect us. He wants to supply our needs and bring special blessings in our lives. He wants to be gracious to us and shower us with peace.

A true husband will sacrifice for his bride and try to make her life special. God is no different with us. He is on a mission to make our lives special. He gave the ultimate sacrifice of Himself to purchase us. We should be encouraged that He is our special Heavenly Groom and we should respond to Him with hearts of love, respect, and gratitude.

Suggested Prayer

Dear Lord,
I often forget that I am Your bride. Forgive me for seeing You as a mean God who is looking to punish me. Give me eyes to see that You love me as a groom loves his bride. Deepen my relationship with You. Let me be loving and respectful. In Jesus' Name, Amen.

I Just Can't Sleep

Job 7:4
When I lie down I say, 'When shall I arise?' But the night is long, and I am full of tossing till the dawn.

Poor Job had many sleepless nights. He is not alone, is he? You and I lay in bed, exhausted; yet we cannot sleep. You share your burden with your friend, and your "spiritual" friend says "Just give it to Jesus, that's what I would do." Obviously, your friend has not been in your shoes.

Job tossed and turned all night with a heavy heart. Sleepless nights are part of the grieving process. Sleepless nights lead to sleepy days at work because you are just exhausted physically, mentally, emotionally, and spiritually. Some people have so much energy at night that they sleep only a few hours and get up and exercise. Your body is out of sync and it is terrible. As you toss and turn you see that empty place in the bed where your spouse used to sleep. You probably do not realize it but in the next bedroom there is a little boy or girl crying his or herself to sleep every night. It's horrible!

It will take some time for your mind to process everything that has happened to you. Eventually you will sleep a little longer each night. It will not be quick, but your body will get back in sync. Your children will experience healing too, but it is a process. There are no shortcuts. Be honest with your boss and explain to him or her why you are so tired at work. Take the time to see how your children are faring. My son cried himself to sleep every night for months. I did not know this until six years later. He finally broke down one evening and told me about it. Your homework today is to hug your children and tell them that you love them. Your term paper is to check up on them daily to see how they are doing.

Suggested Prayer
Lord,
I can't sleep at night or stay awake during the day. Lord, heal my broken heart and worn-out body. Heal my children too. Lord, please have mercy on us and bring healing. You are the Great Physician, so I call on You. Amen.

God Comforts the Discouraged and Depressed

2 Corinthians 7:6
But God, who comforts the downcast, comforted us by the coming of Titus.

Everyone gets discouraged and depressed. It is our nature to get bummed out from time to time. Thank God, He has a way of comforting us when we are cast down. God has and uses many ways to comfort His children. One way is by sending someone our way to lift our spirit. As you reflect on your Christian life, how many times has God sent someone to encourage you? It usually happens when you least expect it, and it comes from an unlikely person. Either way, God shows His great love to us by sending someone our way. Brothers and sisters, if you are discouraged today God has someone coming your way to encourage you.

Decide today to be a blessing to someone else. Pray and ask God to show you who needs encouragement. Make a list of these people and plan on visiting or calling them, or sending a text their way. A simple text lets that person know that you are thinking about them. Determine to make a difference in someone's life today.

Perhaps you know someone who is going through a divorce. You know exactly how they feel, and you can be a major source of encouragement to them. Do you remember how you felt after someone encouraged you? Pass that good feeling on to someone else. It is not difficult to be a blessing to others. The hardest part is determining that you will do it. Once you make that call or visit, the Holy Spirit will do all the work. He will give you the boldness and the words to say.

Suggested Prayer
Father,
I remember when I was depressed and discouraged. At my weakest hour You sent someone to talk to me. Lord, I want to be a blessing to others. Let me be a comforter to those who are cast down. In Jesus' Name I pray, Amen.

No More Burdens to Bear

Psalms 81:6
I relieved your shoulder of the burden; your hands were freed from the basket.

One of the greatest events of the Old Testament was when God delivered the children of Israel out of Egypt. Our text tells us that God relieved their shoulder from their heavy burdens and freed their hands from the basket. In His time God relieved them and set them free. Make no mistake, God saw every tear. He heard every cry. His chosen people were suffering as slaves in Egypt. They were beaten, and many died. They were Pharaoh's slaves and the situation was bleak. At the right time God sent Moses to deliver them from the hands of Pharaoh. There were years of suffering, but there came a day when the slaves were set free. The burden of Egypt was a thing of the past.

This is exactly what God did for us spiritually. We were the devil's slaves and at the right time God sent Jesus to deliver us. If the Son makes you free, you are free indeed (John 8:36). Are you a Christian, but under some kind of heavy burden? God sees this burden and He sees the problems that lie ahead of you. There is coming a day when God will relieve your shoulder and free your hands. Hang in there, at the right time you will be set free. Be encouraged today that God sees your tears and hears your cries. One day soon there will be no more burdens to bear. We are going to a city whose Maker and Builder is God. It will be worth it all when we see Jesus face to face. Deliverance is coming! Amen! Praise God! Here comes Jesus to deliver you!

Suggested Prayer
Dear Lord,
I am under a heavy burden. Free my shoulder and hands so I can serve You. Lord, in Your time send deliverance. I long for the day when there will be no more burdens to bear. Thank you, Jesus; Amen.

Gracious Supply

Psalms 81:10
I am the LORD your God, who brought you up out of the land of Egypt. Open your mouth wide, and I will fill it.

God is awesome, and He is a God of grace. In this text we see possession with the pronoun "your." He is a personal God who owns us, and we own Him. There is a mutual possession that takes place when we trust Him. God, in His infinite grace, owns us and has fellowship with us. Our biggest need is to be owned by our gracious Father.

Not only is there possession, there is power in this scripture. God said, "I brought you up from the burden of Egypt." Our God brought us out of a life of sin and into the kingdom of His Dear Son.

Not only is there possession and power, there is also preparation in the verse. God said, "open your mouth wide." This speaks of preparation on our part. When we are opening our mouths wide we are exercising faith. We are believing that God is going to do something on our behalf.

Today there are many closed mouths, denoting that people are not really expecting God to work on their behalf. They have become discouraged and do not seek Him by faith anymore. Is your mouth opened or closed today? If it is open, is it opened a little, or is it wide open? If your mouth is closed today, let me encourage you. The God who saved you wants to do mighty things through you. He wants to bless you and supply all your needs. Confess your doubts and reach out by faith to Him.

Not only is there possession, power and preparation, there is also provision. To the mouth that is open wide, God said, "I will fill it." When our mouths are open wide it shows total dependence on Him. Imagine some baby birds in a nest waiting for the mother to feed them. They are totally looking to the parent to feed them. We cannot look to ourselves for answers. God promises to fill our need, whatever it may be. Friends, God will graciously supply your needs.

Suggested Prayer
Lord,
I see that You bought me with Your blood. Let these needs of mine draw me closer to You. By faith I totally depend on You to supply my needs. Thank You for being my God and thank You for the gracious supply that is coming my way. In Jesus' Name, Amen.

The Kingdom of God

Romans 14:17

For the kingdom of God is not a matter of eating and drinking but of righteousness and peace and joy in the Holy Spirit.

God's kingdom includes many things. It includes all of God's people accomplishing His purposes for the universe. It is being a part of the kingdom as well as inviting others to come to this kingdom.

Our text tells us what the kingdom is not, as well as what it consists of. The kingdom is not "a matter of eating and drinking" or outward observances. Some refrain from certain foods or refuse to drink certain things. Many people and churches are worried about trivial matters that are not the kingdom of God. Some will not allow certain types of music into their churches. Some people will not go out to eat on Sunday or go to a movie any day of the week. Paul says these things are not the kingdom of God. These are the things that cause division and keep us from seeking the kingdom. The kingdom of God is not an outward observance!

The verse tells us what the kingdom of God is: "righteousness and peace and joy in the Holy Spirit." As we turn our hearts into the ways of the Spirit, we begin to see that we have an imputed righteousness and a practical righteousness. We then begin to have peace and joy in our lives. As the Spirit controls us we become better citizens of the kingdom. We also begin to do kingdom works. We share our faith. We help those with needs. God's will is being done on earth. It happens because it is the Spirit of God accomplishing the kingdom of God through us.

Suggested Prayer

Dear Lord,
I am off base in my walk with You. I want my life to count for Your kingdom. Holy Spirit, I yield my heart to You. Take the things out of my life that are hindering Your kingdom and replace them with things that will advance Your kingdom. In Jesus' Name, Amen.

NOVEMBER 7

The Devil Has Your Best Interests in Mind

Proverbs 27:12

The prudent sees danger and hides himself, but the simple go on and suffer for it.

Notice that I did not say that the devil has his best interests in mind. Let me clarify my title. The devil sees what our focus and interests are in life, and this is where he will attack. So yes, his best interest is in mind too. He is out to destroy your Christian walk and testimony.

Solomon says the prudent person or sensible person sees the trap and hides himself from the sin. The foolish person does not discern that a trap is laid before him, and he takes the bait. The foolish man will suffer for the poor choices that he made.

Let's talk real life. The devil sees your loneliness and sees you praying for a spouse. He sees you spending endless hours looking at dating sites. The devil has his person answer the email that you sent out. Satan is bringing you the person that will bring you down. The devil used your best interest in mind so you would not recognize the trap. After all, didn't you pray about it? His best interest is now working to bring about your demise.

There was a young single minister who was an interim pastor of a church, and he was leading the congregation quite well for his lack of experience. One Sunday a single mom attended the services with her four children. The next day she called the young preacher and explained that she was attracted to him. In his weakness he began to date the lady. Long story short, his loneliness caused him to make a series of poor choices, and he felt compelled to resign his position at the church.

Friends, give your weaknesses to God and pray for discernment. God's strength is made perfect in our weaknesses. Let us be discerning to the evil forces that are working around us. Hide yourself from the trap that is laid out before you.

Suggested Prayer

Dear Lord,
I am already a victim to falling into the snares of the devil. Lord, I have made seeking a spouse my main interest and I see now how I have fallen prey. Forgive me and release my spirit from these traps. I give my weaknesses to You. Give me wisdom to keep from falling into these traps. In Jesus' Name I pray, Amen. Protect me, Lord.

I Am Full of Disgrace

Job 10:15
If I am guilty, woe to me! If I am in the right, I cannot lift up my head, for I am filled with disgrace and look on my affliction.

Job was full of shame, disgrace, and confusion. His friends were even more confused. With divorce comes shame, disgrace, and confusion—it is part of the territory. Confusion sets in because we wonder how and why this happened to us. God is not the author of confusion (1 Corinthians 14:33); it must come from Satan working through our sinful natures. We feel shame and disgrace and we wonder if people are talking about us. We ask ourselves, "what do the neighbors and my coworkers think about me?" I just cannot show my face in town because I might see someone that I know. I am tired of explaining my side of the story. I am not going in that restaurant by myself.

I was in Orlando, Florida recently and I was faced with two choices. I could starve for three days because I was too embarrassed to go eat at a restaurant by myself or I could force myself to eat at a table alone. There I was, a thousand miles from home, knowing no one, yet I was ashamed to eat alone. After much internal debate and deliberation, I decided to eat at a table by myself. It was an ordeal, but I did it anyway. I ate very fast, paid, and got out of there as fast as I could. I have not eaten in a restaurant by myself since then and I don't plan on it, either. Sometimes it is hard to lift my head and be seen in public. Church is difficult for me too. It seems like I am the only one that enters those doors by myself. Are people staring at me? Everyone else is sitting with their families except me. I am all alone.

Dear reader, if you have similar thoughts and feelings, it does get better. Eventually you will see that people come to church and eat out alone all the time. You will think less and less about your neighbor's opinions and more and more about what God thinks of you. As you walk with God, He will take the confusion, shame, and disgrace away. I do not mind doing many things by myself, but I am not about to sit alone in a restaurant unless I absolutely have too.

Suggested Prayer
Dear Lord, I have experienced much shame and confusion through this divorce. Lord, it is getting better; I thank You for challenging my faith. I know this is from the enemy because confusion does not come from You. Lord, I give the shame to You and ask that I could lift my head in public, knowing that You are on my side. Thank You, O Lord. Amen.

Success and Suffering

Acts 9:15-16

But the Lord said to him, "Go, for he is a chosen instrument of mine to carry my name before the Gentiles and kings and the children of Israel. For I will show him how much he must suffer for the sake of my name."

It seems like success and suffering go hand and hand. There is a crown to be won, but there is a cross to bear. The Apostle Paul was called to be a special apostle to the Gentiles. He was also to witness to the Jews and high-ranking officials in the Roman Empire. Paul was a church planter and overseer of the churches he established. He also wrote a great portion of the New Testament. In his spare time, he made and sold tents to support his ministry. The successes were great as he carried out the ministry that God had for him.

The suffering was also great. Paul was stoned in one town. He experienced beatings, shipwrecks, hunger, thirst, lack of adequate clothing and shelter, and several other hardships. Did I mention that he was arrested and thrown in prison? Paul was eventually executed by the Roman government for his faith. He was guilty of trusting Jesus Christ as his personal Savior. Most of the things Paul suffered were for the cause of Christ and fulfilling the ministry that God had for him. I can honestly say that most of my suffering has been because of my own sin and poor decision-making.

Paul gave himself completely to the will of God. We too must give ourselves completely to Him. The successes will be great, but so will the suffering. It is better to suffer and do something for God than to have a life of ease sitting on the sidelines. Make a commitment to our Heavenly Coach and ask Him to put you in the game.

Suggested Prayer

Dear Lord,

My life seems empty. It seems like I am not serving You and I am just coasting through life. Lord, I give myself to You today. Let Your will be done in my life. Use me in a special way, even if it involves suffering. I might not be used like Paul was used, Lord, but I want to make a difference in people's lives. Use me today. Amen.

A Powerful Affirmation

Micah 3:8

But as for me, I am filled with power, with the Spirit of the LORD, and with justice and might, to declare to Jacob his transgression and to Israel his sin.

We need to be reminded from time to time that we are new creations in Christ Jesus. With conversion comes the third Person of the godhead residing in our hearts, the Holy Spirit. Micah reminded himself that he was filled with the Holy Spirit and power and courage to declare to Israel his transgression. He knew that in his bosom resided the power to accomplish God's will.

As our minds begin to weaken and we run into some hard decisions, we need to remind ourselves of this verse. We have power and courage to do God's will because we have the Holy Spirit. When you need courage to lead your home in the ways of God, remember that the Spirit is with you. When you must deal with your ex-spouse about a situation with the children, remind yourself that the Holy Ghost will give you the words to say and give you counsel for the problem. At work when you must give that oral presentation, you can speak with boldness because you have the Holy Spirit. The Spirit wants to control and lead you into all the will of God.

We sometimes forget we have Him, and we think we are alone. We get discouraged because we think that only our abilities reside in us. We forget that God is with us. Make that tough decision with confidence, knowing that the Holy Spirit is with you. He is here, so let Him be dominant—not dormant, in your life.

Suggested Prayer

Dear Lord,
I have felt all alone. I have tried to figure all this out by myself. I have made some half-confident, weak decisions. Today I want to recognize that I have the Holy Spirit so I can make bold, confident decisions for You. Thank You, God, for sending Your Holy Spirit. In the Name of Jesus I pray, Amen.

Come Home

Zechariah 1:3
Therefore say to them, Thus declares the LORD of hosts: Return to me, says the LORD of hosts, and I will return to you, says the LORD of hosts.

Today you might find yourself way out of God's will and far away from where you need to be as a Christian. Perhaps you have been discouraged and just do not care anymore. Maybe your sins are so great that you feel like there is no way back to God. The devil would like to remind us of our sins and failures. We need to understand that our righteousness is based on Jesus Christ and not on our own works or efforts. We are sinners. So, what do sinners do? We sin!

There is no hole that God cannot get us out of. No matter how bad it looks today, God says return. Return to God and He will return to you. The only condition on our part is to return. He did not say return and tithe, or return and give away your possessions. He said return. If we would simply return, He will return. He can and will forgive us of every sin. He will restore your broken relationship with Him. He will cleanse your mind and conscience, and give you joy and peace. He can restore broken fellowship.

God can restore financial losses that may have occurred because of the divorce. Leave all that to Him. Let Him cleanse and restore. All you need to do is return. Let Him work out all the details. When Israel returned from Babylonian captivity, the first thing they established in the land was temple worship. The most important thing for us today is to return and renew that broken fellowship. Will you come home today? God will accept you with arms wide open. He will show you what you need to do.

Suggested Prayer ——————————————————————————
Dear Lord,
I have sinned and messed up a lot of things. I do not know how to fix it all. Today I want to come home. Lord, I return to You, confessing my sins. I rededicate myself to You and ask that You would restore our relationship so I can walk with You. In Jesus' Name I pray, Amen.

We Must Die So Jesus Can Live

2 Corinthians 4:10-11

...always carrying in the body the death of Jesus, so that the life of Jesus may also be manifested in our bodies. For we who live are always being given over to death for Jesus' sake, so that the life of Jesus also may be manifested in our mortal flesh.

It is strange to grasp—this idea that Jesus Christ lives in us. You see, Jesus wants to live out His life and purpose through us. He wants to be our hands and feet. He wants to love people through us. He wants to use our mouths to say encouraging words to others. He wants to take us to distant places to get the gospel out to those who have not heard. There is no greater honor than a life that is used by God to accomplish His will on earth.

We all want to see this world changed and come to know Jesus as Savior. The ironic thing is that Jesus lives inside of every Christian. So why isn't the world being changed? The problem has never been with God. The problem lies in our sinful flesh.

For Jesus to live and work through us a death must take place. What needs to die is our sinful flesh. We must die to our sinful passions and sometimes even our hopes and dreams. When we die to ourselves we can truly live. We are not perfect and will never reach perfection in this life.

Is the life of Jesus apparent in your life? We must die daily. As we deny ourselves, the Father, Son, and Spirit begin to work in our lives and bring about a change that will cause our lives to have a godly purpose and direction. Today and every day, plan out your own funeral so you can walk in newness of life. It is time that we get fed up with living ordinary lives that have no impact for the kingdom of God.

Suggested Prayer

Dear Lord,
I am the problem. There is no manifestation of Jesus in my life. I die to my sins and selfishness. I empty myself so I can be filled with You. Let my life be your hands and feet to accomplish Your will. In Jesus' Name I pray, Amen.

Soar to New Heights

Isaiah 40:28-31

Have you not known? Have you not heard? The LORD is the everlasting God, the Creator of the ends of the earth. He does not faint or grow weary; his understanding is unsearchable. He gives power to the faint, and to him who has no might he increases strength. Even youths shall faint and be weary, and young men shall fall exhausted; but they who wait for the LORD shall renew their strength; they shall mount up with wings like eagles; they shall run and not be weary; they shall walk and not faint.

One thing I have noticed about people going through a divorce is that they are just plum wore out (a little southern, not exactly proper English). I see these people and they are exhausted. The surrender flag in their heart is waving because they have just given up. I see it in their eyes. They are only existing. They are dying souls in a living corpse. An AED would not restart their broken heart. Divorce is such a discouraging time and you simply tire out. There seems to be no more strength for the day.

Thank God there is help! God never gets tired and He wants us to have divine strength. God will give us His power. In our own strength we will eventually tire out and fall by the wayside, but we can exchange our strength for His strength. As we wait on Him, God begins to renew our strength. When this happens, we will not tire or grow weary. The Christian life is not a forty-yard dash, it is a marathon. We can walk and run in the power of God and not grow weary.

We can soar like eagles. Have you ever noticed that when this majestic bird is soaring high in the sky it looks like he is sailing effortlessly? The eagle might flap a wing here and there. They are riding on air currents, and it looks so easy. Our air current is the Holy Spirit. When we tap into His current, we can soar to new heights. It will seem effortless because we are relying on Him and not ourselves. As we soar to new heights, we get closer to Him and earth's problems seem smaller and smaller. Today exchange your strength for His strength—and soar to new heights!

Suggested Prayer

Dear Lord, I am tired and I have given up. I am exhausted and I have no more strength. Lord, I exchange my strength for Your strength. Let me catch the wave of the Holy Spirit and soar to new heights. In the Name of my Savior I pray, Amen.

Faith's Characteristics

Hebrews 11:1-3

Now faith is the assurance of things hoped for, the conviction of things not seen. For by it the people of old received their commendation. By faith we understand that the universe was created by the word of God, so that what is seen was not made of things that are visible.

Hebrews chapter 11 is the great faith chapter of the Bible, and it describes how many Old Testament saints lived by faith. As we take a bird's-eye view of the chapter, we see that there are 40 verses. The number 40 denotes testing in the Bible. For example, it rained 40 days and nights during the flood; Israel spent 40 years in the wilderness; Jesus was tempted 40 days and nights; Goliath taunted the armies of Israel 40 days. The whole point is that our faith will be tested.

What is faith? Faith is simply taking God at His Word and acting on it. God speaks and by faith we respond in obedience. It sounds simple enough but it is very hard to live out in this world. Faith is like our foundation or title deed. Faith is our conviction or belief that God will do what He has promised in His Word. Faith controlled the thoughts and actions of the people mentioned in this chapter. Faith understands that God created everything, no matter what some scientists may teach. Faith also understands the new creation in Christ Jesus. Faith accepts Him as Lord and Savior. Every person who has ever been saved has been saved by faith, not some ritualistic practice. Faith looks to His second coming.

Faith is our guiding principle through life. At one point you took God at His Word and believed in Jesus, and He wiped out all your sins of the past and made you a new creation. We really do not have a problem trusting God about our home in heaven or His second coming. The problem lies not in the past or the future, but in the present. Today, exercise your faith in the present. What has God promised you in His Word? Take Him at His Word and act upon what He has promised. Faith is not a 'I hope so' sort of thing. Faith is solely based on the Word of God (Romans 10:17).

Suggested Prayer ────────────────────────

Dear Lord, my faith seems non-existent at times. I trusted You as Savior, and I believe You have a home in heaven for me. Lord, I am struggling today. I am having great difficulty taking You at Your Word. I am being tested, so please give me the faith to trust You through this test. In Jesus' Name, Amen.

A Faith That Still Speaks

Hebrews 11:4

By faith Abel offered to God a more acceptable sacrifice than Cain, through which he was commended as righteous, God commending him by accepting his gifts. And through his faith, though he died, he still speaks.

Abel probably died over 6,000 years ago but his faith still speaks to us today. Wouldn't you like to be remembered as a person of faith long after you are gone? Wouldn't it be awesome if your faith was an example for the generations to come? So, what is the whole deal with this Cain and Abel thing? Basically, God's requirement for a sacrifice was a lamb (Genesis 3:21). By faith Abel offered up a lamb as a sacrifice to God. He took the Lord at His word and made this offering. He repented and by faith believed in God. The result was righteousness and a relationship with God.

On the other hand, Cain offered his own sacrifice. His offering was some vegetables from the ground. God even gave Cain another chance to offer a lamb, but he insisted on his own way and would not repent. The result of Cain's sacrifice was religion and rebellion while Abel experienced righteousness and a relationship. Cain, in a jealous rage, murdered Abel. The first murder was over religion. You see that there is nothing new under the sun.

God has prescribed only one way to obtain salvation; that is by trusting Jesus as Savior. This is God's method. The results of God's plan are righteousness and a relationship with Him. Mankind offers its best, yet it only results in rebellion and religion. There is a vast difference between a religion and a relationship with Jesus Christ. Do you want your faith to be an example for generations to come? It is simple. Take God at His word. Respond in faith. As you take God at His word and respond in faith you will touch lives now and leave a legacy of faith for the generations to come.

Suggested Prayer

Dear Lord,
I want my faith to be an example to my children and my grandchildren and many more generations to come. I purpose to read the Word of God and respond in faith. In Jesus' Name I pray, Amen.

An Impossible Faith

Hebrews 11:11

By faith Sarah herself received power to conceive, even when she was past the age, since she considered him faithful who had promised.

Abraham and Sarah were a unique couple. God promised that they would have a son, and yet they had no children. God said a great nation would come through this promised son and that the whole world would be blessed through him. Here is Abraham (which means father of a multitude) with no son. He is almost 100 years old and Sarah is 90. Their ability to have children was gone decades ago. For them to have a son it would take a miracle. It was physically impossible for them to have a child. Yet God promised them a son that would come from their own bodies. There would be no adoptions or foster parenting. They would have a baby.

We always hear about the faith of Abraham, but our text tells us that Sarah was a woman of faith too. She was also a spiritual giant, like her husband. Sarah took God at His word. She did not look at the circumstance or her inability to have children. She trusted God, and He brought it to pass.

What has God promised you that looks impossible today? Do not look at your ability or your circumstances. Simply believe what God has said and respond in faith. God specializes in the impossible. You cannot supply your needs, but God can. You can't seem to find a new spouse, but God can send someone. Do you lack transportation? God can get you a vehicle if that is what you need. The impossible becomes possible through faith.

Suggested Prayer

Dear Lord,
I have a great need and You promised to supply my needs. I need a miracle today. I am not looking at what I can do. I am simply trusting You. Do the impossible through me. In Jesus' Name I pray, Amen.

An Unlikely Faith

Hebrews 11:31
By faith Rahab the prostitute did not perish with those who were disobedient, because she had given a friendly welcome to the spies.

Rahab was a Gentile prostitute. Not only was she immoral, she was considered an outcast because she was not Jewish. Did we forget that God loves everyone, and nothing is impossible with Him? Rahab had heard how Jehovah had delivered Israel from Pharaoh. God sent the two spies to her house; these two men were to survey Jericho before Israel would invade the city. Rahab learned how God had promised Israel the land and how her city would be destroyed. She responded to all that God said by faith. She put her trust in God and hid the two spies when the soldiers of Jericho came looking for them.

She helped the spies escape by hanging a red makeshift rope from her window on the city wall. The spies instructed her to put the rope out her window and to bring her household into her apartment. Before Israel invaded Jericho they were instructed not to harm the woman or her family. Her faith saved her life and her family's lives. She began to walk with God. She became the great-grandmother of King David. Jesus Christ Himself would be born from the lineage of a Gentile woman, a former prostitute.

There are so many lessons to learn from Rahab. The key to her success was that she simply took God at His word. Do you want a faith that will save your life and your family's lives? Like Abel and Rahab and the people mentioned in Hebrews chapter 11, do you want your faith to influence generations to come? Do you want your life to count for the King? It is as simple as taking God at His word and responding by faith.

Suggested Prayer
*Dear Lord,
I am an unlikely person to make a difference in this world. If you can use Rahab, You can use me. Lord, I believe in Your Word. Help me respond to it. Let it save my life and the lives of my family. Then let it reach out to this world. Father, into Thy hands I commit my spirit. Amen.*

322 | PRESSING ON

Faith, a Two-Edged Sword

Hebrews 11:34, 37

...Quenched the power of fire, escaped the edge of the sword, were made strong out of weakness, became mighty in war, put foreign armies to flight. They were stoned, they were sawn in two, they were killed with the sword. They went about in skins of sheep and goats, destitute, afflicted, mistreated...

In these verses we see that some saints "escaped the edge of the sword." They trusted God for deliverance and God spared their lives. When the Assyrians surrounded Jerusalem, King Hezekiah and the Prophet Isaiah prayed. God sent an angel one night and the angel slew 185,000 Assyrian troops. The Israelites escaped the edge of the sword by trusting God. In verse 37 we read that some "were killed with the sword." In Acts chapter 12 we read how the Apostle James was killed with the sword. There have been many pastors, missionaries, and other Christians who were executed for their faith.

These two verses almost seem to contradict each other. The people who were delivered trusted God. The people who died were executed trusting God. We must conclude that the outcome was not dependent on their faith. The outcome was determined by God Himself. Sometimes He delivers and sometimes He allows death. One person believes for healing from cancer and survives. Another person believes for healing and dies of cancer.

We must recognize that the sovereignty of God plays a major role in our lives. We must accept His determined outcome. Our responsibility is to pray and take God at His word. These verses are not meant as a discouragement. They are meant to encourage our faith. The next time you pray and it does not materialize, it is not because you did not have faith. It is because God had different plans. While waiting in line at the post office, I told the gentleman in front of me that they are always slow. He responded by saying that this is a reminder that we are on God's timetable and not our own. Don't beat yourself up if things do not go how you planned. God has a different plan.

Suggested Prayer

Dear Lord, today I decide to trust You. If you deliver me or not, I am going to trust You. Help me not to be discouraged if things do not work out as I hoped they would. Lord, I accept Your will in my life. In Jesus' Name I pray, Amen.

Dr. Hua's Wise Counsel

Proverbs 27:9
Oil and perfume make the heart glad, and the sweetness of a friend comes from his earnest counsel.

In 2005 God gave me a very special friend named Hua Mo. He is a brilliant man and holds a PhD in chemistry from the prestigious Rice University. One day while we were at lunch together, I was telling him about my desire to remarry and the role that children play in a second marriage. He explained to me the five levels of a stepfather or stepmother in a new relationship.

Level 1 is where the kids will look at you as their own parent. You would be no different than their biological parent. Level 2 is where you would be their close friend. They might not see you as a parent, but they will see you as a good friend. Level 3 is where the stepchildren see you as a neighbor. They are not necessarily opposed to you, but they are not exactly running to you with open arms. Level 4 is where the kids treat you as a stranger. You are someone distant from them. Level 5 is where you are the enemy. The house was fine till you showed up. The ideal situation is level 1 or 2.

If you are operating in levels 3-5 there is a good chance that this is not the right situation for you. Keep in mind that the leading cause of divorce in second marriages is the children. It takes God and a whole lot of patience to blend families together, and yes, it can be done. As you date and look for a future spouse see which level they fit into with your children. Then see which level you fit in with their children. This simple process could save you a lot of heartache down the road.

Suggested Prayer ———————————————————————
Dear Lord,
Thank You for Dr. Hua and his wise counsel. Lord, use these five levels to help me and others. Lord, may You give good friends like Hua to other people who might be struggling. In Jesus' Name I pray, Amen.

O Come All Ye Thankful!

1 Chronicles 16:34
Oh give thanks to the LORD, for he is good; for his steadfast love endures forever!

We are entering the holiday season in the United States. We have three big holidays that are not far apart on the calendar: Thanksgiving, which is always the fourth Thursday in November, then Christmas, which is December 25th. Then we have New Year's Day, always January 1. Holidays are meant to be a time of family, friends, food, and fellowship. However, this time of year in America is very difficult for many people, especially those who are divorced.

Are you thankful? Of course you are! Do you believe God is good and that He loves you? The answer is undoubtedly yes. Then why do you feel so bad during the holidays? Your family was torn apart and these festivities remind you of what is missing in your life. Many of your friends have treated you like you have leprosy since your breakup. Why would you cook a turkey for just you and your children when they will be at the other home the next day? What would you do with all that leftover food?

Thanksgiving arrives and you are all alone because it is not your year to have the kids for this holiday. Holidays are tough! In December you are invited to a Christmas party and if you go you will be the only single person attending. Then comes January 1—the day that represents your being alone.

There are a million other things I would rather do than go through the holiday season, but let me add that it does get better as God heals you. You learn to accept and embrace things. You will find that His grace is sufficient. At the time of this writing this will be my ninth holiday season as a single father. It does not bother me anymore. God still loves me and cares for me. With His grace this too (the holiday season) shall pass. After the holidays, spring will be just around the corner with plenty of Son-shine.

Suggested Prayer
Dear Lord,
These holidays are tough. I want You to know, Lord, that I am thankful and I believe that You are a faithful, loving God. I believe You are good. Lord, I am just asking for grace to get through this tough season. I also ask that one day I would look forward to holidays again. In Jesus' Name, Amen.

Call on the Elders

James 5:14-15

Is anyone among you sick? Let him call for the elders of the church, and let them pray over him, anointing him with oil in the name of the Lord. And the prayer of faith will save the one who is sick, and the Lord will raise him up. And if he has committed sins, he will be forgiven.

It is not wrong to call on the elders of your church to have them pray over you. What is wrong is keeping all the hurt and sadness bottled up inside. God has given you a group of men at your church that He would have you call on. You might be thinking that your divorce is not the physical sickness that James was talking about in these verses. I do believe that the verses are talking about a physical sickness in its most literal sense. However, I believe a divorce is a cancer in its own right. It effects our souls and spirits, and this often brings sickness to our bodies. Sickness can come from the stress of a divorce.

Not only can your elders pray for you, they also have valuable insight into the Word of God. An elder's prime responsibility is the Word of God and prayer (Acts 6:4). Let them pray for you! That is why God gave them to your congregation. I jokingly say if you need to be saved call on your Baptist friend, but if you need healing call on your Pentecostal friend. The truth of the matter is that we serve a God who heals and restores.

At the time of this writing my eldest brother is very ill. He could not call on the elders, so I brought an elder (Pentecostal) to him. This elder prayed over my brother and he seemed to get worse. Then suddenly he began getting better and better each day. Friends, do not go through this battle alone. Your spirit and soul are sick. Call on your elders, keeping in mind that you might not feel better right away. In fact, you might get worse. However, the Great Physician heard the prayers of your elders. Help and healing are on the way. Let God heal you in His time and in His way. You will be happier after you have met with your church leadership. You will also see the supernatural power of God working in your life.

Suggested Prayer —————————————————————————

Dear Lord, This is a heavy burden and I cannot take it anymore. Lord, I am going to call on the elders of my church. As they pray over me, please bring healing. May they give me some insight into the scriptures that will help me. Lord, heal me so You can use me to heal others. In Jesus' Name, Amen.

Release the Beasts

Malachi 4:2
But for you who fear my name, the sun of righteousness shall rise with healing in its wings. You shall go out leaping like calves from the stall.

The calves are all penned up in the stall, and then the rancher comes by and opens the gate. The calves suddenly rush out into open pasture, leaping and full of energy. They have been waiting on him to set them free all day, and now the moment arrives; they go in a burst of energy. This is how God describes us when He heals us. We have been penned up in the stalls too long. Our lives have been miserable and restricted. We remember how we used to roam freely. Our stall is our own home as we sit within its walls like a prisoner.

When God opens the stall door you will go out running and leaping, full of the Holy Spirit (Acts 3:8). There is coming a day when the Sun of Righteousness will heal you and set you free. It is a process that starts when we honor His Name. Honoring the Name of the Lord means that we believe that God is, and we believe in everything that He stands for. We have a godly fear or respect for Him. Then God responds by rising to our cause with healing in His wings.

Everyone's healing is as unique as a fingerprint. Do not be discouraged if someone heals faster than you or gets remarried faster than you. We are all on God's time. Although healing is unique, there are some common elements involved. There must be forgiveness, prayer, Bible reading, church attendance, and support from others. We must also keep in mind that God is healing our children too. Your children must also be ready for a new person to come in their lives. Be encouraged today that the Son will set you free (John 8:32). The feeling is indescribable when you are finally released and set free.

Suggested Prayer ———————————————————————
Dear Lord,
I have been a prisoner in my own home. I have been bottled up and downtrodden too long. I realize that You are healing me, and I trust that You will keep healing me. Today I commit myself anew and afresh to You and trust that Your healing will have its perfect work. Heal all my family, Lord. Thank You, Father. Thank You, Jesus. Thank You, Holy Spirit. Amen.

Hand Picked by the King

Esther 2:17

...the king loved Esther more than all the women, and she won grace and favor in his sight more than all the virgins, so that he set the royal crown on her head and made her queen instead of Vashti.

It is amazing how the Bible is a living book, and there is always more to learn. As a lady was talking to me today, she was expressing how King Ahasuerus picked Esther out of all the other women. This dear lady recently found out her husband has been talking to another woman. She was trying to encourage herself in the Lord through this trial, and she was sharing her heavy burden so I could pray for her. The Holy Spirit gave me a word for her, and I had never thought about this aspect of Esther until the words rolled out of my mouth.

Esther was a beautiful woman. The king could have the bride of his choice, and his choice was this beautiful Jewish orphan woman. As I looked at my dear struggling friend, I told her that she too was handpicked by the King. I told her that she was beautiful in the King's eyes. I also told her, "Of all the people He could have picked, He chose you." I told her how she too had found favor and grace in the King's sight.

Today, my friends, King Jesus has picked you out of all the people to be His bride. Ladies, you are beautiful in His sight. Sir, Jesus loves you too. You were precious in the King's sight, and He loved you enough to die for you. You have found favor and grace in the sight of Jesus. He has called you to be His special bride. Praise God for His great love toward us.

Suggested Prayer

Dear Lord,
Help me realize that I am special in Your eyes. When I am down, let me see the great love that You have for me. Thank You for choosing me. Thank You for my salvation. Lord, help me be an obedient child, and may Your will be done in my life. In Jesus' Name I pray, Amen.

A Pitiful Hope

1 Corinthians 15:19
If in Christ we have hope in this life only, we are of all people most to be pitied.

Some people's hopes are pitiful at best. Paul reminds us that since Jesus rose from the grave, we too will rise and spend eternity with Him. Paul says that the most pitiful hope is one that has Christ for this earthly life only. Jesus did not die for our sins only for this life. When we die, we will spend eternity somewhere. We will either be with God or away from Him in hell. Jesus died, was buried, and rose again so we do not have to spend eternity in hell. He did not merely die so we could just experience this life on earth.

He often allows us to enjoy a great life here, but there is a greater life ahead. It is so sad when people have no hope of the future. It is horrible to think that this is all that there is. What an encouraging thought that we will spend eternity with God. Although the deaths of family and friends are discouraging, there is a hope that lies beyond the grave. It will be so awesome to spend eternity with family and friends as we worship the Lord together.

A Christian hope is not a pitiful hope. It is a living hope in a living resurrected Savior whom we will live with forever. Unfortunately, we Christians may find ourselves in some pitiful situations. We might even want someone to have pity on us. Thank God Jesus had pity on us and paved a way for us to spend eternity with the Father. Do things look pitiful in your life? Remind yourself that there is more to life than this earthly existence. This life is a short span of time in comparison to eternity. The next world will be indescribable. Are you living for this world or the world to come?

Suggested Prayer
Lord,
Things have looked bleak recently and I have been way beyond discouraged. Lord, help me get my heart and mind on You and the age to come. Let me see my sufferings as only temporary. Lord, let me live for eternity. In Jesus' Name, Amen.

It's a Whole New World Out There

Psalms 137:1-4

By the waters of Babylon, there we sat down and wept, when we remembered Zion. On the willows there we hung up our lyres. For there our captors required of us songs, and our tormentors, mirth, saying, "Sing us one of the songs of Zion!" How shall we sing the LORD'S song in a foreign land?

The Jewish people of the Southern Kingdom, consisting of the tribes of Benjamin and Judah, were overthrown by the Babylonian Empire. Many of the Jewish survivors were taken captive and sent to Babylon. There was a series of three invasions with survivors exiled to this vast empire. It was a whole new world to these poor Jews. Their hearts were in Jerusalem but their bodies were in a strange land. There were no songs in their hearts anymore. Their homes, jobs, temple worship, friends, and family were all gone. They literally had to start over in a new land.

Does this sound familiar? Your heart was broken. Your family and friends have forsaken you, and now you are all alone, left to fend for yourself. Life as you knew it is gone. Everything is new, and you are literally starting over. You are like a fish out of water. You do not know how to act or think. It was like you were dropped off on a deserted island with no idea of how to get back home.

There is good news. God brought these captives back to the land of Israel in a series of three returns. When God had fulfilled His purpose, He brought His people back to their land. When they returned, temple worship was restored and they began to live normal lives again. Dear friends, God is going to restore you when He has accomplished His purpose in your life. Someday soon you will find yourself on familiar soil.

Suggested Prayer ————————————————————

Dear Lord,
I am like a lost sheep. I do not know where I am in life or where I am going. Lord, I need You to help me find my way. Work out Your purpose in my life and use me in a special way to help others who got lost along the way. In Jesus' Name, Amen.

The Impossible Made Possible

Zechariah 4:6

Then he said to me, "This is the word of the LORD to Zerubbabel: Not by might, nor by power, but by my Spirit, says the LORD of hosts.

Zerubbabel was the leader of the first return of the Jews back to their homeland from Babylonian captivity. The scene was a city that was ransacked and deserted. Jerusalem means city of peace. There was no peace there, only pieces of rubble. The temple was destroyed and the walls of the city were broken down. Slowly but surely the Jews rebuilt the temple. Later Ezra came and restored the Word of God to the people, then Nehemiah rebuilt the walls of Jerusalem. Eventually Jerusalem was a restored city.

How was it all accomplished? It was not by the might or power on the part of the Jews; it was by the precious Holy Ghost. Some of us do not have peace and are looking at all the scattered pieces. The Holy Spirit will restore you, so yield to Him today.

Imagine that you are that broken city of old. The first thing to be restored was the temple. So, today renew your worship and prayer life. The second thing was a restoration of the Word of God. Begin reading and obeying the scriptures. Then the walls were rebuilt. Set up some standards that will keep the enemy out. Now sit back and watch the Holy Spirit restore you and give you peace. In His time you will be like that city, the joy of the whole earth. You will not just be surviving, you will be thriving by the Spirit's renewing power.

Suggested Prayer ────────────────────────────

Dear Lord,

My life is in pieces. I ask that You pick up the pieces and restore me. Holy Spirit, restore my worship. Holy Spirit, speak to me through the Word. I commit myself to live by Your Word and Your precepts. Renew, refresh, and revive my spirit. In Jesus' Name, Amen.

Free Yourself

Hebrews 13:5-6

Keep your life free from love of money, and be content with what you have, for he has said, "I will never leave you nor forsake you." So we can confidently say, "The Lord is my helper; I will not fear; what can man do to me?"

Debt weighs our spirits down and makes us slaves to our creditors. Financial experts will tell you to sell everything that you can to get out of debt. It might be time to sell that new car and buy one that you can pay cash for. Divorce is a painful process, and I have personally sold most of my earthly possessions to keep a roof over my head. There is great advice for us in this verse.

Free yourself from the love of money. Money is a tool to reach your desired goals in life. Money is not the goal, it is one of the avenues to the goal. Another related idea is to be content with what you have. Covetousness can be described as an itch for more. Be content with your house, cars, clothes, furniture, etc. How many things will you take to heaven? It is just stuff. That is all it is. It is not worth being in debt and all the associated stress that comes with it.

Another thing to remember is that God is with you and He will supply all your needs. He will never leave you or forsake you. People and possessions have wings—they fly into our lives and fly out as well. God never flies away. God also wants us to be confident that He is our Helper. Every time we charge an item that we cannot pay for, we are relying on self instead of God. Today have confidence and faith that He is your Helper. When we apply these principles to our lives, we are not afraid of the creditor knocking at our door. There will not be an eviction notice. They will not repossess your car in the middle of the night. It is great to see our Helper supply our needs. As you live by His principles, He will get you debt free so you can freely serve Him.

Suggested Prayer ——————————————————————

Dear Lord,
I need to be set free. I am in debt because I love money and things. Lord, I have been paying the consequences for my bad choices. I will sell all and make the necessary adjustments I need to make so I can live freely for You. Lord, forgive me and help me to be content with You. In Jesus' Name I pray, Amen.

Psalms 46:10

"Be still, and know that I am God. I will be exalted among the nations, I will be exalted in the earth!"

We live in a fast-paced world with many demands on our time. We are rushing to work, taking the kids to school and soccer practice, cooking dinner, supervising homework and baths, taking twenty minutes to relax, and then off to bed. I feel exhausted writing the previous sentence.

Some translations of this verse convey the idea of "stop striving." The idea of the verse is to be still before the Lord and to recognize that He is sovereign. We should then surrender to Him whatever is bothering us. Many people are striving and rushing around, not in a physical sense but in their hearts. Their hearts are racing with thoughts of a new spouse. They try every effort to find someone. They go to work and church, trying to see who is single. They spend hours on dating sites. The loneliness is so intense they are putting forth every effort to find someone. They are frustrated because nothing seems to work. Then a still, small voice says, "Be still, and know that I am God." Suddenly they realize that God wants to be God in their lives and that He is in control. God has been trying to say to them, "I've got this." So, they decide to stop striving and hand it over to Him.

Dedicate yourself to Him, no matter what, even if it means staying single. The good news is that the striving in your heart will be gone. The Lord has taken away the stress and anxiety away and has replaced it with peace and contentment. You are beginning to enjoy life. You are at the place in your life where God can send someone. Sometime soon God will send a companion. What happened? You let God be God and allowed Him to work. Friends, if I have described you, it is high time that you let God be the Sovereign Lord of your life. When this happens, you will see Him quickly do what you have spent months and years trying to do in your own strength. Stop striving. Be still and know that He is God.

Suggested Prayer

Dear Lord,
I am worn out and frustrated trying to find a new spouse. Today I stop my striving. Take the stress away and send peace and contentment. I give it over to You, and may Your will be done. In Jesus' Name I pray, Amen.

Prepare Your Heart for the Blessing

Hosea 10:12

Sow for yourselves righteousness; reap steadfast love; break up your fallow ground, for it is the time to seek the LORD, that he may come and rain righteousness upon you.

God wants to bless us, so we must clear our minds of negative thoughts that would hinder our blessings. Our hearts are like soil. In the parable of the sower Jesus describes four types of soil or four conditions of the heart (Matthew 13:1-23). We must breakup our fallow ground or soil that has not been plowed. We must let the Word of God and the Spirit of God plow our hearts over and over. There is hardness and indifference that must be dealt with if we are to receive the blessing. There is also bitterness that must be broken up.

Once the soil of our hearts has been plowed and the weeds are all gone, the Master Husbandman can work with our heart. This plowing process begins when we determine to seek Him daily. As we read our Bibles and pray He prepares the soil of our hearts for a blessing. Once the soil is finally ready the seeds of blessing can be planted. We sow the seeds of righteousness and we reap a harvest of love. God will send down the rain to water the seeds.

A farmer must patiently watch and wait for the harvest. The farmer does all he can by preparing the soil, but it is God Almighty who sends the showers and allows the crops to grow. Allow God to break up the soil of your heart. The plowing of the soil is where most of the work is done. The better the soil, the bigger the crop. Then sow those seeds of righteousness. The showers will come, and you will reap a harvest of blessing. There shall be showers of blessings. Oh, that this might be the day that you reap a harvest of blessings!

Suggested Prayer

Dear Lord,

Help me realize that You truly want to bless me. Lord, I give You my heart. May the Spirit of God and the Word of God work together to break up my hard heart. Then let me sow and watch and wait for the harvest to come. Thank You, Lord Jesus! Amen.

NOVEMBER 30

They Are Out to Arrest You

John 10:39
Again they sought to arrest him, but he escaped from their hands.

The Jewish authorities wanted to kill Jesus, but He evaded their arrest; it was not time for Him to be crucified. They were upset because Jesus claimed to be God. The devil was out to destroy Jesus.

God calls us to be wise as serpents and harmless as doves in our dealings with this world. As you get back into the dating scene, beware of the schemers and con artists who are the devil's pawns. They are out to destroy you, not because you claim to be God but because you believe in the Son of God. The deceivers are both men and women.

I recently heard of a man who would meet a woman online and then setup a dinner date. He would tell her to order whatever she wanted. They would eat steak and lobster and drink the finest wine. Later, he would tell her to order whatever dessert she desired. He would suddenly have to take a phone call, and then he would slip out of the restaurant, leaving her with an enormous bill to pay. He had done this to several poor women. He needs to be punished. God saw his wrong-doing and He will judge him accordingly. There are other men who supposedly fall on hard times and they have several women sending them money. Some men and women are just looking for an extra check to come their way. A friend of mine told me about his friend, a Christian man who was recently divorced. He started dating online and met several nice ladies. One night his date told him that she was going to give herself completely to him. In his weakness he took her to a hotel. She suddenly needed to go to her car to get her cigarettes. She returned with two big men who robbed him and left him stranded there with nothing but his boxers. It was a horrible lesson for this man to learn.

Friends, be very careful when you are lonely; it is easy to be deceived. Ask God for wisdom and ask Him to keep your emotions in check. Evade the schemers and deceptive ones that would arrest you and bring you down.

Suggested Prayer
Dear Lord,
Please give me wisdom and a spirit of discernment when it comes to dating. Protect me from being a victim. Lord, give me eyes that see and ears that hear, and a heart that understands. Keep me from the evil one. In Jesus' Name, Amen.

Can You Agree?

Amos 3:3
"Do two walk together, unless they have agreed to meet?

Two people cannot walk together unless they agree to meet. Two people really cannot walk together as a couple unless they can agree on some fundamental things. The most important thing to agree on is Jesus Christ. Is your "friend" (potential spouse) a Christian? If so, is he or she a dedicated Christian? Consider the children. Does he or she have kids? Do they want kids? Do you want more kids? Can you accept his or her kids? Can he/she accept yours?

Then you must see if your goals are compatible with his/her goals. If there is a major disagreement in these three areas, it might be best for both of you to end the relationship and find a more suitable partner.

No two couples are completely compatible, and no one agrees on everything. However, you must agree on the major things if you are going to walk together.

I dated a very nice lady, and we got along well. In fact, I got along with her better than any person including my wife of nineteen years. We would cook together, spend hours talking, and going for walks. She is still an awesome lady, but there came a day when we could not agree on a major issue. She had pursued a career as a lawyer, and after making her money she wanted to have a baby or adopt a baby. I, on the other hand, had raised two boys (I am 48 at this time) and I just could not see myself starting over. She was going to be miserable in life if she could not raise a child. After several attempts to make it work, I saw that I was holding her back from her goals and dreams. We had to let each other go. She wanted a family and I already had one. My future goal was to serve the Lord in the ministry with the time I have left on earth. It was painful to go our separate ways, but it had to be done.

Take time to ask the key questions. If you cannot agree on the major things, set each other free before the relationship gets too serious. Date, have fun, do great things, but be true to yourself and the other person. Do not try to force a relationship that will not work for either party.

Suggested Prayer

Dear Lord, I ask that You lead all the readers of this devotional into the relationships that You want for their lives. Protect them from the schemers and those good people who are just not compatible. Lead and guide them. Keep them from heartaches and sorrow. Give them a spouse that they can walk together with on the major issues of life. Give them someone who loves You and has the same desire to serve You. In Jesus' Name, Amen.

Friendly Wounds

Zechariah 13:6
And if one asks him, 'What are these wounds on your back?' he will say, 'The wounds I received in the house of my friends.'

Jesus received many wounds both emotionally and physically from the Jewish people. It is puzzling that Jesus was God's only begotten Son, yet the Father allowed His chosen people to abuse His Son. Jesus was accused of many things; He was belittled, mocked, made fun of, beaten, had His beard plucked out, and was crucified. Jesus had a rough life and died a horrible death. Our text states that His wounds happened in the house of His friends. The Jews rejected Him, the disciples denied Him, the Romans crucified Him. Our sins put Him on the cross, yet we are His friends.

Jesus had a purpose for all His suffering—it was to redeem all of us. God allowed His friends to do some horrible things to accomplish His will. Through it all Jesus was never bitter toward anyone. He kept His eye on the Father's will. You see, friends, it was not the Romans or the Jews or even you or I who crucified Jesus. God the Father allowed this, and the Father, Son, and Spirit agreed on this before the earth was ever created.

How are you and I doing today? We have been wounded by our "friends." It hurts but it will never compare to the hurt Jesus experienced. Today I would like us to see that God allowed these people to wound us that He might bring about a bigger purpose in our lives. The deeper the wound the greater the glory. We must not become bitter toward our friends that have hurt us. God is doing something for His Kingdom through you. Remember, the servant is not greater than his Master. If they persecuted Jesus, they will persecute you. Perhaps you should make a list of those who have hurt you. Then go down that list and forgive each and every one on that list. Then turn that list into a prayer list and pray for these people. Your wounds will be worth it if some of your friends and family become Christians.

Suggested Prayer
*Dear Lord,
I have had some friends hurt me deeply. Lord, there must be a purpose in all of this. Forgive them and let me begin praying for them. Save those who have hurt me. Accomplish something great for Your Kingdom through my wounds. Amen.*

Fasting

Matthew 6:16

"And when you fast, do not look gloomy like the hypocrites, for they disfigure their faces that their fasting may be seen by others. Truly, I say to you, they have received their reward.

Fasting can take many forms. It can be skipping food and water for a day to spend time with God and pray about a specific concern in your life. It may be that you skip a meal once a day for several days. The idea is that you are giving up something so you can spend extra time with God.

It would be wise to consult your physician before you decide to fast. In a church I pastored there was a lady in the congregation who was diabetic and she could not fast in the traditional sense. If you have a job that is outdoors, it might not be good to forgo drinking water. If you cannot do a food or water fast, perhaps you can get creative—like skipping TV to spend time with God.

From time to time we need to fast to find the will of the Lord. Journal your fast. For example, write down the specific problem in the journal. Then have some specific headings: insights, related scripture, solutions, resolutions. I have fasted several times and God has always directed me. Fasting is putting God first. He always honors us when we put Him first. A friend of mine spent forty days skipping breakfast so she could pray for our president. We can spend forty days complaining about the president or we can pray for him and our other officials (1 Timothy 2:1-5).

A fast helps us put all our focus on God. It is very difficult to hear a still small voice these days. We must be still and attentive if we are going to hear a word from God about our situation. As I fasted about my loneliness, God showed me that it is a universal problem. I made a list of the people I knew who were alone, and I started contacting them to encourage them. Study the topic of fasting in the scriptures and see for yourself how God honored those who fasted. God will honor you too.

Suggested Prayer

Dear Lord,

You know my health. Please lead me into a fast that will help me figure out what is going on in my life. Give me a renewed spirit of hope and revive me. Renew me so I can rise above my circumstances to do Your will for my life. In Jesus' Name, Amen.

I Sat Where They Sat

Ezekiel 3:15-17

And I came to the exiles at Tel-abib, who were dwelling by the Chebar canal, and I sat where they were dwelling. And I sat there overwhelmed among them seven days. And at the end of seven days, the word of the LORD came to me: "Son of man, I have made you a watchman for the house of Israel. Whenever you hear a word from my mouth, you shall give them warning from me.

Ezekiel sat among the Jewish captives who were exiled to Babylon. He sat there astonished for seven days. At the end of those seven days God made him a watchman over the Jewish exiles. Ezekiel was to warn the people as well as admonish them to follow the Lord. He was God's instrument to deliver God's message to God's people. However, he first had to sit where they sat. He had to see, hear, feel, and experience their pain. Before he could address the people, he had to identify with them.

Before Jesus redeemed us He became one of us. There are people all around you that are going through a divorce. You have sat where they sat. You can identify with these people and help them because God has helped you. Is God calling you into a special ministry for divorced people? Pray about helping your church if it has a Divorce Care or similar program. If your church does not have a program, pray about starting one. Are you qualified to do this? Let me say that you have sat where they sat and of all people you can identify with these individuals.

God has been faithful to give you insight into your problem. Now it is time to be a watchman or watch-woman to help those who are hurting. God did not help you for it to end there. He wants you to share the love of Christ with others. He will bless you for all your good efforts. When that struggling person comes into your life you can say, "I sat where you sat, and I know how you feel and what you are going through."

Suggested Prayer ——————————————————————————

Dear Lord,
Thank You for all the help that You have given me. Lord, I know how these people feel who are going through or thinking about a divorce. Lord, use me in Your service. Lead me to a group of people I can share Your love with. In Jesus' Name, Amen.

It's OK to Stay at Home

Numbers 9:15-17

On the day that the tabernacle was set up, the cloud covered the tabernacle, the tent of the testimony. And at evening it was over the tabernacle like the appearance of fire until the morning. So it was always: the cloud covered it by day and the appearance of fire by night. And whenever the cloud lifted from over the tent, after that the people of Israel set out, and in the place where the cloud settled down, there the people of Israel camped.

When Israel left Egypt they were tent dwellers, and this speaks of the brevity of life. We are just pilgrims passing through this life to the next one. The tabernacle was in the center of the camp, and all other tents revolved around it. This speaks of how the Lord should be at the center of everything that we do. The cloud by day and the appearance of fire by night spoke of the Lord's comfort and guidance. Today we have the Holy Spirit for comfort and guidance.

The Jewish people were to stay put until the Lord lifted the cloud off the tabernacle. Houston, we have a problem! Most divorced people do not want to stay put or stay at home or even be home. They fill their lives with activities to keep them away from home. Eventually we all must come home. Perhaps all the activities that we occupy our time with keep our minds off our problems. Those four walls remind us of our great loss and what used to be. Home should be a place of peace and rest, not a prison. It is acceptable to not have a date and to spend the evening at home. Sometimes you need to just *do you* until the Holy Spirit leads you into another direction. Staying home can give you time to spend with God so He can continue to heal you.

Make your home inviting, perhaps with your favorite music, foods, or even some nice candles. Make a list of some projects to do at home. There are some inexpensive projects that you can do that will help you feel better about your home. Let Jesus be the center of your home and make Him the priority. It is time to take back our homes from the clutches of Satan. As God heals, you will discover that it is fine to be by yourself at home. God is the only One that can give you peace and contentment, so yield to Him today. Let the Holy Spirit guide and direct you. Stand still and see the salvation of the Lord.

Suggested Prayer

Dear Lord, It is hard to go home. Lord, I put You in the center of my life. Father, I yield to Your plan for me. Holy Spirit, lead me and direct me into all the will of God. Lord, make my home a place of peace and rest. Amen.

Parties, Parties, Parties

Mark 6:21
But an opportunity came when Herod on his birthday gave a banquet for his nobles and military commanders and the leading men of Galilee.

B irthday parties will never be the same at your home. Do your best with what you have to make your child's birthday special. Do not criticize or become jealous of your ex-spouse if he or she is able to do more for your child than you can. It is not a competition, it is your child. In the not-so-distant future, you and your ex-spouse will be grandparents, so keep that in mind. Your children and future grandchildren deserve your respect; you must prepare for dealings with your ex at these events.

Jesus attended parties, weddings, and the Jewish feasts. He entered the homes of the outcasts of society. Jesus always put the Father's interests first, everywhere He went. In the United States we are surrounded by parties this time of year, usually revolving around Christmas and New Year's Day. There will be parties with your family, church, friends and work colleagues. These parties can be depressing as you think about what you have lost. You used to go with your husband or wife, and now you are headed out the door with your three best friends: me, myself, and I. It would be so much easier just to stay home.

If you decide to stay home, I think God understands. I also think that if you force yourself to go you could be a blessing to someone there. There might be someone you can encourage or show the way of salvation. Jesus always used feasts and weddings as teaching opportunities. On the other hand, there might be someone there that can encourage you in your spiritual walk. We need other people in our lives. The devil would have us isolate ourselves from everyone and get us down. Whether you decide to go to the party or stay at home, remember that Jesus loves you and accepts you no matter what decision you make. Be sensitive to the Holy Spirit's leading because He might have a divine appointment for you to share your faith.

Suggested Prayer ————————————————————————————————
Dear Lord,
Parties should be a time of rejoicing, but I just do not like them anymore. Lord, help me honor You wherever I go. Help me make my children and grandchildren feel special on their birthdays. Lord, use me to be a blessing to my family, church, and work associates. In Jesus' Name, Amen.

You Have a Choice

Numbers 36:6

This is what the LORD commands concerning the daughters of Zelophehad: 'Let them marry whom they think best, only they shall marry within the clan of the tribe of their father.

In this portion of scripture God wanted the daughters of Zelophehad to marry whom they thought best for them, but only within the same tribe so as not to mar the allotted land inheritance. The point I want to make is that they were given a choice within certain boundaries.

As believers our boundaries are the scriptures. The age-old question has been, "Does God send that perfect person to me or do I have a choice?" I think the answer is yes to both aspects of this question. At times God has handpicked couples and put them together, like Boaz and Ruth. He also has allowed people to make their own choices, like King David and Bathsheba. There are no easy answers, and one of the key elements is not to hurry. Allow God to work on you and the other person.

Do not make a rash decision or feel like this one person may be your only available choice. You made a choice in the past and it did not work out, so please use extreme discernment. A widow friend of mine has been single for over thirty years. Her prayer was something like the following: "Lord, either send me someone or send peace if I am to stay single." The Lord sent her peace and she never remarried. One elderly man signed up for an online dating site, and set up a few dates. The very first lady he went out with impressed him so much that he canceled the other dates. In a very short time he was married. Still another man had a lady recommended to him and they talked over the phone for a solid month before they finally met. When they met, he simply was not attracted to her. He called me asking for advice because he did not want to quench the Spirit of God if this was a divine path for him. I told him that looks are not everything, but they are something. I further explained that if you are not attracted to her, do not force the relationship. He decided to just be friends with her and within weeks he met the lady he felt God wanted him to have.

What is my advice? 1. Heal. Let God heal you. 2. Heed. Does your situation match the scriptures? 3. Halt. Slow down and sort your emotions. 4. Hear. What is God telling you? How does the other person feel? 5. Hold up. If you are not sure, do not do anything until you are.

Suggested Prayer ——————————————————————————
Dear Lord, dating is complicated to me. Please heal me and lead me in the right path for my life. Help me to know and be confident that I am making the right choice. In the Name of Jesus I pray, Amen.

A Higher Standard

Genesis 39:9-12

He is not greater in this house than I am, nor has he kept back anything from me except you, because you are his wife. How then can I do this great wickedness and sin against God?" And as she spoke to Joseph day after day, he would not listen to her, to lie beside her or to be with her. But one day, when he went into the house to do his work…she caught him by his garment, saying, "Lie with me." But he left his garment in her hand and fled and got out of the house.

Joseph's brothers sold him as a slave, and he eventually ended up in Potiphar's home as a servant. Potiphar saw that Joseph was different and that he had God's favor, so he made Joseph manager of his entire household. Joseph was a handsome young man, and Potiphar's wife wanted to be intimate with the young servant. She approached him day after day. Finally, when all the other males were out of the house, She grabbed Joseph by the coat and he fled out of the house. He lost his coat but kept his character. Joseph had passed an important test. God removed Joseph from the situation by allowing him to be arrested and thrown into prison. He had passed one test, now he had one more test (prison) before God would promote him as prime minister of all of Egypt.

Sometimes what looks like a step backward is actually God's path to protecting and promoting us. Things got a whole lot worse for Joseph before they got better. God was protecting him and making him the man He wanted him to be. How did Joseph resist the temptation day after day? He had already made up his mind that he would be faithful to God. You see, if we do not make up our minds for God the world will make up our minds for us and we will sin against God. A night of fun can become a lifetime of frustration and regret. Many enter adult life with no set standards and the world and the devil work them over. Why? They did not set themselves to live by a higher standard.

A single young man in our area got two girls pregnant within weeks apart. Now he is paying child support for both children and neither girl wants anything to do with him. What encouragement would you give this young man? We, like Joseph, need to determine to live for God and to commit ourselves, body, soul, and spirit to Him. In God's time He will send someone to you. You may have to pass the test or several tests before it all comes together.

Suggested Prayer

Dear Lord, I do not want to fall by the wayside. Lord, my life is already a mess and I don't want it to get any worse. I commit myself to You. I determine to live by Your Word. If things get worse, let me know that you are protecting me and preparing me. In Jesus' Name, Amen.

Behind Closed Doors

John 20:19

On the evening of that day, the first day of the week, the doors being locked where the disciples were for fear of the Jews, Jesus came and stood among them and said to them, "Peace be with you."

After Jesus rose from the grave the disciples locked themselves in a house; they were afraid that the Jewish authorities would arrest them or have them killed. They sat behind locked doors in deep fear, hoping they would not be discovered. Then Jesus, in His resurrected body, walked through those locked doors and said, "Peace be with you." This whole scene shows us how God is sovereign or in complete control. Nothing would happen to those fearful disciples unless God allowed it. God took away all their fears with His presence.

Dear friends, many people are behind locked doors in an emotional sense. The door of their heart is locked shut. They have been hurt so badly through their divorce that they will not let anyone get too close to them. They do not want to go through that pain again. They might date and honestly love a person, but they cannot give their heart over to this new person. Others will never date again. It is sad and there are no easy answers. If you are dating someone like this, you will need to exercise patience with them as they slowly open up to you.

The only person who got through those locked doors was Jesus. You might not be able to let a man or a woman through those doors, but allow Jesus to come in. Invite Him into the situation. He knows all about it anyway. He is still the Great Physician and has the proper remedy. Jesus will show you that He is sovereign. He will eventually take all the fears, hurts, and apprehensions away. The healing process may take a long time but eventually you will have peace. When Jesus has done His perfect work you will be able to allow that person access to your heart.

Suggested Prayer

Dear Lord,
I cannot describe my pain, but You know all about it. Lord, I cannot trust any person, but today I trust You. I give You my heart. Unlock my heart and make and mold me into the person You would have me to be. Let me see and believe that You are sovereign. Help me to trust again. In Jesus' Name, Amen.

Don't Let a Kidney Stone Remind You

Hosea 8:12-14

Were I to write for him my laws by the ten thousands, they would be regarded as a strange thing. As for my sacrificial offerings, they sacrifice meat and eat it, but the LORD does not accept them. Now he will remember their iniquity and punish their sins; they shall return to Egypt. For Israel has forgotten his Maker and built palaces, and Judah has multiplied fortified cities; so I will send a fire upon his cities, and it shall devour her strongholds.

A few years back I had a kidney stone and my urologist, Dr. Joseph Sonstein, prescribed a daily pill and told me to drink eight to ten glasses of water a day. I am truly fascinated with the work that he does. He sees many patients daily, performs surgeries, and trains new doctors. He is truly a great physician. However, we have even a Greater Physician. At my annual checkup recently I told him that I don't always drink enough water. Dr. Sonstein replied by saying, "Well, don't let a kidney stone be a reminder." Those words echoed in my heart, and it reminds me to take that daily pill and to drink all that water. When I think back on the pain of the kidney stone, not to mention the cost of surgery, I do not want to go through that again. Hopefully another kidney stone will not be my reminder to drink enough water.

The Greater Physician has given us the Word of God to keep us from sinning against Him and making poor choices. His Word should echo in our hearts to remind us to follow Him. After repeated warnings, God remembered the sins of Israel and Judah and brought them into captivity. When a kidney stone forms it is too late—you are going to experience some extreme pain. When God judges the Christian, it is too late and he or she will have to suffer the consequences. The judgment of God (your kidney stone) will be your reminder that God is serious about His Word. Do not let His judgment be your reminder to keep His Word. You have come too far in your journey to turn back now. Yes, God is a loving, patient, wonderful God, but when He has had enough and He sends judgment, it is too late.

Suggested Prayer ——————————————————————————————

Dear Lord, Help me to love You and to live by Your Word. Lord, let me not be judged by sinning against You. I know You are patient, but let me not tempt You. If I must suffer let it be for good and not because of my own sins. In Jesus' Name, Amen.

Blessed Be The Name of The Lord

Nehemiah 9:5

Then the Levites, Jeshua, Kadmiel, Bani, Hashabneiah, Sherebiah, Hodiah, Shebaniah, and Pethahiah, said, "Stand up and bless the LORD your God from everlasting to everlasting. Blessed be your glorious name, which is exalted above all blessing and praise.

It is good to bless the Lord both publicly and privately. I hope you attend a church where you can worship the Lord without any hindrances. Worship is more than just a Sunday event; it should also be done privately too. Worship is a lifestyle as well as an act. It might be a raised hand or rearing a child in the ways of God. Worship is praising God for who He is and what He stands for.

I challenge you to make a list from A to Z with names of our Lord. Each name describes something about His character and nature. Develop this list as you do your daily Bible reading, then use your list as a form of praise. I sing or praise God when I am alone, so I won't be distracted and so my kids won't think I went off the deep end.

He is: A-Almighty, Amen, Anchor, Adonai, Advocate, Ancient of days, God of Abraham, Isaac, and Jacob, The God of Abraham, Isaac, and Israel, Alpha and Omega, Author and Finisher of our faith, Author of Life, Altar of Incense, Ark, Awesome God, Abba-Father, The Angel of the Lord. B-Branch, Bridegroom, Bread of Life, Brazen Altar, Beginning and the End, Bright and Morning Star, Buckler, Balm in Gilead. C-Carpenter, Christ, Christ Jesus, Christ Jesus our Lord, Comforter, Counselor, Consuming Fire, Creator. D-Deliverer, Door, Defender, Despised and Rejected of men.

E-Everlasting God, Everlasting Father, Eternal, Emmanuel, Elohim, El Shaddai, El-Elohe-Israel, the Mighty God of Israel. F-Faithful, Firstfruits of Them that Slept, First and Last, Faithful and True, Fortress, Firstborn of the Dead. G-God, God of gods, Great God, the God of Israel, the God of the Jews, the God of the Gentiles, the God of Glory, Good, Glory, Good Shepherd, Golden Lampstand, Grace, Great Physician. H-Helper, High and Lifted Up, Holy, Holy One, the Holy One of Israel, Harmless, Hope, Holy Spirit, Holy Ghost, Holy Servant Jesus. I-I Am, Immortal, Invisible, Immutable, Infinite, Indescribable, Immanuel. Praise Him from A to I today and tomorrow praise Him from J to Z.

Suggested Prayer ——————————————————————————

Dear Lord, I praise Your glorious, wonderful Name today. May my life and may my lips bring forth praise to Your Name. Amen! Praise the Lord!

Praise Him! Praise Him!

Revelation 22:13

I am the Alpha and the Omega, the first and the last, the beginning and the end."

As you praise the Lord with your list of names it is overwhelming to think about the One who is all together glorious. Jesus said He was "the Alpha and Omega." The Alpha is the first letter of the Greek alphabet and the Omega is the last letter. In English we might say He is the A and the Z. He is everything in between.

He is: J-Jesus, Jesus Christ, Joy, Jealous, Just, Jehovah, the Righteous Judge. K-Kind, Kinsman Redeemer, King, King of Kings. L-Lamp, Lawgiver, Light, Love, Lion of the tribe of Judah; the Lamb, Lovely, Light of the World, Living God, Longsuffering, Living Water, Lord, Lord God, Lord Jesus Christ, Lord God of Hosts, Lord of Lords.

M-Maker, Messiah, Mighty God, Mighty One, Mercy, Most High God. N-Name Above All Names. O-Omnipresent, Omniscient, Omnipotent, Omega, Only Begotten Son, Only Wise God. P-Priest, Prophet, Peace, Pure, Present, Prince, Prince of Peace, Prince of Life. Q-Quick. R-Redeemer, Rock, Rock of Israel, The Rock of Your Stronghold, Rod from the Stem of Jesse, Refuge, Righteous, Resurrection and the Life, Root of David, Root of Jesse.

S-Savior, Servant, Shield, Sovereign, Spirit, Spirit of Jesus, Spirit of the Lord, Spirit of Truth, Strong Tower, Separate from sinners, The Strength of Israel, Son, Son of Abraham, Son of God, Son of Man, Son of David, Son of the Blessed, Shepherd, Man of Sorrows. T-True Vine, Table of Shewbread, Truth, the Way and the Truth and the Life. U-Unspeakable Gift, Unsearchable. V-Vine, Veil. W-Wonderful, Wisdom, Wise, Word, Word of God. X-God of King Xerses. (The only word in the Bible that starts with X is Xerxes. The heart of the king is in the hand of the Lord [Proverbs 21:1].) Y-Yahweh. Z-Zeal.

Take a name or several names for God and begin to praise Him. Think about these names and what they mean. May the Lord give you insight into His character and nature as you praise Him. As you lift your thoughts and heart upward, you will discover that your problems will get smaller and smaller. You will also see that you serve a big God and that nothing is impossible for Him. May the Lord direct you into all the will of God for your life.

Suggested Prayer

"Worthy is the Lamb who was slain, to receive power and wealth and wisdom and might and honor and glory and blessing!" (Revelation 5:12). Amen. Praise the Lord. Praise Him! Praise Him!

O Little Town of Bethlehem

Micah 5:2

But you, O Bethlehem Ephrathah, who are too little to be among the clans of Judah, from you shall come forth for me one who is to be ruler in Israel, whose coming forth is from of old, from ancient days.

As the Christmas season approaches it is interesting to see how many prophecies in the Old Testament were fulfilled with the coming of Christ. This verse tells us that Jesus would be born in Bethlehem, that He would be a King, and that His origins were from eternity past. Micah predicted the birthplace of our Lord hundreds of years before it came to pass. Someone has said that Bethlehem is a mere comma in the sentence that would describe the Lord. This means that He existed in eternity past, was born (*the comma*), lived, died, rose again, and lives throughout all eternity. All of these prophecies give us a glimpse into the life of our Lord Jesus Christ.

The point I want to make is that God knows everything, and He knows all about you too. He knew what town you would be born in. He knew what year you would be born. He knew whom you would marry, and when you would divorce. He knew you would get a divorce long before you were ever born. God knows every detail about you. Nothing you have said or done has caught Him by surprise. With this knowledge comes His gracious love and healing power. In short, God has your life under His complete control. My encouragement for you is to trust the Lord today and tomorrow, and the next day and every day. You can trust Him now and for your future.

Do you believe this verse? Do you believe that God knew His Son would be born in Bethlehem? If you can believe this verse I want you to believe all the verses of the Bible, especially the ones that speak of His provision and healing. God is going to do great things for you. Can you take Him at His Word?

Suggested Prayer —————————————————————

Dear Lord,
It is so easy for me to believe this verse. It is easy for me to believe that Jesus is my Savior. Lord, I am struggling with the verses about You supplying my needs, and I am struggling with the thought of whether You will give me another spouse. Lord, I believe; help my unbelief. Amen.

The Outcast's Hope

Psalm 16:8-9

I have set the LORD always before me; because he is at my right hand, I shall not be shaken. Therefore my heart is glad, and my whole being rejoices; my flesh also dwells secure.

At the time of this psalm David had been anointed king, but Saul was still on the throne. Saul knew that David would be king, so he was hunting him down every day to kill him. David fled and was hiding anywhere he could to escape death. He had left his family and all the comforts of home, and was running like a fugitive. David was on the run, but God was with him. David had put God first and knew that the Lord was at his right hand. In the Bible, the right side always speaks of power and the right. David knew he would be king one day, and that the God of the universe was at his right side to make it happen. David knew that he would be safe because God was on his side. David's heart was glad and his whole being rejoiced in God. Outwardly there was peril and persecution, but inwardly there was peace. His flesh was secure; he rested in hope.

A Christian's hope is anchored in the Lord. We are secure in Him. We rest in hope because we know that God is in control of our lives. As our world crumbles around us, we too can have hope. Hope is the inward workings of God in our hearts as we trust in His Word. The world's hope is outward and based solely on circumstances. We hope to get a raise. We hope they will go out with us. We hope we will be able to pay our bills. We hope to go on a cruise.

Of all the people who should have been hopeless, it should have been David. The king of the land had a personal vendetta and had issued a death warrant on David. The authorities were on high alert to capture this fugitive. Yet David rested in hope. He was promised by God that he would be King of Israel. When God promises you something it will come to pass, despite the circumstances. We have a steadfast hope which is the anchor of our souls (Hebrews 6:19). David had to ignore the outward circumstances and concentrate inwardly on the Lord. Today ignore the circumstances and concentrate on the Lord. The result will be an inward transformation that will give you hope.

Suggested Prayer

Dear Lord, I also feel like an outcast. I am looking at those who hurt me and looking at my bills and I am nervous. Lord, change my heart and put a hope in me that will give me faith through these tough days. Let me focus on Christ and not on circumstances. In Jesus' Name, Amen.

The Only Hope

Psalms 71:5
For you, O Lord, are my hope, my trust, O LORD, from my youth.

As a kid my favorite movie was Star Wars. Now that I am a 52-year-old kid my favorite movie is still Star Wars. When Princess Leia and the Rebel Alliance were in deep trouble, she sent a message to Obi-wan Kenobi through the droid R2-D2. The crux of the message was "Help me, Obi-Wan Kenobi. You're our only hope."

No one knows exactly who wrote this psalm, but most agree that the pen is that of an elderly man. The psalmist had put his faith in God as a child and had learned to trust Him through the years. He had probably put his faith in people, and one by one they let him down. He put his hope in circumstances, but they all fell short. Eventually, after setbacks and disappointments along the way, he realized that his only hope and trust was in the Lord. He could reflect and see how God had been faithful to him as a child. He could see how God had helped him through the various stages of life. At the end of his days and after great accomplishments, as well as some blunders, he goes on record as saying God is our only hope.

People, possessions, fame and family are all temporary and will eventually fail. God is your permanent family and He will never fail you. When you said "yes" to Jesus He put a living hope inside of you that gave you assurance of salvation, a secure home in heaven and a steadfast hope for the trials of this life. Hope in any person or situation is doomed for failure. Through these trials put your trust and hope in Jesus. All other hopes will eventually disappoint you. If you want to be inspired watch Star Wars. If you want help from God you might need to say, "help me Jesus, You're my only hope."

Suggested Prayer
Dear Lord,
You are our only hope. You have helped me in the past. You have a home for me in heaven in the future. Lord, I need help today. Lord, I need to see that You are working on my behalf today. Let my trust and hope be in You only. Amen.

The Obvious Hope

Psalms 119:116

Uphold me according to your promise, that I may live, and let me not be put to shame in my hope!

Psalm 119 is a song about the Scriptures. Every verse speaks about the Word of God. As Christians our hope comes from the Word of God. Everything we know about God comes from the Scriptures. The Holy Spirit takes the Word of God and changes our hearts and minds as we apply it to our lives. The reason we lack faith and hope is because we have not obeyed the Scriptures, merely reading them instead of allowing the Spirit to do an inward transformation.

The psalmist knew that the Word said God would sustain him and that he would live, but he was also concerned that he might be put to shame because of his hope in the Lord. We all have been embarrassed because of our sins and failures but we should not be ashamed of the hope that is in us. God has never failed one of His children that was trying earnestly to live for Him. Your enemies may try to put you to shame or make you look bad for your hope, but God will uphold you.

The world may deny your hope and laugh at it but one day they will all have to face the Lord. There will be no laughing on that day for the lost. Christ is the judge of unbelievers and they all will receive a guilty sentence. None of them will be pardoned on that day. At the time of judgment they might think back to those times when they laughed at your hope. Everyone will eventually believe in Jesus, but the unbeliever's belief will come too late.

Today our obvious hope is the written Word that tells us about the Living Word, Jesus Christ. Your hope is anchored in Christ through the Holy Scriptures. You will never need to be put to shame for your hope in God. Everything that is recorded in the Scriptures is truth and will come to pass. May the Holy Spirit take the Scriptures and change us so we will not be ashamed.

Suggested Prayer

Dear Lord,
Forgive me for those times when I should have stood up for You. Lord, let me not be ashamed of my hope. Holy Spirit, change my heart as I read the Word and let me be bold for Jesus. Amen.

D ECEMBER 17

The Onward Hope

Psalms 130:7
O Israel, hope in the LORD! For with the LORD there is steadfast love, and with him is plentiful redemption.

P salm 130 is one of the fifteen psalms known as the Songs of Degrees. These psalms are Psalms 120-135, and they were sung as Jewish citizens made their three annual pilgrimages to Jerusalem. These fifteen songs were sung as an encouragement for the travelers as they went onward in their journey to the Jewish temple. God has put a song in our hearts that encourages us as we march onward; that song is hope in our God.

There was a collective hope, as Israel as a nation was encouraged to hope in the Lord. They had a unique privilege based solely on God's love and redemption for them. Their relationship was not based on works that could merit Jehovah's favor. The verse says, "For with the LORD is steadfast love, and with him is plentiful redemption." Israel was a nation that had its roots based on redemption. God first redeemed them from Egypt and then they journeyed to the promised land. This redemption was saturated in His great love. As the nation went onward they could hope in their God to accomplish what He had promised them.

The Christian today has a hope based on redemption. God sent Jesus to redeem us because of His great love for us. We too are on a journey, not to a physical temple but to a heavenly tabernacle. As we journey onward, let us hope in this Great God who redeemed us because of His love. We are just pilgrims passing through this life. We are looking for a city whose builder and maker is God. What keeps us going through the difficulties of life? The hope in a Savior who spurs us on to live for Him until the day when faith will be sight and hope will be realized.

Suggested Prayer —————————————————
Dear Lord,
I sometimes forget that I am just a pilgrim here. Lord, I forget that my relationship is based on the redemption of Jesus because of Your great love for me. Today I ask for a hope that will spur me onward and upward to do great things for You. In Jesus' Name, Amen.

The Obtained Hope

Psalms 146:5
Blessed is he whose help is the God of Jacob, whose hope is in the LORD his God.

The last five psalms in the book of Psalms are the hallelujah chorus. They encourage us to praise the Lord. All five of the psalms start off with praise to the Lord. At this time, God had brought the Jews back from captivity. The temple had been rebuilt, the walls and the city of Jerusalem had been rebuilt, and the city was back to normal. It was time to praise the Lord. Their hope of returning to the land and serving God in Israel had become a reality. God had promised to restore them and bring them back to the land, and God was faithful to His promises.

It is an exciting time when hope is realized, and faith becomes sight. This psalm reminds us that God is our Creator. It also reminds us that He feeds the hungry, sets the prisoners free, the blind receive sight, He helps the fatherless and widows, and He brings justice. It even says that He lifts those who are bowed down. This psalm should give you hope because most of us can relate to God's workings in the Jews in this psalm. Hope was obtained because God did everything that He promised He would do as the Creator God and Covenant God of Israel. There was now nothing left to do but praise the Lord.

Friend, today I want you to hope in the Lord. He has promised to bring justice, to feed you, and to restore you too. The obtained faith has its ultimate fulfillment when we go to be with the Lord in heaven. At that time faith will be sight. Until that happens, hope in the Lord. Your enemies will fall. You and your children will be taken care of. God will heal your soul and restore your losses. That special person will come into your life if that is His plan. The hope of the nation of Israel was God Himself. The hope of the Christian is God too. Like the psalmist we need to break out in praise, "Praise the LORD! Praise the LORD, O my soul!" (Psalm 146:1).

Suggested Prayer ——————————————————————————
Lord,
We praise You! You are our Creator! You are our Redeemer and the Supplier! Lord, I put my hope in You! I thank You in advance for the things that will become a reality for me. Praise the Lord! Praise Him! Praise Him! Praise Him! Hallelujah!

It's Just Me and the Dog These Days

Ephesians 5:16
...making the best use of the time, because the days are evil.

My ex-wife wanted a dog and she finally found one that she was not allergic to. He was a double-dapple miniature dachshund named Duke. When she left, the dog stayed because he was not allowed in her new husband's home. Well, Mr. Duke was a blessing in disguise. I would take him on many walks, as I would spend time praying and walking. He slept in the boys' beds and he was a great source of comfort to all of us.

I dated a lady and she said the dog must go if I was going to be her husband. Well, I decided that she needed to go, and we kept the dog. When I was looking at a dating site I stumbled across a picture of an Asian lady, clinging to her small dog. The caption under her picture said, "must like dog." I laughed and laughed. I probably missed my sign and should have contacted her. I have spent several nights at home with just me and the dog when the boys were at their mother's home.

Truly we live in evil days and these are evil times. However, I chose to use my time to get closer to God. Those were dark days when it was just me and the dog, but I determined in my heart that I would be faithful to the Lord. God used those lonely times to change me.

There is a reason why a dog is called man's best friend. Dogs are loyal to their masters. Your wife or husband may leave, but your dog will never leave. Everyone may leave you, but the Lord will never leave you or forsake you. So, use your time wisely and may you deepen your relationship with Him as you go through these evil days. Oh yeah, don't forget to take your dog on a walk.

Suggested Prayer ───────────────────────────────
Dear Lord,
We live in some evil times. Lord, I determine to love and serve You. Help me use my time wisely to draw closer to You. In Jesus' Name, Amen.

An Unlikely Choice

1 Samuel 16:6-7

When they came, he looked on Eliab and thought, "Surely the LORD's anointed is before him." But the LORD said to Samuel, "Do not look on his appearance or on the height of his stature, because I have rejected him. For the LORD sees not as man sees: man looks on the outward appearance, but the LORD looks on the heart."

God had rejected Saul from being King of Israel. He sent Samuel to the home of Jesse, in Bethlehem, to anoint one of his sons as the new king. Samuel examined seven sons of Jesse, but the Lord did not choose any of them. Finally, Jesse's last son David, a young teenager, was chosen and anointed as the new king. Samuel learned an important lesson that day. He learned that God looks at the heart and not the outward appearance or physical abilities. The other seven sons were more qualified for the job outwardly, but inwardly they were not qualified. The heart of the King of Israel had to be a man after God's own heart, like King David.

Today we can learn a valuable lesson about finding a new spouse. As much as possible, we need to see if they have a heart for God. You should want God's choice and not your own choice. Dear lady, God's choice for you might not be the most handsome or the wealthiest man. Dear sir, God's choice for you might not be the prettiest girl that you have dreamed of dating. Friend, God's choice for you will be someone with a good heart for God, you, and your children.

I have been out with a couple of wealthy ladies—not God's choice for me. I have also been out with one of the most beautiful ladies I have ever seen (my teenaged boys even thought she was a knockout)—also not God's choice. One day I surrendered my thoughts and expectations about a future spouse to God. I told Him that I wanted His choice and He put a lady in my life that lived approximately 8,500 miles away from my home. I fell in love with her because she has an awesome heart, she loves Jesus, her daughter, and me and my family. She is not the wealthiest lady or even the prettiest lady, but she is beautiful to me. I could not be happier with anyone else because this lady is God's choice for me. Friends, surrender to God and let Him choose for you.

Suggested Prayer

Dear Lord, today I pray for Your will to be done in my life. Help me to look at the heart and not the outward appearance or ability. Lord, I do not know who is right for me so send me Your choice. Give me the discernment to know Your will. Lord, I am excited to see what You are going to do, and I already receive Your will for me. In Jesus' Name I pray, Amen!

It Is Not Your Battle

2 Chronicles 20:17

You will not need to fight in this battle. Stand firm, hold your position, and see the salvation of the LORD on your behalf, O Judah and Jerusalem. Do not be afraid and do not be dismayed. Tomorrow go out against them, and the LORD will be with you.

In verse 16 of this chapter God tells us that it is not our battle. The battle is the Lord's and has always been the Lord's. When my wife left I frantically read the scriptures, trying to find something to help me. As The Holy Spirit showed me this verse, and this portion of scripture became my anchor. This was the answer that I was looking for. God clearly showed me that this was not my fight. I was to position myself in the Word of God and prayer. I was to stand still and see the salvation of the Lord. These were the instructions given to King Jehoshaphat as the enemy approached. Instead of relying on weapons of war, Israel broke out in songs of praise and stood still. The enemy was defeated before their very eyes and they saw the Lord's deliverance.

There are people who have hurt us and we might feel like harming them, but our weapons are spiritual and they will bring down strongholds. Your weapon is the Word of God. Stand still and position yourself in the Word. Pray and praise God. Then you will experience the extraordinary power of the Lord. He will bring about a great deliverance in your life.

Did I experience deliverance overnight? No. However, angels were dispatched from heaven even before my ex-wife dropped the bomb on me. I believe this verse with my whole heart. I quit trying to fight God's battle. I kept reading, praying, praising, going to church, and serving Him. In God's time and in His way, He delivered me from the hurt and heartache. He restored my finances and brought peace and contentment.

Ask God to give you a portion of scripture to lead you through the pain and hurt. This might not be your verse, but you can make it your verse. You do not need to fight. You need to stand still and position yourself in the things of God; sit back and let Him fight His battle. You will experience great deliverance.

Suggested Prayer

Dear Lord, Forgive me for trying to fight your battle. Today I put down my weapons of revenge and the arm of my flesh. I leave the battle to You since it belongs to You. Forgive me for taking Your battle from You. It never has belonged to me. I see that You love me and want to fight my battle for me. I pick up the Word of God and position myself in You. I will stand still and experience Your deliverance. In Jesus' Name I pray, Amen.

A Drunken Stupor

1 Corinthians 15:34
Wake up from your drunken stupor, as is right, and do not go on sinning. For some have no knowledge of God. I say this to your shame.

I s it possible to be in a drunken stupor without alcohol? Paul is describing a Christian as though he were drunk. What he means is that our minds are in such a fog that it is like we are in a drunken stupor. We are so consumed with our problems and the pressures of life that we cannot function properly. Our sins cloud our minds where we cannot think properly. Sin destroys body, soul, and spirit. The result of all this is we are walking around and going through life like alcoholics.

The reason that we need to sober up is because there is a whole world of lost people around us that do not know God. These people are perishing before our very eyes, but we are too drunk to notice their lost condition. We ourselves are sinning because we are living in a state of mind that Paul describes as a drunken stupor. We desperately need to sober up and confess our sins. We need to be led by the Spirit of God.

God is interested in the whole world and wants everyone to be saved. His heart yearns for the lost people of the world to be saved by trusting Jesus Christ as their Savior. He has designed the gospel in such a way that you and I are to go out and tell the world the good news about Jesus. Some will perish, never having had the opportunity to hear the name of Jesus one time.

When was the last time you shared your faith with someone? When was the last time you gave someone a Bible or gave an offering for a missionary? If it has been awhile, perhaps you are in a drunken stupor and need to repent and wake up. It does not take much for the enemy to get us distracted. The goal of all churches should be that Christians share Jesus with people and teach them the Word. Today I invite you to sober up and start sharing your faith with others.

Suggested Prayer
Dear Lord,
I feel like I am a drunk person. I cannot make the right choices. Lord, I am involved in sin and I feel ashamed. People around me are perishing and I don't seem to care. Today I confess my sin and ask that You help me share my faith with someone today. Lord, let me begin by sharing my faith with family and friends. In Jesus' Name I pray, Amen.

DECEMBER 23

A Challenge from God

Jeremiah 32:26-27
The word of the LORD came to Jeremiah: "Behold, I am the LORD, the God of all flesh. Is anything too hard for me?

Jeremiah is known as the weeping prophet. He warned the people that the Babylonians were coming to destroy the land if they did not repent. The nation did not listen to the words of the prophet. Jeremiah experienced the iniquities of Israel and the invasion of the Babylonians. In a very short time everything was destroyed and the nation was scattered. It is interesting that God issued Jeremiah a challenge. God refers to Himself as Jehovah God, meaning the self-existent God who made a covenant with Israel. He also refers to Himself as Elohim, the Creator God.

Our God is the Lord of all mankind. He knows everything and He owns everything. There is no task that is too difficult for Him. As you see yourself as a recipient of wrongdoing and all the associated troubles that came with it, God wants to challenge you. Is there anything too hard for God? Can He not restore your financial losses? Can He not supply your needs? Can He not send you a husband or a wife? God can restore your losses! God can supply your needs! God can send you that special person even if they are on the other side of the world. They may be from another country and culture and speak a different language. They might even be in your city or your congregation. There is nothing too hard for God and He will make it happen. It is not too difficult for God to bring them to you.

Today I want you to write a detailed list of your problems. Then ask yourself if the problems on that list are too difficult for God. Take that list to God and pray about it. Tell Him all about it. Then sit back and watch Him work. Prayer is not some mystical formula or a spell of good fortune. No, no, it is talking to the Master Problem Solver, the God of all mankind, the Covenant God, the Creator God. Today God wants to challenge you like He did to Jeremiah some 2,500 years ago. He wants to solve your problems so you will see how great He is and in return you will magnify His greatness with praise. You will proclaim to others about the Great God that we serve. I am excited for you today because He is going to do great things for you.

Suggested Prayer
Dear Father, I sometimes doubt You and my problems look too big. However, today I give You my problems. I can't do it myself. Let this trial bring me closer to You and may others be saved whey they see Your power working in my life. Amen.

The Eve of Deliverance

Exodus 12:11

In this manner you shall eat it: with your belt fastened, your sandals on your feet, and your staff in your hand. And you shall eat it in haste. It is the LORD's Passover.

It is Christmas Eve and tomorrow will mark the day that Jesus was born to bring about our deliverance. In our text today Israel is on the eve of a great deliverance from Egypt. God has seen enough! His people have suffered too long! God instructed the Jewish people to observe the Passover. They were to sacrifice a lamb without blemish and apply the blood to the doorposts, because that very night God would send one last plague. God would kill all the firstborn of Egypt. If the blood was applied to a Jewish family's door, God would pass over them and the firstborn of the home would not die. In other words, those therein would be spared from His great wrath. God commanded that the Passover would be observed every year to remember God's great deliverance of His people.

The New Testament tells us that Jesus is our Passover Lamb without blemish (1 Corinthians 5:7). The blood of the Lamb is now applied to our hearts, not our homes. The Jews were to eat this meal by faith, with their bags packed and sandals on their feet in anticipation. That very night they ate the meal, then God sent the last plague and Pharaoh let them go.

Today I am afraid we are celebrating without packed bags and our sandals are off. Yes, we believe in Jesus. Yes, He saved our souls, but with our bags not packed, we are not expecting Him to deliver us from the effects of divorce. Today I want you to pack your bags and put those shoes on because you are on the eve of a great deliverance. God has seen your trials and your tears. He has had enough! Do you want to see the awesome delivering power of a resurrected Savior? Do you want to be delivered from bitterness, depression, and the spiritual slavery of divorce? If you want deliverance by faith, pack those bags and shod your feet by trusting in the delivering power of the blood of Jesus. Friends, you are on the eve of deliverance.

Suggested Prayer

Dear Lord, I am discouraged and disappointed today. It is Christmas Eve and I am all alone. Lord, I have lost all faith in You delivering me. Help me see that You care and want to make Your delivering power known in my life. By faith I believe You will deliver me. Lord, I anticipate a great deliverance. Thank You for delivering me. Amen.

A Merry Christmas Somewhere

Luke 2:10
And the angel said to them, "Fear not, for behold, I bring you good news of great joy that will be for all the people.

As the shepherds watched over their flocks an angel appeared to them, bringing great news. This news would be a source of joy to the whole world because the Savior was born. Christmas is a nice holiday and a sure source of joy as we reflect on Jesus Christ our Savior, who died for our sins. Christmas is a great family time too. Wait a minute! I don't have a family anymore. In fact, what should be a joy is now the worst day of the year for some people. Holidays are tough! Oftentimes we reflect on what we have lost, and the pain outweighs any joy that we may have. It is hard to fake a smile when your heart is torn apart.

Try to remind yourself that you win. God will give you the victory in Jesus. Instead of counting your losses, concentrate on the Lord. Wait another minute! It is not just you who feel bad. Your children are now torn between two houses. Today might be a good time to reassure them of your love for them. Let them know that they are loved by both homes.

The only thing merry about Christmas is that it will be over soon. There are no easy answers for this problem. As you grow in grace and God heals you, it will be easier to go through the holidays. Will your holidays ever be the same? Who knows? They may even be better. Tell the Lord about your pain and ask for His help. He will get you through the holidays. The joy of the Lord is your strength, so let Him restore the joy in your life. True joy is having a Savior who loved you enough to die for you. I wish there were immediate answers for those who are hurting. I do not have the answers, but I know God is faithful and He will help you.

Suggested Prayer
Dear Lord,
This day is horrible. It should be a time of joy, but all I feel is sorrow. Give me the grace to get through this day and please bring the joy of Your salvation in my life. In Jesus' Name I pray, Amen.

He Brought Us Through

Deuteronomy 2:7

For the LORD your God has blessed you in all the work of your hands. He knows you're going through this great wilderness. These forty years the LORD your God has been with you. You have lacked nothing.

I n the book of Deuteronomy Moses is restating the Law, giving a farewell address, and making final preparations for the Jews to enter the promised land. Those forty years were tough as they wandered in the wilderness. Two things stand out about God in this verse—one is His presence and the other is His miraculous provision. God was with them through this journey. He knew their wanderings, hurts, sorrows, needs, and their sins. Many times the people questioned whether God was with them or not.

Sometimes it seems like God is not with us, but His presence has always been with us. The miraculous provision was there too. The only way to receive a miracle is to be in the place where you need a miracle. You must have your own wilderness experience to witness His miraculous power and provision. These people were privileged to see the power of God work in their lives. Don't tell the major shoe manufacturers, but their shoes lasted forty years. After forty years their sandals were as fresh as the day they were made. And don't tell Macy's, but their clothes did not wear out. When they needed water in the desert, God brought water from great depths. When they needed food, God sent the manna and the quails. When they needed guidance God sent Moses, Aaron, Miriam, Joshua, Caleb, and elders. When they needed a word, God gave them the Law. These people did not lack one thing in the wilderness.

It has not been easy, but God has brought me through this wilderness of divorce. I was never late on a bill and never missed a meal. Praise God! You might not be out of the wilderness yet, and that is fine. God might have a little more healing He wants to accomplish in you. You will make it through. God has given you two great things—His presence is with you and His provision is there for you too.

Suggested Prayer ─────────────────────────────────

Dear Lord, It does not seem like you are with me at times. Today I trust that Your presence and provision are with me. Lord, I am tired, but I believe that You will see me through. Let Your presence be strong and let me have faith in Your provision. I thank You that You will see me through. In Jesus' Name, Amen.

A Man's Life Verse

Jeremiah 33:3

Call to me and I will answer you, and will tell you great and hidden things that you have not known.

Last night my neighbor called to tell me that his father, Larry Earles, had just passed away. Mr. Earles' favorite verse is our text before us. The context of this verse is very important. Jeremiah was in prison. He had preached his heart out with tears flowing, trying to get Israel to repent. God had given him a message that was quite simple: repent or else the Babylonians are coming to destroy the land. The sermon was not popular, and Jeremiah was rewarded with a prison sentence for his fine preaching. In this prison, and against all odds, God spoke to him and reminded him that He was the creator of the universe, and if he would call on God he would see some great things. Jeremiah did just that and saw many future events.

Mr. Earles seemed to be an ordinary man, but he had learned how to call on the God of the universe. God came to Larry Earles and showed him some great things. He was instrumental in starting three churches, served as interim pastor in a few places, and filled vacant pulpits on several occasions. Yes, he seemed to be an ordinary man, but he had an extraordinary God who used him in a mighty way.

Today, friends, your circumstances may look bad. Perhaps your prison is divorce or depression or loneliness. Perhaps you are in a financial prison. The odds are not in your favor, but God is in your favor. He will speak to you and remind you of His greatness. He created everything and controls everything. Call on Him and He will do great things for you too. You can be used in a mighty way if you will learn how to call on Him.

Suggested Prayer ————————————————

Dear Lord,
Today I find myself in need of You. Lord, I am facing some horrible circumstances. I believe that You are the Creator and Controller of everything. So today, Lord, I call on You and ask that You do great things through me. Lord, do something way beyond what I could ask or think. In Jesus' Name, Amen.

Far Reaching Consequences

Romans 5:12

Therefore, just as sin came into the world through one man, and death through sin, and so death spread to all men because all sinned…

I have two wonderful sons who were both saved at a young age. As I started winding down this devotional book, I asked my boys, "if there was one thing you would like people to know, what would it be?" My youngest said something about the dog, and my oldest said that people need to realize that their decisions effect everybody. My oldest son was a momma's boy. It broke his heart when she left. He cried himself to sleep every night and began eating way too much. He could not concentrate at school and his whole world was rocked. Both of my boys hardly have any dealings with their mother because she let them down. When they needed her the most she was not there for them.

When Adam sinned, we all became sinners, and he let the human race down. God forgave Adam and Eve, but the whole world changed. We will continue to feel the effects of their sin until the day when Jesus comes back and makes all things new. Jesus died on the cross so we would not have to perish. We cannot change our past. When the dust settles, we must pick up the pieces.

My exhortation for us today is that we make right biblical choices. You have suffered enough. Your kids have suffered enough. Your family and friends have suffered enough. Today let us be problem solvers and not problem makers. If you find yourself out of the will of God today, repent before something worse comes upon you. Today if you find yourself in the will of God, then keep keeping on. We are tempted to let off the gas and coast through life. We are tempted to sin to ease the pain. Sin is a temporary high. When you come down from that high you will find that you ruined yourself and those around you. Your decisions do not affect just you, they impact everyone and everything.

Suggested Prayer ───────────────────────────────────────

Dear Lord,
Thank You for Your forgiveness of sins. Lord, I know that You forgave me, but I also know I must face the consequences. So today I ask that You forgive me, and in Your wrath, please remember mercy. Help me make the right choices in life. Let me be part of the solution and not part of the problem. In Jesus' Name I pray, Amen.

Pressing On

Hosea 6:1-3

"Come, let us return to the LORD; for he has torn us, that he may heal us; he has struck us down, and he will bind us up. After two days he will revive us; on the third day he will raise us up, that we may live before him. Let us know; let us press on to know the LORD; his going out is sure as the dawn; he will come to us as the showers, and the spring rains that water the earth."

Sometimes it is hard to press on. We try and try and there seems to be no progress. Hosea encourages us to return and to press on in our walk with God. The Lord promises to heal us and to bind up what He has torn down. God caused or allowed these things to happen to us that He might heal us and make us the people He wants us to be. It is not an easy road, but it is the straight and narrow road that God asks us to walk on. He has also promised to revive us and to raise us up so we can live before Him. Hosea says God will come to us like the showers and the spring rains. These rains speak of God's faithfulness. Just as the crops need the spring rains to bring a full harvest, God is sending rain on your spirit that you might bring forth fruit for Him.

After seven long years of (yes, you guessed it) just me and the dog, I have experienced God's healing power. God has revived my spirit and raised me up. Glory has come down and filled my soul. Right about now I need to let out a shout of praise to our God. You must keep pressing on and keep getting to know God. It took Moses eighty years to get to the place where God could use him.

There is an older man in our church named Van. It took most of his adult life for God to get him to the place of complete surrender, the place where God wanted him to be. Van presses on to know the Lord and he is so full of God. Van's goal is to refresh the saints of God. I have come home and written down many things that Van said because God was talking to me through him. Press on! Press on! Do not be discouraged, God is going to do great things through you!

Suggested Prayer

Dear Lord,
Forgive me for my faults and failures. Today I determine in my heart to press on with You. Please heal me and raise me up. Then send the showers that I might be fruitful for You. In Jesus' Name, Amen.

A Divine Calling

Jeremiah 1:4-5
Now the word of the LORD came to me, saying, "Before I formed you in the womb I knew you, and before you were born I consecrated you; I appointed you a prophet to the nations."

P oor Jeremiah tried every excuse to avoid the calling of God on his life. He tried to tell God that he was too young to be a prophet. God specifically spoke to this young man, and the scriptures say that God came to him.

There seems to be a biblical pattern in this calling of Jeremiah. God has already chosen His people for a task before they are ever born. At the right time the word of the Lord comes to His chosen servants. God knew Jeremiah before he was ever formed in the womb. That is deep and beyond any human comprehension. God consecrated him and set him apart for this great task, then God sent him to be His prophet to the nations. Both Jews and Gentiles would benefit from the ministry of Jeremiah.

There seems to be a threefold pattern with God when He calls people for His work. First, there is a selection on God's part; secondly, there is a separation from other things so the person can accomplish God's plan. Thirdly, there is a sending by God for the great work.

The things that have happened to you were no accident. God knew all about you before you were born. God has something for you. Thank God that He did not save you just to let you go through this life alone and without a divine purpose. Do not be surprised if someday soon a still small voice comes to you. He will put something on your heart. You will be burdened about a group of people. You will have a desire to help them. The Holy Spirit will speak to you. He will separate you for the great work and then send you out. The burden of your heart will match the call of God. You will be selected, set apart, and sent by God Himself. Amen! That's exciting! God is going to use you!

Suggested Prayer ——————————————————————————
Dear Lord,
It has been a tough year, but I know that You have been with me the whole time. Lord, I want to do all of Your will for my life. Heal me and give me a burden for someone or something. God, let me hear You speak to me. I will separate myself for this task; please send me. Enable me to do Your will. In Jesus' Name I pray, Amen.

A New Journey Awaits You

Acts 13:2-3

While they were worshiping the Lord and fasting, the Holy Spirit said, "Set apart for me Barnabas and Saul for the work to which I have called them." Then after fasting and praying they laid their hands on them and sent them off.

It is New Year's Eve (just me and the dog here), and you might be thinking about what you will change in the coming year. Perhaps you need to lose a few pounds or want to read your Bible more. Maybe you have plans for paying off that credit card. Perhaps you are thinking this is the year you will be remarried.

Today I want you to consider your service with God. Paul and Barnabas were worshiping and fasting as usual when the Holy Spirit spoke to them. Three things (compare Jeremiah's call with these verses) stand out in these verses. First, they were selected. The Holy Spirit selected them to be missionaries. They were called to the mission field. The Holy Spirit has selected you to a ministry too. How will you know that you are selected? As you worship and pray and develop a pattern of fellowship with God, the Holy Spirit will speak to you.

Secondly, they were not only selected, they were separated. They had to cut ties with friends, family, and many other comforts to meet God in His work. The great guitarist Joe Bonamassa knows nothing of sports or any other worldly interests. He only knows how to play a guitar, and he is an expert at it. The great Olympic champions separate themselves from everything to excel in their sport. The great preacher and author John Phillips said he would have trouble changing a light bulb. All he knew was how to study, teach, and write about the Bible.

Lastly, not only is there selection and separation, there is also sending. The early church sent Paul and Barnabas out with prayers and laying on of hands. There will be some prayer warriors out there and some people to encourage you along the way. There will be financial backing if you need it. Your mission field might be in your own home or city. Not all are called to the foreign fields. You have been selected for something. Separate yourself for this great work. Your church will send you with the support you need. Ultimately, it is God who is sending you and empowering you.

Suggested Prayer

Dear Lord,
Here am I, send me!

A Final Word

***

Psalms 118:24
This is the day that the LORD has made; let us rejoice and be glad in it.

I hope the book has helped you and brought some healing to your heart. I tried to write it in such a way to bring about a balance to your life through the scriptures and prayer. You might not have noticed but I wrote the devotional in a series of triplets. January through June the pattern was one day in the Old Testament followed by two days in the New Testament. From July to December I spent two days in the Old followed by one day in the New. I used all sixty-six books of the Bible.

I also put a relevant topic for each month on the 14th through the 18th of each month. For January the topic was prayer, February was finances, March was loneliness; April was the Bible, May was time, June was waiting. July was dating and remarriage, August was the hands of God, September was the children; October was love, November was faith, December was hope. My desire is that people would gain a new respect for God and His Word, especially the Old Testament. My prayer is that Christians, Jews, Muslims, and all people would be encouraged by the writings.

Let me say that God loves you. If you cannot rejoice in anything, you can rejoice in Him today. If you find yourself still struggling each day, do not be ashamed to visit a good Christian counselor. Do not be ashamed to be on antidepressants. Do not be ashamed to sign up for a Divorce Care program at a local church. There is great healing power in the Word of God and prayer. I also wanted you to see that the Holy Bible speaks to your problems. The Bible is timeless, and I used every book to show you its relevance. I offered up "Suggested Prayers" for you *and* myself.

May God bless you richly! It has been a long, tough journey, but God got me through the wilderness of divorce. Every day I write down those two important words: "you win." Jesus is still on the throne and He loves you. I believe He will heal, restore, revive, and send you out for some special task. You have been called. God bless you!

One last prayer: ————————————————————————
Dear Lord,
I ask that You bless the readers of this book. Bless their children too. Lord, heal them and supply all their needs. Call them for Your special service, and may they bring help and healing to this dying world. In the Name above all Names, Jesus, I pray. Amen.

You Win, My Friends!

CPSIA information can be obtained
at www.ICGtesting.com
Printed in the USA
FSHW020239240621
82609FS